We Still Walk in Their Footprint:
The Civilian Conservation Corps in Northern Arizona, 1933-1942

Rock Culvert Construction Hualapai Mountain Park, August 8, 1936. Courtesy NARAMD, RG 79/150/35/17/07 Box 5.

By Robert W. Audretsch

© 2013 Robert W. Audretsch
All Rights Reserved.

No part of this publication may be reproduced, stored in a retrieval system, or transmitted, in any form or by any means, electronic, mechanical, photocopying, recording, or otherwise, without the written permission of the author.

First published by Dog Ear Publishing
4010 W. 86th Street, Ste H
Indianapolis, IN 46268
www.dogearpublishing.net

ISBN: 978-1-4575-1783-9

This book is printed on acid-free paper.

Printed in the United States of America

Cover design by Ron Short Studios, Santa Fe, NM, www.ronshortstudios.com

Front Cover:
F-28 CCC Enrollees On Board Truck, circa 1938. Courtesy Kaibab National Forest.
Hualapai Mountain Park Horse Trail Construction, July, 1934. Courtesy NARAMD RG 79/150/35/17/07 Entry 95 (PI #166) Box 5.
Road Construction Prescott National Forest, CCC F-39, Verde, photograph by J.T. Bonner, January, 1938. Courtesy US Forest Service, Southwestern Regional Office.

Back Cover:
Four Different Working Crews (Schultz Pass Camp?) by Creston F. Baumgartner.
Photograph of painting courtesy NARAMD RG 121/650/21/18/04 Box 1 E-142.

DEDICATION

To Lee Benson, Alfred H. Kelly and Charles B. Dew, Wayne State University Department of History Faculty, 1961-1964, who sparked my first inspirations to research and write history.

Contents

Dedication iii

List of Illustrations vii

Acronyms and Terms ix

Preface xi

Acknowledgements xii

Chapter 1	**CCC to the Rescue!** 1	
	Two Wasted Resources 3	
	The CCC Comes to Arizona 3	
Chapter 2	**Petrified Forest National Monument (NM-2, NM-2, NP-8)** 8	
	Sidebar: What Do the Numbers Mean? 19	
Chapter 3	**Flagstaff Area National Monuments (NM-5, NP-12)** 20	
	Flagstaff City, Coconino County 20	
	The New Deal at the Monuments 20	
	Civilian Conservation Corps, Mt. Elden 20	
	Wupatki 23	
	Walnut Canyon 24	
	Sunset Crater 25	
	Sidebar: Diversity in the CCC 30	
Chapter 4	**Coconino National Forest** 33	
	The Forest Service and the CCC: An Overview 33	
Chapter 5	**CCC Artists Program** 60	
Chapter 6	**Kaibab National Forest** 63	
Chapter 7	**Prescott National Forest** 75	
Chapter 8	**Division of Grazing Camps, Yavapai County** 94	
	Division of Grazing and the CCC: An Overview 94	
	Congress Junction (DG-47) 94	
	Yava (DG-8) 96	
Chapter 9	**Camp Newspapers** 101	
Chapter 10	**John A. Thompson Ranch (SCS-27)** 107	
	Soil Conservation Service and the CCC: An Overview 107	

Chapter 11	**Parker Dam (BR-17, BR-18, FWS-1)**	109
	BR-17 (Parker Dam)	
	BR-18 (Upper Parker Dam)	109
	FWS-1	110
	Sidebar: Health and Safety in the CCC	*111*
Chapter 12	**Hualapai Mountain Park, Kingman (SP-8, SP-9, CP-2)**	113
	State Parks and the CCC: A Short Overview	113
	Sidebar: Camp Controversy	*122*
Chapter 13	**Round Valley (DG-46)**	125
Chapter 14	**Kingman (DG-133 and G-133)**	134
Chapter 15	**St. George (DG-45)**	140
	Sidebar: Showdown at Black Rock	*151*
Chapter 16	**Short Creek (G-135)**	154
Chapter 17	**Pipe Spring (DG-44)**	157
Chapter 18	**Antelope Valley (G-173)**	170
Chapter 19	**Fredonia (G-170)**	174
Chapter 20	**End of the CCC in Arizona**	177
Appendix 1	CCC Enrollment Periods	180
Appendix 2	List of CCC Camps in Study Area	181
Appendix 3	Camp Newspaper Poems and Song	185
Sources		188
Selected Bibliography		189
Index		192

List of Illustrations

Title Page. *Rock Culvert Construction Hualapai Mountain Park* i
Figure 1. *Relief Caravan on the Way* i
Figure 2. *Looking North Across Wolf Hole Lake* 2
Figure 3. *70 HP Diesel Buried In Mud* 3
Figure 4. *CCC Company 831, Petrified Forest, August 7, 1934* 8
Figure 5. *Oil and Paint Storage Building Construction, ca. 1936* 10
Figure 6. *CCC Blue Forest Foot Path Construction, April, 1937* 11
Figure 7. *Walnut Canyon Residence Under Construction, 1940* 24
Figure 8. *Road Construction, Camp F-5, Flagstaff, July 2, 1936* 38
Figure 9. *Camp F-6-A, Company 863* 43
Figure 10. *Prairie Dog Extermination, Coconino National Forest* 44
Figure 11. *Typical CCC Water Development Project, Possibly Little Leroux Spring* 45
Figure 12. *Leroux Spring Forest Nursery, F-75 at Work* 48
Figure 13. *Beaver Creek Ranger Station Barn-Garage* 50
Figure 14. *Monument to Battle of Big Dry Wash, May, 1941* 51
Figure 15. *Snow Bowl's Hart Prairie Lodge* 54
Figure 16. *Creston F. Baumgartner, circa 1930* 60
Figure 17. *Three Boys on Their Way to Work(?)* 61
Figure 18. *CCC Company 851, F-27, Bellemont* 63
Figure 19. *Grandview Lookout Cabin, circa 1936* 67
Figure 20. *Moqui Ranger Station Under Construction, June, 1940* 70
Figure 21. *Increasing Height Check Dam Hayfield Draw* 78
Figure 22. *Juniper Crib Check Dams* 79
Figure 23. *New Crown King Ranger Station Dwelling* 81
Figure 24. *Shelter on Horsethief Basin Campground* 83
Figure 25. *Granite Basin Dam* 87
Figure 26. *Typical Raising a Phone Line Pole* 96
Figure 27. *"Page of Dirt" from Forest Desert, Company 3342 Newspaper* 104
Figure 28. *Typical CCC Tank Construction* 108
Figure 29. *Shovel and Truck Working on Bill Williams Truck Trail* 111
Figure 30. *Hualapai Mountain Park CCC Camp SP-8?,,,* 114
Figure 31. *Hualapai Mountain Park CCC Camp, SP-9* 114
Figure 32. *Rock Culvert Construction Hualapai Mountain Park* 117
Figure 33. *Overnight Cabin Recently Completed at Hualpai Mountain County Park* 117
Figure 34. *Petition Dated April 16, 1939* 123
Figure 35. *Petition Dated April 16, 1939 continued* 124
Figure 36. *Company 2865, Camp DG-46A, Round Valley* 126
Figure 37. *DG-46 Emergency Work, Democrat Mine Road* 127
Figure 38. *Buck and Doe Side Camp* 128
Figure 39. *DG-46 Dam* 129
Figure 40. *DG-46 Sloping a Cut on Round Valley-Hackberry Truck Trail* 129
Figure 41. *Fifty Posts, 100 Stays Per Shift* 130
Figure 42. *Mokaac Spring Corral, Pipeline, Storage Tank* 141
Figure 43. *215 Foot Suspension Bridge Over Ft. Pierce Wash* 143
Figure 44. *Heavy Going on Wolf Hole Road* 144

Figure 45.	*DG-44, Clay Hole, Partially Completed Corral Project*	*158*
Figure 46.	*Pipe Spring Camp, Company 2557*	*159*
Figure 47.	*Bull Rush Bridge Work*	*159*
Figure 48.	*Bull Rush Bridge on Completion*	*160*
Figure 49.	*Hack Canyon Spike Camp*	*160*
Figure 50.	*Small Band of Wild Ones*	*161*
Figure 51.	*Band of Eleven Wild Horses Already in the Trap*	*161*
Figure 52.	*House Rock Spike Camp*	*162*
Figure 53.	*Typical CCC Fence Construction*	*162*
Figure 54.	*DG-44 Soap Creek … Partially Completed Corral*	*164*
Figure 55.	*Honorable Discharge from Civilian Conservation Corps*	*178*

Acronyms and Terms

8th Corps	Army Corps headquartered at Fort Sam Houston, Texas, consisting of Texas, Oklahoma, Colorado, New Mexico, Arizona, Wyoming (less Yellowstone National Park)
AHSLA	Arizona Historical Society Library & Archives, Tucson, AZ
ASLAPR	Arizona State Library, Archives and Public Records, Phoenix, AZ
Arizona Strip	Part of the state of Arizona that is north of the Colorado River, comprising parts of Mohave and Coconino counties, including the towns of Fredonia, Littlefield, and Short Creek (Colorado City)
BLMKN	Bureau of Land Management Kingman Field Office
BLMSTG	Bureau of Land Management St. George Field Office
BLMSTG–*RIRB*	Bureau of Land Management St. George Field Office *Range Improvement Record Book*
BR	Bureau of Reclamation
CCC	Civilian Conservation Corps
CCCL	Civilian Conservation Corps Legacy
CIR	Camp Inspection Report
CP	County Park
CRL	Center for Research Libraries
CWA	Civil Works Administration; New Deal federal agency established through the hard winter of 1933–1934 putting unemployed to work in building schools, airports, bridges, and the like
DG	Division of Grazing
DOI	Department of the Interior
ECW	Emergency Conservation Work; official agency name established in 1933. The name Civilian Conservation Corps became popular even in 1933. In 1937, Congress changed the name by statute to Civilian Conservation Corps.
FANMA	Flagstaff Area National Monuments Archives
FDR	Franklin Delano Roosevelt
FERA	New Deal program established by Congress on May 12, 1933, that gave cash grants to state and city work relief projects
FP	Federal Project
FS	Forest Service
FY	Fiscal Year
G	Department of Grazing
GCNM	Grand Canyon National Monument
GCNP	Grand Canyon National Park
GCNPMC	Grand Canyon National Park Museum Collection
GCNPRL	Grand Canyon National Park Research Library
GPO	Government Printing Office
KNF	Kaibab National Forest
LEM	Local Experienced Man; enrollee hired locally for his work and supervisory skills. LEMs were not subject to the normal age and marital requirements and were expected to be wholesome role models for the junior enrollees.
LO	Lookout
MMHA	Mohave Museum of History and Arts, Kingman, AZ
NARACA	National Archives and Records Administration, Riverside, CA
NARACO	National Archives and Records Administration, Denver, CO
NARADC	National Archives and Records Administration, Washington, DC
NARAMD	National Archives and Records Administration, College Park, MD

NARAMO	National Archives and Records Administration, St. Louis, MO
NAU	Northern Arizona University, Flagstaff, AZ
NIRA	Omnibus New Deal legislation that included NRA, FERA, and PWA with $3.3 billion funding
NPS	National Park Service
NRA	National Recovery Administration; New Deal federal agency that tried to end unfair competition by setting prices and creating codes of "fair practices"
PWA	Public Works Administration; New Deal federal agency, 1933–1939, that focused on reducing unemployment, typically through large-scale projects such as dams, bridges, public buildings, and municipal water and sewage systems
SCS	Soil Conservation Service
SNMAHA	Smithsonian National Museum of American History Archives
SMR	Superintendent's Monthly Report
SMNR	Superintendent's Monthly Narrative Report
SP	State Park
TT	Tree Tower
USDA	United States Department of Agriculture
USDI	United States Department of Interior
USFS	United States Forest Service
USGS	United States Geological Survey
WPA	Works Progress Administration; largest New Deal federal agency, 1935–1943; employed many through public works projects and arts and literary projects

Preface

AFTER FIVE YEARS OF CCC research, it is apparent that the largest problem in telling the CCC story is the fact that they did an extraordinary amount of work. To get one's hands around their accomplishments is a great challenge. Their work went from the pedestrian to the magnificent. Not a part of Arizona was unaffected.

Once I made the decision to take on the rest of northern Arizona beyond the boundaries of Grand Canyon National Park, it was evident that there was a lot to understand and that the evidence available varied from company to company, from locale to locale. It was an immense disappointment that the records of the CCC–Indian Division housed in the National Archives represent only a small part of what was accomplished. So I made the decision not to include work of the Indian Division in the hopes that another researcher will find enough to tell its story. With the exception of Petrified Forest, the area of this monograph is the counties of Coconino, Mohave, Yavapai, and Prescott. For the CCC work at Grand Canyon National Park, readers are directed to my earlier monograph, *Shaping the Park and Saving the Boys: The Civilian Conservation Corps at Grand Canyon, 1933–1942* (Dog Ear Publishing, 2011). For the CCC work along the Mogollon Rim, readers are directed to Robert J. Moore's *The Civilian Conservation Corps in Arizona's Rim Country: Working in the Woods* (University of Nevada Press, 2006). With the exceptions of the Indian Division and work in Arizona done by Nevada CCC companies, I believe I have presented a comprehensive view of CCC work in these counties.[1] In just one instance in this region, Montezuma Castle National Monument, other New Deal programs such as the CWA and PWA were sufficient for the labor needs of the local agency, and the CCC was not used.[2]

The CCC story is many faceted. The effect of the program on the boys and their families and the participation of the military in the CCC program are areas for future studies. For me, the most tantalizing area is documenting the work that was accomplished. However, before I could do that I had to establish the baseline data—specifying as exactly as possible when and where each company was located as well as when they completed their tenure. So this monograph focuses greatly on the work projects. Yet, when possible, I have added some of the human element and the names of the main actors if those were in the records. And, I hope I have given a true flavor of what the enrollees were communicating in their camp newspapers.

Sifting through the records in archives is but one part of the research process. Once I got into the field with competent guides such as St. George Utah BLM archeologist John M. Herron, I began to see that a great deal of the CCC work is still in use today and that the CCC work was made to last. The Civilian Conservation Corps, along with other New Deal agencies, was responsible for unprecedented federal land agency infrastructure growth in northern Arizona. At Petrified Forest, we often use the road alignments and trails the CCC first built. In the Prescott and Kaibab National Forests, Petrified Forest, Walnut Canyon, and Wupatki, we still use the buildings the CCC (often with other New Deal agencies) built. In the Kingman area and the Arizona Strip, we frequently use CCC-built roads, trails, fences, and stock tanks. The first reliable roads from St. George, Utah, to Wolf Hole, Arizona, and from Fredonia to Mount Trumbull were CCC constructed. Indeed, the Taylor Grazing Act of 1934, the first law for the "orderly use of the range," was not meaningful until CCC labor was introduced. In the case of Petrified Forest, the CCC and other New Deal agencies transformed it from a backwater to a real national park. Throughout the Prescott, Kaibab, and Coconino National Forests, many of the road alignments we use today were first built by CCC boys. Hualapai Mountain Park's buildings and trails surely would not exist today if not for the CCC. These forty-four CCC companies completed an astounding number of projects, accomplishing as much as fifty years' work in less than ten years. However, this study is not a detailed road map. It is a sign post. I hope other researchers and scholars will use my work as a springboard to dig deeper into the CCC story.

A note about terminology and names: from time to time the historical records use terms that are confusing today—for example, the use of early term "ECW" for the latter-day term "CCC." Newspapers as well as official reports often used variant spellings of Hualapai, Schultz, Abineau, Schnebly, and the like. So I have taken the liberty of substituting the current terms in order to lessen confusion. Whenever possible when a personal name was not complete in the records and first names or initials were available, they have been supplied.

---

1. For a capsule view of the CCC archeological work at Rampart Cave, Mohave County, see Roman Malach's *Home on the Range,* 33–39. For a look at the CCC work at Lake Mead, see McBride, *Hard Work and Far from Home* and Kolvet, *Civilian Conservation Corps in Nevada.*
2. See Protas, *Past Preserved in Stone,* 100–104.

Acknowledgements

MY RESEARCH FOR THIS BOOK took me from the Atlantic to the Pacific, south to Tucson, Arizona and north to Denver, Colorado over a two year period. Inevitably with so many CCC companies to learn about many people and institutions were critical to this project. John M. Herron, St. George Utah BLM archeologist, opened up the agency files without limitation. He answered my many questions. He suggested changes in my chapters dealing with the Arizona Strip. And he took me to numerous CCC sites on the Arizona Strip. To see the CCC work, often still sturdy after more than seven decades, was enlightening and refreshing after so much time looking at reports and photos. Bill Parker of Petrified Forest National Park drew my attention to the notion that CCC and New Deal improvements were so comprehensive and well-planned that we frequently still walk in their footprint. Gene Morris of the National Archives at College Park Maryland assisted me on numerous occasions answering my questions and helping me find my way through the complexities of the agency's filing system. Michael I. Smith and Jim Steely on many occasions answered my questions kindly and steered me to other sources of information. John Irish gladly shared his large collection of CCC photos. For many months I sat in the Arizona Historical Society library indexing newspapers day after day. Katherine Reeve and her staff were always helpful and courteous. Rick Martinez of the National Archives in Denver deftly steered me through their files. Margaret Hangan, Kaibab National Forest archeologist, gladly opened her agency files to me without limitation and answered many questions. At Petrified Forest National Park Matt Smith and Stephanie Pieper opened their files, answered my many questions and suggested areas to research.

I want to acknowledge the assistance of Gwenn Gallenstein of the Flagstaff Area National Monuments, Peter J. Pilles, Jr. and Mark Swift of the Coconino National Forest, Shannon Clark, Jane Jackson, Tim Watkins of the Kingman Area BLM, Kathleen Duxbury, Dave Lorenz, Bob Moore, Sheila Poole and Ashley Cummings of the Forest Service Southwest Regional Office, Richard Melzer, Ron Short, Rose Houk, Susan Deaver Olberding, and Andrea Bornemeier of Pipe Spring National Monument. John and Vivien Baumgartner kindly shared their photos of CCC Artist Creston Baumgartner.

Many other librarians and archivists were critical to my work including the staff of the Grand Canyon National Park Research Library, Grand Canyon National Park Museum Collection, University of Arizona Library, University of Arizona Special Collections, Flagstaff City-Coconino County Public Library, Arizona State University Special Collections, St. George Branch Washington County Library, Kanab City Library, Smithsonian National Museum of American History Archives, and Williams Public Library. I want to acknowledge the kind assistance of Randy Thompson and Jennifer Albin of the National Archives at Riverside, California; Pat Foley and Dan W. Messersmith of the Mohave Museum of History and Arts; R. Sean Evans of the Northern Arizona University Cline Library Special Collections; Steve Gregory of the Fort Huachuca Museum and Bill Creech of the National Archives Washington, DC. Margaret Audretsch Scoville helped me trace CCC death records. Sharon Hunt, as always, is a wonderful editor to work with. Matt Murry and his co-workers at Dog Ear Publishing were always patient and helpful.

Without these many individuals and institutions this book would not have been possible. But I alone am responsible for any errors.

CHAPTER 1

CCC to the Rescue!

When big emergencies came, —
Wind, rain, dust, floods, blizzards, fires, insect pests —
Always the public turned to the CCC.
The boys came, they would help,
Organized into cheerful and salvage crews —
They always came.

Blizzards swept sage flats and pinyon hills of Utah,
Cutting off sheep, snowbound herders, prospectors,
Back in the hills, away from food and fuel.
The CCC boys opened roads, dug out sheep,
Cattle, herders, and prospectors,
Got them out to food and safety.
—From *Emergencies* by John D. Guthrie[1]

THE WINTER OF 1936–1937 SAW record snowfalls across northern Arizona. The January 22, 1937, issue of the *Coconino Sun* noted that seventy-four inches of snow had fallen in Flagstaff. In the Hualapai Mountains outside Kingman, four feet of snow was on the ground, necessitating the movement of the Hualapai Mountain CCC camp down to the lower elevations of the Round Valley CCC camp.[2] And at Round Valley, their Francis Creek spike camp men were moved to the main camp because of snow.[3] But, like other CCC camps, Round Valley had a Caterpillar, and they went to the rescue of stranded ranchers. Enrollees rescued the Day family in the Francis Creek area, and they took out twenty-six people from the Democrat Mine area who had been stranded for two weeks.[4] The Kanab, Utah, newspaper declared it the "Worst Storm in Dixie's History." Temperatures were said to be 30° to 40° below and snowdrifts from St. George, Utah, to the Nevada line to be 15′ high.[5] Communities such as Fredonia, Wolf Hole, Short Creek, and Mount Trumbull on the Arizona Strip were cut off from the outside world. The St. George newspaper estimated that at least thirty-five men and twenty thousand to thirty thousand sheep in the Wolf Hole and Mount Trumbull area were stranded and out of food.[6] Grand Canyon enrollees worked for over two weeks to open the snowbound road to Supai, where Indians isolated since Christmas were in need of critical medical supplies.[7]

Figure 1. Relief Caravan on the Way, DG-45, 1937. Courtesy NARACO, RG 49/15/C/6/1 Box 62.

Heavy snow stretched from the New Mexico to the Nevada state lines and beyond. A rescue party from the Boulder City, Nevada, CCC camp plowed through snowdrifts up to 8′ deep for two days to reach isolated miners at the Kelly Mine ninety miles away.⁸ Near Holbrook, the Petrified Forest CCC camp took two days to open six miles of road so two ranchers could feed their starving cattle.⁹ The deep snow fell as far south as the CCC camp at Yava, where it reached up to 3′ deep. Here, Camp DG-8 curtailed most regular activities to focus on plowing roads to isolated ranchers and, in one case, getting a sick person out to medical care. They also helped feed stranded wildlife. (See chapter 8, *Division of Grazing Camps, Yavapai County*.) The Mayer CCC boys were feeding quail as well as plowing the roads. The Pipe Spring camp was cut off from the outside from December 18 until late January, but that did not keep them from aiding ranchers by clearing roads, day and night. (See chapter 17, *Pipe Spring [DG-44]*.)

Of the Arizona rescue work, the most exhaustive was that of Camp DG-45 on the Arizona Strip. Snow started on December 28, 1936, at St. George, Utah, with a 2′ snowfall; after a few days, 30″ of snow was on the ground. By January 10, sheep and cattle were dying. Besides the snow, man and beast had to deal with temperatures so cold they broke previous records. Temperatures as low as 30° below were reported at Mount Trumbull. The combination of heavy snow covering the shrubs and grasses and extreme cold was a lethal mixture for livestock. On January 7, a CCC caravan of eight trucks and their R-5 Caterpillar left St. George for Little Tank some fifty-two miles south into Arizona. In two days, they reached the Wolf Hole spike camp twenty-eight miles south. At that point the caravan, which included four private cars and trucks, stayed at Wolf Hole while the Caterpillar plowed ahead alone, averaging only three miles a day. However, another snowfall covered the road behind the Caterpillar. The R-5 turned around, hooked one heavily loaded truck to it, and in two days finally reached Little Tank. "People there were almost out of food and all grain was gone." The weather moderated a bit, and the "Cat" returned to Wolf Hole, bringing the remaining caravan to Little Tank, where they arrived on January 15. Some twenty-five thousand sheep were said to be within ten miles of Little Tank. The twelve tons of grain and cottonseed cake were a welcome sight. The R-5 was having mechanical problems, so it returned to St. George on January 18. An appeal to Salt Lake City by the camp resulted in the loan of a seventy-horsepower diesel Caterpillar to join the now-repaired R-5.

On January 22, a second caravan left St. George, totaling twenty-two trucks and pickups. DG-45 contributed three trucks, and the CCC camps at Zion and Veyo, Utah, another eight, while the rest were privately owned.

Figure 2. Looking North across Wolf Hole Lake, DG-45, 1937. Courtesy NARACO, RG 49/15/C/6/1 Box 62.

Meanwhile, more snow had fallen, making the going even harder. Both Caterpillars worked in relays day and night, arriving at Little Tank six days later. By this time ranchers were estimating they had already lost 30% of their sheep. The caravan carried forty tons of feed, and both "Cats" were plowing the way to isolated herds. After a week all the feed was distributed, but the R-5 again broke down as a result of the extraordinary heavy work. Snow again fell, necessitating re-plowing of the road between Little Tank and Wolf Hole.

On February 3, the diesel "Cat" started for Mount Trumbull and arrived two days later. The R-5 was again repaired and with the diesel started another rescue, this time twenty-five miles southwest of Mount Trumbull to two stranded sheep herds numbering some six thousand. Two days out, rain began to fall, eventually melting much of the snow and negating the need to continue. The diesel "Cat" turned around for St. George, but near Little Tank the mud was so deep the "Cat" was buried to its tracks. It took a week to dig it out. The R-5 joined the rescue again, bringing in more grain. From time to time the diesel "Cat" was stuck in the mud, but the lighter R-5 was able to pull it out. By mid-February, the "Cats" made more trips to other isolated Arizona Strip communities as well as Bunkerville, Nevada. Camp Superintendent D.M. Thompson estimated the CCC gave direct relief to thirty thousand sheep and five hundred cattle. Many more sheep and cattle were saved due to the CCC opening the roads and allowing ranchers to come to the rescue.¹⁰

Figure 3. 70 HP Diesel Buried in Mud when Rain Melted Snow, DG-45, 1937. Courtesy NARACO, RG 49/15/C/6/1 Box 62.

Two Wasted Resources

What was the CCC? In summary, this new program was a "catalyst," bringing "together two wasted resources, the young men and the land, in an attempt to save both."[11] Its origins were first in the mind of the new president, Franklin Delano Roosevelt. He was a conservationist and, as the governor of New York, sponsored Temporary Emergency Relief Administration legislation. Under this plan, by 1932, ten thousand men were employed planting trees, fighting forest fires, building roads and trails, and developing recreational facilities throughout New York.[12] Indeed, by the early 1930s, the idea of sending unemployed people to work in the forests had gained acceptance in at least a half-dozen European countries.[13] FDR was sworn into office on March 4, 1933, and after meeting with his advisors March 9–14, draft legislation was introduced to Congress on March 21. On March 31, after overwhelming congressional support, the president signed the legislation creating the Civilian Conservation Corps.[14] Unemployed US citizens were to be employed "in the construction [and] maintenance … in connection with the forestation of [US] lands … which are suitable for timber production, the prevention of forest fires, floods and soil erosion, plant pest and disease control, the construction, maintenance or repair of paths, trails, and fire lanes in the national parks and national forests, and such other work … as the President may determine to be desirable." The authorizing legislation (PL 5-73) and implementing Executive Order 6101 (April 5, 1933) totaled just two printed pages.[15]

To be eligible, a young man had to be between the ages of seventeen and twenty-five, and priority was given to families on relief. (Later in the program the age limits would change slightly, and the relief requirement would be relaxed.) In April 1933, the age requirements were relaxed for people in three broad categories: veterans (Executive Order 6129, May 11, 1933); local experienced men (LEMs), who acted as role models and supervisors; and American Indians, organized into separate Indian Division companies. The prospective young enrollee had to be in good health, a citizen, and unmarried, without a criminal record. He was paid $30 per month. His basic housing, food, and medical care were provided. He was required to send home $25 each month to his family. The War Department was responsible for physical examinations and conditioning of enrollees; organization and administration; transportation; supplies; enforcement of sanitation; provision of medical care and hospitalization; discipline; and the welfare and education of the boys. Enrollees were formed in companies of two hundred.[16] The enrollee while at work was supervised by technical agencies such as the National Park Service and Forest Service.[17] Although the enrollees' lives outside of work were controlled by the military, they were not governed by strict military discipline. Boys enrolled (they did not enlist) for six months, and their service was voluntary. Labor leader Robert Fechner was appointed CCC director on April 5. On April 7, the first enrollee was accepted.[18]

The CCC Comes to Arizona

As the March 1933 debate in Congress over Roosevelt's conservation measure progressed, a few Arizona newspapers weighed in with editorials. The *Arizona Republic* opined that the measure was merely a stop gap and another dole. "It may be that there will never be an adequate return."[19] A *Prescott Evening Courier* editorial took a more positive approach. The president was praised for his "worth while" efforts. Although the program had shortcomings, "delay is fatal to a starving man."[20] The Prescott newspaper, in a later editorial, was more positive, saying enrollees will "feel a source of pride … that they are making a great contribution to the welfare of their country for years to come."[21] The *Phoenix Gazette* was a bit more upbeat than its sister Phoenix paper stating, "Action is the Roosevelt slogan."[22] However, nearly all northern Arizona newspapers failed to editorialize, preferring to report the debates.

On March 31, the president signed the legislation creating the Civilian Conservation Corps. On April 1, "four government departments threw their administrative agencies in to high gear," and Secretary of Agriculture Henry Wallace telegraphed state governors, inviting them to send a representative to an April 6 Washington, D.C. conference.[23] The same day, the *Arizona Republic* noted that Southwest Regional Forester Frank C. W. Pooler was inquiring of all U.S. Forest Service supervisors how many men they could put to work.[24] On April 5, the *Phoenix Gazette* noted that the first twenty-five thousand CCC enrollees would be sent to conditioning camps, with most coming from eastern U.S. cities.[25] The following day the *Arizona Republic* announced that W. W. Lane, former state highway engineer, would be at the Washington meeting as Arizona's representative.[26] Apparently the Washington conference supplied little details beyond the state quota of 1,000 enrollees.[27] (Although the state plan for the first year called for 1,000 juniors, it also called for 825 LEMs, 100 veterans, and 5,484 Indians.)[28]

Even though the April 6 meeting was said to be lacking in details, Arizona officials were quick to announce their plans. The following day in Flagstaff, County Engineer J. B. Wright and Forest Service officials announced ambitious road building plans. Wright stated that three thousand men would be working in the Coconino National Forest when the program was in full swing.[29] On the same day, the *Phoenix Gazette* announced plans for CCC work in the Coronado as well as the Coconino and Tonto National Forests.[30] In Holbrook on April 7, Sitgreaves National Forest Supervisor Lee Kirby announced his list of CCC projects.[31] On the same day, Williams newspaper readers were notified a camp was coming to the area.[32]

However, on April 8, controversy was aired when some Maricopa County state house representatives protested the transporting of out-of-state unemployed men into the state when Arizona already had ten thousand out of work. Their views were aired in a telegram to Senator Henry Ashurst.[33] While Ashurst took the side of those protesting the out-of-state men,[34] Governor Benjamin B. Moeur vigorously defended the president. "There are no state lines regarding this work, as it is national in scope. I sincerely hope that every citizen in the state will co-operate with the President.... We are sorely in need of every outside dollar we can obtain." He stated that ten million dollars would be coming to the state in federal programs and that much of that money would be used for the purchase of food and materials within the state. He concluded that Arizona would receive a generous share of federal monies and credited that to Lane's knowledge of forests and soil erosion and the influence of senators Ashurst and Hayden.[35] The idea of rejecting outside labor was not held everywhere. In Douglas, a business group sent telegrams supporting "even outside labor" for the reforestation program.[36] In Flagstaff, the chamber of commerce supported the reforestation program, fearing that numerous protests would result in a net loss of jobs to the state.[37] Ultimately, the controversy over outsiders was solved by the CCC agreeing to assign Arizona men first to their home state and to assign in Arizona only men recruited in the 8th Army Corps area.[38] They also would give preference to locating CCC camps where local cooperation was evident.

Meanwhile, delays and confusion began to plague the new program.[39] Director Fechner began a quick reorganization. Again, state officials were beckoned to Washington, and Stuart Bailey of the State Board of Public Welfare and T. S. O'Connell, state engineer, flew east.[40] Bailey was designated the first state CCC representative,[41] and soon after, state enrollment agencies began to accept men. (Florence Warner, executive secretary of the State Board of Public Welfare, was listed in the first Washington reports.)[42] On April 21, Fechner announced Arizona would initially be given twenty-eight camps, housing five thousand enrollees.[43] Of these, eight would be in northern Arizona national forests, with five in the Coconino, one in the Kaibab, two in the Tusayan, and three in the Prescott.[44]

But the enrollment of Arizona boys was not going smoothly. The *Arizona Republic* reported on April 26 that the first recruits would leave the following day for conditioning at Fort Bliss. The next day the newspaper reported that the men were delayed indefinitely as Fort Bliss was overcrowded.[45] The Jerome newspaper, in a UP story, faulted the lack of transportation.[46] On May 4, Governor Moeur announced that he had been advised by Fort Sam Houston that Fort Huachuca would take 250 enrollees. Moeur advised the military that Fort Tuthill near Flagstaff would be available for conditioning. (Apparently Moeur did not receive an answer regarding this suggestion.)[47] On May 5, Bailey told the *Arizona Republic* that nearly all 1,000 juniors had been selected.[48] As it turned out, Fechner, the Forest Service, and the War Department needed to streamline what was a slow and convoluted process.

On May 10, Fechner met with the CCC Advisory Council and requested of Colonel Duncan Major, the War Department representative, how the CCC could speed up the process to meet the president's goal of 250,000 enrollees in camp by July. The military requested, and was granted, new powers to cut red tape and hold wide authority over the movement of new enrollees.[49] "Where questions arise not covered by instructions or when necessary to change such instructions you are authorized to act" and report later, commanders were told.[50] Quickly, the military enacted massive decentralization. The military set a goal of enrolling 8,540 men per day, a greater number than processed for World War I. "On June 1st a peak daily enrollment of 13,843 men was reached."[51] Arizona began to enroll men a bit faster. On May 9, Bailey announced that 215 recruits were assembling in Tucson, Nogales, Bisbee, and Douglas for physical exams. Those accepted would be moved by Army trucks that afternoon to Fort Huachuca.[52] Three days later, Governor Moeur requested that Arizona counties aid with enrollee transportation. On May 14, the *Arizona Republic* reported that he was promised the loan of vehicles by ten of fourteen counties. Coconino County promised three dump trucks, three graders, and three tractors.[53] The new enrollees were soon to arrive.

The first CCC companies to be established in Arizona were Company 805 at Safford (F-14, Crook National Forest) and Company 806 at Globe (F-16, Crook National Forest) on May 23, 1933. The following day, Company 807 arrived at Payson (F-23, Tonto National Forest). Many of the men arrived by a special train of 525 men originating in San Antonio, Texas.[54] Of the enrollees at these first three camps, about three-quarters were from Texas, with the rest from Arizona. The first camp established in this study area was Company 851 (F-27, Bellemont, Tusayan National Forest) on May 25. By August 31, 1933, the date of the first military *Location and Strength Report*, a total of twenty-three companies were at work statewide. Of these, eight companies were located in the area of this study.[55] All of the latter were located on national forest lands. (In addition, over thirty Arizona CCC camps were planned for Indian reservations.)[56]

The Army pulled officers and non-commissioned officers from teaching and staff jobs in order to fill the frantic need for camp leaders. Equipment and clothing that had been in storage since the end of World War I were quickly distributed. Sometimes the clothing and equipment were so aged they had to be handled carefully lest they fall apart. Fred Lancaster, an enrollee in a Prescott National Forest camp in late 1933, described walking carefully in his boots lest the soles fall off. He wrote that you "soon became adept to sliding into your bunk from the head, lest putting all your weight on one spot would rip the rotten canvas out of your cot." At first, the meals were outdoors until the kitchen and mess hall were finished, so with a little wind, everything was "well flavored with sand." Enrollees moved into their barracks even before they were finished. Candles supplied the light at night until a light plant arrived. At first, Lancaster reported, all work was done by hand. They built eighteen miles of road and twenty miles of fence with picks, shovels, and wheelbarrows.[57]

---

1. Guthrie, *Saga of the CCC*, 31.
2. "110 Hualapai CCC Boys Are Moved to Round Valley Camp," *Mohave County Miner*, January 8, 1937, 1.
3. "Round Valley CCC Camp," *Mohave County Miner*, January 15, 1937, 5.
4. "CCC Boys Rescue Marooned Family," *Mohave County Miner*, February 5, 1937, 1.
5. "Worst Storm in Dixie's History," *Kane County Standard*, January 22, 1937, 1.
6. "Concern Felt for Safety of Stockmen on Arizona Strip," *Washington County News*, January 14, 1937, 1, 5.
7. "Grand Canyon News," *Prescott Evening Courier*, January 21, 1937, 2.
8. "Heroic Struggles in Snow Told by Rescued Group," *Arizona Republic*, January 18, 1937, 1, 2.
9. PFNM, "SMNR," January 1937, NARAMD RG 79/150/34/12/1 E-1 Box 2332.
10. Quote is from Thompson, D. M., "Report of Emergency Stock Relief on the Arizona Strip DG 45 St. George, Utah Dec. 29th, 1936 to Feb. 15th, 1937," NARACO RG 49/15/C/6/1 Box 62. See also Baldridge, *Nine Years of Achievement*, 345–347. According to historian Baldridge, 428,000 sheep and 27,000 cattle were saved across the state of Utah by eleven CCC camps. See Baldridge, "Final Preparations Being Made for Utah Gathering," *Civilian Conservation Corps Legacy Journal*, Sept./Oct. 2011, 3–4.
11. Salmond, *Civilian Conservation Corps*, 4.
12. J. Smith, *FDR*, 320.
13. Salmond, *Civilian Conservation Corps*, 5.
14. Although the official name of the organization was Emergency Conservation Work in 1933, it quickly became known popularly as the Civilian Conservation Corps. On June 28, 1937, the official name of the agency became Civilian Conservation Corps. In this book, Civilian Conservation Corps is used throughout to lessen confusion.
15. See Paige, *Civilian Conservation Corps and the National Park Service*, Appendix A, for legislation and executive orders.
16. U.S. War Department, *Civilian Conservation Corps Regulations*, 2.
17. For a detailed look at the formative period of the CCC, see Audretsch, *Shaping the Park and Saving the Boys*, 1–3.
18. Salmond, *Civilian Conservation Corps*, 31. Early on when the president asked Fechner how long before the first camp was opened, his response was a month. "The president replied that he wanted one opened within a week. Just seven days after that, Camp Roosevelt, near Luray, Virginia, was opened," said Fechner.
19. "Reforestation and Unemployment," *Arizona Republic*, March 29, 1933, sect. 2, 8.
20. "Criticism of the Roosevelt Relief Plan," *Prescott Evening Courier*, April 4, 1933, 4.

21. "Enrolling the Roosevelt Forestry Army," *Prescott Evening Courier,* April 27, 1933, 4.
22. "Plans for Reforestation," *Phoenix Gazette,* April 1, 1933, 4.
23. "Forestry Projects Studied," *Arizona Republic,* April 1, 1933, 1.
24. "Plan Arizona Work," *Arizona Republic,* April 1, 1933, 6.
25. "First Forestry Workers' Group Ordered to Camp," *Phoenix Gazette,* April 5, 1933, 1.
26. "Lane to Attend Forestry Meet," *Arizona Republic,* April 6, 1933, sect. 2, 5.
27. Collins, *New Deal in Arizona,* 208.
28. U.S. Civilian Conservation Corps, *Second Report of the Director of Emergency Conservation Work,* 20.
29. "Army of 200 Men Will Work in the Forests Here under Roosevelt Plan," *Coconino Sun,* April 7, 1933, 1.
30. "Enlisted Workers Coming to Arizona" and "400 Will Work in the Coconino Forests," *Phoenix Gazette,* April 7, 1933, 1.
31. "100 Forest Workers Will Arrive Here April 15th," *Holbrook Tribune,* April 7, 1933, 1.
32. "Government Employment Camp near Here," *Williams News,* April 7, 1933, 1.
33. "First Reforestation Recruits Are Sent to Conditioning Camps," *Arizona Republic,* April 8, 1933, 1. See also "Senator Ashurst Protests Opening State Forests to Outside Labor," *Phoenix Gazette,* April 10, 1933, 7.
34. "Ashurst Would Aid Arizona's Jobless," *Coconino Sun,* April 14, 1933, 2.
35. "U.S. Program to Put $10,000,000 in the State," *Arizona Republic,* April 9, 1933, 1. While Peter Booth in his thesis on the CCC in Arizona is critical of Moeur's lack of support of the federal efforts, William Collins states Moeur did all he could. See Collins, *New Deal in Arizona,* 209. Moeur offered the use of state highway equipment and suggested Fort Tuthill as a possible CCC reconditioning center. Moeur's secretary, H. H. Hotchkiss, took a position as a CCC procurement officer (*Arizona Republic,* April 13, 1934, 3). It appears to this author that Moeur supported the CCC. Moeur's papers at the state archives contain only a few letters relating to this subject, including two letters from Major General Frank R. McCoy, 8th Corps Army Commander. Both are very cordial in tone. On July 15, 1933, McCoy directed Arizona Army commanders "to develop, with regard to your [state] work and problems, an interest and understanding" and inviting Moeur and other state officials to visit camps. In his letter of September 25, 1933, McCoy indicates Moeur had visited with Army officers and asks for "your continued interest in the camps." See Governor Moeur Papers, ASLAPR RG 1 SG 11, Box 5A, CCC Camps. Moeur took an active involvement in early CCC matters, publicly recommending CCC sites to the National Park Service (*Arizona Republic,* August 10, 1933, 3); visiting CCC camps at Williams and Grand Canyon (*Arizona Republic,* August 25, 1933, 10), as well as Bellemont (*Happy Days,* September 16, 1933, 12); visiting Fort Huachuca to discuss CCC matters (*Arizona Republic,* August 18, 1933, 5); and publicly recommending as well as writing to counties that they request CCC winter camps (*Arizona Republic,* August 31, 1933, 1, 3 and *Phoenix Gazette,* August 31, 1933, 2). Moeur spoke at the dedication of the Papago Park CCC camp saying, "There is being more good done through the CCC camps than in any other organization of mankind in many years" (*Arizona Republic,* December 11, 1933, sect. 1, 4).
36. *Arizona Republic,* April 9, 1933, 4.
37. "Flagstaff Approves Reforestation Plan as Trade Stimulus," *Coconino Sun,* April 14, 1933, 1, 3.
38. Booth, *Civilian Conservation Corps in Arizona,* 20. "Priority Due Arizonians…," *Arizona Republic,* May 2, 1933, 1, indicates Secretary of Labor Frances Perkins communicated to State Highway Commissioner C. E. Addams that "Arizona people will be placed in Arizona camps before outsiders are brought in."
39. Booth, Ibid., 18–21; "Forestry Recruiting Retarded," *Arizona Republic,* April 10, 1933, 1.
40. "Officials Going East by Plane," *Arizona Republic,* April 10, 1933, 4.
41. Booth, *Civilian Conservation Corps in Arizona,* 26.
42. U.S. Civilian Conservation Corps, *Second Report of the Director of Emergency Conservation Work,* 17.
43. "State Given Allotment of Forest Camps," *Arizona Republic,* April 21, 1933, 1.
44. "Arizona Gets 28 Reforestation Camps," *Coconino Sun,* April 28, 1933, 6.
45. *Arizona Republic,* April 26, 1933, 1, and April 27, 1933, 1.
46. "Reforestation Plans Change," *Verde Copper News,* April 28, 1933, 3.
47. "Huachuca Gets Arizona Recruits," *Prescott Evening Courier,* May 4, 1933, 2.
48. "State Forest Quota Raised to 1,825 Men," *Arizona Republic,* May 5, 1933, 1.
49. Salmond, *Civilian Conservation Corps,* 37–40.
50. Sherraden, "Military Participation in a Youth Employment Program."
51. Major, "Mobilizing the Conservation Corps," 35, 37.
52. "Movement of Arizona's Recruits Begins Today," *Arizona Republic,* May 9, 1933, sect. 2, 1.
53. "Counties Aid Forest Work," *Arizona Republic,* May 14, 1933, 3.

54. "Forest Camps to Be Opened," *Arizona Republic,* May 23, 1933, sect. 2, 6.
55. U.S. War Department, Location and Strength of CCC Companies, 1933–1942, NARAMD RG 35 530/65/22/04/05.
56. "33 Camps Will Be Placed on Reservations," *Phoenix Gazette,* May 3, 1933, 1.
57. *Pinecroft News,* June 1939, Fiche MN #0519, CRL Newspapers.

CHAPTER 2

Petrified Forest National Monument (NM-1, NM-2, NP-8)

ACCORDING TO HISTORIAN GEORGE M. Lubick, "For the usually neglected national monuments like Petrified Forest, the New Deal years represented a watershed in their history." Soon the meager monument budget would be dwarfed by federal monies.[1] Even before the CCC arrived at Petrified Forest, the effect of the New Deal had already being felt. As early as November 1933, the *Holbrook Tribune* noted the monument was to get CWA funds. Later, newspaper articles reported that as many as 210 CWA men would be working. On December 8, 1933, the Flagstaff newspaper noted that Petrified Forest had been allocated $47,587 in CWA funds.[2] On April 20, 1934, the Holbrook newspaper noted (page 3) the CWA improvements included thirty miles of drift fence, campground improvements, ruins restoration, landscaping, and archeological surveys. CWA work ended on April 19, 1934.[3] The article also noted that PWA funds were to be allocated for road construction. PWA monies were also said to be used for footpaths and bridges.[4] The arrival of the CCC at the monument was announced publicly on June 6, 1934, noting that a fifteen-enrollee fly camp had arrived from Phoenix to improve a site for the arrival of the full camp. Finishing the CWA work, trail construction and soil erosion control were said to be its work.[5]

1934

NM-1, formerly SP-3A, was officially occupied by Company 831 on July 3, 1934. The camp was located on the south bank of the Rio Puerco below the highway bridge. It was delayed coming until a successful well was finished with a flow of 3,500 gallons per day, the Army minimum. The commanding officer was Capt. J. R. Worthington; he was succeeded by Capt. H. H. Geisser. E. A. Campbell was the first educational advisor, and W. H. Collie was the first project superintendent.[6]

Even though the men were "well behaved," there was a concern about damage to the pictograph area nearby. However, the importance of the site was explained, and no problems were noted. Work began July 8 with 88 men, but then the workforce increased to full company strength.[7] On July 7, the camp was inspected by Special Investigator James C. Reddoch, and he rated morale as "excellent."[8] On July 19, CCC Director Robert Fechner, with Capt. Paolo Sperati, sub-district commander, inspected the work projects.[9] During July, the local newspaper noted the camp was to receive a CCC Artist, Earl Darry (or Darrey). However, no records of Darry's work have been found by this author.[10]

During August, four projects were underway. The trans-monument telephone line connecting with the line along US Route 66 was progressing with both above- and underground installation. Other projects were Newspaper Rock Road, general cleanup, and construction of one of the Antelope reservoirs.

On the morning of August 27, enrollee Henry (Hinio) Santistevan, 37, was returning to camp on the Santa Fe Railway and injured badly. He was not found until four hours later. He was taken to the camp doctor by railway employees but died at the Winslow hospital. He had one leg severed and other serious injuries.[11]

On August 31, Company 831 had a total of 166 men (from Texas and Arizona, with 7 African Americans). The army staff consisted of a reserve captain, a reserve 2nd lieutenant, a contract physician, and an educational advisor.

During September, the nineteen-mile-long trans-monument telephone line, one Antelope reservoir, Newspaper Rock

Figure 4. CCC Company 831, Petrified Forest, August 7, 1934, Rio Puerco Camp. Courtesy Petrified Forest National Park Museum Collection, #34822.

protective fencing, and the Newspaper Rock Road were completed.[12] Also during September, the *Holbrook Tribune* (page 7) noted that the park was using PWA funds for trails to rock art sites. Unfortunately, tragedy struck again on September 30 when a CCC truck returning to camp from Holbrook overturned, injuring eight and killing New Mexico enrollee Casiano Salazar, 27.[13]

On October 27, the camp was moved to the headquarters area[14] and into new winter buildings. A generator supplied electricity to the camp.[15] On September 17–20, W. H. Wirt of the NPS Forestry Division inspected the camp and submitted a six-page report with details of the work completed. He noted that the company was organized for firefighting, but adequate water was still a problem. Educational Advisor Campbell had fifteen teachers, but there was still no adequate meeting places for classes. Camp NM-1 is "well organized" and "doing efficient work."[16] At the end of October, the camp had 191 enrollees (evenly divided between those from Arizona and Texas, with 3 African Americans).

During November, a large number of men were sick, averaging 12%, leaving an average of 135 men were available for work. Ongoing projects included Rio Puerco water development, Blue Forest Road, a footpath to the pictographs, and landscaping.[17] By December, organized educational classes for enrollees were underway, with twenty-two subjects taught by fourteen instructors, with the largest group attending grade school classes.[18]

During December, work continued on the Rio Puerco water development, a minor road to the Blue Forest foot trail, a foot trail to pictographs near headquarters, and Antelope Reservoir No. 2.[19] During the summer, the camp had fielded a baseball team, and the year ended with the local newspaper noting a CCC basketball team was forming.[20] A year-end report showed the following projects and man days: Rio Puerco Pipe Line (484), Agate Bridge Water System (780), Blue Forest Road (3,836), Pictograph Rock Foot Trail (1,410), cleanup (3,332), and three parking areas (1,288).[21]

1935

January opened on a positive note, with the community invited to a camp open house on January 11.[22] During the month, work continued on the Rio Puerco water development, a minor road to the Blue Forest, the Antelope reservoir near Highway 260, landscaping, and cleanup.[23] At the end of January, company strength was 200 (all white enrollees, almost evenly divided between those from Texas and from Arizona).

During February, in addition to the ongoing projects, five hundred cottonwood cuttings were set in the sedimentary fill east of the Rio Puerco Bridge.[24] Associate Forester W. H. Wirt, in his mid-February inspection, in addition to the latter-mentioned project, noted a total of eight projects, including obliteration of seven miles of old road from Rio Puerco to US Route 66. He found the camp "to be clean, well organized and free from fire hazards."[25]

In March, the special investigator noted that the well was only supplying salt water and the camp was hauling two thousand gallons of fresh water daily. He recommended a 5kw light plant, stating that the 3kw plant was not enough.[26] During April, company strength dropped to 100, but with new enrollees and re-enlistments strength went back to 200. Work continued on the water lines from the Rio Puerco and the ten-thousand-gallon storage tank.[27] In May, the three new checking stations were completed under the PWA grant. CCC work included the stone masonry pumphouse on the Rio Puerco. The latter work included a skilled mason assisted by the enrollees. Other work included sewer lines and septic tanks on the Rio Puerco, Pictograph Road, flagstone walks with boulder curbing, sodding and seeding at the wildlife reservoirs, and obliteration of old roads.[28] In June the pumphouse was completed. This included the skilled mason doing some training of the enrollees in masonry. The mason said that three of the enrollees were now so skilled he would hire them if he had the need.

With the completion of the pumphouse, water was supplied to the comfort station, headquarters area, and CCC camp. The sewer line at Rio Puerco was completed and a sewer line at Agate Bridge begun. Good progress was made on Rio Puerco riprap and bank protection this month.[29] Associate Forester Wirt inspected the camp on June 24–25 with Commanding Officer Lt. L. M. Linxwiler and found company strength at 210, with only 1 AWOL. He noted a new work project: seven enrollees doing guide and educational work.[30] On June 30, company strength was 205 (most from Arizona).

During July, much work was concentrated on stabilizing the banks near the Rio Puerco Bridge. Selected enrollees were successfully doing the work of education, guide, and contact work with the public. Work continued on the Agate Bridge water system, and the pictographs truck trail was nearly complete. Progress was made on the survey of petrified wood. Another enrollee death occurred on July 3 when Calvin Jones "was gone from camp and killed by a railway train in Winslow."[31]

Conditions were said to be "very good" in August. "The men are generally well satisfied, and radical activities are practically non-existent." Six enrollees continued the petrified wood survey. Six enrollees were now doing public contact work. A flagstone walk adjacent to the headquarters campground was completed.[32]

In September, enrollees painted the Rio Puerco steel bridge. Work on the Agate Bridge water and sewage system was nearly complete.[33] Associate Forester Wirt inspected the camp on September 1–2, 1935, and noted strength at 170, with 1 AWOL. He noted twelve enrollees were recently sent to a forestry camp at Eagle Creek. The new educational advisor, K. C. Chatwin, had just arrived, and Wirt had high hopes for him. Wirt noted that the cottonwoods and willows planted on the Rio Puerco seemed to be doing well.[34] A September 30 work report for the period beginning April 1 listed nineteen projects totaling 16,772 man days. The most man days, 3,447, was devoted to placing boulders to restrict vehicle access at parking lots, picnic areas, etc.[35]

On October 4, enrollee Jimmie Peralta made the front page of the Holbrook newspaper from being bound over in court for auto theft. In November, as in previous months, an enrollee was using the power grader on monument highways. Work continued on the Blue Forest scenic road.[36] A visit by Special Investigator Reddoch near month's end indicated no problems.[37] W. H Wirt inspected the camp November 29–30 accompanied by the camp doctor and Project Superintendent Roer and found the camp "very well kept" with "a neat appearance." Of the 170 men in camp, he noted that 81 had come about a month ago from camp F-22 at Los Burros. A survey of petrified wood that had been inactive was to be resumed soon.[38] At year's end, Company 831 had 205 enrollees (94 from Oklahoma, 72 from Arizona, and 39 from Texas, with 6 African Americans).

1936

January marked some serious difficulty with the CCC mess. On January 10, there was a near strike, and three men were discharged who were considered ringleaders by the Army investigators. Major Whitlock, 8th Corps area commander, stated "that there are complaints in every company regarding the mess." Work continued on the Blue Forest scenic road, Rio Puerco bank protection, headquarters coal shed, and the boundary survey. Two enrollees assisted the park naturalist in the stabilizing of a special petrified tree, exposing about fifteen feet of a standing tree "(in the side of marl hill)," other impressions such as ferns, and what appeared to be leaves of a tree.[39]

During February, work continued on the January projects. Three enrollees were assisting the park naturalist in the collecting of fossils for the museum collection.[40] In March, a decision was made in Washington, D.C., to cut the number of Arizona camps effective April 1.[41] However, Petrified Forest would not be abandoned on April 1 as ordered because the new location for Company 831 was not yet ready. They would remain until May 1.[42]

In April, the excavation of the standing petrified tree made national news.[43] An April 1936 progress report from October 1 to April 30 listed a total of 17,253 man days in seventeen broad work projects. Educational guide work totaled 1,206 man days, while only 72 man days were devoted to the petrified wood survey and 48 man days to geological research.[44] The men departed the week of May 8 for Emma, Colorado, according to the *Holbrook Tribune* (page 4). In July, the *Arizona Republic* summarized the twenty-two-month-long work in a lengthy article, along with photos, of Company 831 at the park.[45]

Figure 5. Oil and Paint Storage Building Construction, circa 1936. Courtesy Petrified Forest National Park Museum Collection, #15866.

In October, the Army Quartermaster Corps came in to recondition the CCC barracks. All the new enrollees arrived by October 12, some by truck and others by train from Colorado (Company 805).[46] The camp was officially occupied October 11, with actual work beginning October 19.[47] November work was slow due to lack of qualified foremen. Projects included the underground phone line to Painted Desert, razing undesirable structures, Blue Forest and Agate Bridge foot trails, and public contact work.[48]

December work was slow due to sickness, snow, and men on holiday leave. Work included razing undesirable Painted Desert structures, resurfacing Blue Forest Road, and public contact at the museum.[49] At year's end, Company 805 had a total of 147 men (more than half from Colorado, and the remainder from Arizona, Oklahoma, and Texas, with 1 African American).

1937

For much of January, intense cold and snow slowed work. On January 25, two stockmen, Spurlock and Thompson, walked some miles to the park, requesting assistance in opening the snowbound road to their starving cattle out to Highway 260. Project Superintendent Collie, several trucks, and a crew of enrollees were sent out and, after two days of arduous work, opened six miles of road, helping save the cattle. With a break in the weather the last week of the month, projects included Dry Creek Wash flood control and riprap, trail maintenance, diversion ditches, and public contact work.[50] The officers' and technicians' quarters that burned on January 22 were rebuilt and reoccupied about February 17. The pre-fabricated building (120' x 20') was shipped from Linden, Texas.[51] Work projects during January included tree planting, flood control and riprap, Blue Forest Road, diversion ditches, and public contact work.[52]

During March work went "nicely." Projects included constructing the oil storage building and the employee cabin, riprap and flood control, Blue Forest Scenic Road, Agate Bridge Foot Path, and public contact work.[53] The March 26 *Holbrook Tribune* (page 4) noted the camp had invited the community to its April 4 open house. NPS Landscape Architect Alfred H. Kuehl inspected area work during February and March and called the quality of work "excellent." He noted that an invitation for bids to remodel the Painted Desert Inn were sent out to thirty-seven firms, but resulted in only one submission, from Olds Brothers of Winslow for $67,500.[54] On March 23, Assistant Forester H. L. Bill visited Petrified Forest, apparently at the request of NPS Superintendent Charles Smith, to access the damage porcupines had done to CCC-planted cottonwood seedlings along the Rio Puerco. He noted

Figure 6. CCC Blue Forest Foot Path Construction, April 1937. Courtesy NARACO, RG 79.

forty to fifty thousand seedlings had been set, but that the porcupine damage did not warrant control measures at that time.[55] An October through March progress report noted eighteen CCC projects totaling 11,335 man days. Blue Forest footpaths (1,378 man days), the oil storage building (1,609 man days), and riprap work on Highway 63 (1,577 man days) were the largest projects.[56]

April work included assigning enrollees to assist the PWA remodeling of the Painted Desert Inn. Flood control work on Dry Creek continued, and enrollees were assisting in the collection of specimens for the Geology Museum.[57] May work was concentrated on riprap and flood control, the headquarters employee cabin, ditch excavation, and remodeling at Painted Desert Inn.[58] In June, skilled stone masons were employed at Painted Desert Inn. The remodeling was quite complex. Sitgreaves National Forest donated logs, poles, and vigas (about five hundred, with a maximum diameter of 15"). The Apache Indian Agency donated more than five thousand savanas (quaking aspen poles). To assist in acquiring the timber, an enrollee crew of fifteen was located at the Los Burros CCC camp. This was excellent cooperation between agencies. Ongoing work included ditch excavation for the 6" water line at Painted Desert Inn.[59] On June 30, Company 805 had 137 men (slightly more than half from Oklahoma and the remainder from Arizona, Colorado, and Texas, with 1 African American).

In July, enrollees unloaded about a dozen carloads of materials and supplies destined for the Painted Desert PWA work. Enrollee-dug ditches were being used by the contractor, Lewis Brothers, for the water and sewage line installation. Painted Desert Inn work included thirty enrollees assisting three skilled stone masons. Ongoing work included riprap and flood control, headquarters employee cabin, ditch excavation, and public contact work.[60]

On July 28, Special Investigator A. W. Stockman visited the camp and noted some Oklahoma enrollees were dissatisfied because they were working outside their home state. He noted that many of their buildings were slowly falling apart. The mess was "most satisfactory." He noted much of the CCC work in detail in his report. Five thousand cubic yards of stone had been quarried for road work. Stockman noted that over four hundred steel rails had been driven in flood channels with pile-driving equipment.[61]

In August, CCC work centered on the Painted Desert area. Much work still was required in digging ditches, with one across the highway by the Painted Desert Lodge measuring 12' deep.[62] On September 17, one hundred enrollees, spic and span in their best uniforms, participated in the Constitution Day parade in

Holbrook. The American Legion led, followed by the American Legion Auxiliary, and then the CCC. Louis Purvis, assistant to the technician, left on September 25. Many men left at the end of the month, leaving total strength at 51 enrollees.[63] During October, work again was concentrated at Painted Desert. Enrollees came up to full strength by month's end.[64] November work was carried on "in a very good manner." Painted Desert Lodge showed "very good progress." Work continued on building repair, landscaping, Blue Forest Road, and riprap.[65] December work included the Painted Desert Lodge and riprap work. Many men were absent for the holidays.[66] At year's end, Company 805 had 184 men (more than half from Texas, and the remainder from Arizona, Colorado, and Oklahoma, with 1 African American).

1938

Fine weather in January allowed CCC work to proceed "at a good rate." The park superintendent noted a "great showing" to the Painted Desert Inn alterations. Other projects included the Painted Desert Power House project; stone riprap and flood control on the monument highway and the entrance road at the new Rio Puerco CCC camp site; erection of new camp buildings; and renovation and painting at the headquarters museum.[67]

During February, an average of thirty-two enrollees assisted Army personnel erecting the new NM-2 buildings at the Puerco River.[68] Thirty enrollees continued to assist at the Painted Desert Inn. Work continued on the power house, and the museum had been completely repainted. Public contact work continued and new museum cases were being assembled.[69]

During March, an average of thirty-nine enrollees assisted Army personnel erecting the new NM-2 buildings at the Puerco River. NM-1 was to be abandoned on April 2. About thirty enrollees were assisting at the Painted Desert Inn alterations. All headquarters residences were being repainted.[70] April saw enrollees assisting with Painted Desert Inn alterations, the Painted Desert power house, fencing, riprap and flood control, and fine grading. Nine enrollees were doing education and public contact work.[71]

During May, two large flood control and riprap projects along the highway were completed. Work continued on the Painted Desert Inn alterations and the Painted Desert Power House project. Nine enrollees were on public contact work. Company strength was only at 130. On May 29, CCC Director Robert Fechner and CCC Inspector John H. Haile Jr. inspected the monument CCC work, and Fechner was "well pleased" with "all activities."[72]

During June, work continued on ongoing projects. New projects begun included the camp service road, salvage of the abandoned CCC buildings, general landscaping, and a Painted Desert Inn service lane, as well as terraces, walks, and walls there.[73]

July had little CCC activity, as only thirty-seven enrollees were available for work. The new company was expected August 2.[74] Soon after the new company (3342) arrived, a few enrollees had to be discharged, including one who had a quantity of petrified wood in his luggage. He was taken to the U.S. commissioner, held in jail one night, and then released. Work continued on the Painted Desert Inn as well as salvaging the former CCC buildings. A great deal of ditch digging and landscaping was done.[75]

By August, the new enrollees had become accustomed to conditions there and were performing "efficient work." Much work at the Painted Desert Inn had been finished. An enrollee crew of eleven was sent to the Los Burros CCC camp in the Sitgreaves National Forest to get more poles to finish the inn. A number of enrollees were engaged in public contact work, enabling rangers and naturalists to complete other work.[76]

October found all the plastering at the Painted Desert Inn finished, and stone flagging was being laid on floors. Much other work continued, including public contact work.[77] On October 28 and 29, Special Investigator Stockman visited the camp. His report was mixed, to say the least. "Poor mess hall and recreation equipment, an unsatisfactory liberty trip once a week, and drab environment most likely are factors in homesickness that is general." He noted that there had been eleven dishonorable discharges in the past three months "for refusal to work in order to gain a discharge." But morale was good, he noted, and their Army officers were held in high esteem.[78]

In December, work included 9,000′ of trenching for the pipeline from the Rio Puerco to the storage reservoir near headquarters.[79] At the end of the year, Company 3342 had only 85 men (all but 3 from Pennsylvania).

1939

In the middle of January, new recruits came from Philadelphia. From 100 to 125 enrollees were digging trench for the 3″ pipeline, with about 13,500′ having been dug so far. Painted Desert Inn landscaping and exterior walls work continued, and a few enrollees were doing public contact work.[80]

During February, nearly 3,400 man days were accomplished, with 2,436 digging the trench from the Rio Puerco to the storage reservoir .5 mile from headquarters. From 100 to 130 enrollees were on this project, which totaled 20,000′ excavated so far. Other work included painting the inside of the Painted Desert Inn, 160 man days of public contact and guide work, and remodeling the old CCC infirmary into employee quarters.[81]

In March, substantial work was done on the pipeline, with 2,230 man days of a total of 3,750 worked. Walks, terraces, and walls accounted for 988 man days. Public contact work was 265 man days.[82] On March 31, the *Holbrook Tribune* (page 2) noted the community was invited to a camp open house on April 2.

During April, 2,982 man days were worked, with 1,485 devoted to trench work. So far 33,550′ had been dug. The Painted Desert Checking Station was painted, landscaping was done, and 265 man days devoted to public contact work. Painted Desert walks, terraces, and walls accounted for 688 man days.[83]

During May, a total of 3,279 man days were logged, with the largest share, 1,939, spent on pipeline work. Landscaping accounted for 282 man days; walks, terraces, and walls accounted for 545 man days; and public contact work accounted for 272 man days.[84] At the end of June, many men went home, leaving only forty-six, with the Army keeping twenty-two for overhead. (Almost all the enrollees were from Pennsylvania.) A total of 2,239 man days went to project work, with 1,295 for pipeline work. The total distance of trench dug was 6.8 miles, and 4.9 miles of pipe had been laid. Other work included 300 man days for landscaping and 214 for public contact work.[85]

In July, new men did not arrive until July 24. A total of 1,242 man days were worked. The pipeline installation (two miles remaining) took 962 man days. Public contact work and work on the Painted Desert Checking Station accounted for the remainder.[86]

In August, 3,442 man days were worked, with 2,892 spent on water supply work. Trenches of 42,000′ were dug and 41,000′ of pipe was laid. Forms for the fifty-thousand-gallon concrete reservoir were set. The Painted Desert Checking Station was completed, and 345 man days were devoted to education, public contact, and guide work.[87]

In September, 2,817 man days were worked, with 2,033 devoted to the water system. Much of the concrete had been poured at the reservoir, 45,000′ of trench was dug, and 41,000′ of pipe was laid. Public contact work totaled 239 man days.[88]

At the end of October, sixty-five enrollees were sent to assist the sheriff in the search for a lost boy, Bruce Crozier, near Winslow. The search included as many as six hundred people at one point, and eventually, seven days later, the boy walked into a hunter's camp twenty-five miles away. Petrified Forest CCC totaled 260 man days searching. A total of 3,311 man days were worked, with 1,879 devoted to the water system. Boundary fence work accounted for 500 man days. Work at the Painted Desert Inn, the store room, and Residence No. 1 was accomplished.[89]

During November, 3,406 man days were worked, with 1,860 spent on water system work, 631 on the boundary fence, as well as work on Residence No. 1, the storeroom, and the museum.[90] On November 13, Leonard J. Maicki, 19, a Pennsylvania CCC cook at the camp, was killed by a train.[91]

In December, work was reduced due to holiday leave of many enrollees. Only 1,021 man days went to project work, including the water supply system, boundary fence, landscaping, Painted Desert Inn, and public contact work.[92] At the end of the year, Company 3342 had 71 boys (all but 3 from Pennsylvania).

1940

On January 16, the company was up to full strength, and much energy was devoted to the water system and completing the Painted Desert Inn. Total man days were 2,496, with 1,873 devoted to the water system and 142 to the Painted Desert Inn. In addition, 246 man days went to work on walks, terraces, and walls.[93] The new men who arrived in January were said to be "the most industrious group of enrollees we have ever had." A weekly class in natural history was being attended by an average of 23 enrollees. Company strength on January 31 was 201 enrollees (nearly all from Pennsylvania). Total man days for February were 3,418, with 2,420 spent on the water system. All pipe was laid to the reservoir, for a total of 61,834′. (The distance of 11.71 miles was said to be the longest of any pipeline project throughout the National Park Service area.)[94] In addition, 5,620′ were dug in the headquarters area. Painted Desert Inn work totaled 364 man days, and 232 man days were spent at Residence No. 2.[95]

The month of March saw 1,521 man days spent on the water system, out of a total of 3,284 man days for the month. Much landscaping was done at the reservoir and the Painted Desert Inn, totaling 600 man days. Other work at the Inn totaled 653 man days, and 381 man days were devoted to Painted Desert Inn Residence No. 2. Public contact work totaled 80 man days.[96]

During April, 2,983 man hours were devoted to projects, including 550 for the water system; 963 for Painted Desert walks, walls, and terraces; 574 to the Painted Desert Inn; 527 to the Painted Desert Inn gas and oil station; and 132 to public contact work.[97] During May, most CCC work was concentrated on the pipeline and the Painted Desert area. Landscaping and curbstone were done at the inn. A large new entrance sign was being built, and a crew of twelve worked on road and trail repair all month.[98] On May 31, the company had 164 enrollees (nearly all from Pennsylvania, with 2 veterans).

In June, work was curtailed with the end of the enrollment period; many men were ending their stay, and by June 15, only sixty enrollees were in the park. All the men were working at the Painted Desert Inn. One of the employee dwellings was completed, except for the sewer connections.[99] On June 30, Company 3342 dropped to 59 men (nearly all from Pennsylvania, with 2 veterans). A NPS Fiscal Year 1940 report credited the CCC with "developing and improving the area" enough to show results in "increased travel and longer time spent in the Monument by each visitor." The Painted Desert Inn was said to be "one of the finest buildings of its type in existence," with almost all its work done by the CCC.[100]

On July 31, company strength was 187 men (most from Pennsylvania, with 2 veterans). Company strength stayed high for the next four months, but dropped to 65 at the end of the year. During August, large crews were working on the Painted Desert reservoir landscaping project. All of the furniture for the Painted Desert Inn was completed. Residence No. 1 was complete, and Residence No. 2 was expected to be ready October 1. CCC enrollees were doing road maintenance, and "guide and contact men have been used all month at the checking stations and museums."[101]

During September, the *Superintendent's Monthly Report* noted that the Painted Desert Inn was "100% complete at the end of the month." Work was nearly complete on the Painted Desert reservoir, and work continued on the gas and oil station. Work was begun on the Painted Desert equipment building. This monthly report noted that "a crew has been busy the entire month quarrying rock" for these buildings. Sign painting was in progress at the Inn. Enrollees were making visitor contacts all month.[102]

During October, most of the CCC work was concentrated in the Painted Desert area. The Painted Desert gas and oil station was nearing completion. Enrollees were doing landscaping, road maintenance, and backfilling pipeline excavations. Others were assisting visitors. The report noted: "Company strength has been well up the entire month and all active projects have moved at top speed."[103]

At year's end, the last monthly report noted that eight CCC projects were completed. Work continued on the gas and oil station and on the equipment shed. A small survey crew was active on the boundary setting correct lines for fencing, and some fencing was completed near Third Forest. Another crew finished installation of the gas butane system. CCC guides were "active at Rainbow Museum, Puerco Station and east entrance of Painted Desert."[104]

1941

In January, work started on the new headquarters residence. A crew of thirty-five worked on fence construction, and a crew of fifty were working on the Painted Desert pumphouse road. Enrollees continued public contact work at three locations.[105] On January 31, Company 3342 had 199 men (most from Pennsylvania, with 1 veteran). Company strength stayed somewhat high through the end of May.

In February, large crews continued work on the Painted Desert pumphouse road, fence construction, headquarters dwelling, rock quarry, and Painted Desert equipment shed. Small crews were doing landscaping, public contact work, and painting. Company strength was high at 197, but only 136 were working, as many were out with colds, pneumonia, and the like.[106]

In March, permission was given for construction of a coal storage room. A crew of thirty enrollees was doing landscaping and associated work; another crew of twenty-five was doing various projects in the Painted Desert Inn area; a crew of thirty to forty was excavating the basement and quarry rock for the new residence; a crew of twenty-two was doing road construction; and a crew of fifteen was doing fence construction. Enrollees continued public contact work at three locations.[107]

During April, average company strength was 180. Enrollees were doing public contact work at six locations, including museums, checking stations, Newspaper Rock, and Agate Bridge. Large crews were at work on the previous month's projects such as road and fence construction and rock quarrying.[108]

In May, twenty-five to forty enrollees were detailed to the Army for camp improvement work such as flood control and road maintenance. Enrollees did public contact work, road construction, boundary fence construction, masonry work, and stone quarrying.[109]

During June, CCC work came to a standstill as one hundred enrollees were being discharged, so an average of only fifty-nine men were available each day. Work consisted of public contact work (143 man days), headquarters dwelling construction (358), Painted Desert pumphouse truck trail construction (357), headquarters garage construction (152), and boundary fence construction (98).[110] On June 22, Company 3342 was replaced by Company 1837, which had previously worked at Tucson Mountain Park. Instead of Pennsylvania boys, now the enrollees were largely from Arizona, with some from Texas.

In July, the park noted its highest July visitation ever with 42,651 visitors. The lack of trained enrollees limited CCC work for the month. A side camp of twenty men was located in Phoenix, constructing "table and bench combinations." Total man days for field work during the month totaled 1,706, with major work on headquarters dwelling construction (386 man days), Painted Desert pumphouse truck trail construction (304 man days), curb and gutter construction (416 man days), public contact work (105 man days), and fence and sign construction.[111] On July 31, Company 1837 had 135 men (almost evenly divided between those from Texas and from Arizona).

During August, an average of 139 enrollees was present; at the end of the month there were 167. Enrollees were active on the headquarters dwelling construction and rock quarrying, the pumphouse truck trail, and the two parking areas at the inn. They finished the sign at the east entrance of Painted Desert Rim Drive. Public contact work continued, and a small crew was assisting with the excavation at the Indian Cave near the CCC camp.[112]

During October, the average company strength was 126. However, due to the lack of qualified supervisors, some work was curtailed. One foreman came on loan from Grand Canyon for thirty days. In the Painted Desert area, enrollees were working on curbing, truck trail construction, signs, road gutters, and fences. In the headquarters area, work continued on the residence and the garage. Public contact work continued at five locations.[113]

November work was noted as progressing "satisfactorily," with an average of ninety enrollees working daily. At the Painted Desert area the gutter work was nearly complete. Here, enrollees were doing landscaping and truck trail construction. At the headquarters area, work continued on the residence and garage. A new rock quarry was opened near the CCC camp, and a small crew was working there. Public contact work continued.[114]

In December, an average of 114 enrollees was working daily. At the Painted Desert area enrollees were doing landscaping, sign work, and truck trail construction. At the headquarters area, work continued on the residence and garage. One crew worked throughout the month at the rock quarry near the CCC camp.[115] On December 31, there were a total of 116 men in the company (about a third from Arizona and the remainder from Texas, with 3 veterans). In the previous five months, the company was seldom near full strength, listing 170 enrollees on September 30, 1941. With the advent of the world war, any government program not contributing directly to the war effort was soon to be questioned. Superintendent's monthly reports noted that park staff was guarding area bridges against possible sabotage.

1942

In January, company strength was cut to 50 enrollees in the middle of the month, resulting in postponing some work. During the month, public contact work continued, and work continued on Residence No. 5 headquarters, Painted Desert signs and pumphouse road, and graveling the Blue Forest Road.[116] January camp strength totaled just 50 at month's end, with 5 veterans.

In February, only an average of 38 men was available. Public contact work was limited to two guides at Painted Desert Information Office. "Good progress" was made on Residence No. 5 headquarters and the garage. A veteran enrollee was temporarily detailed from NP-12 in Flagstaff to install water and sewer lines in the residence.[117] On February 28, Company 1837 had only 41 men (mostly from Arizona and a few from Texas, with 5 veterans).

On March 7, the camp was officially abandoned. The park assigned a caretaker to safeguard the buildings and equipment until the War Department decided on their disposition.[118] The park superintendent noted that "reviewing the many necessary projects completed by the CCC in Petrified Forest, at least 90% of the development, with the exception of highway development, was accomplished by the Corps. The loss is keenly felt and it is hoped that as soon as world affairs return to normal, a CCC camp will again be assigned to this area." Decades later, historian George Lubick noted that because the Petrified Forest facilities "were so shabby, the CCC construction resulted in dramatic improvements from one end of the reserve to the other." Petrified Forest, "once the source of embarrassment and derision—had improved immensely thanks to the PWA, CCC and CWA," says Lubick. This dramatic change was critical to Petrified Forest becoming a national park.[119]

Unless otherwise noted, any reference to the number of enrollees in a company, the location of the company, or company supervisors are from U.S. War Department, Location and Strength of CCC Companies, 1933–1942, NARAMD RG 35 530/65/22/04/05

1. Lubick, *Petrified Forest National Park,* 116.
2. "US Parks Allocated Civil Works Funds," *Coconino Sun,* December 8, 1933, 1.
3. Lubick, *Petrified Forest National Park,* 118.
4. Ibid., 116.
5. "CCC Camp Moving to Rio Puerco," *Holbrook Tribune,* June 1, 1934, 1.
6. Wirt, W. H., *Report to the Chief Forester on ECW Work at Petrified Forest, July 5–July 7, 1934,* Correspondence & Subject Files 1928-1959, NPS, Branch of Forestry, NARAMD RG 79/570/81/34/3 Entry 84 Box 212.
7. Work may have started as early as July 3. See Fiscal 1935 Report, NPS National Monuments Central Classified Files 1933–1949, NARAMD RG 79/150/34/12/1 P10-B Box 2331.
8. PFNM, Camp Inspection Reports, NARAMD 35/530/65/23/04 Entry 115 PI 11 Box 11.
9. PFNM, *SMNR, July 1934,* NARAMD RG 79/150/34/12/1 E-1 Box 2332.

10. "Artist to Be Placed in Petrified Forest CCC Camp near Here," *Holbrook Tribune,* July 20, 1934, 7. "C.C.C. Artists Are Assigned to Flagstaff Camps," *Coconino Sun,* July 27, 1934, 6. Nearly one hundred artists were assigned to CCC camps nationwide by Washington, D.C., but frequently no records remain for many of these artists. Of the three said to have been assigned to Arizona, only minimal information has been located regarding work by Creston F. Baumgartner in the Coconino National Forest.

11. PFNM, *SMNR, August 1934,* NARAMD RG 79/150/34/12/1 E-1 Box 2332; "CCC Worker Dies after Falling from Train," *Holbrook Tribune,* August 31, 1934, 1. He apparently was riding the train illegally, a common occurrence during the Depression. The newspaper identified him as Santistevan, 45, of Winslow, former CWA worker. Arizona Death Records, State File No. 249, Registered No. 69.

12. PFNM, *SMNR, September 1934,* NARAMD RG 79/150/34/12/1 E-1 Box 2332.

13. Salazar died on October 1. "CCC Enrollee Is Killed, Nine Others Injured in Wreck," *Coconino Sun,* October 5, 1934, 8. See also *Report of Truck Accident which Occurred September 30, 1934.* The CCC special investigator reported that the accident was the result of the driver passing another vehicle too far to the right. One injured enrollee was transferred to the Army Hospital at Fort Bliss, and all others were released. PFNM, Camp Inspection Reports, NARAMD 35/530/65/23/04 Entry 115 PI 11 Box 11; Arizona Death Records, State File No. 270, Registered No. 78.

14. PFNM, *SMNR, October 1934,* NARAMD RG 79/150/34/12/1 E-1 Box 2332.

15. *Holbrook Tribune,* November 2, 1934, 1.

16. Wirt, W. H., *Report to the Chief Forester on ECW Work at Petrified Forest, September 17–20, 1934,* Correspondence & Subject Files 1928–1959, NPS, Branch of Forestry, NARAMD RG 79/570/81/34/3 Entry 84 Box 212.

17. PFNM, *SMNR, November 1934,* NARAMD RG 79/150/34/12/1 E-1 Box 2332.

18. *Holbrook Tribune,* December 14, 1934, 5.

19. PFNM, *SMNR, December 1934,* NARAMD RG 79/150/34/12/1 E-1 Box 2332.

20. *Holbrook Tribune,* December 14, 1934, 6.

21. U.S. DOI, NPS, *ECW Supplemental Work Project Progress Report,* Records of the CCC, NARAMD RG 22/150/03/01/01 Entry 193 Box 6.

22. *Holbrook Tribune,* January 11, 1935, 5. The February 1 newspaper (page 7) noted seventy-five people attended.

23. PFNM, *SMNR, January 1935,* NARAMD RG 79/150/34/12/1 E-1 Box 2332.

24. PFNM, *SMNR, February 1935,* NARAMD RG 79/150/34/12/1 E-1 Box 2332.

25. Wirt, W. H., *Report to the Chief Forester on ECW Work at Petrified Forest, February 18–19, 1935,* Correspondence & Subject Files 1928–1959, NPS, Branch of Forestry, NARAMD RG 79/570/81/34/3 Entry 84 Box 212.

26. PFNM, Camp Inspection Reports, NARAMD 35/530/65/23/04 Entry 115 PI 11 Box 11.

27. PFNM, *SMNR, April 1935,* NARAMD RG 79/150/34/12/1 E-1 Box 2332.

28. PFNM, *SMNR, May 1935,* NARAMD RG 79/150/34/12/1 E-1 Box 2332.

29. PFNM, *SMNR, June 1935,* NARAMD RG 79/150/34/12/1 E-1 Box 2332.

30. Wirt, W. H., *Report to the Chief Forester on ECW Work at Petrified Forest, June 24–25, 1935,* Correspondence & Subject Files 1928–1959, NPS, Branch of Forestry, NARAMD RG 79/570/81/34/3 Entry 84 Box 212.

31. PFNM, *SMNR, July 1935,* NARAMD RG 79/150/34/12/1 E-1 Box 2332; *Holbrook Tribune,* July 5, 1935, 2. See also *Report of Contract Physician Regarding Death of Calvin Jones* and accompanying *Proceedings of Board of Officers.* The latter report indicates Jones was absent without leave and under the influence of alcohol at the time of his death. PFNM, Camp Inspection Reports, NARAMD 35/530/65/23/04 Entry 115 PI 11 Box 11.

32. PFNM, *SMNR, August 1935,* NARAMD RG 79/150/34/12/1 E-1 Box 2332.

33. PFNM, *SMNR, September 1935,* NARAMD RG 79/150/34/12/1 E-1 Box 2332.

34. Wirt, W. H., *Report to the Chief Forester on ECW Work at Petrified Forest, September 1–2, 1935,* Correspondence & Subject Files 1928–1959, NPS, Branch of Forestry, NARAMD RG 79/570/81/34/3 Entry 84 Box 212.

35. U.S. DOI, NPS, *ECW Supplemental Work Project Progress Report,* Records of the CCC, NARAMD RG 22/150/03/01/01 Entry 193 Box 6.

36. PFNM, *SMNR, November 1935,* NARAMD RG 79/150/34/12/1 E-1 Box 2332.

37. PFNM, Camp Inspection Reports, NARAMD 35/530/65/23/04 Entry 115 PI 11 Box 11.

38. Wirt, W. H., *Report to the Chief Forester on ECW Work at Petrified Forest, November 29–30, 1935,* Correspondence & Subject Files 1928–1959, NPS, Branch of Forestry, NARAMD RG 79/570/81/34/3 Entry 84 Box 212.

39. PFNM, *SMNR, January 1936,* NARAMD RG 79/150/34/12/1 E-1 Box 2332.

40. PFNM, *SMNR, February 1936,* NARAMD RG 79/150/34/12/1 E-1 Box 2332.

41. "CCC to Disband 21 State Camps," *Arizona Republic*, March 20, 1936, 8. The Arizona action was part of a larger plan by President Roosevelt to disband seven hundred camps nationwide. A revolt within his own political party resulted in FDR backing off from the executive order. See "Solons Stop CCC Closing," *Arizona Republic*, March 22, 1936, 1, 6. FDR agreed to keep nationwide enrollment at 350,000 through March 31, 1937.
42. PFNM, *SMNR, March 1936*, NARAMD RG 79/150/34/12/1 E-1 Box 2332.
43. "Excavation of Petrified Tree Supports New Forest Theory," *Arizona Republic*, April 1, 1936, sect. 2, 1.
44. U.S. DOI, NPS, *ECW Supplemental Work Project Progress Report*, Records of the CCC, NARAMD RG 22/150/03/01/01 Entry 193 Box 6.
45. "Ages Preserve Story Inscribed in Stone," *Arizona Republic*, July 19, 1936, 3.
46. "State Will Get More CCC Men," *Arizona Republic*, October 4, 1936, 7. 153 were said to be coming to Petrified Forest from Walden, Colorado.
47. Fiscal 1937 Report in NPS National Monuments Central Classified Files 1933–1949, NARAMD RG 79/150/34/12/1 P10-B Box 2331.
48. PFNM, *SMNR, November 1936*, NARAMD RG 79/150/34/12/1 E-1 Box 2332.
49. PFNM, *SMNR, December 1936*, NARAMD RG 79/150/34/12/1 E-1 Box 2332.
50. PFNM, *SMNR, January 1937*, NARAMD RG 79/150/34/12/1 E-1 Box 2332.
51. "Camp to Erect New Building," *Arizona Republic*, January 27, 1936, sect. 2, 1.
52. PFNM, *SMNR, February 1937*, NARAMD RG 79/150/34/12/1 E-1 Box 2332.
53. PFNM, *SMNR, March 1937*, NARAMD RG 79/150/34/12/1 E-1 Box 2332.
54. U.S. NPS, Records of the NPS, Branch of Plans & Design, Monthly Narrative Reports, 1936–38, NARAMD RG 79/150/35/7/7 Box 15.
55. *Daily Report from H. L. Bill, Assistant Forester, March 23, 1937*, Correspondence & Subject Files 1928–1959, NPS, Branch of Forestry, NARAMD RG 79/570/81/34/3 Entry 84 Box 212.
56. U.S. DOI, NPS, *ECW Supplemental Work Project Progress Report*, Records of the CCC, NARAMD RG 22/150/03/01/01 Entry 193 Box 6.
57. PFNM, *SMNR, April 1937*, NARAMD RG 79/150/34/12/1 E-1 Box 2332.
58. PFNM, *SMNR, May 1937*, NARAMD RG 79/150/34/12/1 E-1 Box 2332.
59. PFNM, *SMNR, June 1937*, NARAMD RG 79/150/34/12/1 E-1 Box 2332.
60. PFNM, *SMNR, July 1937*, NARAMD RG 79/150/34/12/1 E-1 Box 2332.
61. PFNM, Camp Inspection Reports, NARAMD 35/530/65/23/04 Entry 115 PI 11 Box 11.
62. PFNM, *SMNR, August 1937*, NARAMD RG 79/150/34/12/1 E-1 Box 2332.
63. PFNM, *SMNR, September 1937*, NARAMD RG 79/150/34/12/1 E-1 Box 2332.
64. PFNM, *SMNR, October 1937*, NARAMD RG 79/150/34/12/1 E-1 Box 2332.
65. PFNM, *SMNR, November 1937*, NARAMD RG 79/150/34/12/1 E-1 Box 2332.
66. PFNM, *SMNR, December 1937*, NARAMD RG 79/150/34/12/1 E-1 Box 2332.
67. PFNM, *SMNR, January 1938*, NARAMD RG 79/150/34/12/1 E-1 Box 2332.
68. According to landscape architect Kuehl, the move was to facilitate work on the Painted Desert Inn. U.S. NPS, Records of the NPS, Branch of Plans & Design, Monthly Narrative Reports, 1936–38, NARAMD RG 79/150/35/7/7 Box 16.
69. PFNM, *SMNR, February 1938*, NARAMD RG 79/150/34/12/1 E-1 Box 2332.
70. PFNM, *SMNR, March 1938*, NARAMD RG 79/150/34/12/1 E-1 Box 2332.
71. PFNM, *SMNR, April 1938*, NARAMD RG 79/150/34/12/1 E-1 Box 2332.
72. PFNM, *SMNR, May 1938*, NARAMD RG 79/150/34/12/1 E-1 Box 2332.
73. PFNM, *SMNR, June 1938*, NARAMD RG 79/150/34/12/1 E-1 Box 2332.
74. PFNM, *SMNR, July 1938*, NARAMD RG 79/150/34/12/1 E-1 Box 2332.
75. PFNM, *SMNR, August 1938*, NARAMD RG 79/150/34/12/1 E-1 Box 2333.
76. PFNM, *SMNR, September 1938*, NARAMD RG 79/150/34/12/1 E-1 Box 2333.
77. PFNM, *SMNR, October 1938*, NARAMD RG 79/150/34/12/1 E-1 Box 2333.
78. PFNM, Camp Inspection Reports, NARAMD 35/530/65/23/04 Entry 115 PI 11 Box 11.
79. PFNM, *SMNR, December 1938*, NARAMD RG 79/150/34/12/1 E-1 Box 2333.
80. PFNM, *SMNR, January 1939*, NARAMD RG 79/150/34/12/1 E-1 Box 2333.
81. PFNM, *SMNR, February 1939*, NARAMD RG 79/150/34/12/1 E-1 Box 2333.

82. PFNM, *SMNR, March 1939,* NARAMD RG 79/150/34/12/1 E-1 Box 2333.
83. PFNM, *SMNR, April 1939,* NARAMD RG 79/150/34/12/1 E-1 Box 2333.
84. PFNM, *SMNR, May 1939,* NARAMD RG 79/150/34/12/1 E-1 Box 2333.
85. PFNM, *SMNR, June 1939,* NARAMD RG 79/150/34/12/1 E-1 Box 2333.
86. PFNM, *SMNR, July 1939,* NARAMD RG 79/150/34/12/1 E-1 Box 2333.
87. PFNM, *SMNR, August 1939,* NARAMD RG 79/150/34/12/1 E-1 Box 2333.
88. PFNM, *SMNR, September 1939,* NARAMD RG 79/150/34/12/1 E-1 Box 2333.
89. PFNM, *SMNR, October 1939,* NARAMD RG 79/150/34/12/1 E-1 Box 2333.
90. PFNM, *SMNR, November 1939,* NARAMD RG 79/150/34/12/1 E-1 Box 2333.
91. *Holbrook Tribune,* November 17, 1939, 1. According to *Happy Days,* November 18, 1939, 1, he was "hopping" the train. Arizona Death Records, State File No. 297, Registered No. 62.
92. PFNM, *SMNR, December 1939,* NARAMD RG 79/150/34/12/1 E-1 Box 2333.
93. PFNM, *SMNR, January 1940,* NARAMD RG 79/150/34/12/1 E-1 Box 2333.
94. *Happy Days,* March 30, 1940, 7.
95. PFNM, *SMNR, February 1940,* NARAMD RG 79/150/34/12/1 E-1 Box 2333.
96. PFNM, *SMNR, March 1940,* NARAMD RG 79/150/34/12/1 E-1 Box 2333.
97. PFNM, *SMNR, April 1940,* NARAMD RG 79/150/34/12/1 E-1 Box 2333.
98. PFNM, *SMNR, May 1940,* NARAMD RG 79/150/34/12/1 E-1 Box 2333.
99. PFNM, *SMNR, June 1940,* NARAMD RG 79/150/34/12/1 E-1 Box 2333.
100. "Fiscal 1940 Report," NPS National Monuments Central Classified Files 1933–1949, NARAMD RG 79/150/34/12/1 P10-B Box 2331.
101. PFNM, *SMNR, August 1940,* NARAMD RG 79/150/34/12/1 E-1 Box 2333.
102. PFNM, *SMNR, September 1940,* NARAMD RG 79/150/34/12/1 E-1 Box 2333.
103. PFNM, *SMNR, October 1940,* NARAMD RG 79/150/34/12/1 E-1 Box 2333.
104. PFNM, *SMNR, December 1940,* NARAMD RG 79/150/34/12/1 E-1 Box 2333.
105. PFNM, *SMNR, January 1941,* NARAMD RG 79/150/34/12/1 E-1 Box 2333.
106. PFNM, *SMNR, February 1941,* NARAMD RG 79/150/34/12/1 E-1 Box 2333.
107. PFNM, *SMNR, March 1941,* NARAMD RG 79/150/34/12/1 E-1 Box 2333.
108. PFNM, *SMNR, April 1941,* NARAMD RG 79/150/34/12/1 E-1 Box 2333.
109. PFNM, *SMNR, May 1941,* NARAMD RG 79/150/34/12/1 E-1 Box 2333.
110. PFNM, *SMNR, June 1941,* NARAMD RG 79/150/34/12/1 E-1 Box 2333.
111. PFNM, *SMNR, July 1941,* NARAMD RG 79/150/34/12/1 E-1 Box 2333.
112. PFNM, *SMNR, August 1941,* NARAMD RG 79/150/34/12/1 E-1 Box 2333.
113. PFNM, *SMNR, October 1941,* NARAMD RG 79/150/34/12/1 E-1 Box 2333.
114. PFNM, *SMNR, November 1941,* NARAMD RG 79/150/34/12/1 E-1 Box 2333.
115. PFNM, *SMNR, December 1941,* NARAMD RG 79/150/34/12/1 E-1 Box 2333.
116. PFNM, *SMNR, January 1942,* NARAMD RG 79/150/34/12/1 E-1 Box 2333.
117. PFNM, *SMNR, February 1942,* NARAMD RG 79/150/34/12/1 E-1 Box 2333.
118. PFNM, *SMNR, March 1942,* NARAMD RG 79/150/34/12/1 E-1 Box 2333.
119. Lubick, *Petrified Forest National Park*, 122–123.

Sidebar:
What Do the Numbers Mean?

Throughout the literature on the CCC, one sees terms like F-27A, Company 851, and so on. All of the terminology was created by the military for ease of travel, finance, administration, and supervision.[1] First, the War Department divided the country into nine ***Corps*** areas. The 8th Corps consisted of Arizona, Colorado, New Mexico, Oklahoma, Utah, and Wyoming (excluding Yellowstone National Park). Generally, Corps areas were somewhat autonomous.

The most basic organizational unit of the CCC was the ***company.*** Frequently, but not always, a company consisted of 200 enrollees; it could go as high as 220 enrollees. (The term ***enrollee*** was deliberately used for the young men entering the CCC so as not to sound military-like. Military terms such as *enlistment* were also discouraged when referring to non-military enrollees.)

Three or four military officers and five enlisted men were the cadre, or company staff. Officers consisted of a commanding officer, second in command, medical officer, and educational officer. Enlisted men included a first sergeant, supply sergeant, mess sergeant, company clerk, and cook.[2] In the early years of the CCC, the officers were active duty military personnel. Within a short time enlisted men were no longer used and the educational duties were assigned to a civilian educational advisor. Quickly, reserve officers took the place of active duty personnel. Late in the program, many of these leadership positions were held by civilians.

A typical company also had technical staff, or work supervisors, who were frequently LEMs (***local experienced men***). The top technical man was called the ***superintendent*** or ***project superintendent.*** Fifteen to twenty of the enrollees were appointed leaders or assistant leaders. Leaders and assistant leaders were paid premium pay over other enrollees.

Company numbers had their own logic. These three- or four-digit numbers were defined by the Army Corps area. Arizona was in the 8th Corps, so company numbers began with 8 or 18, 28, and so on. Generally, a lower number gave a clue that that particular company was formed early. So, in the first few years, the 8th Corps had company numbers beginning with an 8 or 18. Not until 1940 were 8th Corps companies designated by numbers beginning in 48.

Early in the program, enrollees were generally sent near where they enrolled, perhaps because it was much easier, cheaper, and faster to send men to someplace close. Later in the program, more and more of the work to be done was in the West, where much federal land existed. By this time, it was not unusual to see a company formed in the East, such as 3348, go to the 8th Corps. If a company consisted of veterans, the company number was followed by **V**; if the company was composed of African Americans, the company number was followed by **C**. In the area of this study, there were two veterans companies and no companies composed entirely of African American men.

Each physical camp location had its unique ***camp designation.*** Camps were designated by their supervising agency or landowner. NP signified a National Park location, NM a National Monument location, F a National Forest location, DG a Division of Grazing location, and SP a state park location, along with thirty other such designations. In the case of the Coconino National Forest, the first camp to be designated by the Army was F-5, or Flagstaff. Generally, a letter designation added to the camp designation identified the state in which the camp was located. So NP-12A was Arizona, while NP-4NC was a Great Smoky Mountains National Park location in North Carolina. Every camp designation, such as NP-12 (or NP-12A), had a particular mailing address, railroad location, and telegraph location. Generally the camp designation—in effect, its address—did not change when a new company replaced an earlier one. For example, F-28 did not change, even though Companies 848 and 1826V were stationed there. (See Appendix 2 for a complete list.)

The calendar organization of the CCC, generally six months, was the ***enrollment period*** (not enlistment period). The First Enrollment Period (April 5, 1933, to Sept. 30, 1933) and the Nineteenth Enrollment Period (April 1, 1942, to June 30, 1942) were the only ones not six months in length. Typical enrollment periods began in October or April and ended in March or September. (See Appendix 1 for a complete list.)

---

1. For another summary of basic CCC organization, see Jolley, *"That Magnificent Army of Youth and Peace,"* 23–26. War Department regulations were printed in U.S. War Department, *Civilian Conservation Corps Regulations*.

2. Smith, "The Army's Role in the Success of the CCC," 33.

CHAPTER 3

Flagstaff Area National Monuments (NM-5, NP-12)
Flagstaff City, Coconino County

THE FLAGSTAFF AREA BENEFITED GREATLY from the CCC. Forest Service camps were nearby, such as Schultz Pass, Mormon Lake, and Bellemont. The town also benefited indirectly from the National Park camps at Grand Canyon and the Forest Service camps at Williams. Although somewhat short-lived, the Mt. Elden camp supported the city in at least two ways. Camp and enrollee expenditures put money directly into the local economy and improving the infrastructure of the nearby national monuments helped increase future tourist visitations. In addition, local officials discussed, and sometimes tried, to get CCC camps for a number of other endeavors unsuccessfully.

On April 13, 1934, the Flagstaff *Coconino Sun* reported that the city of Flagstaff had applied for a CCC camp on the Peaks to develop Abineau Spring water. If approved, the camp would build a road and pipeline from Abineau to the Inner Basin and connect to the present city system.[1] On May 25, 1934, the newspaper reported that work had begun on the road and pipeline, but with Schultz Pass CCC boys.[2] It is unclear how much of this finished project was accomplished by the CCC. (The city received a FERA grant of $30,472 for the water line.)[3] A year later, the Flagstaff City Council heard of three possible CCC proposals, totaling $41,800, from J. B. Wright, county engineer. Those were a 40-acre reservoir and dam at Switzer Canyon; improving roads in the 160-acre city park; and sanitation and drainage work in the park.[4] In 1939, the city applied for a CCC camp for 1940 after a 1939 request was not approved. It included enlarging a park dam; enlarging the ball park; adding bleachers, and handball and horseshoe courts; park drainage; and road and trail work.[5] Apparently, the latter was also not approved.

During 1938 and 1939, the present-day Grand Canyon Caverns was considered for possible CCC work. In November 1938, the *Coconino Sun* reported the county was using WPA funds to construct a road to the caverns.[6] The following month, the *Williams News* reported the caverns might become a state park, as NPS representative C. D. Carter was investigating.[7] A favorable decision was said to make it eligible for a CCC camp. However, in 1939, county involvement was ended after the expenditure of $5–6,000 in WPA monies.[8]

The New Deal at the Monuments

As early as 1933, New Deal monies were funding work at the Flagstaff-area national monuments. On December 8, 1933, the *Coconino Sun* announced a $5,599 CWA allocation to Wupatki National Monument for excavation and restoration work. The article reported that a CCC camp was planned there for the near future.[9] Walnut Canyon was allocated $2,308 from the CWA.[10] At Wupatki, twenty-one men were doing excavation work and planning on the completion of the survey started the previous summer. Walnut Canyon had six men to start on December 26 with a ruins survey, and evacuation and restoration, weather permitting.[11] At the same time, the *Coconino Sun* reported there were plans to establish a CCC camp at Wupatki in the near future. The reported camp was to be "a spur camp for the Grand Canyon with 10 men to which will be added 11 men" from CWA.[12] Less than a year later, NPS engineers were said to be half-done with surveys of Walnut Canyon trails and ruins restoration, and the Sunset Crater entrance road and parking, with the Wupatki survey unfinished.[13] On April 29, 1935, it was announced that the three Flagstaff-area monuments had been awarded $40,000 for the construction of homes and buildings.[14] (Apparently these were PWA funds that were allocated for Wupatki Residence No. 1 and Walnut Canyon Residence No. 2, and administration and museum buildings.)[15] However, in June 1935, Wupatki was rejected as a permanent CCC camp site, as Heiser Spring was reported to have insufficient water. Equipment at Heiser was moved to Desert View.[16] Apparently, the PWA funds were kept until CCC resources could be obtained three years later.

Civilian Conservation Corps, Mt. Elden 1938

On March 18, 1938, the Flagstaff newspaper announced a CCC camp was being planned for work at the area's national monuments. The site for the new camp was said to be near the old Greenlaw Mill, but did not yet have water and electricity.[17] (A crew led by Hugh Miller had been inspecting possible sites during March.)[18] On April 22, the newspaper announced that a forty-five-man CCC contingent had arrived to erect the new camp. These men were said to be from SP-11 (Saguaro National Forest outside Tucson). It was suggested that the new camp would first be tents. Once the buildings that were previously used at Grand Canyon's Desert View arrived, the tents would be replaced.[19] Finally, on August 2, 1938, the 195 new enrollees of Company 3345 arrived from Tobyhanna, Pennsylvania. Capt. Charles Norman was the commanding officer and Lt. John F. Sanchez the junior officer.[20] As soon as they arrived, the enrollees were working at all three area monuments.[21]

On October 24, 1938, Special Investigator A. W. Stockman inspected the camp and wrote of numerous problems. Morale was low, resulting in many administrative and dishonorable discharges. Stockman reported that the poor mess was in need of immediate change. The junior officer should be changed, he charged. The mess steward and cooks were inexperienced. His report included a detailed list of the mess problems. While he was there, Stockman phoned the Army district commander, and the junior officer was immediately transferred out and a new officer appointed. Stockman reported there were numerous complaints by enrollees that they were being charged 35 cents a month for a program of old and unappealing movies.[22] On December 31, 1938, camp strength was 92 enrollees (all but 2 from Pennsylvania). Supervisors were an Army captain, a contract physician, and an educational advisor.

1939

Happy Days reported that the company educational advisor, Joe V. Sachen, had organized a crack boxing team, and as of April 1, it was still undefeated.[23] The team traveled as far away as Prescott to participate in competition.[24] News from the camp was not all good, as the May 5 *Coconino Sun* reported the arrest of an enrollee for the theft of gas.[25] Apparently, the camp had made a good impression on the town, as they were invited to a Mothers' Day breakfast by the K. of C.[26] In early June, enrollees assisted the Wildlife Department in the capture of antelope for transfer to Tucson.[27] On June 14, the *Prescott Evening Courier* reported that the Mt. Elden camp sent 200 enrollees to Oak Creek Canyon to fight a forest fire. A total of 320 were on the fire near the Oak Creek Lodge.[28] The June 30, 1939, monthly report listed the same supervisors, but only 78 enrollees (75 from Pennsylvania). On July 10, 120 new Pennsylvania enrollees arrived, bringing camp strength to 197. All enrollees went through a three-day Army conditioning and then intensive fire training.[29]

Although Special Investigator Stockman visited the camp again in January, it was not until June that the camp's problems came to a head. In March, Lt. Charles E. Miller was abruptly transferred to Mt. Elden from Camp F-32, Sedona, and put on probation for his harsh treatment of the Sedona enrollees. Miller did not improve. Miller's commander noted he "continued to be gruff and discourteous in his dealings with enrollees," and he was relieved of his Mt. Elden duties in May. However, the next commander, Lieutenant Sagaser, was not liked. On June 18, Stockman reported the "majority of enrollees do not feel kindly towards Lieut. Sagaser, because of the strict disciplinary measures he has felt necessary to adopt and apply." Enrollees complained of long inspections on Saturday and excessive fines. Enrollees said they were promised trips to Grand Canyon and Petrified Forest, but did not get them. In addition, the mess was improved, but still unsatisfactory. Stockman reported that enrollees and the technical staff complained of the inadequacy of the food, poor food preparation, and the lack of variety. He reported the mess staff was the same as in October and had not received any new training. All were leaving July 1. Mess equipment was lacking. Stockman noted the camp project superintendent asserted that enrollee work output was down greatly because of the food situation. "The work program has suffered because of the food situation," Stockman reported. At this point, Frank Pinkley, who supervised the Arizona national monuments, and the Army commanders asserted that the food was not as bad as some said and could not cause significant loss of work output. One Army inspector asserted the project superintendent was unable to cooperate with the commanding officers of the camp, he was highly nervous, and his statements regarding the mess were highly exaggerated. By the end of June, former KPs were running the mess, and 125 enrollees asked to return home to Pennsylvania.

On June 30, the *Coconino Sun* reported the camp was to have a new commander: Lt. James McCormick Jr.[30] On July 10, the replacements from Pennsylvania included a mess steward and two to three cooks, and the situation was expected to improve. Two days earlier, an Army district inspector had arrived at camp and was to stay until the situation was alleviated. Stockman reported the enrollees in camp that did not return home appeared to have high morale. They "are popular in Flagstaff and welcomed. Their deportment is unusually good." Over sixty men attended the Catholic Church service, and the Catholic priest reserved three pews for enrollees and visited camp quite often.[31]

Stockman inspected the camp again September 6–7 and reported: "Much advancement in morale, mess and other camp features have been made since then, but many improvements are still possible, especially in mess." The new officers were said to be "striving for attainment." A new project superintendent had been appointed, and cooperation between him and the commanding officer was satisfactory.[32]

On August 25, the *Coconino Sun* reported that former NM-5 enrollee Willard Fox of Philadelphia attempted suicide while in the county jail. He was to be sent to the state prison for auto theft.[33]

On September 30, a controversy occurred when CCC Director Robert Fechner received a complaint that NP-12 was using CCC enrollees instead of skilled tradesmen such as carpenters. The local Plasters' Union also complained of CCC labor on Walnut Canyon plastering. This complaint brought a reprimand from Washington. Apparently, there was a problem with carpentry, as the camp agreed to hire a carpenter for a month. One high NPS official wrote: "I am inclined to believe that we have been caught in Flagstaff in the back wash of some sort of dissension between the Union and the camps at Grand Canyon."[34] On October 6, the *Coconino Sun* reported that a new commanding officer was coming, Lt. Harry J. Kieling, who had supervised the building of the camp in 1938. His second in command was to be Lt. William L. Finney, presently the temporary commander.[35] On October 20, the camp received 52 new Pennsylvania enrollees, bringing the camp to 205 boys. The Mt. Elden camp was now designated a year-round camp.[36]

On October 30, NP-12 was asked to assist in the search for a lost seven-year-old boy, Bruce Crozier, near Promontory Point in the Sitgreaves National Forest. A total of 107 enrollees as well as camp supervisors participated over a period of five days. The boy walked into a hunter's camp safely. A total of 413 enrollee man days were used.[37] On December 31, Company 3345 reported a total of 107 enrollees (all but 3 from Pennsylvania). At that time the camp designation changed from NM-5 to NP-12.

1940

During the first half of the year, the number of enrollees gradually went from 198 enrollees on January 31 to 139 on May 31 to 63 on June 30 (all of the men were from Pennsylvania, except 2 from Arizona and 1 from Texas). Company 3345 had no African American enrollees during its time at Mt. Elden.

Early in the year, the camp started planning for a camp open house. Typically, the open houses were on April 7, the date that the first enrollee was sworn in during 1933.[38] During the period June 19–25, the camp participated in firefighting at Long Valley in the Coconino National Forest, sending drivers, supervisors, and five trucks, using 34 CCC man days.[39] On July 26, a special train brought 416 new Pennsylvania enrollees to Flagstaff, with 136 to Mt. Elden and the remainder to the Flagstaff Forest Service camp and the Grand Canyon North Rim camp.[40] In August, the camp completed plans for the next three years. The monument and CCC staffs were quite optimistic for a lengthened stay.[41]

At 3:00 p.m. on October 21, tragedy struck when a CCC truck carrying enrollees from splitting rails for Walnut Canyon overturned, killing enrollee Chester S. Mastalski, 19, from Pennsylvania. The accident occurred sixteen miles southwest of Flagstaff on the Fernow Road. Twenty-four enrollees were sitting on seats on the truck's rear when the driver attempted to pass a logging truck and lost control, flipping the truck twice. A NPS investigator faulted the driver, William D. Brown, for excessive speed and for passing the logging truck even though he had been warned not to pass them. All of the enrollees in back were thrown out. Luckily, the other enrollees only had minor injuries.[42]

On November 1, it was announced the camp commander, Lt. Harry Kieling, had been called to Army active duty and the second in command, Lt. George Tyson, would be the new commanding officer.[43] From July to November, the camp had between 176 and 205 enrollees, with either 1 or 2 veterans. On December 31, the camp had just 53 enrollees, with 2 Arizona veterans. Throughout the year's last half, nearly all the enrollees were Pennsylvania boys.

1941–1942

In January and February, the camp had 198 and 181 enrollees (nearly all from Pennsylvania, with 1 or 2 veterans). Like many other CCC camps, enrollees were given basic noncombatant military training such as marching.[44] On March 28, it was reported that the monument work and the camp were inspected by local welfare officials. They called the road work at Walnut Canyon "remarkable improvements." Paul Beaubien, Walnut Canyon custodian, led the monuments tour, while Lt. Oscar Wingren led the barracks area tour. M. B. Stevenson was the project superintendent, Dr. Isaac Rogers was the camp doctor, and Prof. Ellsworth Schenebley was the educational advisor.[45] On March 31, Project Superintendent Stevenson wrote the superintendent of the Southwest Monuments, Hugh M. Miller, complaining that NP-12 was handicapped because its enrollees were from the 3rd Corps (Pennsylvania, Maryland, Virginia, and Washington, D.C.). "The maximum it is able to obtain from the six months enrollment period is four months actual work and sometimes drops as low as three and one half months." He said that each six months all key enrollees such as truck drivers and clerks must be completely replaced.[46] On April 30, there was no company listed for Mt. Elden in the location and strength reports, indicating Company 3345 was either disbanded or transferred out.[47]

Company 3838 (an 8th Corps company) arrived at Mt. Elden officially on May 10, 1941, and at the end of the month, it had 153 enrollees (65 from New Mexico, 85 from Texas, 1 from Pennsylvania, and 2 veterans from Arizona). Supervisors were two Army officers, a contract physician, and an educational advisor. In

June, camp enrollment totaled 135 and then increased to 170 on July 31 (106 from Texas, 55 from New Mexico, 7 from Arizona, 1 from Pennsylvania, and 1 from Colorado, with 4 veterans). During August, enrollees began work on the rehabilitation of the airfield at Winona. This was part of CCC National Defense work. The work was estimated at 100 man days and was largely the removal of rocks from the airfield.[48] From August 31 to October 31, camp strength dropped, as it typically does at the end of an enrollment period, from 185 to 143.

On October 2, a U.S. Army Air Corps B-18 bomber crashed on Agassiz Peak during a snowstorm, with the loss of all six men on board. Sheriff deputies and others went to the scene. According to the *Coconino Sun*, CCC enrollees and Ranger Ed Oldham brought out most of the bodies.[49] On October 9, Project Superintendent Stevenson, with two foreman and seventy enrollees, went to the Spruce Canyon Trail to begin construction of a 1.5-mile trail to the crash site in order to recover as much of the plane wreckage as possible. By 3 p.m. that day, the trail was completed to the 11,000' elevation level, and Army mechanics were disassembling the plane. Enrollees carried wreckage to the Spring Cabin Road till nightfall. On October 10 and 11, seventy enrollees returned to carry out more wreckage.[50] Once the wreckage parts were carried down to the 10,000' elevation level, they were loaded onto trucks that hauled the material to the Snow Bowl Road.[51]

On December 31, the camp had 130 enrollees (with 2 veterans). By February, the camp was down to 72 enrollees (32 from Texas, 27 from Arizona, 12 from New Mexico, and 1 from Colorado, with 3 veterans). NP-12 was disbanded on March 21, 1942, with 30 men transferred to NP-2 at Grand Canyon South Rim and 33 being discharged.[52]

Wupatki
1938

On June 15, 1938, well before the new Pennsylvania enrollees arrived, six enrollees assigned to erecting the Mt. Elden buildings assisted with putting an Electrolux into the "refrigerator room."[53] Beginning August 18, enrollees were working on the entrance road by way of the Citadel, mostly removing rocks.[54] During September, a ten-enrollee crew was working on small jobs such as cleanup, road scraping, and picking juniper berries. On September 20, a CCC crew digging a clay pit discovered a burial.[55] On September 29, 1938, Wupatki was notified that $7,750 in PWA monies had been allocated for the custodian's residence, utility building, and sewage system.[56] (Typically, the PWA funds were used for materials and skilled labor while the CCC supplied the unskilled labor.) In October a stone water trough at Wupatki Spring was completed.[57] This job was only one of many, according to the *Coconino Sun*. They reported that Project Superintendent Clay Parker promised winter work, including a parking lot, ruins stabilization and repair, and a new custodian's residence, museum, and utility building.[58] On December 20, boys began work on the water system, custodian's residence, and excavating for the administration building and Residence No. 2.[59]

1939

In January, work was progressing on the custodian's residence (41' x 47') and water system. The latter was said to include a small sump below the spring, with water pumped to the reservoir above the house.[60] The water system included a 4,000-gallon storage reservoir, 1,300' pipeline and a 10 x 10' pumphouse.[61] In February, preparations were underway to set up a twenty-five man spike camp at Heiser Spring.

During April, enrollee guides were reported doing "a very good job of protecting the monument and keeping it neat." However, forty men were reported hospitalized with the flu.[62] At the end of May, the water system reservoir and pipeline were complete, and work started on the pumphouse.[63] During June and July, work continued on the road.

The spike camp buildings and infrastructure were finally completed on September 5. During September, two enrollees were mounting botanical specimens and were being trained in other museum techniques.[64] The month before it was reported that enrollees were collecting reptiles for the monument, and there was hope they could be trained to compile a bird list.[65] The *Coconino Sun* reported on the Wupatki improvements, noting that the new residence, garage, and workshop were made from the local Moenkopi sandstone to blend into surroundings, to be unobtrusive as possible, and to appear like ruins. Even the masonry of ruins has been studied to be duplicated in the new construction.[66] By November, roofs were erected on all the new structures, and the spike camp shut down at the end of the month until January. The December *Southwest Monuments Reports* report noted that enrollee William Coleman wanted to be a wildlife technician and during the winter would study the area's small mammals.[67]

1940

On January 15, enrollees re-occupied the spike camp and started to work on the septic tank and sewer line.[68] From February through June, enrollees also worked on the custodian's residence and utility room. The June report noted the custodian's residence cabinets were completed.[69] As of June, the enrollees were said to have worked on a total of ten miles of roads and trails and a two-stall garage and workshop (22 x 30').[70] During August, enrollees began digging the footings for the administration building. Also in August, the carpenter shop was producing signs and map cases for Wupatki. August and September was a time for a great deal of enrollee work on the roads, after heavy rains.[71] By November, the custodian's residence was complete, except for the installation of appliances.[72]

1941

As of March 1941, a total of $5,546 in PWA funds was noted in the final construction report for the residence, utility building, water system, and sewer system. The report noted that CCC labor, calculated at $2 per man day, would total $14,726.[73] Unfortunately, this author was not able to locate more information.

Figure 7. Walnut Canyon Residence under Construction, 1940. Photograph by Paul Beaubien. Courtesy Flagstaff Area Monuments Museum Collection, WACA #5558.

Walnut Canyon
1938

As soon as the new enrollees arrived in August 1938, they went to work on building roads and trails, quarrying rock, and finishing camp buildings; they even fought one small forest fire. In September, enrollees started work on one of the two new residence buildings, and work on the Island Trail was said to be "progressing satisfactorily." During this month, drawings for a 1.9-mile-long northern boundary fence were approved, estimated at 8,000 man days. The original application called for 1,100 logs for this "pitchy pine" fence.[74] On September 30, Walnut Canyon was notified that $17,200 in PWA funds had been allocated for an administration building and employee residence.[75] Enrollees were working constantly at the "Headquarters Quarry," and four enrollees were guiding tourists.[76] During October, work began on a second residence building.[77]

1939

In January, foundations were laid for the ranger residence (36 x 52') and partially laid for another building, and the museum site was leveled.[78] The ranger residence of stone construction including a garage was 36 x 52'.[79] Also in January, work was going on in earnest on the 6.5-mile-long water line connecting the monument into the Mt. Elden Water Users and Pipe Line Association main. The job required much blasting, and fifty to sixty men were working on it.[80] During March, two CCC guides started work, and work began on Residence No. 2 (30 x 50', made of stone).[81]

From April through July, work continued on the water line, residences, and administration building. Some guide training also occurred. An August monthly report noted three enrollees were training to be guides and another eight to nine were interested. "Our CCC camp at Walnut Canyon is humming with activity and gives the promise of being one of our best camps," said monument acting custodian Paul Beaubien's summary.[82]

By September 30, 812 CCC man days had been spent guiding visitors.[83] During September, the 1,200-gallon-sump was worked on, and the sewer line and sump system were 90% complete. The masonry walls for the utility area yard were completed.[84] The November monthly report noted progress on both residence buildings. The five-thousand-gallon sewage septic tank concrete was being poured, and the walls of the administration building exhibit room were 95% complete.[85]

On December 1, the Flagstaff newspaper printed a lengthy article detailing Walnut Canyon work. The newspaper called the activities an "extensive improvement program." Plans indicated that "Walnut Canyon is intended to be a real gateway to southwestern national monuments." William Stevenson was said to be the camp superintendent and Dr. Lester Mermel the camp physician. The CCC camp was reported to have school rooms, gym, library, hobby shops, and mechanical and carpenter shops.[86]

The December summary was positive: "The Flagstaff camp is doing a good job of getting set before winter strikes," wrote

Beaubien. All but 1,000' remained on the water line. Enrollees were installing the beams in the administration building.[87]

1940–1941

During January, work resumed on the two residence buildings and the split rail fence. Work began on landscaping along the pipeline.[88] According to former NP-12 enrollee Frank T. Wisniewski, work on the residences was largely hand labor, including splitting cedar shakes, installing hand-hewn posts and rafters, and adding stone blocks fashioned by hammer and chisel.[89] During March, it was reported that rock quarry work was continuous, fence rails continued to be stockpiled, and work continued on residences and the administration building. Custodian Beaubien noted that three enrollees were being used as guides and "they receive many compliments."[90]

In April, the pipeline was finished, turned on, and working fine. (Upon completion. the pipeline was said to be 34,300' long and have required 13,584 man days.)[91] Boundaries were being surveyed for fencing.[92] The May report noted that pipeline landscaping was complete. (By the time the camp was abandoned, 2,494 man days were put into landscaping work.)[93] Enrollees were participating in a two-day fire suppression course. Ruins stabilization under Paul Ezell was begun, with enrollees hauling down clay, water, etc.[94]

During June, work continued on the administration building and two residences. The sewer system to headquarters was reported completed. (The sewer system required 5,368 man days.)[95] One mile of fencing was said to be complete. Ruins stabilization continued on seven rooms. (Apparently, only four rooms were completed, with the CCC using 685 man days.)[96] Three enrollees were working as guides.[97]

In addition to the work mentioned above, a June 30 NPS report reported 34 man days for firefighting. Four-tenths of a mile of rail fence was up, and enrollees had completed five signs. One-half mile of trail was complete, and six hundred cubic yards of limestone had been excavated. Enrollees had constructed log tables and benches.[98] Except for July when the number of enrollees available was limited, work continued through the summer on the residences, fence line, quarry work, the administration building, and comfort station.

In September, one residence was reported completed, with only interior work remaining on the other.[99] (The employee residence was completed October 1940, requiring 3,566 man days.)[100] The October report noted that comfort station work was nearly complete. (The comfort station was completed in November, using 1,157 man days.)[101] However, the fence work was halted due to the fatal truck accident. Monument records indicate that 75% of the fence was completed by the CCC, with the remainder completed using regular monument funds. The total fence was reported to be 3.4 miles long, with the CCC work completing 1.9 miles. Of the original estimate of 8,063 man days, the CCC worked 5,671 man days.[102] It appears that portions of the pitchy pine fence existing in 2012 are original CCC work.[103]

In November, enrollees were being used as guides. Roads to the residences were being constructed. Interior work at the administration building continued, and enrollees were maintaining the entrance road.[104] It appears the administration building was not completed until March 1941, requiring 5,700 man days.[105]

During early 1941, enrollee work included maintaining the roads at Walnut Canyon.[106] By the time the camp was abandoned, enrollees had put in 5,712 man days on road maintenance, including snow plowing.[107] In addition, by May 1941, enrollees had put in 3,847 man days improving the entrance road.[108] Plans called for the CCC to construct a drinking fountain, fireplaces, garbage pits, and signs for a picnic area, but due to the camp being abandoned, those jobs were not started.[109] The abandonment of the camp left the Island Trail work 80% complete, using 1,716 man days.[110]

Sunset Crater
1938

Even before the Pennsylvania enrollees arrived, the enrollees assigned to erecting the Mt. Elden buildings assisted at Sunset Crater, when three enrollees assisted putting out a small lightning fire.[111] During August and September 1938, enrollees constructed a new visitor map and register.[112] During October, enrollees assisted a stranded motorist stuck in the cinders on the monument road.[113]

1939

It appears there were plans for more improvements for an administration building, a museum, and a ranger station, but funding was uncertain.[114] On May 13, 1939, twenty enrollees assisted the Forest Service on a fire call in the cinder hills northeast of the crater. Twenty man days were required, with the Forest Service remaining another ten days to extinguish the fire completely.[115] During the summer, enrollees worked on the entrance road, with it being reported "the small crew has improved the road considerably."[116]

1940–1941

As of June, one NPS memo summarized Sunset work from August 2, 1938, to June 30, as "truck trails & minor rds. – 1 mile."[117] Apparently, a main duty of the enrollees in 1941 was grading the road to Sunset Crater.[118] According to one former enrollee, a spike camp was located at the Painted Desert, constructing roads and doing cleanup.[119] Another former enrollee reported that he worked digging cinders in the Sunset Crater area that were used for the roads at Walnut Canyon.[120] Little information about work projects at Sunset Crater after 1940 was located.

Unless noted otherwise, any reference to the number of enrollees in a company, the location of the company, or company supervisors are from U.S. War Department, Location and Strength of CCC Companies, 1933–1942, NARAMD RG 35 530/65/22/04/05.

1. "Civilian Corps Camp Sought to Develop Water," *Coconino Sun,* April 13, 1934, 1, 5.
2. "Contract Let for Aubineau Project Pipe," *Coconino Sun,* May 25, 1934, 1.
3. "Much Federal Money Spent in This County in Last Two Years," *Coconino Sun,* October 18, 1935, 8.
4. "Plans CCC Recreation Projects," *Coconino Sun,* May 24, 1935, 1, 6.
5. "No CCC Camp for Flagstaff," *Coconino Sun,* March 24, 1939, 1; "May Get City Park CCC Camp," *Coconino Sun,* April 28, 1939, 1; "May Get Help for City Park," *Coconino Sun,* May 5, 1939, 1. The application was part of a five-year city council plan. See *Flagstaff Journal,* May 5, 1939, 4.
6. F. M. Guirey, "Coconino Caverns," *Coconino Sun,* November 18, 1938, 5.
7. "Coconino Caverns May Become State Park," *Williams News,* December 8, 1938, 1.
8. "County Ending Partnership with Caverns Company," *Coconino Sun,* May 5, 1939, 1.
9. "Recovery Funds Are Allocated for Work at Wupatki Monument," *Coconino Sun,* December 8, 1933, 6.
10. "US Parks Obtain Civil Works Funds," *Coconino Sun,* December 8, 1933, 1.
11. "Work at Wupatki and Navajo Monuments Underway by Archeological Expeditions," *Coconino Sun,* December 22, 1933, 1.
12. "Recovery Funds Are Allocated for Work at Wupatki Monument," *Coconino Sun,* December 8, 1933, 6.
13. "Surveys Begun for Projects at Monuments," *Coconino Sun,* October 26, 1934, 1, 8.
14. "Three Monuments to Get $40,000," *Flagstaff Journal,* April 29, 1935, 2; *Arizona Republic,* April 29, 1935, 2.
15. U.S. NPS, "October 1938 Monthly Narrative Report to Chief Architect by H. H. Cornell," Branch of Plans and Design, Monthly Narrative Reports, 1936–38, NARAMD RG 79/150/35/7/7 Box 16. Unfortunately, the subsequent records are unclear regarding the exact funding of the Flagstaff-area monument buildings. Apparently it was a mix of other New Deal funds such as WPA and PWA and CCC funds. This was a common occurrence at other Arizona national parks and monuments.
16. "Two Local CCC Sites Ruled Out," *Coconino Sun,* June 7, 1935, 1, 6; "Move CCC Stuff Now Haul Water," *Coconino Sun,* July 12, 1935, sect. 2, 4.
17. "National Park CCC Camp Is Being Planned," *Coconino Sun,* March 18, 1938, 1.
18. "Walnut Canyon," *Southwest Monuments Monthly Reports, March 1938.*
19. "Mt. Elden CCC Camp Moving in," *Coconino Sun,* April 22, 1938, 1; "Grand Canyon News," *Coconino Sun,* April 22, 1938, 1.
20. "Pennsylvania CCC Men Arrive," *Coconino Sun,* August 5, 1938, 1.
21. For a delightful look at the human side of Mt. Elden camp life including the camp newspapers and excerpts from oral history interviews, see Jackson, "Monumental Tasks."
22. U.S. CCC, Camp Inspection Reports, NARAMD RG 35/530/65/23/04 Entry 115 (PI #11) Box 11. As an enrollee's total spending money was $5.00 per month, this complaint was not trivial. Often, movie program participation was mandatory. This type of complaint was not uncommon in other camps.
23. *Happy Days,* February 18, 1939, 15 and April 1, 1939, 15.
24. *Happy Days,* December 30, 1939, 11.
25. "Personals," *Coconino Sun,* May 5, 1938, 5.
26. *Happy Days,* May 27, 1939, 11.
27. "Mt. Elden CCC Help Capture Baby Antelope," *Coconino Sun,* June 9, 1939, 7. Eighty-nine man days were expended. See Job. No. 36, "Job Completion Report," FANMA.
28. "Canyon Blaze Is Controlled," *Prescott Evening Courier,* June 14, 1939, 1.
29. "Walnut Canyon National Monument," *Southwest Monuments Reports, July 1939,* 34.
30. "Change Command at CCC Camp," *Coconino Sun,* June 30, 1939, 5.
31. U.S. CCC, Camp Inspection Reports, NARAMD RG 35/530/65/23/04 Entry 115 (PI #11) Box 11.

32. U.S. CCC, Camp Inspection Reports, NARAMD RG 35/530/65/23/04 Entry 115 (PI #11) Box 11.
33. "Prisoner Makes Suicide Attempt in County Jail," *Coconino Sun*, August 25, 1939, 1. The article reported that Fox had a previous Pennsylvania conviction for grand theft. It did not note that would have made him ineligible for CCC enrollment.
34. Herbert Maier to the Director, 11 November 1939, U.S. NPS, Arizona National Monuments, NARACO RG 79 8NS-79-94-139 39/4/6:3-39/10/2:6 Box 85. For background on the Grand Canyon dispute, see Audretsch, *Shaping the Park and Saving the Boys*, 12.
35. "Back to Command Camp He Built," *Coconino Sun*, October 6, 1939, 1.
36. "New CCC Boys at Elden Camp," *Coconino Sun*, October 20, 1939, 1.
37. Job No. 41, "Job Completion Report," FANMA.
38. "Open House at Mt. Elden CCC Camp," *Coconino Sun*, March 29, 1940, 7.
39. Job No. 48, "Job Completion Report," FANMA.
40. "416 New Men for CCC Camps Arrive Saturday," *Coconino Sun*, July 26, 1940, 2.
41. "Mt. Elden CCC Camp Plans Work for Three Years; Hope to Get Approval for Extended Stay Here," *Flagstaff Journal*, August 22, 1940, 1.
42. "CCC Enrollee Killed Monday in Truck Wreck," *Coconino Sun*, October 25, 1940, 8; Carl A. Taubert, "Investigation Report USCCC 91062 Truck Accident Causing Death of Chester Mastalski and Injuries to 24 Other Enrollees 10-21-40," U.S. NPS, Arizona National Monuments, Accidents Folder, NARACO RG 79 8NS-79-94-139 39/4/6:3-39/10/2:6 Box 85; Arizona Death Records, 1940, State File No. 46, Registrar's No. 62.
43. "Lt. Harry Kieling Called to Army Air Service," *Coconino Sun*, November 1, 1940, sect. 2, 1.
44. Albert Spudy interview in Stein, *New Deal at Walnut Canyon*, 16.
45. "Fine Work Being Done by CCC Boys," *Coconino Sun*, March 28, 1941, 1, 8.
46. M. B. Stevenson to Hugh M. Miller, 31 October 1940, U.S. NPS, Arizona National Monuments, CCC Camp Sites Folder, NARACO RG 79 8NS-79-94-139 39/4/6:3-39/10/2:6 Box 85.
47. According to former enrollees, Company 3345 next went to a SCS CCC camp at Davenport, Washington. See Albert Spudy and Joseph Michalsky interviews in Stein, *New Deal at Walnut Canyon*, 16, 26.
48. U.S. NPS, Airfield Sites, NARACO RG 79 8NS-79-91-139 079-52G-0100; Job No. 65, "Job Completion Report," FANMA.
49. "Plane Crashes on Peaks," *Coconino Sun*, October 10, 1941, 1, 6.
50. M. B. Stevenson to Charles A. Richie, 15 October 1941, U.S. NPS, Arizona National Monuments, CCC Camp Sites Folder, NARACO RG 79 8NS-79-94-139 39/4/6:3-39/10/2:6 Box 85.
51. "Bomber Parts Salvaged and Taken to Tucson," *Coconino Sun*, October 17, 1941, 5.
52. "Elden CCC Camp Will Disband Tomorrow," *Coconino Sun*, March 20, 1941, 1.
53. "Wupatki National Monument," *Southwest Monuments Monthly Reports, June 1938*.
54. "Wupatki National Monument," *Southwest Monuments Monthly Reports, August 1938*.
55. "Wupatki National Monument," *Southwest Monuments Monthly Reports, September 1938*.
56. Demary to Pinkley, telegram, 29 September 1938, "Southwestern National Monuments Final Construction Report on Public Works Project O.P. 752-05-183, Wupatki National Monument," FANMA.
57. "Wupatki National Monument," *Southwest Monuments Monthly Reports, October 1938*.
58. "Improvements at Wupatki Ruins," *Coconino Sun*, October 7, 1938, 1.
59. "Wupatki National Monument," *Southwest Monuments Monthly Reports, December 1938*.
60. "Nat'l Monuments Building Bids to Be Readvertised," *Coconino Sun*, January 20, 1939, 1.
61. U.S. NPS, Arizona National Monuments, NP-12, "CCC Work Accomplished ... 8-2-38 to 6-30-40," NARACO RG 79 8NS-79-94-139 39/4/6:3-39/10/2:6 Box 85.
62. "Wupatki National Monument," *Southwest Monuments Monthly Reports, April 1939*, 256.
63. "Wupatki National Monument," *Southwest Monuments Monthly Reports, May 1939*.
64. "Wupatki National Monument," *Southwest Monuments Monthly Reports, September 1939*.
65. "Wupatki National Monument," *Southwest Monuments Monthly Reports, August 1939*.
66. "Work Starts on Wupatki Developments," *Coconino Sun*, September 1, 1939, 1, 8.
67. "Wupatki National Monument," *Southwest Monuments Monthly Reports, December 1939*, 412. The *Southwest Monuments Monthly Reports, February 1940* (page 120) noted Coleman had "proven to be very capable of making a study of skins of small mammals of this area."
68. "Wupatki National Monument," *Southwest Monuments Monthly Reports, January 1940*.
69. "Wupatki National Monument," *Southwest Monuments Monthly Reports, June 1940*. The residence was completed

during the summer of 1941. See Jackson, "Monumental Tasks," 297.

70. U.S. NPS, Arizona National Monuments, NP-12, "CCC Work Accomplished … 8-2-38 to 6-30-40," NARACO RG 79 8NS-79-94-139 39/4/6:3-39/10/2:6 Box 85.
71. "Wupatki National Monument," *Southwest Monuments Monthly Reports, August 1940; September 1940*.
72. "Wupatki National Monument," *Southwest Monuments Monthly Reports, November 1940*.
73. "Final Construction Report on Public Works Project O.P. 752-05-183, Wupatki National Monument," FANMA.
74. Walnut Canyon National Monument, *Historic Structure Report, Ranger Cabin & Boundary Fence*, Preservation Studies Program, College of Architecture & Landscape Architecture, University of Arizona (March 2007), 4.
75. Demary to Pinkley, telegram, 29 September 1938, "Southwestern National Monuments Final Construction Report on Public Works Project O.P. 752-05-183, Wupatki National Monument," FANMA.
76. "Walnut Canyon National Monument," *Southwest Monuments Monthly Reports, September 1938*.
77. "Walnut Canyon National Monument," *Southwest Monuments Monthly Reports, October 1938*.
78. "Nat'l Monuments Building Bids to Be Readvertised," *Coconino Sun,* January 20, 1939, 1.
79. U.S. NPS, Arizona National Monuments, NP-12, "CCC Work Accomplished … 8-2-38 to 6-30-40," NARACO RG 79 8NS-79-94-139 39/4/6:3-39/10/2:6 Box 85.
80. "Walnut Canyon National Monument," *Southwest Monuments Monthly Reports, January 1939*.
81. "Walnut Canyon National Monument," *Southwest Monuments Monthly Reports, March 1939*.
82. "Walnut Canyon National Monument," *Southwest Monuments Monthly Reports, August 1939*, 83.
83. Job. No. 3, "Job Completion Report," FANMA.
84. "Walnut Canyon National Monument," *Southwest Monuments Monthly Reports, September 1939*, 173.
85. "Walnut Canyon National Monument" *Southwest Monuments Monthly Reports, November 1939*.
86. "Mt. Elden CCC Constructing Fine Group of Stone Buildings at Walnut Canyon Monument," *Coconino Sun,* December 1, 1939, 1, 5.
87. "Walnut Canyon National Monument," *Southwest Monuments Monthly Reports, December 1939*, 404.
88. "Walnut Canyon National Monument," *Southwest Monuments Monthly Reports, January 1940*.
89. Frank T. Wisniewski, "Civilian Conservation Corps," 3, CCC Collection, P-AZ-02, ANMAHA.
90. "Walnut Canyon National Monument," *Southwest Monuments Monthly Reports, March 1940*, 178.
91. Job No. 13, "Job Completion Report," FANMA.
92. "Walnut Canyon National Monument," *Southwest Monuments Monthly Reports, April 1940*.
93. Job No. 54, "Job Completion Report," FANMA.
94. "Walnut Canyon National Monument," *Southwest Monuments Monthly Reports, May 1940*.
95. Job No. 11, "Job Completion Report," FANMA.
96. Job No. 17, "Job Completion Report," FANMA.
97. "Walnut Canyon National Monument," *Southwest Monuments Monthly Reports, June 1940*.
98. U.S. NPS, Arizona National Monuments, NP-12, "CCC Work Accomplished … 8-2-38 to 6-30-40," NARACO RG 79 8NS-79-94-139 39/4/6:3-39/10/2:6 Box 85. Five tables and benches were constructed using 207 man days. Job No. 5, "Job Completion Report," FANMA.
99. "Walnut Canyon National Monument," *Southwest Monuments Monthly Reports, September 1940*. The ranger residence, Job No. 4, was reported as requiring a total of 9,350 man days. "Job Completion Report," FANMA.
100. Job No. 26, "Job Completion Report," FANMA.
101. Job No. 52, "Job Completion Report," FANMA.
102. Job No. 10, "Job Completion Report," FANMA.
103. "Walnut Canyon National Monument," *Southwest Monuments Monthly Reports, October 1940*; "Walnut Canyon National Monument," *Southwest Monuments Monthly Reports, September 1940*, 4.
104. "Walnut Canyon National Monument," *Southwest Monuments Monthly Reports, November 1940*.
105. Job No. 22, "Job Completion Report," FANMA.
106. Joseph Michalsky interview in Stein, *New Deal at Walnut Canyon*, 26.
107. Jobs No. 16 and 63, "Job Completion Report," FANMA.
108. Job No. 12, "Job Completion Report," FANMA.
109. Jobs No. 6 through 9, "Job Completion Report," FANMA.
110. Job No. 13, "Job Completion Report," FANMA.
111. "Sunset Crater," *Southwest Monuments Monthly Reports, July 1938*.
112. "Sunset Crater," *Southwest Monuments Monthly Reports, September 1938*.
113. "Wupatki National Monument," *Southwest Monuments Monthly Reports, October 1938*.
114. "Nat'l Monuments Building Bids to Be Readvertised," *Coconino Sun,* January 20, 1939, 1.
115. Job No. 19, "Job Completion Report," FANMA.
116. "Sunset Crater," *Southwest Monuments Monthly Reports, July 1939; August 1939*.
117. U.S. NPS, Arizona National Monuments, NP-12, "CCC Work Accomplished … 8-2-38 to 6-30-40," NARACO RG 79 8NS-79-94-139 39/4/6:3-39/10/2:6 Box 85.

118. Albert Spudy interview in Stein, *New Deal at Walnut Canyon*, 17.
119. Joseph Michalsky interview in Stein, *New Deal at Walnut Canyon*, 28.
120. Joseph Cmar interview in Stein, *New Deal at Walnut Canyon*, 47.

**Sidebar:
Diversity in the CCC**

During the 1930s, minorities, such as African Americans and American Indians, lived a life almost always segregated from white Americans. The most that they might expect to attain was a "separate but equal" existence. But the Great Depression sometimes hurt minorities more than whites. CCC officials knew that they could not ignore the needs of minorities.

African Americans

At first, some CCC companies were integrated, especially in places such as Arizona where few African Americans lived. But by 1935, complaints convinced the CCC director, Robert Fechner, to forbid integration. He ordered "complete segregation of colored and white enrollees." Even though the law creating the CCC forbid discrimination "on account of race, color, or creed," Fechner held that "segregation is not discrimination."[1]

The CCC's goal was to enroll a percentage of black enrollees that reflected the percentage of blacks in the state population in the 1930 census, and none more. By 1936, nearly all African Americans in the CCC were in segregated companies, designated by a "C" and supervised by white officers. Only the states of Wisconsin and Vermont appeared to defy Washington's dictum by keeping mixed companies of both African Americans and whites.[2] There were other exceptions. Veterans Company 1826V, formed in July 1933 and ultimately disbanded in northern Arizona in 1942, always had about ten African American members. In northern Arizona, Company 822 had black members until 1939. Company 819 at Grand Canyon's South Rim, as well as Company 863 in the Coconino National Forest, also had a few black enrollees as late as 1938.[3] In Arizona after June 30, 1939 the only company reporting African American enrollees was 1826V.

Generally, "blacks were segregated into their own quarters and often assigned the worst jobs to perform in the camps."[4] Indeed, at the Horse Thief Basin spike camp of Company 822, "the colored enrollees are grouped in their own tents, mess tables, and also on the work job."[5] But in at least one case in northern Arizona, African American enrollees were sometimes doing the same work as white enrollees. At Grand Canyon, a former African American Company 818 enrollee, John B. Scott, commented that the few blacks were usually forced to be cooks or domestics. However, he noted that at Phantom Ranch, black enrollees frequently did the same trail work as the whites.[6] Once Scott reached the status of seasoned trail worker, a new enrollee was assigned for Scott to monitor. Louis Purvis writes that on one occasion Scott saved a new recruit's life by pulling him away from an impending rock fall.[7] Scott also assisted with the camp newspaper, *Ace in the Hole*.[8]

But life was not always easy for African American enrollees at the canyon bottom. Manuel Fraijo, a former Company 818 enrollee at Phantom Ranch, wrote of their company in 1933–1934 having six black enrollees, all but one from Texas. In the company were a "group from Texas that hated the black boys and would make their lives miserable. But occasionally the black boys in the privacy of their own tent and with their banjos and ukuleles would sing their southern ballads and religious hymns. Gradually the whole camp would gather outside their tent to hear their beautiful melodies."[9] Unfortunately, we know little about other northern Arizona African American enrollees.

It is this writer's opinion that the CCC survived, indeed it was successful, because of many factors. The CCC was flexible and adaptable. In the rush to get the CCC program off the ground in 1933, the military was willing to break with convention. At Grand Canyon National Park, in Company 819 during the First Enrollment Period, a number of the leaders giving orders to the nearly all-white company were African American officers and non-commissioned officers from Fort Huachuca, Arizona.[10]

Camp newspapers occasionally printed jokes demeaning to blacks, reflecting the dominant societal attitudes. When enrollees expressed opinions in camp newspapers or oral history interviews about differences, they were more likely to emphasize them if an enrollee was from a state different from their own.

At the CCC's end in 1942, there were over 165 companies nationwide composed of African Americans. Over the CCC's existence, about 250,000 African Americans served.[11] For many African Americans, the CCC offered new skills and hope. As one North Carolina enrollee said: "The CCC was the best life I ever lived. It was beautiful."[12]

Hispanics

In Arizona, discrimination against Hispanics occurred, but may not have been widespread.[13] (See chapter 12 sidebar, *Camp Controversy*.) Former Grand Canyon enrollee Manuel Fraijo remembers choosing Company 818 after an unfriendly Company 819 sergeant asked for volunteers. As soon as they stepped off the train on the South Rim, the "sergeant proceeded to hassle us about our national heritage (Hispanic), and tell us how lucky we were to be a part of his camp." Fraijo immediately volunteered for Company 818 at the bottom, saying, "I wanted very little to do with the sergeant."[14] In his detailed study about the CCC in New Mexico, Richard Melzer found no evidence of discrimination against Hispanics in selection, in camp placement, or in promotions.[15]

American Indians

Among Native Americans, CCC work was frequently independent of Washington's rules. Some scholars, such as Peter MacMillan Booth, consider the CCC work with Indians as its most successful aspect. Unlike most of the CCC enrollees, Indians did not travel far, but rather worked on their own reservations. Projects were frequently picked by local tribal officials. Males above age eighteen were eligible, single or married. Most CCC Indian Division projects were for resource development, such as soil conservation, and building infrastructure such as roads, fences, and telephone lines.[16] At the program's end, 177,436 Native Americans and Territorials participated.[17] One Michigan Native American enrollee said he "was treated better in the CCC than [in the nearby city] or in the Army."[18]

Veterans

Also hard hit by the economic chaos were veterans of World War I. Many veterans, wounded both physically and mentally, were unable to find any employment. On May 11, 1933, FDR issued an executive order authorizing the enrollment of veterans into special camps without marital or age limits.[19] While their work was sometimes modified because of their disabilities, their projects were nearly the same as those of the "juniors." Veterans' camps were designated with a "V," and there were about 250 camps nationwide by program's end. Over 225,000 veterans served, including even a few veterans of the Spanish American War![20] Arizona had a total of three veterans' companies and, of these, two, 1823V and 1826V, served in the area of this study.[21]

---

1. New Deal Network, "African Americans in the CCC." See also Salmond, *Civilian Conservation Corps*, 88–101; Otis et al., *Forest Service and CCC*, 7.
2. CCCL, "CCC Camp Lists," http://www.ccclegacy.org/ camp_lists.htm. Vermont and Wisconsin are the only states to have companies signified by "M" for mixed.
3. U.S. War Department, Location and Strength of CCC Companies, 1933–1942, NARAMD RG 35 530/65/22/04/05.
4. Collins, *New Deal in Arizona*, 210. See also Otis et al., *Forest Service and the Civilian Conservation Corps*, 29.
5. U.S. CCC, Camp Inspection Reports, NARAMD RG 35/530/65/23/04 Entry 115 (PI #11) Box 8.
6. Greer Price, e-mail message to author, November 25, 2009. In at least two Grand Canyon photos of North Rim work, a single African American enrollee is working with whites doing pest control work, that is "locating infected trees, felling, barking and burning of the infected trees." "Narrative Report for Fifth Enrollment Period … 1935…," GCNPMC Cat. #29853. For an image of black and whites doing the same Clear Creek Trail work, see GCNPMC Cat. #53489.
7. Purvis, *Ace in the Hole*, 104–105.
8. *Ace in the Hole*, Company 818 newspaper, December 25, 1935, GCNPMC Cat. #53496.
9. Fraijo, "Days of C.C.C.," 3, GCNPMC Cat. #99251.
10. Audretsch, *Shaping the Park and Saving the Boys*, 9.
11. Enrollment of African Americans is variously estimated from 200,000 by Salmond to 250,000 by the New Deal website. The latter estimates 150 "colored" companies, but counting the "colored" companies on the "CCC Camp Lists" pages of the CCC Legacy website totals 165. These diverse numbers point to the need for a detailed scholarly look at African Americans in the CCC.
12. Jolley, "*Magnificent Army of Youth and Peace*," 120. See Melzer, *Coming of Age*, 238, for a similar quote from a Pennsylvania boy enrolled in New Mexico.

13. See Otis et al., *Forest Service and the Civilian Conservation Corps*, 7.
14. Fraijo, *Days of C.C.C.*, 1, 3, GCNPMC Cat. #99251.
15. Melzer, *Coming of Age*, 249–253.
16. Salmond, *Civilian Conservation Corps*, 33; Peter MacMillan Booth, e-mail message to author, March 28, 2008.
17. U.S. Federal Security Agency, *Final Report of the Director of the Civilian Conservation Corps*, 108–109.
18. Hivert-Carthew, *Proud to Work*, 79.
19. Salmond, *Civilian Conservation Corps*, 36; Executive Order 6129.
20. Salmond, Ibid., 36–37.
21. U.S. War Department, Location and Strength of CCC Companies, 1933–1942, NARAMD RG 35 530/65/22/04/05.

CHAPTER 4

Coconino National Forest

The Forest Service and the CCC: An Overview

THE U.S. FOREST SERVICE WAS involved in the planning for the CCC soon after the 1932 election. At that time, FDR's team contacted Chief Forester Robert Y. Stuart to begin planning to put young men to work in federal forests.[1] Early on, forestry professionals were predicting incredible advancement for their profession. "Some foresters believe that the CCC has advanced forestry 20 years," proclaimed the 1937 textbook *CCC Forestry*.[2]

As soon as the CCC legislation was passed by Congress, the Forest Service was in the center of publicity. Just the day after the congressional vote, Southwest Regional Forest Supervisor Frank C. W. Pooler was said to have been queried about how many men he could put to work by mid-April.[3] (Pooler had already directed the region's nine forests to select projects and the like.)[4] A few days later, Fred Winn, Coronado National forest supervisor, was quoted as saying he had fifty projects such as trail building and fire control ready to start.[5] Just weeks later, Pooler stated that there was no "difficulty in finding an abundance of profitable work." Potential CCC projects included fire suppression, forest health, range improvements, recreational development, assistance with livestock use, eradication of undesirable plants and rodents, and improvement of fish and game conditions.[6]

Pooler worked with state officials meeting with Stuart Bailey, of Arizona's Secretary of the State Public Welfare Board, not long after he had flown to Washington for the very first CCC briefing.[7] A few days later, Pooler announced that Aldo Leopold had been named as CCC technical advisor. Leopold was reported to have been at Safford previous to the first enrollees coming to the Crook National Forest on May 23.[8] Two days later, the Phoenix newspaper announced camp locations in the Coconino, Prescott, and Sitgreaves National Forests.[9] By June 1933, Pooler was touting the CCC program's benefits, saying that enrollees "will return to their homes better men mentally and physically. We want to contribute to their self-respect and want to give them a more wholesome outlook in life as a result of their contact with the great outdoors of the forests."[10]

When the First Enrollment Period ended, Pooler again promoted the CCC work in the region's forests with a list of statistics.[11] Forest supervisors—such as T. T. Swift of the Tonto, J. C. Nave of the Prescott, Ralph W. Hussey of the Coconino, and Leo Kirby of the Sitgreaves—were speaking to local groups such as the Rotary, explaining and promoting the CCC camps. And once work was accomplished, Forest Service officials were quick to sing its praises. Cattlemen were told by regional Forest Service official D. A. Shoemaker that the CCC and NRA in "the past year was able to complete range improvements that normally would have required 10 years."[12] Cattlemen also took up the banner. Arizona cattlemen at their 1934 annual convention in Phoenix passed a resolution that CCC work repairing fences "be made general throughout the state."[13] CCC crews were also lauded for their contribution to firefighting. Because of their strategic locations and their training, they were said to respond quicker than pick up crews.[14] Coronado Forest Supervisor Winn said that CCC "workers are completing projects that forest officials had estimated would take until 1943."[15] Even some military commanders picked up the positive message. Major Ray C. Rutherford, Globe sub-district CCC commander, boasted: "Park and forest recreational areas of the country are 20 years ahead in their development as a result of the $255,000,000 CCC program."[16] At the national level, the American Forestry Association was quoted as saying many state forestry programs had been advanced ten to twenty years.[17]

In Arizona, the Forest Service jumped out of the starting gate with twenty-one of the twenty-three First Enrollment Period camps and twenty-two of the thirty Second Enrollment Period camps. The Forest Service almost always remained enthusiastic about the CCC.[18] Five years into the program, Pooler was still spreading the word of the CCC benefits. "The CCC, one of the greatest forces for conservation in our nation's history" made realities that "which we could not have reached for years." CCC "has helped us far along … to the still distant goal of balanced use of natural resources … We will need the CCC camps for years to come … We look to the next five years of the CCC with great expectations."[19]

Ultimately, "roughly 75 per cent of all CCC camps worked on projects administered by the Department of Agriculture."[20] Indeed, throughout the program the Forest Service "always had the majority of CCC camps."[21] At the CCC program's ending, Forest Service camps were 42% of the state total.[22] Of all the non-Indian federal land agencies, the Forest Service was the most vigorous in the use of New Deal funds. National forests in Arizona were frequently the recipients of CWA, PWA, and WPA grants.

Many Forest Service projects, such as road building, required significant unskilled labor. So, besides the CCC, Arizona national forests pursued the use of labor from transient camps. Transient camps were frequently established at fairgrounds, and northern Arizona sites included Prescott, Flagstaff, and Williams. The camps were first funded by the CWA, and later FERA even had portable camps. In late 1935, twelve National Forest projects employing 2,400 transients were approved.[23]

Some have said that the New Deal era was a watershed in Forest Service history. In the beginning, much of the national forest CCC work was managing resources, such as timber. With increased New Deal funding, the Forest Service was able to increase the development of recreation and the enhancement of its transportation networks. When the CCC ended, says one researcher, "more conservation and recreation work had been accomplished by one organization than in any period in American environmental history."[24]

It should be noted that the National Archives and Records Administration has considerable detailed work records for the Coconino National Forest. Sadly, records like this for the other Arizona national forests appear to no longer be available. So, the Coconino Forest information for this study surpasses that of the Kaibab and Prescott National Forests.

Summer Season, 1933

Just a week after the CCC legislation was signed into law, Coconino National Forest officials and county engineer J. B. Wright announced possible projects for the CCC boys. Under consideration was converting the broken trail over Schultz Pass into an 11-mile-long "first class road" and building an 18-mile-long Anderson Mesa Road connecting Mormon Lake east to Hay Lake and Soldier Lake. Timber thinning and rodent control were also anticipated.[25]

Wright announced five possible camp locations in the Coconino: Schultz Pass, Double Springs at Mormon Lake, Clover Springs in Long Valley, Baker Butte on the Mogollon Rim, and Woods Ranch south of Munds Park. He emphasized that a reliable water supply was most important, with one thousand gallons per day a minimum, but up to six thousand gallons more desirable.[26] During May, both the Forest Service and the Army were inspecting possible camp locations. By May 26, plans called for 1,100 enrollees coming to five camps in the county, including Schultz Pass.

Wright said he had finished engineering details of the Schultz Pass Road, and the county engineer's office would be assisting the Forest Service through the summer. Wright further said he was looking for volunteer trucks and autos to transport the new enrollees from the railroad station to the camps. George Fleming, clerk of the board of county commissioners, said that idle road equipment, including three tractors, three graders, and six dump trucks, would be at the disposal of the CCC.[27]

The first Coconino National Forest group to arrive was Company 821 (172 Arizona men), for F-5, Schultz Pass, on May 28. On June 2, Company 863 (175 Texas men) arrived for F-6, Double Springs. On June 3, Company 860 (175 Texas men) arrived for F-9, Wood Springs.[28]

The Forest Service hired a veteran forester, E. A. McNamara, along with four aides, to supervise the work program.[29] In order for the Army to communicate to the Flagstaff area, they were transferring a small three-man portable field radio detachment from Fort Bliss capable of communicating up to 600 miles.[30] A week after the detachment's arrival, Maj. Pearl L. Thomas arrived in Flagstaff, heading a fifteen-man detachment supervising the ten northern Arizona camps. He was said to be leasing buildings at the city park.[31] As the Army was arriving, Forest Supervisor E. G. Miller was explaining the CCC to the Rotary.[32] In early July, Schultz Pass and Mormon Lake enrollees fought a forest fire at Long Valley.[33]

F-5, Schultz Pass

The first thirty-five enrollees left Fort Huachuca on May 27 and arrived in Flagstaff on May 28. A firsthand account by one of the first arrivals described how they drove down a poorly constructed road for five miles and unloaded their baggage and tents in a grove of pine trees, where they were greeted by Supervisor Miller and Chief Ranger Ed Oldham. "There were no buildings, no company street, no headquarters—in fact, the only thing to see in Camp now which met their view is one little lonesome water faucet." The tents were quickly erected. They slept on straw tick mattresses and had little hot water at first. They awoke in the mornings to frozen tent ropes.[34]

Schultz Pass camp monthly work reports were available, except for the month of July. For the June through October period, three miles of the roughest section of the Schultz Pass Road were constructed. Supervisor Miller stated that without the CCC "it would have required several years to accomplish the goals that have been reached in a single summer."[35] The four months of work reports indicate 3,369 man days on the road construction, 223 man days on roadside cleanup, 439 man days doing erosion control (constructing rock dams), and 41 man days plugging sinkholes in Lake Mary. They spent 1,824 man days doing timber stand improvement and 1,298 man days doing timber stand improvement at the Fort Valley Experimental Forest outside Flagstaff.

They spent considerable time poisoning rodents, a practice opposed by the National Audubon Society at the national level.[36] Killing porcupines totaled 1,252 man days, and killing prairie dogs in the Rogers Lake and Lake Mary areas totaled 358 man days. Mexican pocket gophers were eradicated over a 24.5-square-mile area. Poison weed control (milkweed, loco weed) accounted for 330 man days.[37] A *Coconino Sun* summary article reported work on 5,600 acres, with 225 check dams of erosion control work; 94,000 acres porcupine and prairie dog control; 1,470 acres poison plant control; and construction of four structures, including a 110′-long store room.[38] On August 31, F-5 (Company 821) reported 180 Arizona enrollees (with 3 African Americans). Camp supervisors were four Army officers (including a medical officer) and three Army enlisted men. On September 30, they reported 131 enrollees (with 2 African Americans). Company 821 departed F-5 on November 2 and moved to F-35, Clarkdale.

F-6, Double Springs (Mormon Lake)

The first commanding officer of F-6 was Capt. J. A. Smith, and the first project superintendent was L. R. Elmore.[39] Only one monthly report for F-6 for this period has survived, that of July 31, 1933; however, monthly reports for August through October labeled F-51 appear to be Company 863. The Double Springs camp reported roadside cleanup along the Weimer Springs Road and over two hundred acres of forest culture completed. Major resources were put into rodent control, with a fifteen-man crew working north of Weimer Springs Road shooting 157 porcupines and putting out 1,865 poison stations for the same. Another crew of ten were eradicating prairie dogs over ten thousand acres of the Anderson Mesa area by putting out 350 quarts of poison. A twenty-man poison plant crew worked two weeks curbing milkweed and motherworth weed. A road construction crew of eighteen to twenty-four finished the last 3 miles of the road into Kinnikinick Lake and completed .5 mile of the Picket Lake Road. A campground crew built twenty-six fireplaces and twelve camp tables, and distributed eight toilets.[40] The Flagstaff newspaper summary included 97,000 acres of porcupine and prairie dog work; 15 miles of telephone line and 13 miles of road work; extensive campground improvements, including a water system with a large concrete dam and a rock spring house; 175 campground conveniences, such as benches, fireplaces, etc.; five small buildings constructed; and two water projects completed.[41]

During August through October, road construction work was done on Pickett Lake Road and Anderson Mesa Road (three miles). Road maintenance was done on the Double Springs Road, Mormon Lake–Sheep Springs Road, and Tombler's Lodge Road. During this three-month period, substantial work was put into eradicating porcupines, with 558 shot, 5,668 poison baits put out, and 26,660 acres covered. During August and September, prairie dog eradication crews of eight to ten enrollees put out 510 quarts of bait and 690 quarts of prebait on Anderson Mesa, covering 21,200 acres. Forest culture work covered 1,960 acres. Enrollees eradicating milkweed had a crew of twelve to fifteen with scythes on Anderson Mesa in August and an area north of Mormon Lake, also using 500 pounds of calcium chlorate. That crew worked a fifty-acre area north of Bass Point pulling milkweed. Fence work during the three-month period included 1.25 miles of the G-4 drift fence and 4 miles of the Anderson Mesa Rim Fence. Substantial time was put in at Dairy Springs doing recreation development, installing picnic tables and toilets as well as constructing a 55,000-gallon reservoir, a 1-mile pipeline, and a pumping plant. In October, a five-man crew was working on the water system for the new F-51 camp.[42]

On August 31, F-6 (Company 863) reported 184 enrollees (150 from Texas and the rest from Arizona, with 7 African Americans). Camp supervisors included three Army officers, three non-commissioned officers, and a contract surgeon. On September 30, they reported 102 enrollees (with 1 African American). Company 863 departed F-6 on November 1 and moved to F-51, Beaver Creek.

F-9, Wood Springs

For this time span, it appears the work reports for Wood Springs are complete, covering June 6 to October 31. From June 6 to July 31, the Wood Springs camp fought five fires (48 man days) and did telephone line construction near Schnebly Hill (528 man days). The Lee Butte lookout trail was started. The Lee Butte Cabin tower excavations were started (71 man days). Lee Spring was cleaned out, walled, and fenced, with rough-hewn log troughs placed and the area cleaned up. The Sheep Springs development included clearing out and walling in the spring, fencing in the area below the spring as a campground, fencing the side spring, changing the road a short distance, relocating the troughs, and cleaning up the area (175 man days). The G-4 holding corral was started. Enrollees did range grass reseeding (239 man days). Nearly 3,000 man days were spent cutting fence posts and maintaining 26 miles of fence. The Ralston-Guyberg Division Fence (1,116 man days) and the Munds Park Ranger Station Fence were completed (3,251 man days). The Munds Park telephone line was worked (226 man days). Pingue eradication work was started near Pine tanks and moved to Wood Springs and Clay Park, taking 948 man days. Roadside cleanup totaled 520 man days, and forest culture work totaled 956 man days. Porcupine eradication involved shooting 31 and putting out 1,695 poison blocks.

Major effort was put into road construction, with 6.9 miles nearly complete on the Foxboro–Rattlesnake Truck Trail (3,386). The Foxboro–Munds Park Road Betterment with the Munds Park Bridge was started, and ten men were under the supervision of the Coconino County Highway Department, with three span bridges completed. Total man days on this project were 681.[43] The Flagstaff newspaper summary included four buildings built, 16,640 acres of rodent control, and 1,700 acres of poisonous plant eradication.[44] On August 31, F-9 (Company 860) reported 185 enrollees (141 from Texas and the rest from Arizona, with 6 African Americans). On September 30, 101 enrollees were reported. Company 860 departed F-9 on November 1 and moved to F-32, Clear Creek.

Winter Season, 1933–1934
F-32, Clear Creek

We have project reports for Company 860 from November 1, 1933, to March 31, 1934, but none for the reminder of its time until it departed on May 1. On March 31, the 4-mile telephone line from Woods Spring to Lee Butte was 80% completed. The Lee Butte Lookout Tower was completed in November. Road construction of 11.5 miles (Schnebly Hill and Sedona Clear Creek Roads) and road maintenance of 11 miles were noted. (The latter work included construction of nine bridges.) Horse trail work included Woods Canyon (4.3 miles) and Howard Trail (.5 mile). Campgrounds at Pine Tree Flat, Slide Rock, Purtyman, Banjo Bill, and Harding were cleaned. Other campground work included thirty latrines, ninety wood tables, and fifty-seven cooking fireplaces constructed, and wells dug at Pine Flat and near Pine Tree Flat. Fence construction included 6 miles of range fence (Page & Fain Division Fence), and 10.5 miles of fence were maintained including the D.K. Fence and the Ralston Pasture Fence. John Lee Spring was developed. Seeds were gathered and replanting done. Erosion control work near D.K. Pasture totaled 2,368 dams on 2,216 acres, and one corral was constructed at the Sedona Ranger Station. The Clarkdale Indian Ruin Restoration consisted of cutting and hauling timbers for restoration three miles east of Clarkdale.[45]

On December 31, enrollee George B. Kinnerly, 19, of Texas and Naomi Webb, 15, of Clarkdale were killed when two CCC trucks collided on Highway 79 in Yavapai County near Clarkdale.[46] On March 14, 1934, enrollee Candido Mostiero, 23, from Jerome died from pneumonia at Fort Whipple Veterans Hospital.[47]

On November 30, Company 860 reported 195 enrollees (with 7 African Americans). On January 31, it reported 189 enrollees (with 6 African Americans). Company 860 departed F-32 on May 1 and moved to F-62, Prescott National Forest.

F-35, Clarkdale

Work reports exist for the whole period, November 6, 1933, to May 1, 1934. Company 821 did substantial road construction during this time. On the Mud Tank Road No. 142, 2.2 miles were completed, requiring 4,468 man days. Road No. 121 required 1,339 man days to complete 6.2 miles. The Bullpen Road No. 215 required 199 man days to complete 1.5 miles. Other road construction totaled 590 man days. Erosion control work required 7,469 man days, resulting in 1,395 dams, 1,336 plugs, 300 yards of willow planting along Clear Creek, and .25 mile of riprap. Fence work totaled 776 man days cutting 1,713 posts and telephone stubs from Strawberry Hill, resulting in 4.8 miles of fence construction, including the Back & McDonald Allotment, the Coconino-Tonto boundary, and the Calkins and Richards Fence. Telephone line construction (184 man days), construction of a fence around the ranger station building, water line improvements (252) and revegetation work (293) were other projects.

Rodent control work required 331 man days to distribute (an astounding!) 5,452 pounds of poison grain over 31,340 acres. (For rodent control, a typical monthly work report included a two-page mimeographed Rodent Control Report with details of money spent, poisons used, and how many of each species were killed per acre. Poisons noted by this author were zith thallium and strychnine alkaloid. Poisons were mixed with bread crumbs or grain and salt. Rodent nests were also dug out and the animals killed.)[48]

On November 30, Company 821 reported 192 enrollees (all but 3 enrollees from Arizona, with 2 African Americans). On January 31, the report showed 192 enrollees (nearly all from Arizona, with 2 African Americans). On May 1, the company moved back to F-5, Schultz Pass.

F-51, Beaver Creek

Detailed monthly work reports exist for Company 863 from November through April. During November, much of the work seemed to be getting the camp area habitable and continuing some of the projects begun while they were at Double Springs. A crew of fifteen to twenty enrollees moved all the road machinery to the new location and then constructed 2 miles of road into the camp. A road maintenance crew of twenty widened three hundred yards of the road on the Blue Grade from 12′ to 21′, all by hand. Another crew of ten used five dump trucks to haul three hundred loads of gravel. A crew of sixteen to twenty worked on the Anderson Mesa telephone line construction, completing 10 miles. Erosion control continued with a crew of about eighty building 434 rock dams on 118 acres. A range improvement crew of nine worked two weeks gathering native seeds and planting a 1.3-acre site near Stoneman Lake.

In December, a crew of thirty-five was constructing the road between camp and the junction with the Stoneman Lake–Verde Valley Road, with the bulk of the crew in the vicinity of the Red Tank Wash approach. Three bridges were built (24′ long x 16′ wide). One road betterment crew of fifteen (five were dump truck drivers) surfaced .75 mile of the Stoneman Lake–Verde Valley Road about 3 miles east of the Blue Grade. Another crew of eighteen was widening (from 12′ to 18′) the Blue Grade sector of the Stoneman Lake–Verde Valley Road about 6 miles above the Beaver Creek camp. The latter road section was said to be one of the most hazardous in the forest. A crew of fifteen set 350 posts on the Walker Division Fence. Three crews averaging twenty men were constructing erosion control dams (including 84 large Type 16 dams), completing 295 smaller dams. Also, a camp garage was constructed.[49]

From January through March, the road construction crews of up to thirty-five worked the Beaver Creek–Clear Creek Road, completing over 6 miles in the Walker Creek vicinity. Highlights of the work included 6′-high retaining walls at the Beaver Creek Bridge and a 22′ bridge span across Beaver Creek just above Camp F-51. Two road betterment crews worked on the Stoneman Lake–Verde Valley Road, one on the Blue Grade sector and the other on the "Through the Cedars" section. The latter work involved resurfacing using five county dump trucks and a county Caterpillar. The Blue Grade work included widening the road from twelve to sixteen feet, resurfacing, digging ditches, and constructing sidewalls as high as twenty feet. According to the work report, this road "is considered one of the most hazardous on the entire Coconino Forest because of its inadequate width, being located on a steep mountainside and traversing, as it does, a decent of almost 1,000 feet in 3 miles from the top of the Mogollon Rim."

A crew of fourteen was constructing the Walker & Bell Division Fence near the Red Tank Wash crossing. A crew of fourteen completed 2 miles of the Bell-Ralston Division Fence, and they then moved to the Bell-Hollingshead Boundary Fence .5 mile west of the Beaver Creek Ranger Station where it follows the rim. By the end of March, they had completed about .75 miles of construction. The same crew constructed .75 miles of pasture fence at the Beaver Creek Ranger Station and did one hundred yards of the Bell Fence at Soda Springs.

Erosion control crews often averaged three twenty-man crews; during the three-month period, they constructed 1,590 dams of various sizes. A bridge construction crew of seven to nine completed three 26′-long spans across Red Tank Wash and a diversion dam across Beaver Creek south of camp. A water development crew of eight worked at Hance Spring, cleaning it, enclosing it in a 3 x 7′ concrete structure, laying five hundred feet of pipe, and building two concrete watering troughs. A carpenter crew of four spent the entire months of February and March constructing a building at the Beaver Creek Ranger Station. The range improvement crew "planted tamarisk in the neighborhood of Coffee Creek."[50]

During April, the road construction crew completed over 2 miles of road between the ranger station and the guest ranch, while the road betterment crew finished their work on both the Blue Grade and the "Through the Cedars" sections of the Stoneman Lake–Verde Valley Road. The erosion control crew of thirty-four built 201 dams, benefiting 135 acres. The carpenter crew installed a sewer system and built an eight-hundred-gallon water tank for the Beaver Creek Ranger Station.

On November 30, Company 863 reported 210 enrollees (almost evenly split between men from Arizona and from Texas). On January 31, they reported 196 (with 1 African American). Company 863 departed F-51 on May 1 and moved to F-6, Double Springs.

Summer Season, 1934
F-5, Schultz Pass

In mid-April, the Flagstaff newspaper reported that the Schultz Pass camp was again approved and that the city was seeking Arizona congressional approval of a plan to have the CCC build a road and a pipeline from Abineau Springs to the Inner Basin and connect it to the present city water system. A camp on the Peaks was also advocated. On April 20, a crew of eight to ten men was readying the camp for occupancy. On May 4, the *Coconino Sun* announced the arrival of the two Coconino National Forest companies.[51] Company 821 officially occupied F-5 on May 1. Three weeks later, the newspaper reported the CCC camp would participate in the water project by building the road while the city would lay the pipeline.[52] Detailed monthly work reports are available for the camp occupancy May through October.

During the May 1 through July 25 period, Company 821 constructed the Schultz Pass Road, using 1,935 man days, and the Abineau Springs–Inner Basin Road, using 1,377 man days. In addition, they constructed a 4.5-mile telephone line to the Inner Basin in 213 man days. Timber stand improvement accounted for 1,494 man days, and timber stand improvement at the Fort Valley Experimental Station involved 467 man days. (The latter work included collecting pine cones, planting the seeds, tending the seedlings, and preparing the seedlings for transplanting.)[53]

Enrollees also began work in June and July improving Little Leroux Spring, by first cleaning out the spring and then digging ditch and laying pipeline, using 305 man days. During the three-month period, porcupine control accounted for 481 man days, other telephone line construction took 215 man days, and roadside cleanup required 179 man days. F-5 reported 820 man days fighting forest fires. This is a high sum and may be related to June fires reported near Riordan Peak and Kendrick Peak requiring CCC assistance.[54] Enrollees did erosion control work, including in the Pump House area, totaling 411 man days. Fence construction totaled 233 man days at Black Spring and Griffith Spring and Lake Mary.[55]

On July 21, Special Investigator James C. Reddoch visited camp and noted 203 men in camp. Apparently, since May 1, there were 12 dishonorable discharges (7 elopement, 5 work refusal) and 46 honorable discharges. Candles were being used for light, but an electric line was coming soon. There were no serious problems.[56] Also during July, Robert Fechner, director of the CCC, visited Flagstaff and viewed the CCC as a potentially permanent organization. It is "far too valuable an institution to let lapse. Not only has it saved millions of dollars worth of timber, but it has restored the faith of hundreds of thousands of boys in themselves."[57]

In the July 26 through October 26 period, F-5 reported 92 man days worked by camp artist Creston Baumgartner. (See chapter 5, *The CCC Artists Program*.) Enrollees did their last work on the Abineau Springs–Inner Basin Road, noting 5.5 miles completed during the summer using 589 man days. Schultz Pass Road construction work accounted for 1,912 man days, and roadside cleanup (mostly in Oak Creek Canyon) totaled 406 man days. Timber stand improvement was 1,414 man days, and work at Fort Valley Experimental Station was 758 man days. Telephone line construction was 739 man days, and fence construction was 150 man days. Porcupine control was reported at 490 man days. Fighting forest fires was 203 man days, while fire prevention (burning brush) was 253 man days. Seventeen erosion control dams in the Pump House area accounted for 149 man days. Enrollees took 46 man days to construct a thousand-gallon tank for firefighting at Little Leroux Spring, along with a trough for wildlife. They reported 170 man days for construction of a 2.2-mile trail from Leroux Springs to Viet Road. Twenty-one man days were reported for the search for a lost woman at Walnut Canyon.[58] She was reported found by Company 821 enrollees.[59] On August 31, Company 821 reported 175 enrollees (99 from Arizona and the rest from Texas, with 3 African Americans). Also in August, the camp newspaper reported the camp finally got electricity to replace their lanterns.[60]

Figure 8. Road Construction, Camp F-5, Flagstaff, July 2, 1936. Photograph by Carson. Courtesy Coconino National Forest.

The camp received official orders to move in mid-October, and fifty-one enrollees were sent to F-35 to prepare the camp for the company arrival. Tragedy struck during this time when L. C. Daniels, 18, an African American man enrolled from NcNary, Arizona, drowned in Clear Creek.[61] On October 29, Company 821 moved officially from Schultz Pass to F-35, Clarkdale.

During November, the *Coconino Sun* reported that even though the Schultz Pass Road was not completed, a temporary road allowed access to Route 89. The road was reported as being constructed for fire suppression, but recreational access was available. Its completion was anticipated for the following summer.[62]

F-6, Double Springs

While we have a final report for the May 1 through November 1 work, we only have three of the detailed monthly reports. Camp 863 did substantial road work on the Mormon Lake–Munds Park Road, completing 6 miles. Twenty-three enrollees were working two shifts with a compressor during May. They noted that 1.5 tons of powder was needed on one difficult section. Two miles of the Mud Springs Road were completed. Seven miles of Kinnikinick Road were resurfaced. Roads were also maintained around Mormon Lake, Weimer Spring, and

Ashurst Lake. Forest stand improvement (pruning and thinning) accounted for 2,560 man days, often using a crew of fifty. Fence work included rebuilding 7.5 miles of the Sawmill Springs Drift Fence and constructing three miles of the Bell-Goswick Division Fence, a .5 mile of the old G4 Drift Fence, 4 miles of the Bell-Apache-Maid Division Fence, and 2 miles of the Zalesky Allotment Fence. Enrollees cleaned 8.5 miles of roadway and seined 35,000 fish. The campground development crew of fifteen did plugging of sinkholes in the Lake Mary bottom as well as painting and constructing toilets and tables. Two of the monthly reports noted eight to ten enrollees working at the Colter Ranch Experimental Station. Fire suppression totaled 262 man days. Porcupine eradication continued, with a crew of seven to eight enrollees covering an area north to Lake Mary, south to Hutch Mountain, east along Anderson Mesa to Sawmill Springs, and west to Horse Park. Enrollees cleaned out the Mormon Lake rearing ponds. Spring development included work at Double, Pilgrim's Playground, and Wallace Springs. At Winsor Spring and Navajo Spring, springs were cleaned out and concreted, with overflow pipes installed. Tinney Spring was cleaned, concreted, and piped to a thousand-gallon storage tank.[63] Special Investigator Reddoch visited the camp on July 21 and summarized the work progress, finding no serious difficulties.[64] On August 31, Company 863 reported 164 enrollees (91 from Texas and the rest from Arizona). Company 863 departed F-6 on October 29, 1934 and moved to F-51, Beaver Creek.

Winter Season, 1934–1935
F-35, Clarkdale

Company 821 arrived on October 29 and on October 31 reported 181 enrollees (102 from Texas and the rest from Arizona, with 3 African Americans). For the period October 29, 1934, to May 11, 1935, we have nearly complete work reports, with only one monthly report missing. Road construction work included 1,080 man days to construct 1.7 miles of the Mud Tank Road No. 142 and 1,402 man days to construct 1.5 miles of the Bullpen Road No. 215. The Walker Basin Road work reported 2,496 man days to complete 3.7 miles with equipment days as follows: truck (199), Caterpillar (148), and compressor (221). Road maintenance, such as the Clear Creek–Sedona Road, was 739 man days for road resurfacing, blading, and drainage improvement such as culverts and ditches. For fence work, 1,439 man days were worked, building 9.25 miles of range fence, 2.25 miles of erosion fence, and eight steel gates. Enrollees cut a total of 2,133 posts and 3,000 stays.

Erosion control work was substantial, with 5,060 man days, and erosion maintenance work totaled 1,529 man days repairing gulley plugs and dams. Enrollees constructed 159 wire dams, 45 loose rock dams, and 125 gulley plugs; built 227 cubic yards of rock diversion walls; excavated 900 cubic yards of contour ditch; and constructed 700 linear feet of baffles. Along Clear Creek, enrollees installed 400′ of riprap and planted 250 willow cuttings. At the Clear Creek Ranger Station, enrollees lowered and repaired the well, raised the road grade, and constructed a mile of pasture fence. The work of the camp artist was reported at 37 man days.[65]

On January 31, 1935, Company 821 reported 173 enrollees (with 3 African Americans). For the first time, supervisors included an educational advisor. Company 821 returned to F-5, Schultz Pass, on May 19, 1935.

F-51, Beaver Creek

Company 863 arrived on October 29 and on October 31 reported 189 enrollees (145 from Texas and the rest from Arizona). From November 1, 1934, until May 14, 1935, when the company moved, we have detailed work records. They did substantial work on the Foxboro-Rattlesnake Road with crews as high as fifty-six enrollees, sometimes working double shifts, completing 3.5 miles of road. A great deal of work throughout this period went into the Red Tanks–Rimrock Post Office Road, with crews as high as thirty-one enrollees grading 4.5 miles. They installed ten culverts and built twenty cubic yards of headwall, making the road complete from the Beaver Creek Ranger Station to the Rimrock Post Office. They also worked the Red Tanks Wash Rim Road, grading 2.5 miles.

Road maintenance during this period included a twenty-three-man crew resurfacing 2.5 miles of the Stoneman Lake–Verde Valley Road, sometimes working a double shift. They resurfaced the Stoneman Lake Road and maintained 10 miles of the Beaver Creek–Clear Creek Road. They resurfaced 2.75 miles and cleaned ditches on the Beaver Creek–Sedona Cutoff. A smaller crew averaging thirteen maintained the Hollingshead Stock Trail (many switchbacks, much blasting, and placing forty water bars), the Soda Springs–Beaver Creek Stock Trail, and the Casner Mountain Stock Trail. A crew of twelve placed ten miles of stock driveway monuments from Beaver Head to the Verde River.

The bridge construction crew of ten enrollees completed a 16′ span bridge near Walker's Ranch and an 18′ span bridge near Wickiup. Fence crews averaged eight to ten enrollees and completed 1.5 miles of the Bell–Apache Maid Division Fence and 7 miles of the Lawrence Goswick Division Fence. In some instances, pack mules brought in posts and wire for the 4.25 miles of the Bell–Lawrence Division Fence. The rodent control crews averaged five to eight and did considerable work in the

Big Park area, poisoning kangaroo rats, antelope mice, and field mice. Some Big Park areas were covered as many as three times, covering nearly 15,000 acres and putting out 2,520 quarts of poison. Another area of 7,000 acres was treated with 1,000 pounds of poisoned grain. An additional crew put out 344 pounds of poison in a 14,680-acre area.

The erosion control crews were frequently as high as fifty-six enrollees and did some other work such as water development at Foster Springs. In all, they constructed 859 smaller rock dams, 32 wire dams, and 102 gully plugs. The range revegetation crews ranged from six to twelve enrollees, and plantings included desert willow, chamise, bunch grass, and winter fat over forty-six acres, with Clear Creek and Wickiup Flat as some of the areas noted.

The bridge construction crew was noted working for two months completing Bridge No. 1 west of the Beaver Creek Ranger Station and beginning work on Bridge No. 2. The former had a 16′ span with eight cubic yards of concrete for the abutments. Enrollees tore down the old Beaver Creek Ranger Station and did much of the work for the new ranger station, such as digging the basement area, pouring the concrete, and working as helpers for the carpenters and bricklayers. They also built the hydroelectric power house and installed the water wheel.[66] The new ranger station was nearly complete when the company moved back to F-6 on May 14.

On January 31, Company 863 reported 196 enrollees (57 from Arizona and 139 from Texas, with 2 African Americans). The supervisor's report listed an educational advisor for the first time. On March 11, 1935, Special Investigator Reddoch visited the camp, summarizing their work and noting no problems at the camp.[67]

F-32, Clear Creek

Company 860 returned from the Prescott National Forest on November 5, 1934. On October 31, while at F-62, they reported 177 enrollees (half from Texas and half from Arizona, with 10 African Americans). Unfortunately, we only have two monthly work reports for this period, so our knowledge of their work during this time is quite incomplete. During November and December, enrollees were working on the Schnebly Road construction, expending 1,310 man days to construct 6.2 miles. Clear Creek–Sedona Road construction was noted to be 545 man days. Oak Creek twig blight work was 443 man days. In December, their report noted the Sedona Ranger Station barn was almost complete. The company installed a pipeline and drinking fountains to the Sedona School.[68]

On March 11, Special Investigator Reddoch visited the camp and noted its work projects as road construction and maintenance; ranger station and barn construction, including well and water tank; recreation area development with water system, flush toilets, concrete tables, and benches; erosion control; rodent control; and range revegetation, with seed gathering and the planting of native grasses and shrubs. He noted the enrollees had a food strike on November 18, 1934, over the poor mess.[69]

On January 31, Company 860 reported 196 enrollees (109 from Texas and the rest from Arizona, with 11 African Americans). Company 860 departed F-32 on May 19 and moved to F-62, Prescott National Forest.

Summer Season, 1935
F-5, Schultz Pass

Company 821 returned to F-5, Schultz Pass, on May 19, 1935. Texas enrollee L. C. Maddux, 18, passed away at Mercy Hospital of pneumonia on June 20, 1935.[70] On June 30, they reported 196 enrollees (53 from Arizona and the rest from Texas, with 3 African Americans). Their supervisors were three Army officers, a contract physician, and an educational advisor.

All monthly work reports for their summer season are available, so we have a relatively clear record of their work. The camp reported 593 man days devoted to maintaining and cleaning up the Schultz Pass Road. Road construction man days were substantial, showing work on the Rogers Lake Road (3,549), the Knob Hill Road (497), and the Woody Lookout Road (1,877). Construction of a 1-mile power line to the Army Camp (most likely Fort Tuthill) totaled 253 man days. Telephone line construction was 588 man days. Range fence and the Knob Hill Fence were 324 man days. Timber stand improvement was 435 man days, while Fort Valley timber stand improvement was 3,660. Enrollees did roadside cleanup (300) and tore down the Greenlaw Mill and Camp (186). The camp assisted the county with a road survey (10), did water development at Campbell Ranch (23), and repaired Lake Mary dams (197). They spent considerable time fighting forest fires (685) and were "proud of their fire fighting record, many times there is a crew of fifty men on the way to a fire within four minutes after a fire is reported."[71] Enrollees spent 311 man days controlling prairie dogs at Fort Tuthill and Walnut Canyon and 826 man days maintaining and cleaning up the Pine Flat campground. One of the more unusual projects of any CCC camp was enrollees spending 68 man days gathering ticks for a U.S. Public Health survey of spotted fever.[72]

On August 17, Texas enrollee Roy L. Hart, 21, died at Fort Whipple Veterans Hospital of pneumonia.[73] On November 1, the *Coconino Sun* (page 1) reported F-5 supervisors were Commanding Officer Capt. Herbert W. Moore, assisted by Ensign Walter Ruland, with Gilbert Cady as the educational advisor and Ed A. McNamara as the project superintendent. Company 821 departed F-5 on November 7 and moved to F-32, Sedona.

F-6, Double Springs

Company 863 returned to F-6 on May 14 and on June 30 reported 197 enrollees (49 from Arizona and the rest from Texas, with 1 African American). Monthly work reports are available for their time at F-6, except for October. As it turns out, some of their work was a continuation of their time at F-51. Throughout the five-month period, we have reports that enrollees constructed the Mormon Lake–Munds Park Road, completing at least 3 miles, with some of the work in the Casner Park area. The Foxboro-Rattlesnake Road was completed in May. Also during May, enrollees did road maintenance on 20 miles of the Antelope Park Road, 5 miles of the Ashurst Lake Road, 5 miles of the Kinnikinick Road, and 5 miles of the Mormon Lake recreation roads. Roadside cleanup included the area near Tombler's Lodge. Erosion control work in May included constructing twenty-five dams and 500' of diversion ditch in the Red Tank Wash near Beaver Creek.

Timber stand improvement included 200 acres near Mormon Lake, about 750 acres near Coulter Ranch and Thomas Springs, and 670 acres in the Newman Canyon drainage. Fence construction included 1 mile of the Bell-Lawrence Division Fence and over 5 miles of the Zalesky Allotment Fence. CCC Artist Creston Baumgartner was reported as working during May, June, and August. Spring development consisted of cleaning out the spring and constructing cement boxes and piping to water troughs at Howard and Mormon Lookout Springs. Campground development included constructing 2,000' of a 18 x 18" stone wall, six cooking fire places, five culverts, one 10 x 14' (inside) stone building, and one 12 x 20' frame building in the Lake Mary area. Enrollees cleaned out the Ashurst Lake Drainage Ditch, and about sixty-five men worked for a month at Lake Mary, including fill on the Riordan Dyke. Enrollees participated in fish seining at Lake Mary. Poison plant control included milkweed eradication on over thirty-five acres in areas near Pickett Lake, Mormon Lake, Clark's Well, and Clarks' Valley. Enrollees worked through May and June finishing the construction of the Beaver Creek Ranger Station. Company 863 departed F-6 on November 1 and moved to F-51, Beaver Creek.

Winter Season, 1935–1936
F-32, Sedona

Company 821 officially arrived at F-32, Sedona (twenty-eight miles northeast of Clarkdale) on November 7, 1935. On December 31, they reported 154 enrollees (76 from Arizona, 52 from Texas, and 26 from Oklahoma, with 3 African Americans). On November 25, Special Investigator Reddoch visited the camp and noted no major problems. He summarized their work as road construction and maintenance; bridge construction; telephone line construction; construction of a combination garage, barn, and blacksmith shop; twig blight control; and recreation area development.[74] On December 27, Coconino National Forest Supervisor Hussey announced that a twenty-man CCC crew was presently treating an area of 3,000 acres near Sedona for twig blight and that the crew would be increase to eighty after January 1.[75]

For this time period, we have six monthly work reports (November 6, 1935 to April 30, 1936), so our picture of what the camp was doing appears to be almost complete. Substantial resources were put into Schnebly Hill Road construction, with 11 miles completed, requiring 4,168 man days. Work on the Clear Creek–Sedona Road totaled 3,299 man days. Associated road work included completing Bridge No. 1 on the Clear Creek–Sedona Road (986 man days) and work on Bridge No. 2 on the same road (195 man days) and Bridge No. 1 on Schnebly Hill Road (180 man days).

Enrollees worked through November and December constructing the new Sedona Ranger Station barn and garage and then spent January and February tearing down the old barn. They also landscaped the ranger station area. Enrollees treated 688 acres for twig blight, totaling 2,244 man days. They constructed 13 miles of Schnebly telephone line, requiring 908 man days, constructed a 1.5-mile power line to the Sedona Ranger Station (121 man days), and fought fires on A-1 Mountain and in the Fisher Point area (220 man days). Erosion control work included building erosion fences and water gaps in the Coffee Creek area (84 man days). They also assisted Company 863 working on the Dry Beaver Creek Bridge. On February 20, F-32 enrollee Doler Pirtle, 26, died at Fort Whipple Veterans Hospital of pulmonary edema.[76] Company 821 departed F-32 on May 1, 1936, and moved to F-5.

In March, Coconino National Forest Supervisor Hussey wrote to J. D. Walkup of the Coconino commissioners stressing the continuation of the CCC program. Even though the forest already had three camps, the "needed work in the vicinity of these camps has scarcely been scratched." The camps have "at least two full years of much needed work available." Hussey listed the needs for the camps. He wrote that in the Schultz Pass area the Fort Valley Munds Park telephone line needed reconstruction; Barney Pasture Road needed more construction; and the Mt. Elden and the San Francisco Peaks needed recreational and protective roads. For the Mormon Lake area, he listed Bakers Butte twig blight control work, Mormon Lake to Long Valley telephone line, Mormon Lake campground maintenance, and recreational and protective roads for Mormon

Lake to Munds Park and Hay Lake to Kinnikinick Lake. Even though the Wood Springs camp was not in use, it could be reopened. In this area, he listed the following needs: complete the Schnebly Hill Road; build vista points on rim near Schnebly Hill; complete the Woods Spring to Stoneman Lake Road; improve the Woods Spring to Lee Butte Road; and build a campground for Stoneman Lake.77 At the same time Ed Raudebaugh, the Forest Service CCC work supervisor, said they expected to resume recreational work soon at Oak Creek Canyon, including widening and leveling of the highway near the cattle guard before the hill descent and constructing a wide parking lot with a stone wall for viewing at the same location.78

F-51, Beaver Creek

Company 863 officially arrived at F-51 (thirty miles east of Clarkdale) on November 1. On December 31, they reported 184 enrollees (54 from Arizona, 45 from Oklahoma, and 85 from Texas, with 3 African Americans).79 Special Investigator Reddoch visited the camp on November 25 and noted no serious problems.80

For this time frame, we have access to all the monthly work reports except January. Work accomplished during this period was substantial. Road construction included forty to sixty enrollees working for two months on the Apache Maid Ranger Station Road along a 3.5-mile section, including drilling and shooting and installing culverts and bridges. A crew averaging sixty-five competed nearly 2 miles of the Beaver Creek–Clear Creek Road. A crew averaging fifty graded 2 miles of the Sedona–Clear Creek Road No. 121, including culverts, headwalls, two 14′ bridges, a 20′, and one 6 x 6, 40′-long concrete culvert. Road maintenance included crews working in the areas of the Rimrock Post Office, Stoneman Lake, and Beaver Creek.

Bridge construction included the Beaver Creek Bridge (southwest of the Beaver Creek Ranger Station), Walker Creek Bridge (two 20′ spans), and the Dry Beaver Bridge. The latter project included thirty-five enrollees working a month and completion of the Dry Beaver 6 x 6 culvert (126 man days). Enrollees also repaired and rebuilt a washed-out bridge on the Sedona–Beaver Creek Road (280 man days). Water development was limited to re-piping Hance Spring. Enrollees built .75 mile of fence and built a stone wall, flagstone walks, and steps at the Beaver Creek Ranger Station. The Beaver Creek combination barn and garage and the Clear Creek Ranger Station Barn were completed in March. Work continued on the Stoneman Lake Ditch, with most of the work being done by hand. Twenty-five enrollees spent three weeks cutting timber and brush at Pivot Rock for a future spike camp site. Company 863 moved officially to F-6, Double Springs, on June 1.

Summer Season, 1936
F-5, Schultz Pass

Even before enrollees returned, their projects were laid out in the local newspaper. The Schultz Pass camp would be installing tables and fireplaces at the Oak Creek Canyon vista point and working with the highway department there regarding a protective guard rail. Campground improvements at Townsend and Kit Carson were planned. About sixty enrollees were to be sent to the Fort Valley Experimental Station to construct a nursery.81

In May, three years of CCC work were summarized for newspaper readers. The Schultz Pass camp had constructed 26 miles of roads, including the 13-mile Schultz Pass Road and 5.15-mile-long Abineau Springs Road. They had built 37 miles of telephone line and maintained 100 miles of the same, as well as built a 2-mile power line. They did Oak Creek recreational work and water development at Leroux and Black Springs. They had built ten miles of range fence and performed 250,000 acres of rodent control. The Double Springs camp did Mormon Lake spur roads, the Mormon Lake to Kinnikinick Lake Road, the Mormon Lake to Casner Park Road, and the Ashurst Lake to Clark's Valley Road. They also did spur roads to the Apache Maid Ranger Station and Rimrock Post Office. The Wood Springs camp did 22 miles of road construction, 25 miles of telephone lines, 150,000 acres of rodent control, and 40 miles of range fence maintenance and rebuilding. They also constructed the Lee Butte lookout tower and cabin.82 On May 27, it was announced that the very dry conditions in the forest meant the Schultz Pass camp would have seven-day coverage against fires, with three details of fifteen enrollees in camp on weekends and holidays along with trucks and equipment ready to depart in five minutes.83

Company 821 officially arrived at Schultz Pass on May 1. On June 30, 1936, the company reported 164 enrollees (94 from Texas, 41 from Arizona, 22 from Oklahoma, 2 from New Mexico, and 5 from Colorado, with 2 African Americans). Not long after their arrival, Texas enrollee Doyle Freeman, 17, was admitted to Fort Whipple Veterans Hospital and passed away on June 5 due to nephritis and severe diabetic coma.84 The camp was inspected by a CCC special investigator on July 2, and their work was summarized as twig blight eradication, timber stand improvement, mapping and surveys, road construction, telephone line construction, water work for the nursery and campgrounds, recreation facilities, and fire suppression work. The camp seemed to be on an "even keel" and was "ably administered." There were no enrollee complaints, and enrollee behavior in town was said to be good.85

During this five-and-a-half-month period, monthly work reports are only available for May through July. During this time, they built roads to their cement and powder storage areas (153 man days) and performed Rogers Lake Road construction (1,205 man days). They spent considerable time fighting forest fires (839) and also did fire pre-suppression (178). They did construction on the Deadman Lookout Tower (15). Twig blight control in Oak Creek took 878 man days. Telephone line construction totaled 810 man days, including a line to Fort Valley. Enrollees built a road into the Southwest Nursery (603) and began work on a reservoir for the nursery (1,439).[86] The latter project was a two-hundred-thousand-gallon concrete structure at Little Leroux Spring.[87]

In late June, while enrollees were burning tree limbs with twig blight near Oak Creek, the fire went out of control and burned thirty-five acres. A crew of sixty was needed to suppress it.[88] On July 10, sixty-five F-5 enrollees were fighting a two-thousand-acre fire in the Bellemont area.[89] Because of the lack of monthly reports, F-5 work in the latter part of the summer is largely unknown. In about September 1936, Company 821 leaders were Lt. Ernest L. Massad, commanding officer; Lt. Thomas P. Holmes, exchange officer; Dr. James M. Walsh, camp surgeon; and Gilbert L. Cady, educational advisor.[90] Company 821 departed F-5 on October 19 and moved to F-32, Sedona.

F-6, Double Springs

Company 863 arrived on June 1. On June 30, they reported 168 enrollees (97 from Texas and the rest from Arizona, Colorado, and Oklahoma, with 2 African Americans). On July 3 and 6, a CCC special investigator visited the camp and summarized their work as twig blight control (1,500 acres), road maintenance (25 miles), and drain ditch maintenance (.75 mile). There was "splendid cooperation" between the Army and the Forest Service staff. Enrollees were welcome at all places nearby, such as dances. Enrollees showed "perfect demeanor and deportment, except in very rare initial cases." There were 40 men in camp and 124 at the Pivot Rock spike camp some forty-five miles away.[91]

During June, enrollees were erecting a stone monument and two bronze plaques at the site of the last battle between Apaches and soldiers at Big Dry Wash near General Spring. One plaque is on the stone monument and the other at the road junction.[92] As soon as the camp was occupied, 120 enrollees were moved to the Pivot Rock spike camp. As of September 4, ninety enrollees were doing twig blight eradication.[93] The 1936 *Official Annual* reported enrollees had spent 3,320 man days on this project, pruning 19,433 trees on 638 acres.[94] Generally, spike camps or fly camps were twenty-five or so enrollees, so this large number was quite unusual. Pivot Rock was quite isolated, located seventy-five miles south of Flagstaff along the Mogollon Rim. Mail for the spike camp was retrieved in Pine, Arizona,

Figure 9. Camp F-6-A, Company 863, Double Springs, 1936. Courtesy Coconino National Forest.

below the Rim.⁹⁵ In about September 1936, Company 863 leaders were Capt. Greer B. Nelson, commanding officer; Lt. Charles K. Felder, exchange officer; Dr. John R. Smith, camp surgeon; and James T. Collins, educational advisor.⁹⁶

Four monthly work reports are available for this time period, giving us a limited picture of their work. Twig blight control seems to have been the overriding project, with from 115 to 75 men cutting, pruning, and burning. It appears much of this work was in the Baker Butte area, and their October 6 report says 788 acres had been covered, including 100 acres for a second time. The Stoneman Lake Ditch work was in all the reports with at least 4,200 feet covered, with some sections requiring drilling and blasting. Firefighting was reported at 131 man days. Some road maintenance was done.⁹⁷ Company 863 departed F-6 on October 16 and moved to F-51, Beaver Creek.

Figure 10. Prairie Dog Extermination, Coconino National Forest, date unknown. Courtesy Coconino National Forest.

Winter Season, 1936–1937
F-32, Sedona

Company 821 arrived at F-32 on October 19, 1936. On December 31, they reported 163 enrollees (134 from Texas, 22 from Oklahoma, and 7 from Arizona). Their supervisors were an Army officer, a contract physician, and an educational advisor.

Unfortunately, we only have the April 1937 monthly work report, so our knowledge of their work for this time is quite limited. On February 27, it was reported that the F-32 mess hall and cook house had burned. A garage was the temporary eating place until a new portable mess hall and kitchen was shipped from Texas.⁹⁸ The April monthly work report noted that an average of forty-one enrollees were working on the Clear Creek–Sedona Road sloping banks, installing riprap and culverts. On the Schnebly Hill Road, a crew of nine worked for two weeks with a compressor and bulldozer widening a bad section of road. The telephone line crew was clearing right of way for the telephone line from the top of Schnebly Hill to Munds Park. Telephone line maintenance included the 30-mile line from Flagstaff to Mormon Lake. At the Sedona Ranger Station, enrollees were building a new gas storage building. A crew of thirteen was installing new toilets at the Manzanita Campground. Another crew of six was installing toilets at Banjo Bill Campground. Enrollees were assisting at the fish hatchery.⁹⁹ Company 821 departed F-32 on May 15 and moved to F-5, Schultz Pass.

F-51, Beaver Creek

Company 863 arrived on October 16. On December 31, they reported 149 (82 from Oklahoma, 46 from Texas, and 21 from Arizona, with 2 African Americans). Supervisors were two Army officers, a contract physician, and an educational advisor.

Monthly work reports are available for every month, allowing us a detailed look at their activities. Road construction in October through December was mostly on Stoneman Lake Road and Apache Maid Road. The former project involved bringing the road up to Forest Service standards by widening it, which included drilling and blasting hillsides and installation of culverts, ditches, and headwalls. Apache Maid work included completing .75 mile of road and clearing 1.5 mile of right of way, which included cutting timber, clearing stumps, etc. These two projects were halted December 16 due to adverse weather.

In January, work resumed on the Beaver Creek–Sedona Road No. 121, bringing it up to Forest Service standards using as many as 2,200 man days in one month. In April, sixty men worked the month on the Sedona–Clear Creek Road installing culverts, headwalls, and the like. In April and May, as many as sixty enrollees were building a new 1.5-mile alignment of the Red Tank Wash section of the Beaver Creek–Sedona Road. The new alignment was said to eliminate dangerous curves. Road maintenance included work on the Beaver Creek–Sedona Road, Beaver Creek–Clear Creek Road, Sheep Springs Road, Rattlesnake Canyon–Munds Park Road, and Turn Pike Road.

Work on the Beaver Creek Bridge started in October, with the bridge completed on January 30. The bridge frequently had a crew of twenty. It was a three-span bridge with 26' spans of 10 x 18". Telephone line construction including cutting poles early in the season; .75 mile of the Beaver Creek–Clear Creek line and 5 miles of the No. 6 of the Beaver Creek and Sedona line were completed by February. A crew of twenty-two started on the Apache Maid–Horse Mesa Division Fence in November, stopped due to snow, and then completed the fence in April.

In October, F-51 reported spending 68 man days helping in the construction of the Hutch Mountain Lookout, clearing the mountain top, and doing road work there. During this month, enrollees worked four days plugging sinkholes in Lake Mary, spent 73 man days digging out thirty-nine culverts on the old Long Valley Highway, spent 22 man days planting fish in Clear Creek, and put in 252 man days finishing the Baker Butte district twig blight work. At the Beaver Creek Ranger Station, enrollees lowered the 1,000' water line (to prevent freezing), erected 100' of 3'-high rock wall fence, and put in water gaps in the fence. Maintenance work was done at Hance Spring, and they planted grasses and plants in erosion control plots.

In April, enrollees assisted the Camp Verde Indian Agency by working on their irrigation canal.[100] Company 863 departed F-51 on May 19 and moved to F-75, Pivot Rock. F-51 was officially abandoned by the Army, with the six buildings going to the Army for CCC use and the remainder to the Forest Service for administrative use.[101]

Summer Season, 1937
F-5, Schultz Pass

Company 821 returned at Schultz Pass on May 15. However, even before the full company returned, a small crew that was readying the camp for occupancy was called to fight a series of forest fires.[102] On June 30, they reported 149 enrollees (107 from Oklahoma and the rest from Arizona and Texas, with 2 African Americans). Their supervisors included a contract clergy, an unusual occurrence. Enrollees returned to work at the Fort Valley Experimental Station, developing a nursery with an annual capacity of one million pines. Enrollees were treating 1,100 acres of old cut for tree stand improvement.[103] On July 22, the camp was inspected by a CCC special investigator, and he noted the enrollees were housed in six pyramid and eight hospital storage tents, all in need of waterproofing and likely having seen their last years of service. "Cooperation between all members of the camp personnel is splendid," said the report.[104]

As we have monthly work reports for the months of June through September, we have a clear view of the camp's major work. Shortly after arriving, F-5 set up a spike camp at Spring Valley, and that appears to have been occupied through late September. The records indicate only ten men were assigned there on June 4 and that was increased to forty on July 6. Their work was road betterment, telephone lines, fences, and fire protection. During this time, the camp appears to not have put a lot of resources in roads, as road crews were between five and fifteen men. That did include work on Spring Valley Road and Rogers Lake Road. Telephone line maintenance appeared on three monthly reports, but that appears to not to have been major. Fence work appeared on two monthly reports with a crew of eighteen. They did complete 2.5 miles of fence between the Moretz Lake and Government Mountain allotments. Fire suppression was reported at 172 man days, and a fire standby crew of six was reported at Knob Hill from July through September. Twig blight control work totaled 1,130 acres. Substantial work appears to have been devoted to campground work, with latrines added to the Banjo Bill campground and work at Kit Carson and Townsend campgrounds.

Figure 11. Typical CCC Water Development Project, Possibly Little Leroux Spring, to Feed Nursery below the Spring, circa 1936. Courtesy Coconino National Forest.

Throughout the summer, men were working at the Southwest Experimental Station. Here, they built a garage and tool house, erected fence (1.2 miles), maintained roads, and did 160 acres of forest stand improvement. Southwest crews averaged twenty-two to thirty enrollees. At the Little Leroux Nursery, crews averaged twelve to thirteen enrollees, and they did planting for two months and constructed one cattle guard.[105] Company 821 moved from Schultz Pass to F-32, Sedona, on October 16.

F-75, Pivot Rock

Company 863 returned to the area on May 19, but as much of the Double Springs area work was finished, Pivot Rock was made into a full camp. Apparently, the Double Springs buildings were used as a side camp of F-75 during summer 1937.[106] But once the decision was made to close the camp, the Forest Service planned on tearing the buildings down and salvaging as much as possible. However, the Mormon Lake community asked that one large building be left as a recreation center and scout camp. Local Forest Service officials agreed and sent that request to Regional Headquarters.[107] The outcome of that request is unclear. On June 30, Company 863 reported 144 enrollees (99 from Oklahoma and the rest from Texas and Arizona, with 2 African Americans).

Work reports for F-75 this season are complete and very detailed. Road construction during the summer totaled 2,544 man days for bringing at least 3.5 miles of Bakers Butte Road No. 300 up to Forest Service standards. The work included bank sloping, digging up old culverts and installing new ones, building headwalls, installing a cattle guard, enlarging ditches, and road surfacing. Road maintenance appears on only one monthly report, indicating 274 man days cleaning culverts and catch basins between Mormon Lake, Stoneman Lake, and Munds Park. Twig blight control totaled 3,503 man days covering 1,630 acres. During a four-month period, over 1,200 man days were reported for telephone line work. That work included clearing right of way for Line No. 4 and No. 6, tearing down 15 miles of old line in the Munds Park area and stringing 10 miles, building stub lines to Hutch Mountain and the Mormon Lake Lookout, and re-stringing 3 miles of the Woodland Ranger Station line. At Lee Johnson Spring, enrollees dug out the spring, built a rock dam, and built a 6 x 6′ storage box (106 man days). Cleaning campgrounds in the Mormon Lake and Lake Mary areas took 200 man days. Fire suppression work totaled 87 man days. They installed the plaques at Big Dry Wash battlefield site, built turkey traps at Buck Springs Ridge, and transplanted fish in east Clear Creek. They also assisted fish and game experts doing surveys at Stoneman, Anderson, and Mormon Lakes.[108] Company 863 departed F-75 on October 16 and moved to F-35, Clear Creek.

Winter Season, 1937–1938
F-32, Sedona

Company 821 occupied F-32 on October 16, 1937. On December 31, they reported 163 enrollees (134 from Oklahoma, 22 from Texas, and the rest from Arizona). Monthly work reports are available from November through April, so we have a somewhat detailed look at their labors. During this time, substantial resources were allocated to the Schnebly Hill Road, with crews as large as seventy-one doing bank sloping; installing culverts, headwalls, and catch basins; resetting some culverts; and doing some resurfacing, including some double shifts with jackhammers. Other road construction was reported on the Munds Park Spur, the road to Crazy Park Tank, and the Red Rock Road. Substantial time was reported on the Clear Creek–Sedona Road installing headwalls and culverts. Road betterment appears to be limited to Road No. 153 from Sedona to Burris Ranch (12.2 miles).

Fence work started with cutting 1,300 posts and 200 stubs on House Mountain, with crews working three months on the Sedona Exempt Stock Allotment Fence. The Bridgeport Boundary Fence was completed with crews averaging eighteen to nineteen enrollees, and nine days were devoted to the Munds Pocket Fence. In November, 200 man days were reported doing cleanup and similar work at the Little Leroux Nursery. Crews worked about four months on Telephone Line No. 6, including clearing five miles right of way. Enrollees did significant campground work at the Oak Creek campground, Manzanita campground, and Pine Flat campground, where they installed fifteen fireplaces and did landscaping. They spent 40 man days dismantling the Wood Springs CCC camp. At the Coffee Creek Ranger Station, they did fence and building maintenance and built a new corral.[109] It appears Company 821 departed F-32 on May 22 and moved to F-5, Schultz Pass; however, the CCC records are not definitive.[110]

F-35, Clear Creek

Company 863 arrived at F-35, Clear Creek, on October 16, 1937. On December 31, they reported 167 enrollees (5 from Arizona, 23 from Oklahoma, and 139 from Texas, with 1 African American). It is worthy of note that Bob Marshall, head of recreation management for the Forest Service and wilderness advocate, hiked the Oak Creek Canyon area, covering forty-one miles in one day. Marshall was on an inspection tour of Forest Service primitive areas such as Blue Ridge and Sycamore Canyon.[111]

Detailed monthly work reports were available October through May, so we have a very adequate picture of their accomplishments. Substantial resources were put into road construction—at least 4,754 man days. On Mud Tank Road No. 142, crews as high as forty-six were working the area 6 miles east of Thirteen Mile Rock toward Mud Tank, sloping banks, installing new culverts, etc. A road maintenance crew of thirty cleaned culverts and ditches on the same road for 10 miles starting at the bottom of the hill at the Fossil Creek Road turn-off working toward Thirteen Mile Rock. Later in the season, double shifts were working with the Rock Crusher on Mud Tank Road, surfacing over 2 miles. The Beaver Creek–Clear Creek Road No. 153 reconstructing was about .5 mile of road between Beaver Creek and Red Tank Wash. Crews as high as thirty enrollees worked two months on Tom's Creek Road, grading, doing bank sloping, building headwalls, and doing drainage work in the areas of Thirteen Mile Rock and Mud Tank. Crews worked one month on the Beaver Creek–Clear Creek Road No. 153 including rocking out a 1-mile section for realignment, with the Rock Crusher going double shifts (at least 1,138 man days).

Crews worked on the Beaver Creek Bridge for three months, with as many as forty damming the channel, digging footings, setting forms, and pouring cement. The two holes for the footings were 8' deep and 12 x 20'. Telephone line maintenance and construction was reported at 2,244 man days. Much of the work was on the No. 6 line, including completing a 5-mile new section to the Clear Creek Ranger Station and tearing down the old line. Work still remained on the Big Dry Wash Monument, with 39 man days reported for building the stone marker at the General Springs Road junction. Twig blight work was reported only for October and November, with four hundred acres covered in the Baker Butte area, using 215 man days.

Enrollees worked on two stock tanks for 507 man days. The Thirteen Mile Stock Tank dam was 125' long and 20' high, requiring hauling 1,000 cubic yards. The stock tank on Mud Tank Stock Driveway about half-way between the river and Mud Tanks was 120' long and required 1,000 cubic yards.

Enrollees worked 563 man days completing 1.5 miles of the Mud Tank Stock Driveway Fence. About two miles of the Duggan-Walker Division Fence (184 man days) were completed. The Sheep Driveway Fence accounted for 1,238 man days, with about 6 miles constructed, including from Verde River east to Mud Tank. About 3 miles of the Coconino National Forest boundary fence were completed along the Verde River south of the mouth of West Clear Creek (515 man days).

Building over fourteen water gates from 50 to 150' long and rebuilding erosion control plot fences totaled 551 man days. The Beaver Creek Ranger Station Power Line construction took 68 man days, thus completing the section from the V Bar B Ranch to the ranger station. A fence survey and mapping of all winter range fences of Clear Creek Ranger District (83 man days) and a timber survey in the vicinity of Wickiup and Mud Tanks (79 man days) were reported. Erosion control work included the lower Verde Valley (78 man days) and checking on dams built in 1934–1935, with most holding well in the vicinity of Fossil Creek Highway (161 man days). Enrollees did irrigation ditch maintenance along Beaver Creek (318 man days), building ditches recently lost in a flood and in the Beaver Creek and Clear Creek Ranger Station areas (251 man days).

Painting and landscaping at the Clear Creek Ranger Station required 170 man days, while considerable work was accomplished at the Beaver Creek Ranger Station. There, they resurfaced the driveway and parking lot, placed 400' of curbstones quarried at Red Tank Wash, painted, landscaped, built a corral, and rebuilt all the fences for 1,242 man days. Enrollees did revegetation work at the Superior Nursery (74 man days) and cut Xmas trees at Baker Butte and hauled them to Flagstaff, Sedona, and Clear Creek (18 man days).[112] Company 863 departed F-35 on May 28 and moved to F-75, Pivot Rock.

Summer Season, 1938
F-5, Schultz Pass

It appears Company 821 moved to Schultz Pass on May 22; however, Company 821 does not appear on the War Department location and strength reports for June 30. This author has not been able to establish any Company 821 existence beyond this time, so they may have been disbanded. This was a bit of a confusing time in Arizona, for camps were disbanding or being split up and put in with other camps to make way for a large influx of Pennsylvania enrollees. However, on July 12, Company 311 arrived from Pennsylvania.[113]

Regrettably, only two monthly work reports for Company 311 are available, May and June 1938. So all we know of their work at Schultz Pass must be gleaned from newspaper records. In a mid-May newspaper article, the summer work plan for Schultz Pass camp was laid out. There would be considerable range fencing, especially the Munds Park allotment. Fulton Spring, Griffin Spring, and possibly two other springs were to be developed. Schultz Pass Road would be maintained, and Rogers Lake Road would be extended and improved. There would be a new campground and recreation area at Kit Carson, and the Townsend area campground was to be improved. Some enrollees would be at the Fort Valley Experimental Station. The telephone line to Fernow Ranger Station would be rebuilt. Two range tanks were planned. The Black Bill Park erosion control project would include terracing and diversion ditches. Firefighting would include a five- to six-man standby crew at Knob Hill Ranger Station.[114]

The May 1938 monthly work report notes thirty-one men were working on the Clear Creek and Schnebly Hill Roads, where they installed culverts, three cattle guards, and, on the latter, bridge guard rails. On the Weimer Spring Road, a bridge was replaced, taking 47 man days. A telephone line from Dry Beaver to Sedona and another line into Baldwin's Ranch were completed. Fences constructed included 5.5 miles of the Bridgeport Boundary Fence and the Munds Pocket Fence. An eight-man crew was razing the old Elden Ranger Station structures and hauling the materials to

Knob Hill. Thirty enrollees were working at the Fort Valley Experimental Station, and a six-man fire patrol was stationed at Knob Hill.[115]

The June 1938 monthly report noted the Elden Ranger Station work was completed and enrollees were mapping Knob Hill. The Munds Pocket Fence accounted for 89 man days, and 148 man days were credited to the Odel Lake Stock Tank and Driveway. The preparation of materials for forest boundary signs took 160 man days. Work was noted on Telephone Line No. 1 and the Doney Park diversion dams. A crew averaging thirty-seven worked the Southwest Experimental Forest, while a crew averaging eight was working at the Little Leroux Nursery. A crew averaging sixteen was constructing the power line to the Little Leroux Nursery.[116]

Figure 12. Leroux Spring Forest Nursery, F-75 at Work, June 1941. Photograph by John D. Guthrie. Courtesy U.S. Forest Service, Fort Valley Experimental Forest.

In mid-July, Coconino National Forest Assistant Edward Groesbeck reported that the Kit Carson recreation project—involving toilets, up to thirty fireplaces, picnic tables, and a parking lot—would start soon. Groesbeck said the CCC might work on the San Francisco Peaks Boulevard improving the road.[117] During August, enrollees were reported to have completed spring development on the Rim at Kehl, Lee Johnson, and General Springs. They continued to work on the Kit Carson recreational development.[118]

In September, the *Coconino Sun* reported that local labor officials had complained to the Labor Department in Washington that CCC enrollees were doing carpenter skilled trades work in the construction of the Knob Hill Ranger Station. Work stopped until regular carpenters arrived.[119] In October, the completion of the Kit Carson campground was announced.

The camp was said to have camping and trailer facilities, parking for twenty-two, fireplaces and tables, and piped city water on ten acres. Twenty-five enrollees were said to have worked on the project since July 18.[120]

CCC work at the Little Leroux Nursery was praised as a source for young trees for planting barren areas. The nursery was said to be located one mile off the Fort Valley Road. Fifteen enrollees were working there through the summer. There were hopes a seventeen-man side camp would be located at the nursery in the spring.[121] Company 311 departed F-5, Schultz Pass, on October 22 and moved to F-32.

F-75, Pivot Rock

Company 863 arrived at Pivot Rock on May 28. On June 30, they reported 209 enrollees (66 from Arizona, 30 from Oklahoma, and 113 from Texas, with 2 African Americans). Regrettably, no Forest Service work reports are available, so our knowledge of work for the rest of the time at Pivot Rock is only from a few newspaper articles. In May, the work plan for Pivot Rock camp was said to be similar to that of Schultz Pass, as well as spring development at General and Kehl Springs, range fences, a telephone line from Long Valley to the Sitgreaves Forest boundary, Tonto Rim road improvements, road improvements to Tom's Creek Road coming into Clover Valley, additional work at the Big Dry Ridge battle site, mapping, boundary signs, twig blight control, and a standby fire crew at Long Valley Ranger Station.[122]

In July, the *Coconino Sun* talked of the camp doing Tonto Rim developments at Kehl and Lee Johnson Springs and road development and a telephone line in Tom's Creek.[123] In August, it was reported the spring development work at Kehl, Lee Johnson, and General Springs was completed. Work then was to proceed with picnic tables, fire pits, toilets, and the like at these same locations.[124] Company 863 departed F-75 on October 22, 1938 and moved to F-35, Clear Creek.

Winter Season, 1938–1939
F-32, Sedona

Company 311 arrived at F-32 on October 22, 1938. On December 31, they reported only 82 enrollees (68 from Pennsylvania, 12 from Maryland, and 2 from Arizona). Unfortunately, only the November monthly work report has survived. As we have only sparse newspaper coverage, two monthly work reports, and a few camp inspection reports, our knowledge of their work is very limited.

During November, enrollees worked improving Road No. 228 (128 man days) to the Casner Park Fence, improving about 2.5 miles. Two stock tanks, Crazy Park and New Tank, were worked (225 man days). A crew averaging seventy-seven was working the Munds Pocket Allotment Fence, and a crew averaging twenty completed 3.5 miles of the Casner Park Allotment Fence. Enrollees spent 8 man days working the experimental plot near House Mountain. They spent 102 man days cutting trees, etc., for the Schnebly Hill Vista Point and Picnic Area.[125]

The December monthly work report noted that a twenty-five-man crew was working Schnebly Hill Road, and road maintenance was done on Road No. 153. Twenty men were working on the A. B. Young Trail, and it was nearly complete to the top of the mountain. Work on the Schnebly Hill Picnic Area was suspended on December 22. On November 30, 2 miles of the Burt Lee Park Fence were completed. About 1.5 miles were completed on the fence near Casner Park on the north boundary of the T-6 Allotment Fence.[126]

In February, three very dissatisfied Company 311 enrollees wrote a letter of complaint to CCC Director Robert Fechner in Washington, D.C. They were complaining of harsh treatment, such as high fines for minor infractions. They alleged the harsh treatment by camp officers resulted in a high number of "refusal to work" discharges so enrollees could be sent home. CCC Special Investigator A. W. Stockman investigated on March 9, accompanied by the district military commander. Stockman wrote that complaints included that the camp officers had little interest in recreational activities for the enrollees, the camp canteen did not have regular hours, the Army commander did not give proper consideration to enrollee complaints and suggestions, and the camp officers and foremen did not mix with the enrollees. Stockman reported that he found the recreation hall inadequate. "Athletics and indoor games have lacked direction from any source." The mess, "including cold field lunches, [is] unsatisfactory in most every respect." The commander was frequently absent from camp. He has been "aloof" from enrollees and is "indifferent in some respects to their welfare." Stockman said the junior officer and the medical officer had an "indifferent attitude towards the enrollees."

On March 25, 1939, Stockman wrote CCC Assistant Director James McEntee that the commanding officer, Lt. Charles E. Miller, was transferred out by the Army and was on probation. The junior officer, Lt. Mathew Hutmaker, was put on probation. The medical officer, Lt. Wealty W. Good, was transferred out. Good's senior Army commander Major Hilldring noted: "His continued service in the CCC will depend on his satisfactory functioning at the next (assigned) camp." Stockman returned to the camp and on June 19 wrote McEntee that Lieutenant Miller had been relieved of any 8th Corps service because of his unchanged attitude. Lieutenant Hutmaker was also relieved because of unsatisfactory services. Medical officer Good was improving at a new location and realized he was at fault, reported Stockman. He reported that enrollees were now satisfied. There were no more group discharges. The mess had improved under the active supervision of Capt. Charles J. Norman. Athletic equipment was increased and improved. "No further apprehension" of this company was needed, noted Stockman. "The change to high morale was evident in every way." He said the project superintendent and the Army commander admire each other and have 100% cooperation. He reported that all problems that were noted earlier (with one minor exception) had been addressed.[127]

On May 19, the *Coconino Sun* reported a summary of the winter work of Company 311 from Forest Supervisor Hussey. According to Hussey, the range was much improved for stockmen. Forest fire control had been enhanced by road improvements and new telephone lines such as the recently completed line from Wood Springs to Lee Butte Lookout. Road maintenance included work on Schnebly Hill Road. Seventeen miles of fence line were constructed. Three new stock tanks were completed at Bert Lee Park, Boynton Canyon, and Apache Maid. Tank repair work included Munds Park and Windmill Ranch. New truck trails included the Wood Springs Road beyond T-6 Spring and Dry Creek near Sedona. Enrollees constructed thirty-four road signs for campgrounds, and eight bridges between Sedona and Beaver Creek got new guardrails. Frank J. Randall was the camp project superintendent and Capt. Norman was the Army commander.[128]

A week later, Hussey lauded the F-32 camp educational program where R. G. Stevenson was educational advisor. "The finest thing is not what the CCC enrollees are doing in the way of material development, but what is being done in the way of developing the enrollees themselves." Hussey continued, "Human accomplishments are of higher value." Cleanliness, citizenship, respect for the rights of others, and good work habits were qualities the program tried to instill in the enrollees. All enrollees took instruction in civics and the U.S. Constitution. Evening classes included general construction, fire prevention and suppression, blacksmithing, handling of explosives, forestry, telephone line construction, and truck operation and care. Thirty-nine enrollees were taking vocational classes such as bookkeeping and typing. Hussey said the main goal was to enable enrollees to get jobs and support themselves.[129] Company 311 departed F-32 on May 20 and moved to F-5, Schultz Pass.

F-35, Clear Creek

Company 863 arrived at Clear Creek on October 22, 1938. On December 31, they reported 182 enrollees (124 from Arizona, 56 from Texas, and 2 from Oklahoma). Unfortunately, no work reports have survived. Special Investigator Stockman visited the camp on March 20, 1939, and noted the camp work included road construction and range fence construction.[130] According to the *Flagstaff Journal*, work for the winter season included erecting 18 miles of fence line and repairing 15 miles of telephone line. Three water reservoirs were constructed, with two of earth and a concrete one at the Mud Tanks allotment that measured 32′ long and 6′ high. A well and windmill developed cooperatively with the rancher supplied water to the reservoir and a 40′ cement trough. (It appears this is Clark Tank.) In the areas of Sycamore Canyon, Hackberry Canyon, Verde River, and Hollingshead Trail, 8 miles of livestock trails were constructed. A total of 10 miles of truck trails were constructed, including 6 miles in the Mud Tank area and 4 miles between Wickiup and Clear Creek.[131] Company 863 departed F-35 on May 27 to move to F-75, Pivot Rock.

Figure 13. Beaver Creek Ranger Station Barn-Garage, Built by CCC. Courtesy U.S. Forest Service, Southwestern Regional Office, #360424.

Summer Season, 1939
F-5, Schultz Pass

Company 311 returned to Schultz Pass on May 20. On June 30, they reported 96 enrollees (87 from Pennsylvania). Only the June monthly work report is available, so we have only a partial picture of what they were doing from newspaper articles. Months before they arrived for the season, Forest Assistant Groesbeck told the *Coconino Sun* the Schultz Pass camp would be improving the snow sport area at Hart Prairie. Plans for the area included the construction of ski and toboggan runs and a large parking area. Work was to continue all summer.[132]

In April, their work was outlined to include two side camps at Little Leroux Springs Forest Nursery (fifteen boys) and the Fort Valley Experimental Station (thirty boys). According to Forest Supervisor Hussey, once approval came, fifteen enrollees would be assigned to developing ski slides at Snow Bowl and thirty to forty would be working the road into the area along the Tackitt Ranch Road. Other projects included fencing portions of Rogers Lake and Lake Mary for duck refuges; work on telephone lines, fences, and fire roads; and work on the forest road to the golf links.[133]

According to the *Coconino Sun*, the Little Leroux Springs Forest Nursery enrollees would be transplanting one million trees planted in 1937 from one nursery area to another using a crew of twenty-five. (Another crop of 750,000 seedlings from 1938 was said to be proceeding nicely.) All labor for the nursery was CCC. The CCC-built reservoir fed the sprinkler system. Ranger Roland Rotty was quoted as saying this was the first nursery crop and the first plantings would be done next fall south of Flagstaff between Lake Mary and Fort Tuthill. Camp F-5 maintained the nursery in the summer months, while Camp F-32 did the winter maintenance.[134]

On May 19, the *Coconino Sun* reported Hussey saying that work on the ski road would start the following week using the F-5 enrollees.[135] On June 2, it reported that two hundred enrollees were working on the Snow Bowl Road, with 7 miles of road completed.[136] On June 9, a crew of ten was working at the local golf course on projects such as cleaning the drainage ditches. The camp had already done maintenance at the Townsend and Kit Carson campgrounds. The camp's largest crew of sixty was building the Snow Bowl Road.[137] On June 16, a forest fire near the Kitridge Ranch in Oak Creek Canyon drew its first firefighters from the Schultz Pass camp, but ultimately, over 500 men brought it under control, with 280 CCC boys coming from as far away as the Pivot Rock camp.[138]

By mid-June, the *Coconino Sun* reported that the Snow Bowl Road work was halfway done to roughing out the road. Two compressors for rock drilling and a small tractor for stump pulling were assisting the boys.[139] By the end of the month, the Snow Bowl parking lot and ski cabin were staked out.[140] The June monthly work report noted 591 man days on the Hart Prairie Road clearing right of way, drilling, and rocking out. The Mormon Lake spike camp accounted for 216 man days. A crew averaging eighteen was working at the Little Leroux Nursery, while a crew averaging twenty was at the Fort Valley Experimental Station. Work there included roadside cleanup, timber stand improvement, artificial reforestation, and brush disposal.

A standby crew of six was at Knob Hill for firefighting. (The latter activity was 414 man days.)[141]

In July, work on the Snow Bowl projects was reported to be slower than expected. Because of a very dry forest, enrollees were being called out to every fire, no matter how small.[142] In late September, the Forest Service was hoping to have the 7-mile Snow Bowl Road finished at season's end. As many as sixty enrollees were working for two months, with 5.5 miles of road roughed out and .5 mile finished with a 20′ wide cinder surface.[143] (The Forest Service continued the Snow Bowl work even after Company 311 had moved for the season.) In mid-November, Coconino National Forest staff returned from Prescott National Forest with four 16 x 20′ cabins to be used as ski shelters.[144] By mid-December, the Forest Service was reporting the area was ready for skiers. (Although the road was said to be "completed," substantial work continued the following summer.)[145] On October 28, Company 311 moved to F-32, Sedona. F-5 was officially abandoned, and buildings were salvaged by both the Army and Forest Service.[146]

F-75, Pivot Rock

Company 863 occupied Pivot Rock camp officially on May 27, 1939, and on June 30 reported 172 enrollees (35 from Texas and 137 from Arizona). No work reports were available, so we have an incomplete view based upon newspaper articles.

Even before they occupied their camp, the Forest Service summarized their work as recreation and campground work along the Mogollon Rim and construction of piers and docks at Mormon Lake using a spike camp at that location.[147] The latter was a tent camp with as many as seventy-five enrollees.[148] They were to improve the recreation area adjoining the Dairy Springs campground, including installing badminton and tennis courts, a baseball diamond, wading pools, sanitary facilities, drinking fountains, a playground with swings, a parking lot with barrier walls, and trails.[149]

Plans for the main camp at Pivot Rock for the summer were extensive. The biggest job was for road crews to build 126 miles of truck trails and minor roads and 25 miles of road work on Rim roads. Minor roads included 16 miles to Milk Ranch Point and the rest on Tom's Creek Road and its spurs. Recreation work included benches, tables, fireplaces, and toilet facilities at Lee Johnson Spring; General Spring campgrounds; and tables and benches at Kehl Spring. Twenty-seven miles of telephone lines were planned, including lines from Baker Butte Lookout to the Long Valley Ranger Station, and from the Long Valley Highway to Apache Maid Ranger Station. Planned range improvements included five small water reservoirs, fifteen corrals on the Long Valley sheep drive, and twenty miles of grazing allotment fencing. There was to be water development at General Spring and Bottle Spring, as well as a water supply system for the Long Valley Ranger Station. Enrollees were to assist Arizona Game and Fish with the planting of thirty thousand trout in West Clear Creek. Capt. Greer B. Nelson was the camp commanding officer, and L. R. Elmore was the project superintendent.[150] Company 863 vacated Pivot Rock on October 28 and moved to F-35, Clear Creek.

Figure 14. Monument to Battle of Big Dry Wash, May 1941. Photograph by F. L. Kirby. Courtesy U.S. Forest Service, Southwestern Regional Office.

Winter Season, 1939–1940
F-32, Sedona

Company 311 arrived on October 22, 1939. On December 31, they reported 93 enrollees (all but 4 from Pennsylvania). In 1940, the War Department went from semi-annual to monthly location and strength reports. On January 31, F-32 reported 190 enrollees, but this number slowly dropped to 139 on May 31 (all but 2–4 enrollees from Pennsylvania). On June 30, 1940, they reported only 61 enrollees. Unfortunately, we only have one monthly work report and a few newspaper articles, so we have only a limited idea of what they did.

The January 1940 work report noted road construction work, including fifty-four men working on the Doodle Bug

Ranch Road No. A95, eighteen men on Road No. 153 Clear Creek–Sedona section, and sixteen men on Schnebly Hill Road. Work started on January 29 on the A. B. Young and Jack's Canyon trails. About .5 mile of the Oak Creek–Windmill Allotment Fence was constructed. A crew averaging seventeen was constructing signs.[151]

In February, the *Coconino Sun* reported the enrollees were constructing new rustic log signs for Snow Bowl.[152] In March, enrollees were "progressing nicely" on the scenic Jack's Canyon Trail. At the same time, it was announced that the Schultz Pass camp was to be replaced by a new camp located 3.5 miles north of Flagstaff.[153] (Work on the new F-80 buildings began in April with the arrival of the building components from Washington. Forty Company 311 enrollees were to take eight weeks to complete the assembly.)[154]

In March, enrollees were planting 250,000 Ponderosa seedlings near Munds Park and near the highway close to Fort Tuthill.[155] In May, more tree planting took place, with ninety enrollees planting seedlings that started from seeds enrollees had gathered in 1936. Eight crews of eleven men were planting the seedlings in rows 7′ apart. Fifty thousand seedlings were being planted on 50 acres north of Fort Tuthill and on the west side of the Oak Creek Road. Another 125 acres were being planted north of Pumphouse Wash. An additional 50 acres were to be planted east of Pumphouse in memory of Robert Fechner, CCC director, who had died in December. The planting area was logged in 1890 and burned over.[156] The planting of 250,000 seedlings was finished May 9, and sixty-five enrollees went for fire training at the nursery.[157] On May 28, CCC Special Investigator M. J. Bowen visited the camp and noted no serious problems. He summarized the work as road and fence construction, nursery and forest stand improvement, and construction of the new camp.[158] Company 311 departed F-32 on June 30 and moved to F-80, Flagstaff.

F-35, Clear Creek

Company 863 arrived on October 28, 1939. On December 31, they reported 163 enrollees (nearly all from Arizona). On January 31, they reported 197 enrollees, but that dropped to 108 on March 31. An influx of new enrollees boosted their total to 186, also changing their complexion to exactly half from Texas and half from Arizona. We know very little of their work, as there are no work reports or definitive newspaper articles. On May 11, 1940, Company 863 moved to F-75, Pivot Rock. On June 13, 1940, Special Investigator Bowen filed a short camp inspection report on Company 863, Clear Creek. It is unclear if he was reporting on the Clear Creek camp or Pivot Rock. He reported: "Camp is in very good condition." Work projects were summarized as "progress very good." He did report a high number of desertions, mostly Dallas boys. He summarized their work as road and fence construction, lookout tower construction, and campground construction.[159]

Summer Season, 1940
F-75, Pivot Rock

Company 863 officially arrived at Pivot Rock on May 11, 1940. On June 30, they reported 134 enrollees (71 from Texas and the rest from Arizona). On July 31, they reported 191 enrollees (134 from Texas and the rest from Arizona). By September 30, they dropped to 121 boys and then rose to 193 on October 31 (157 from Texas and the rest from Arizona).

Our knowledge of their work is sketchy, as we have only a few newspaper articles and one short camp inspection report. A March newspaper article reported their planned work as developing playgrounds and water development at Mormon Lake. A Buck Springs spike camp was planned to construct the dam at Dives Tank. Mogollon Rim work would include water development and campground work. If time allowed, enrollees would install new drainage culverts along the road to Weimer Springs west of Lake Mary.[160] It appears that they would also do tree planting.[161] On July 26, the *Coconino Sun* reported a lightning strike hit a compressor doing road work at the Macks crossing road twenty-five miles from the Long Valley CCC camp and set off 150 dynamite charges.[162] The camp appears to have been involved in the range improvements at Windmill Draw, as the cement water tank has the inscription "8.9.1940 CCC." Besides the water tank at Windmill Draw are remains of the windmill, a cement water trough, and a pond.[163] Company 863 departed F-75 on November 17 and moved to F-35, Clear Creek.

F-80, Flagstaff

Company 311 did not arrive until June 30. When they arrived, they reported only 61 enrollees (all but 1 from Pennsylvania). In July, they reported 201 enrollees (all but 2 from Pennsylvania), dropping to 184 in September and reporting 200 on October 31 (all but 3 from Pennsylvania).

Our only sources for information on enrollee work are local newspaper articles. As early as March, the Forest Service was publicizing the summer CCC projects. They included finishing the new camp buildings and working at the nursery. At Snow Bowl, the road was to be finished and a shelter was to be started. Also listed were finishing the construction of the Rogers Lake to Fernow Ranger Station road and the telephone line from Fernow to East Pocket Knob. Griffith Spring was to be boxed and developed, and a lookout was to be constructed at Fernow.[164] Other planned projects included work at the Little Leroux Springs Nursery and the Southwest Experimental Station, fencing including the T6 range, Mogollon Rim recreation work, completion of the Mormon Lake playgrounds, and rebuilding Mack's crossings on East Clear Creek south of Bly. A spike camp at Buck Springs near Pivot Rock was to work on Dyne's Lake recreation area.[165]

In early August, one hundred enrollees were working the Snow Bowl Road, and they expected to finish the road work and four-hundred-car parking lot by the first snow fall. A crew of five to six enrollees was on firefighting standby at the Knob Hill Ranger Station. Other enrollees were dismantling the old Schultz Pass camp, ten were at the Leroux Springs Nursery, and ten to fifteen were working at the experimental station. The Fernow Road at Garney Pasture was expected to be finished soon.[166] By mid-August, two shifts of enrollees were working the Snow Bowl from 5 a.m. to 9 p.m. Another drill and compressor were added, making a total of three at work. Seven dump trucks were working now, according to Forest Supervisor Hussey. All of the road was roughed out, except for the last half-mile, and half the logs for the shelter were cut.[167] In late September, one hundred men were working at Snow Bowl, and road resurfacing with cinders was nearly complete. Work on the $20,000 25 x 90′ log lodge was to start in a few days.[168] Company 311 departed F-80 on November 30 to move to F-32, Sedona.

Winter Season, 1940–1941
F-32, Sedona

Company 311 arrived on November 30, 1940. On their arrival date, they reported 194 enrollees (all but 3 from Pennsylvania). On December 31, they reported only 66, but that number jumped back up to 198, and they reported 191 on March 31, 1941 (nearly all from Pennsylvania).

No work reports were located, and only one newspaper article described work through the winter months. A "New Road to Open Beautiful Scenic Area" proclaimed the *Coconino Sun*, saying the new road started from U.S. Route 66 two miles west of Flagstaff and then went south through the Barney Pasture area, crossing at the head of West Fork Canyon and Oak Creek Canyon rim.[169] It is unclear which CCC company was doing this work. Unfortunately, this is all we know of possible Company 311 work. They returned to F-80, Flagstaff, on April 16, 1941.

F-35, Clear Creek

Company 863 arrived on November 17, 1940, and on November 30 reported 189 enrollees (153 from Texas and the rest from Arizona). On December 31, they dropped down to 139 and then went up to 186 on February 28. On April 30, they reported 150 enrollees (86 from Arizona and 64 from Texas). Unfortunately, no information was located about their work. They departed F-35 on May 17 and moved to F-75, Pivot Rock.

Summer Season, 1941
F-75, Pivot Rock

Company 863 arrived at Pivot Rock on May 17 and on May 30 reported 134 enrollees (almost evenly split between those from Texas and from Arizona). Company strength varied between 117 and 160, until their last report on October 31 noting 130 enrollees (about one-third from Arizona and the rest from Texas).

We have little knowledge of their work. A June 25 camp inspection report indicated their work was road, fence, and telephone line construction. Special Investigator Bowen rated both the morale and mess as fair, but the lunches as poor. He reported that the mess steward and the commanding officer were "not up to standard" and that Colonel Gordon, the Army district commander, was planning on relieving both the commander and executive officer on July 1.[170] A Double Springs spike camp (occupied May 26 to November 1, 1940) was reported to be doing fence construction and campground work with forty enrollees.[171] The company was disbanded on November 1, 1941, with remaining enrollees and staff to be transferred to other companies.[172]

F-80, Flagstaff

Company 311 returned to F-80 on April 16 and reported 191 enrollees on April 30 and 187 on May 31 (all but 3 or 4 from Pennsylvania). On June 24, 1941, Company 822 was reported at F-80. (They were previously at F-19, Prescott.) It is unclear if Company 311 was disbanded or returned to the 3rd Corps area. On June 30, Company 822 reported 139 enrollees (88 from Arizona, including 1 veteran, 1 from Pennsylvania, and 50 from Texas). Company 822 strength went as high as 177 on July 31, and on November 30, they reported 150 enrollees (85 from Arizona and 65 from Texas). At year's end, enrollment dropped to 94.

Our knowledge of their work is insufficient, as a few newspaper articles are the main source of information. A short time after their arrival, one hundred enrollees did fire training.[173] Camp F-80 did keep a spike camp at Spring Valley from June 6 to November 15 with twenty-six to forty enrollees, with the main duty of fire suppression.[174]

In mid-June, the *Coconino Sun* had a long article about CCC work at the five-acre Little Leroux Nursery, explaining the processes in detail. Seeds were frequently obtained from mature trees downed in the logging process. Work by the enrollees required watering the seedlings daily. Over one million trees were scheduled to be planted in the future. Ranger Roland Rotty was quoted as saying the seedlings were "the trees of 1975 and 2000 A.D."[175]

By late August, the company's most visible project was nearing completion. It was said the rustic Snow Bowl ski lodge would be finished by October 31. It was described as 95 x 24', with three fireplaces and just one-third of the roof to install at end of August.[176] Also at the end of August, four enrollees made a regrettable decision when, against Army regulations, they brought two quarts of wine to camp, got drunk, and threatened the night watchman with a knife. A formal hearing was held the same day, and all were dismissed.[177]

Figure 15. Snow Bowl's Hart Prairie Lodge, Constructed by CCC, circa 1945. Courtesy Coconino National Forest.

In October, F-80 enrollees assisted in the in the body recovery and salvaging of an Army bomber after it crashed on Agassiz Peak. Ranger Ed Oldham and enrollees brought the six bodies out. As the wreckage of the airplane was considered classified, enrollees from both F-80 and NP-12 at Mt. Elden built a two-mile trail from the Spruce Cabin Road to the wreckage and then carried out much of the wreckage. About seventy-five enrollees took part in the total operation, along with volunteers, Forest Service staff, and law enforcement officers.[178]

While the CCC was created as an organization that was not to be highly influenced by the military, by 1940 the deteriorating world situation brought about a change. In June 1940, Congress authorized the training of enrollees in noncombatant skills needed by the military and the defense industry. By October 1941, F-80 had forty enrollees taking courses in radio use, motor repair, carpentry, sheet metal, and welding.[179] At the end of October, the Snow Bowl Lodge was said to be completed on November 1.[180] Company 822 did not leave for F-32, Sedona, until January 4, 1942.

Winter Season, 1941–1942
F-32, Sedona

Company 822 arrived at F-32 on January 4, and on January 30 reported 71 enrollees (56 from Arizona, including 1 veteran, and the rest from Texas). The number and composition of enrollees changed considerably, possibly the result of enrollees from disbanded camps being transferred to F-32. At the end of February, company enrollment dropped to 48 but then went up to 121. On April 30, they reported 69 enrollees (35 from Arizona, including 1 veteran, 29 from Oklahoma, and 5 from Texas).

Unfortunately, we know little of their work, as we have only a short camp inspection report dated March 24–25 where Special Inspector Bowen reported the work to be cutting fence posts, building fences and roads, and making signs.[181] During March and April, the *Coconino Sun* reported enrollees were involved in scrap drives for the war effort. The two-month March effort collected 800 pounds of scrap barbwire, 1,500 pounds of tin and iron, and 25 pounds of aluminum.[182] Company 822 departed F-32 on May 21 and moved to F-75, Pivot Rock.

Summer Season, 1942
F-75, Pivot Rock

Company 822 arrived on May 21 and on May 31 reported 174 (108 from Arizona, including 1 veteran, 40 from Texas, 24 from Oklahoma, and 2 from New Mexico). On May 29, it was reported twenty-five enrollees brought a Cinder Hills fire under control.[183] No other information was found on their work projects. In accordance with the congressional directive to disband, they ended their duties, possibly as late as July 23, 1942. On July 24, the *Coconino Sun* reported the Army had taken over the former CCC buildings and were to adapt them for use at the nearby Navajo Army Depot at Bellemont.[184] At the end of May, F-75 was one of only five CCC camps remaining in the state, of which four were in northern Arizona. Much like the work in the Kaibab National Forest, work in the Coconino progressed from nearly all resource-related work to substantially projects related to recreation. The significant resources put into the Snow Bowl Road and ski shelter would have not happened just a few years earlier.

Unless noted otherwise, any reference to the number of enrollees in a company, the location of the company, or company supervisors are from U.S. War Department, Location and Strength of CCC Companies, 1933–1942, NARAMD RG 35 530/65/22/04/05.

1. Salmond, *Civilian Conservation Corps,* 8–9.
2. Kylie, *CCC Forestry,* 55.
3. "Plan Arizona Work," *Arizona Republic,* April 1, 1933, 6.
4. Booth, *Civilian Conservation Corps in Arizona,* 14.
5. "Enlisted Workers Coming to Arizona," *Phoenix Gazette,* April 7, 1933, 1.
6. "Forests of Arizona to Benefit from Big US Development Plan," *Arizona Republic*, May 5, 1933, sect. 3, 4.
7. "Reforestation to Start about May 15," *Phoenix Gazette,* May 2, 1933, 2.
8. *Arizona Republic*, May 13, 1933, 9; "Reforestation Plans Discussed," *Arizona Republic,* May 20, 1933, sect. 2, 6. By July, Leopold had reached Prescott, where he was said to be in charge of CCC erosion control work and advising the Prescott National Forest for a few days on their planned erosion control projects. See *Prescott Evening Courier,* July 6, 1933, 3.
9. "St. Forestry Work Recruits Are Ready to Leave for Camps," *Arizona Republic,* May 25 1933, 2.
10. "Arizona Has 16 CCC Camp Units," *Prescott Evening Courier,* June 12, 1933, 4.
11. "CCC Crews Improve Forests, Survey Indicates," *Coconino Sun,* October 20, 1933, 6.
12. *Arizona Republic,* February 15, 1934, 4.
13. "Cowmen Adopt 19 Resolutions," *Prescott Evening Courier,* February 14, 1934, 1, 7.
14. "Civilian Corps Spend Hours Fighting Fires," *Coconino Sun,* November 30, 1934, 4.
15. "Forest Camps Proving Value," *Phoenix Gazette,* September 12, 1933, 3.
16. "CCC Aid in Forests Lauded," *Arizona Republic,* May 6, 1934, 1.
17. "President Acclaims CCC Boys–Forestry Work Is Cited in Message," *Arizona Republic,* April 18, 1936, 1, 6.
18. For a slightly different view of the Forest Service, illustrating the diversity of opinions within the agency, see Booth, *Civilian Conservation Corps in Arizona,* 13–17.
19. "Work of CCC in State Related," *Prescott Evening Courier,* May 6, 1938, 11.
20. Salmond, *Civilian Conservation Corps,* 121.
21. Otis et al., *Forest Service and the CCC,* 8.
22. U.S. War Department, Camp Directories, 1933–1942, Records of the CCC, NARAMD RG 35/530/65/11/1.
23. "Forest Work Camps Slated," *Arizona Republic,* December 6, 1935, 3; Collins, *New Deal in Arizona,* 60-61.
24. Putt, *South Kaibab National Forest,* 169. For a Forest Service nationwide look with emphasis on CCC projects, see Otis et. al., *Forest Service and the Civilian Conservation Corps,* passim.
25. "Army of 200 Men Will Work in Forests Here under Roosevelt Plan," *Coconino Sun,* April 7, 1933, 1, 3. The Schultz Pass Road was said to follow an old railroad grade for a considerable distance. See "Schulz Pass Road Will Be Rebuilt as Part of Reforestation Plan," *Coconino Sun,* April 28, 1933, 1.
26. "Schulz Pass Road Will Be Rebuilt as Part of Reforestation Plan," *Coconino Sun,* April 28, 1933, 1.
27. "Five Coconino Camps to Receive 1100 Men Soon under New Plan," *Coconino Sun,* May 26, 1933, 1, 2.
28. "1045 Workmen in Northern Arizona Forests under Relief Plan," *Coconino Sun,* June 2, 1933, 8.
29. "McNamara Directs Field Program of Schultz Pass C.C.C.," *Coconino Sun,* June 2, 1933, 3.
30. "Army Radio Corps Speed Messages for Forest Crews," *Coconino Sun,* June 2, 1933, 8.
31. "Headquarters for Conservation Corps Set Up Here," *Coconino Sun,* June 16, 1933, 3.
32. "Reforestation and Education Themes Rotary Luncheon," *Coconino Sun,* June 9, 1933, 1, 3.
33. "Long Valley Fire Burns 130 Acres of Timber Land," *Coconino Sun,* July 7, 1933, 1.
34. *Echo of the Peaks,* vol. I, no. 1, May 24, 1934; *Echo of the Peaks,* vol. II, no. 1, June 28, 1934, Civilian Conservation Corps Newsletters, Serials Collection AHSLA.

35. "Forestry Camps to Be Evacuated," *Coconino Sun*, September 22, 1933, 1, 2.
36. Maher, *Nature's New Deal*, 170. See also Audretsch, *Shaping the Park and Saving the Boys*, 89–93. The justification for killing porcupines was limiting their damage, which often made the trees unacceptable to the timber industry. The June 8, 1934, issue of the F-5 camp newspaper *Echo of the Peaks* explained the preparation of poison blocks. The article reported one crew shooting 530 porcupines near Flagstaff in a two-month period. Daily shootings ran as high as 67 and 75.
37. U.S. Forest Service, CCC Camp Records, 1933–42, NARAMD RG 95/170/41/16/03 Box 67.
38. "Civilian Conservation Corps Work in Nation and County Wins Praise—Forest Supervisor Declares Camps Accomplishments Exceed Expectations," *Coconino Sun*, November 24, 1933, 8.
39. U.S. CCC, Phoenix District, *Official Annual, 1936, Phoenix District, 8th Corps Area, Civilian Conservation Corps* ([Baton Rouge, LA?]: Direct Advertising Co., 1936), 65. GCNPMC Cat. #70738.
40. U.S. Forest Service, CCC Camp Records, 1933–42, NARAMD RG 95/170/41/16/03 Box 67.
41. "Civilian Conservation Corps Work in Nation and County Wins Praise—Forest Supervisor Declares Camps Accomplishments Exceed Expectations," *Coconino Sun*, November 24, 1933, 8.
42. U.S. Forest Service, CCC Camp Records, 1933–42, NARAMD RG 95/170/41/16/03 Box 67.
43. Ibid.
44. "Civilian Conservation Corps Work in Nation and County Wins Praise—Forest Supervisor Declares Camps Accomplishments Exceed Expectations," *Coconino Sun*, November 24, 1933, 8.
45. U.S. Forest Service, CCC Camp Records, 1933–42, NARAMD RG 95/170/41/16/03 Box 67.
46. "CCC Worker and Girl Killed When Two Trucks Crash," *Coconino Sun*, January 5, 1934, 1; Arizona Death Records, State File No. 459, Registered No. 80.
47. "Mexican Youth Succumbs Here," (Jerome) *Verde Valley News*, March 16, 1934, 1; Arizona Death Notices, State File No. 479, Registered No. 22.
48. U.S. Forest Service, CCC Camp Records, 1933–42, NARAMD RG 95/170/41/16/03 Box 67.
49. Ibid.
50. Ibid.
51. "Civilian Corps Camp Sought to Develop Water," *Coconino Sun*, April 13, 1934, 1, 5; "CCC Preparing Schultz Pass Site for Camp Removal," *Coconino Sun*, April 20, 1934, 8; "400 Civilian Corps Workers Return to Flagstaff," *Coconino Sun*, May 4, 1934, 1.
52. "Contract Let for Aubineau Project Pipe—Schulz Pass CCC Crews Start Work on Road to Water Sources," *Coconino Sun*, May 25, 1934, 1.
53. Otis et al., *Forest Service and the CCC*, 32.
54. "Rangers Check Dangerous Forest Fire," *Coconino Sun*, June 15, 1934, 1, 6.
55. U.S. Forest Service, CCC Camp Records, 1933–42, NARAMD RG 95/170/41/16/03 Box 67.
56. U.S. CCC, Camp Inspection Reports, NARAMD RG 35/530/65/23/04 Entry 115 (PI #11) Box 8.
57. "CCC Leader Sees Project as Permanent," July 27, 1934, 1, 2. According to the F-5 camp newspaper *Echo of the Peaks*, July 25, 1934, Fechner inspected the camp and a spike camp and was "well pleased."
58. U.S. Forest Service, CCC Camp Records, 1933–42, NARAMD RG 95/170/41/16/03 Box 67.
59. "Lost Woman Found by Co. 821," *Echo of the Peaks*, October 10, 1934, Civilian Conservation Corps Newsletters, Serials Collection AHSLA.
60. *Echo of the Peaks*, vol. II, no. 5, August 27, 1934, Civilian Conservation Corps Newsletters, Serials Collection AHSLA.
61. *Clear Creek Clarion*, November 16, 1934, Civilian Conservation Corps Newsletters, Serials Collection AHSLA; Arizona Death Records, State File No. 431. According to the (Jerome) *Verde Copper News* (November 2, 1934), Daniels had been previously warned not to swim alone after he was rescued with cramps. On this occasion, it was said he swam away from the others, and his absence was not noticed.
62. "Schultz Pass Trail Still Incomplete," *Coconino Sun*, November 23, 1934, 1.
63. U.S. Forest Service, CCC Camp Records, 1933–42, NARAMD RG 95/170/41/16/03 Box 67.
64. U.S. CCC, Camp Inspection Reports, NARAMD RG 35/530/65/23/04 Entry 115 (PI #11) Box 8.
65. U.S. Forest Service, CCC Camp Records, 1933–42, NARAMD RG 95/170/41/16/03 Box 67.
66. Ibid.
67. U.S. CCC, Camp Inspection Reports, NARAMD RG 35/530/65/23/04 Entry 115 (PI #11) Box 9.
68. Ibid., Box 9.
69. Ibid., Box 8.
70. "CCC Youth Dies," *Flagstaff Journal*, June 21, 1935, 1; Arizona Death Records, State File No. 61, Registered No. 130.

71. U.S. CCC, Phoenix District, *Official Annual, 1936, Phoenix District, 8th Corps Area, Civilian Conservation Corps* ([Baton Rouge, LA?]: Direct Advertising Co., 1936), 63. GCNPMC Cat. #70738.
72. U.S. CCC, Camp Inspection Reports, NARAMD RG 35/530/65/23/04 Entry 115 (PI #11) Box 8.
73. "Whipple Notes," *Prescott Evening Courier,* August 19, 1935, 3; Arizona Death Records, State File No. 378, Registered No. 266-B. Hart reported sick at camp at 8:30 a.m., was attended by the camp physician, transported by ambulance to Fort Whipple, and died at 8:30 that night. See report in U.S. CCC, Camp Inspection Reports, NARAMD RG 35/530/65/23/04 Entry 115 (PI #11) Box 8.
74. U.S. CCC, Camp Inspection Reports, NARAMD RG 35/530/65/23/04 Entry 115 (PI #11) Box 8.
75. "Two Areas Twig Blight in This National Forest," *Coconino Sun,* December 27, 1935, 1.
76. "Fort Whipple," *Prescott Evening Courier,* February 21, 1936, 3; Arizona Death Records, State File No. 540, Registered No. 138-J.
77. "CCC Camp Work Still a Necessity—Hussey Stresses Its Value to Local Forest," *Coconino Sun,* March 13, 1936, 1, 8.
78. "Scenic Parking," *Coconino Sun,* March 13, 1936, 3.
79. U.S. War Department, Location and Strength of CCC Companies, 1933–1942, NARAMD RG 35 530/65/22/04/05.
80. U.S. CCC, Camp Inspection Reports, NARAMD RG 35/530/65/23/04 Entry 115 (PI #11) Box 9.
81. "Bring Two CCC Camps to Forest—Heavy Schedule Laid Out for This Spring," *Coconino Sun,* April 17, 1936, 1, 8. Constructing the nursery surely refers to the Leroux Spring or Little Leroux Spring Nursery begun in 1936. The CCC built the road, constructed all the nursery buildings but three, constructed the power line to the nursery, built the reservoir and irrigation system and "provided the bulk of the labor" "that operated the nursery." See: Wenkler, Chris T. *Transplanting the Northern Arizona Arboretum, Phase II: Investigating the Prehistoric and Historic Use of Little Leroux Spring.* NAU, Arch. Report No. 1187b, 8-98, pages 58, 59, 65, 67.
82. "Much Valuable Improvement of Coconino Forest and Range Effected By Three CCC," *Coconino Sun,* May 1, 1936, 7.
83. "Organize CCC Men to Fight Fire," *Coconino Sun,* May 27, 1936, 1. During this time, the Forest Service had a 10 a.m. policy, meaning that fires were to be out by 10 a.m. that morning, otherwise 10 a.m. the following morning, etc. (Margaret Hangan, e-mail message to author, August 9, 2012.)
84. "Fort Whipple," *Prescott Evening Courier,* June 8, 1936, 5; Arizona Death Records, State File No. 573, Registered No. 232-J.
85. U.S. CCC, Camp Inspection Reports, NARAMD RG 35/530/65/23/04 Entry 115 (PI #11) Box 8.
86. U.S. Forest Service, CCC Camp Records, 1933–42, NARAMD RG 95/170/41/16/03 Box 67.
87. "Building Water Storage System at Fort Valley," *Coconino Sun,* June 5, 1936, 4.
88. "Blaze at Oak Creek Menace to the Forest," *Coconino Sun,* June 26, 1936, 1, 6.
89. "Bellemont Has 2000 Acre Fire," *Coconino Sun,* July 10, 1936, 1.
90. U.S. CCC, Phoenix District, *Official Annual, 1936, Phoenix District, 8th Corps Area, Civilian Conservation Corps* ([Baton Rouge, LA?]: Direct Advertising Co., 1936), 63. GCNPMC Cat. #70738.
91. U.S. CCC, Camp Inspection Reports, NARAMD RG 35/530/65/23/04 Entry 115 (PI #11) Box 8.
92. "To Commemorate Last AZ Apaches' and Soldiers Battle," *Coconino Sun,* June 26, 1936, 6.
93. U.S. Forest Service, CCC Camp Records, 1933–42, NARAMD RG 95/170/41/16/03 Box 67.
94. U.S. CCC, Phoenix District, *Official Annual, 1936, Phoenix District, 8th Corps Area, Civilian Conservation Corps* ([Baton Rouge, LA?]: Direct Advertising Co., 1936), 63. GCNPMC Cat. #70738.
95. Moore, *Civilian Conservation Corps in Arizona's Rim Country,* 51.
96. U.S. CCC, Phoenix District, *Official Annual, 1936, Phoenix District, 8th Corps Area, Civilian Conservation Corps* ([Baton Rouge, LA?]: Direct Advertising Co., 1936), 63. GCNPMC Cat. #70738.
97. U.S. Forest Service, CCC Camp Records, 1933–42, NARAMD RG 95/170/41/16/03 Box 67.
98. "CCC Mess Hall at Sedona Burns," *Coconino Sun,* February 26, 1937, 1; "New Mess Hall for Sedona CCC," *Coconino Sun,* March 5, 1937, 1.
99. U.S. Forest Service, CCC Camp Records, 1933–42, NARAMD RG 95/170/41/16/03 Box 67.
100. Ibid.
101. "Civilian Conservation Corps Eighth Corps Area, Status Record of CCC Camps Authorized Since Inception of the Program up to … December 31, 1941 … Compiled by Office of Liaison Officer, CCC Fort Sam Houston…," NARACO BLM CCC Directories RG 49 Entry 33, 34 Box 132.
102. "Forest Fires Rage North of Peaks," *Coconino Sun,* May 7, 1937, 4.

103. "Big Young Pine Tract under Experiment at Fort Valley Station," *Coconino Sun,* May 28, 1937, sect. 2, 1, 4.
104. U.S. CCC, Camp Inspection Reports, NARAMD RG 35/530/65/23/04 Entry 115 (PI #11) Box 8.
105. U.S. Forest Service, CCC Camp Records, 1933–42, NARAMD RG 95/170/41/16/03 Box 67.
106. "Move CCC Camps," *Coconino Sun,* September 24, 1937, 1.
107. "Mormon Lake Residents Ask Use CCC Camp," *Coconino Sun,* September 24, 1937, 4.
108. U.S. Forest Service, CCC Camp Records, 1933–42, NARAMD RG 95/170/41/16/03 Box 67.
109. Ibid.
110. "Personals," *Coconino Sun,* May 27, 1938, 2. F-5 was said to have moved "last week."
111. "Wilderness Areas Gain Importance," *Williams News,* December 9, 1937, 7.
112. U.S. Forest Service, CCC Camp Records, 1933–42, NARAMD RG 95/170/41/16/03 Box 67.
113. "Special Train 390 CCC Men Came Tuesday—For Schulz Pass And North Rim," *Coconino Sun,* July 15, 1938, 1, 8.
114. "Local CCC Men Have Big Summer Program Outlined," *Coconino Sun,* May 13, 1938, 6.
115. U.S. Forest Service, CCC Camp Records, 1933–42, NARAMD RG 95/170/41/16/03 Box 67.
116. Ibid.
117. "Planning Work for CCC Men," *Coconino Sun,* July 15, 1938, 6.
118. "Developing Forest Recreation Grounds," *Coconino Sun,* August 26, 1938, 1.
119. "Union Protests Use of CCC Men in Carpentry," *Coconino Sun,* September 2, 1938, 1.
120. "Big Trailer Campsite Completed," *Coconino Sun,* October 28, 1938, 1.
121. "Will Re-Forest Lake Mary-Fort Tuthill Barren Areas with Young Trees from Leroux Forest Service Pine Nursery," *Coconino Sun,* October 28, 1938, 1, 6.
122. "Local CCC Men Have Big Summer Program Outlined," *Coconino Sun,* May 13, 1938, 6.
123. "Planning Work for CCC Men," *Coconino Sun,* July 15, 1938, 6.
124. "Developing Forest Recreation Grounds," *Coconino Sun,* August 26, 1938, 1.
125. U.S. Forest Service, CCC Camp Records, 1933–42, NARAMD RG 95/170/41/16/03 Box 67. Apparently, another recreation area was planned for the Oak Creek area. See "Recreation Area Planned at Schnebley," *Coconino Sun,* November 25, 1938, 1.
126. U.S. Forest Service, CCC Camp Records, 1933–42, NARAMD RG 95/170/41/16/03 Box 67.
127. U.S. CCC, Camp Inspection Reports, NARAMD RG 35/530/65/23/04 Entry 115 (PI #11) Box 8.
128. "Sedona CCC Does Much Good Work," *Coconino Sun,* May 19, 1939, 10; "CCC Lessens Fire Hazards," *Prescott Evening Courier,* May 17, 1939, 8.
129. "Forest Supervisor Lauds Coconino CCC Unit for 'Citizen Building,'" *Prescott Evening Courier,* May 25, 1939, 7.
130. U.S. CCC, Camp Inspection Reports, NARAMD RG 35/530/65/23/04 Entry 115 (PI #11) Box 9.
131. "Range Improvements Made by Clear Creek CCC Camp Last Winter," *Flagstaff Journal,* May 26, 1939, 7.
132. "Snow Sport Area to Be Improved," *Coconino Sun,* February 10, 1939, 1.
133. "Forest Officials Plan Activities for CCC Camps," *Coconino Sun,* April 21, 1939, 1.
134. "Nursery to Plant Many Trees Here," *Coconino Sun,* June 2, 1939, 1.
135. "Start Ski Road," *Coconino Sun,* May 19, 1939, 5.
136. "200 Youths Push Snow Bowl Road," *Flagstaff Journal,* June 2, 1939, 1.
137. "Big Program of Improvements by CCC Underway," *Coconino Sun,* June 9, 1939, 1.
138. "Man-Caused Forest Fire Spoils Beautiful Section of Oak Creek," *Coconino Sun,* June 16, 1939, 1, 8; "Rangers Guard Canyon Blaze," *Prescott Evening Courier,* June 16, 1939, 6.
139. "Clearing Crew Half through on Ski Road," *Coconino Sun,* June 16, 1939, 1.
140. "Recreation Plans Going Ahead at Mormon Lake," *Coconino Sun,* June 30, 1939, 2.
141. U.S. Forest Service, CCC Camp Records, 1933–42, NARAMD RG 95/170/41/16/03 Box 67.
142. "Ski Club Will Be Formed Here—Road to Snow Bowl Is Going Slowly, as CCC Fights Fires," *Flagstaff Journal,* July 21, 1939, 1.
143. "Snow Bowl Development Will Make Flagstaff Headquarters for Southwest Winter Sports," *Coconino Sun,* September 22, 1939, sect. 2, 1.
144. "Ski Area about Ready for Snow Sports," *Coconino Sun,* November 17, 1939, 1.
145. "Everything Ready Now for Ski Sports—Forest Service and CCC Have Road Completed," *Coconino Sun,* December 15, 1939, 1.
146. "Civilian Conservation Corps Eighth Corps Area, Status Record of CCC Camps Authorized Since Inception of the Program up to … December 31, 1941 … Compiled by Office of Liaison Officer, CCC Fort Sam Houston…," NARACO BLM CCC Directories RG 49 Entry 33, 34 Box 132.

147. "Forest Officials Plan Activities for CCC Camps," *Coconino Sun,* April 21, 1939, 1.
148. "Big Program of Improvements by CCC Underway," *Coconino Sun,* June 9, 1939, 1.
149. "Mormon Lake Playground Work to Start," *Coconino Sun,* August 25, 1939, 1.
150. "CCC Develops Rim Facilities," *Prescott Evening Courier,* July 5, 1939, 2.
151. U.S. Forest Service, CCC Camp Records, 1933–42, NARAMD RG 95/170/41/16/03 Box 67.
152. "New Signs for Ski Bowl Planned," *Coconino Sun,* February 23, 1940, 1.
153. "Oak Creek News," *Coconino Sun,* March 8, 1940, 1; "New CCC Camp to Be Built North of City," *Coconino Sun,* March 8, 1940, 3.
154. "Work Starts on New CCC Camp North of City," *Coconino Sun,* April 19, 1940, 1.
155. "Rotty to Plant Quarter Million Pine Trees," *Coconino Sun,* March 29, 1940, 1.
156. "Area North of Fort Tuthill, Replanted By CCC Boys, Named in Honor of Robert Fechner," *Coconino Sun,* May 3, 1940, 1, 7.
157. "CCC Boys Start New Work," *Coconino Sun,* May 10, 1940, 1. Another planting area was northeast of the intersection of Rock Ledge Road and the road on the west side of Mormon Lake.
158. U.S. CCC, Camp Inspection Reports, NARAMD RG 35/530/65/23/04 Entry 115 (PI #11) Box 8.
159. Ibid., Box 10.
160. "Snow Bowl Road to Be Finished, Shelter Built," *Coconino Sun,* March 29, 1940, 1.
161. "CCC Men Move to Mormon Lake," *Coconino Sun,* April 19, 1940, 6.
162. "Lightning Fires String of 150 Dynamite Charges," *Coconino Sun,* July 26, 1940, 2.
163. Mark Swift, e-mail message to author, January 3, 2012.
164. "Snow Bowl Road to Be Finished, Shelter Built," *Coconino Sun,* March 29, 1940, 1.
165. "CCC Work Planned for the Summer," *Flagstaff Journal,* June 4, 1940, 1.
166. "Work 100 Men on Snow Bowl Road Project," *Coconino Sun,* August 2, 1940, 1.
167. "Two Shifts on Snow Bowl Road Project," *Coconino Sun,* August 16, 1940, 1, 3.
168. "Ski Club Lodge and Roadway Will Be Ready," *Coconino Sun,* September 27, 1940, 1. Not long after the double shift was started, it was discontinued, as it deprived some enrollees of their "educational recreational opportunities." Concerned that the road would not be finished for ski season, local groups such as the chamber of commerce "contacted various agencies." Apparently, the chamber secretary contacted the 8th Corps commanding general, and Senator Hayden was involved. Ultimately, after a visit to the camp by Arizona CCC District Commander Colonel Gordon, the double shifts were restored. See "Double Shift of CCC Boys at Work on Ski Bowl Road," *Flagstaff Journal,* August 20, 1940, 1.
169. *Coconino Sun,* December 20, 1940, 1, 7. This appears to be the present-day Woody Mountain Road No. 231.
170. U.S. CCC, Camp Inspection Reports, NARAMD RG 35/530/65/23/04 Entry 115 (PI #11) Box 10.
171. U.S. Forest Service, CCC Camp Records, 1933–42, NARAMD RG 95/170/41/16/03 Box 67.
172. "Disband Camp," *Coconino Sun,* October 31, 1941, 3.
173. "Forest Service Training CCC Men for Fire Duty," *Coconino Sun,* May 16, 1941, 1.
174. U.S. Forest Service, CCC Camp Records, 1933–42, NARAMD RG 95/170/41/16/03 Box 67.
175. "Ranger Roland Rotty and CCC Enrollees Planting Million Trees," *Coconino Sun,* June 13, 1941, 4.
176. "Skiing Lodge at Snow Bowl Nearly Ready—Forest Service Spending over $20,000 at Site," *Coconino Sun,* August 29, 1941, 1, 3.
177. U.S. CCC, Camp Inspection Reports, NARAMD RG 35/530/65/23/04 Entry 115 (PI #11) Box 10.
178. "Plane Crashes on Peaks; Claims Six Lives," *Coconino Sun,* October 10, 1941, 1, 6; "Bomber Parts Salvaged and Taken to Tucson," *Coconino Sun,* October 17, 1941, 5.
179. "Local CCC Camp Sets up Center for Radio Work," *Coconino Sun,* October 17, 1941, 6. For details of this national trend, see Salmond, *Civilian Conservation Corps,* 194–199.
180. "Lodge Construction Work Unaffected by Bad Weather," *Coconino Sun,* October 24, 1941, 2. Tragically, the lodge burned down February 17, 1952. See "Fire Hits Snow Bowl," *Coconino Sun,* February 23, 1952, 1.
181. U.S. CCC, Camp Inspection Reports, NARAMD RG 35/530/65/23/04 Entry 115 (PI #11) *Box 8.*
182. "Sedona CCC Enrollees Sell Collected Scrap Materials for $136.90 to High Bidder," *Coconino Sun,* March 27, 1942, 1; "Forest Men Will Gather Scrap Metal," *Coconino Sun,* April 10, 1942, 1.
183. "Hunter Causes Forest Fire near Cinder Hills," *Coconino Sun,* May 29, 1942, 1.
184. "Army Takes Over Nearby CCC Location," *Coconino Sun,* July 24, 1942, 1.

CHAPTER 5

The CCC Artists Program

THE GREAT DEPRESSION WAS SURELY not easy for artists. On December 10, 1933, the Public Works of Art Program (PWAP) was begun with a CWA grant to the Treasury Department. The program's goals included the production of art work and relief work for artists, but not art education. However, CWA funding ended in the spring of 1934.[1] Not long after, apparently with the active involvement of FDR and Eleanor Roosevelt, the CCC Artists Program was begun. It was "to portray the life and activities of the young men." As many as one hundred enrollees participated each enrollment period.[2] Like its predecessor, this program was administered by Treasury. It went on into 1937. According to researcher Kathleen Duxbury, the "CCC assignments, perhaps not as esteemed [as PWAP], required a person that was physically fit and adaptable to out of doors work." Most of the artists were young, and the emphasis was on documenting the work of the CCC.[3] Each artist had to supply his own materials.[4] In the 8th Corps area, the first assignments were to Wyoming (1), Colorado (2), Texas (1), New Mexico (1), and Arizona (3).[5]

The Arizona artists and camps were Creston F. Baumgartner of Arizona, to the Schultz Pass camp near Flagstaff (Company 821); Floyd Peterson of Colorado, to the South Rim Grand Canyon (Company 819); and Earl Darry (also spelled Darrey),[6] to the Petrified Forest National Monument camp (Company 831). Sadly, this aspect of CCC work appears to be largely unrecognized today. An examination of in-print books on the CCC shows only one author writing about this national program.[7] Records of the CCC Artists Program at the National Archives and Records Administration, College Park, Maryland (NARAMD) show only correspondence with Baumgartner and none with the other Arizona artists. Over a one-year period, Baumgartner served at four northern Arizona camps and sent at least eight paintings to Washington, D.C.[8]

Creston F. Baumgartner was born in Baltimore and graduated from the Maryland Institute of Fine Arts in 1927. He did postgraduate work at the Philadelphia Academy of Fine Arts before coming to Arizona in 1932. Baumgartner participated in the CWA artists program, producing an Arizona Capitol Building mural of flowers and cactus.[9] The mural, not quite 3' high and 18' long, was a "valiant attempt to brighten up an otherwise businesslike space."[10] Baumgartner was indeed a productive artist. His duties as CCC artist began July 12, 1934, and ended September 7, 1935, without interruption. He was stationed at Flagstaff (F-5), Camp Verde (F-35), and Double Springs (F-6), and did temporary duty at Rimrock (F-51).[11] Afterwards, he is noted to be on the teaching staff of the Phoenix Federal Art Center.[12]

Records at NARAMD contain five letters that Baumgartner sent to Edward B. Rowan, superintendent of Treasury's Section of Painting and Sculpture. These letters refer to eight completed art works that were sent to Rowan, and Baumgartner indicates he was working on another. None of these are known to be in federal government hands today.

Figure 16. Creston F. Baumgartner, circa 1930. Courtesy Baumgartner Family.

On October 11, 1934, Baumgartner wrote Rowan that he was sending by mail that day a 3.5' x 5' oil painting showing a "representation of four different working crews—roadside cleanup—porcupine crew under biological survey—road building and telephone crew." (See back cover illustration)[13] In a letter dated December 10, 1934, Baumgartner says he has heard from Rowan and that the painting of the four working crews had not been received in Washington, D.C., so he was enclosing a photo of it as well as his Railway Express receipt. He concluded by asking Rowan to write him at his Phoenix address about the painting. Luckily the photo remained in NARAMD files. What happened to the painting remains a mystery.

On November 17, 1934, Baumgartner wrote Rowan to say that he was sending six small landscapes. In the same letter he indicated he was working on another 3.5′ x 5′ canvas "of three boys on their way to work." On March 15, 1935, Baumgartner wrote Rowan from the Rimrock camp, stating that he was mailing an oil painting of the bridge gang. The April 5, 1935, *Flagstaff Journal* indicates Baumgartner donated a painting of enrollees working at the Beaver Creek camp. The whereabouts of this painting is a mystery.[14]

Figure 17. Three Boys on Their Way to Work(?). Photograph of Untitled Painting. Courtesy Baumgartner Family.

Baumgartner was also doing more pedestrian things. On June 11, 1935, he wrote Rowan to say that he had finished a three-week project fabricating 2′ x 2′ galvanized iron signs in the form of a Forest Service shield. The signs were painted and had a pine tree in the middle. The letter included a drawing of the sign.

An analysis of CCC camp newspapers when Baumgartner was enrolled gives us a few other clues about his work and personality. The July 25, 1934, *Echo of the Peaks* indicates Baumgartner had been assigned to Company 821 and was working under the supervision of Supt. E.A. McNamara. The article stated: "Mr. Baumgartner has already painted some excellent pictures locally."[15] From August 9 through October 10, 1934, Baumgartner was listed as one of the newspaper's artists. During this period, the art work in these mimeographed papers appears a bit more creative than earlier issues. However, there is no evidence that all the illustrations are Baumgartner's work. (One does have his initials.) The August 27, 1934, *Echo of the Peaks* noted in an article titled "Artist Makes Big Showing in His Work" that Baumgartner had completed several paintings, including ones of the San Francisco Peaks, Oak Creek, and other nearby scenes. The article concluded: "We are glad to have him in our camp, he has made sketches which are very natural and beautiful."[16] Company 821 moved to Camp Verde for the winter, and the following appeared in a November camp newspaper:

Baumgartner — What do you think of my new painting? I call it the Melon Patch.

Capt. Lane — But I don't see any melons or even vines.

Baumgartner — Well you see they haven't come up yet.[17]

By 1935, Baumgartner was back near Flagstaff again, and he appears in a joke in a June newspaper.[18] In another issue, Baumgartner is referred to twice. Under the "Personals" page is a quote from the *Arizona Republic* noting: "Creston F. Baumgartner, widely known artist, has entered several of his paintings in an exhibit at the Museum of Northern Arizona." In the same newspaper Baumgartner was, again, part of another joke.

Baumgartner: How did you like my paintings?

Jabbo: Great! That one with the fried egg was so natural it nearly made me hungry.

Baumgartner: Great Scott! That wasn't an egg, that was a sunset.[19]

Another article on the same page mentions that Baumgartner is directing a string band made up of camp musicians that had already played for camp dances.[20]

No art of these three men is presently stored at the Fine Arts Division of the U.S. General Services Administration, the custodian of New Deal art. Baumgartner went on to become a successful Arizona artist. What became of Peterson and Darry and their CCC art?

1. Olson, *Historical Dictionary of the New Deal*, 400; McDonald, *Federal Relief Administration and the Arts*, 365.
2. McDonald, Ibid., 366.
3. "CCC Artists—Who Were They?" http://newdealblog.com/archives/category/art.
4. Edward Rowan to Wade Lane, 29 August 1934, indicates Arizona artist Baumgartner would have to supply his own materials. Rowan says FDR is "adamant" that no funds be

used for art supplies and that Fechner was in agreement. Rowan's letter is sympathetic to the artists' plight and suggests using cheaper mediums. NARAMO letter courtesy of Kathleen Duxbury. McDonald, *Federal Relief Administration and the Arts*, 366, also indicates the artists purchased their own supplies.

5. "C.C.C. Artists Are Assigned to Flagstaff Camps," *Coconino Sun*, July 27, 1934, 6.
6. "Artist to Be Placed in Petrified Forest CCC Camp near Here," July 20, 1934, 7, identifies him as Earl Darrey of Arvada, Colorado. Researcher Kathleen Duxbury indicates in an e-mail message to author, December 6, 2011, that an Earl Darley was a PWAP artist in Denver in 1934.
7. Melzer, *Coming of Age*, 92.
8. U.S. Public Building Service, Records of Public Building Service Concerning Federal Art Activities, NARAMD RG 121/650/21/18/01 Entry 142 Box 1.
9. "Oil Paintings, Mural Turned Out under CWA Program," *Arizona Republic*, April 15, 1934, 3.
10. Bermingham, *New Deal in the Southwest*, 13.
11. From Baumgartner's personnel file, NARAMO files, courtesy of Kathleen Duxbury.
12. Fahlman, *New Deal Art in Arizona*, 26, 28.
13. All references to letters between Baumgartner and Rowan are from U.S. Public Building Service, Records of Public Building Service Concerning Federal Art Activities, NARAMD RG 121/650/21/18/01 Entry 142 Box 1.
14. "CCC Youth Paints Landscape Canvas, Wins High Praise," *Flagstaff Journal*, April 5, 1935, 1.
15. "Artist Assigned to Our Camp," *Echo of the Peaks*, July 25, 1934, 1, AHSLA.
16. "Artist Makes Big Showing in Work," *Echo of the Peaks*, August 27, 1934, AHSLA.
17. *Clear Creek Clarion*, November 16, 1934, AHSLA.
18. *Lakeside Mirror*, June 14, 1935, AHSLA.
19. *Lakeside Mirror*, July 15, 1935, AHSLA. The Museum of Northern Arizona does not own any Baumgartner works at the present time.
20. "String Band Formed," *Lakeside Mirror*, July 15, 1935, AHSLA. Byars, Preslar, Stacy, Terrell, and Suber were said to be its members.

CHAPTER 6

Kaibab National Forest

THE CCC WAS ACTIVE IN the present-day Kaibab National Forest early on, with the establishment of F-27 at Bellemont on May 25, 1933, and F-28 at Williams on May 26. At that time, some of the area was known as the Tusayan National Forest. As this area was combined into the Kaibab National Forest in 1934, it is treated in this chapter as one unit. Although the area known as the North Kaibab National Forest today is quite large, it appears there were no CCC companies located on the North Kaibab.[1] On a few occasions Grand Canyon National Park North Rim CCC companies assisted the North Kaibab in firefighting.[2] This appears to be the only CCC impact in the North Kaibab. For the South Kaibab Forest in 1933, the future appeared limited. "By 1930, the majority of harvestable timber in the Williams area had been logged. Overgrazing, poor logging practices, and forest fires had left the forest on the brink of environmental collapse."[3] Many looked to the CCC for improvements, such as roads and recreation development, to attract tourists.

Bellemont (F-27)

The Bellemont camp was short-lived, and documentation of their work is wanting. The camp was officially occupied on May 25, 1933. Company 851 had 170 enrollees.[4] The camp location was two miles south of the railroad track; the exact location is uncertain, but "very likely" "near Hill Spring, which is now on the Navajo Army Depot."[5] According to Forest Ranger Clyde P. Moose, their work included constructing the telephone line to the camp and the road up Volunteer Mountain. Their work also included the road to Rogers Lake. Both roads were said to include bridges and cattle guards.[6] Moose states they built "a lot of other roads" and "some fences."[7] Moose also states the camp lasted a short time because of the lack of nearby work.

On July 28, the Williams newspaper reported that camp supervisors Capt. Frank W. Halsey and Dr. Merriam visited Williams and reported the camp "is in good condition now, the boys well satisfied and work progressing nicely. The road to the camp is being graveled and soon will be in first class condition."[8] On August 11, they were reported to have entertained fifty people at the camp with music, lectures, and food.[9] On August 31, 1933, the camp reported 185 enrollees (155 from Texas and the rest from Arizona, with 3 African Americans). Supervisors were three Army officers, two Army enlisted personnel, and a contract physician.

During September, Arizona governor Benjamin B. Moeur visited the camp, and the camp baseball team was said to have accumulated nine wins.[10] On September 30, Company 851 had 87 enrollees (24 from Arizona, 63 from Texas with 1 African American); the supervisors consisted of two Army officers, two Army enlisted, and a contract surgeon. On October 6, the Williams newspaper announced the Bellemont camp was moving south.[11] During October, the camp commander, Capt. Frank W. Halsey, was suddenly transferred to Phoenix to set up

Figure 18. CCC Company 851, F-27, Bellemont, October 10, 1933. Courtesy Flagstaff Area Monuments Museum Collection, WACA #5920.

two new camps, and he was replaced by Captain Stonesplice.[12] On October 31, Company 851 departed Bellemont via eight trucks for camp F-34, Cave Creek, in the Tonto National Forest.[13] L.F. Archer was left as custodian of the buildings until they were salvaged for Forest Service use.[14]

Williams (F-28)

In northern Arizona, Williams rivaled Kingman as the most vigorous communities of all to welcome the new enrollees and to involve them in local social activities. From the very beginning of the CCC's arrival, the *Williams News* reported on CCC activities, often with a positive image. And like the Kingman *Mohave County Miner*, the Williams newspaper frequently printed a column written by a CCC company representative.[15] Williams, like Kingman, had an active local chamber of commerce that was closely involved in and supportive of the CCC program.

1933

On April 7, the Williams newspaper reported that Tusayan National Forest Supervisor G.W. Kimball had been notified that a CCC camp was coming to the area. Kimball said there were still many questions to be answered, and he was conferring with officials. Kimball said that while it was too late for tree planting, "there is a great deal of forest improvement work" ready to be undertaken.[16] A week later, Kimball answered some of the questions, stating that a road south to Perkinsville was supported by the town chamber of commerce and appeared to be acceptable to the regional forest officials. A camp site with an acceptable water supply was still a concern. He was still unsure of his source for trucks and equipment.[17] The chamber of commerce expressed support for the road decision and also suggested lateral roads for firefighting and timber cutting.[18] Company 848 enrollees were to arrive officially on May 26, to include 170 enrollees to be joined by 30 local men. The Forest Service was to install three 3,000-gallon water tanks and 2,000 feet of pipe for the camp water supply. Work projects were to include the Summit Mountain–Clarkdale Highway and the construction of trails and fire breaks. The camp location was announced as Little Pine Flats, twelve miles south of town.[19]

No sooner had the men gotten off the train when things changed. The camp location was moved to Barney Flat to access the more reliable water at Lockett Spring. The men moved to camp via Forest Service, county, town, and private trucks. The city was temporarily supplying the camp water. Camp supervisors were Capt. Charles R. Hall, Lt. E.L.(?) Thompson, Lt. Scherer, and three non-commissioned Army officers. Most of the enrollees were from Texas. Many of the enrollees were to go through two weeks of conditioning. However, some work projects started immediately.

During their first week, enrollees fought a fire two miles north of JD Dam. (A ten-man reserve crew was at camp for "ready for instant call to fight fires.") Crews were doing road work near JD Dam and in the Pine Flats country. The town newspaper had earlier expressed concern about having two hundred strangers in the small community. Right away, the prospect of enrollees with spending money and the camp purchasing supplies locally began to change that. The newspaper reported: "Williams will benefit very materially from the presence of the reforestation camp south of the city." Although there was no military drill, the discipline would be the same as "any well regulated work camp."[20]

During July, Forest Supervisor Kimball and Camp Commander Capt. Hall spoke to the Williams Rotary Club. Kimball said at first he doubted if the Army and Forest Service could work together, but they were "working remarkably well." Kimball summarized the work projects: fungus eradication, reworking of the Bill Williams Trail, Summit Spring development, cutting of snags, prairie dog eradication at Garland Prairie, porcupine extermination (girdling of trees makes them unfit for timber harvest), and the possible planting of grass on an overgrazed area south of the JD Lake Road.

Captain Hall noted there were few enrollees going AWOL. He said the only discipline was "by admonitions or persuasive measures." Most of the men are "grateful for the opportunity." But, he said, sanitation "is apparently foreign to many of the boys."[21]

On August 29, F-28 Texas enrollee Oscar Terry Lee was admitted to Fort Whipple Veterans Hospital for a blood transfusion. (Fort Whipple was the nearest federal hospital.) Lee was suffering from lymphatic leukemia and died at Whipple on September 17, 1933.[22]

The first report of Company 848 strength on August 31, 1933, revealed the camp had a total of 180 enrollees (155 from Texas and the rest from Arizona, with 3 African Americans). The supervisors included three Army officers, two non-commissioned officers, and an Army medical doctor. On September 22, the town newspaper reported that a number of dam projects were under consideration. In a letter from Regional Forester Pooler to Williams Chamber of Commerce president James Kennedy, Pooler supported raising the JD Dam five feet. Also under consideration were dams at Pine Flats, Dog Town Wash, and other locations. The *News* noted that these new reservoirs would be good for stockmen and tourists.[23]

On September 29, the newspaper reported a housewarming where the enrollees were said to be "good entertainers." Camp Commander Capt. Hall noted 130 enrollees were intending to re-enroll. He said many had gained weight and the "whole attitude of men has changed."[24] On September 30, Camp F-28 reported 104 white enrollees. In October, enrollees were doing road construction north of the Verde River. Others were doing timber stand improvement and building fences.[25] Company 848 was given the orders to move south at the end of the month, and on October 24, many local people visited camp for an evening of music and socializing. Rev. A.W. Gray of the Williams Methodist Community Church performed the ceremony.[26]

On October 31, Company 848 moved to F-30 in the Coronado National Forest. On November 17, the town newspaper reported that the town council and chamber of commerce had drafted a letter to Forest Supervisor Kimball asking for 400 enrollees in the future. The letter listed needed work projects, including the raising of JD Dam.[27] Meanwhile, work on the Perkinsville Road continued with PWA labor.[28]

1934

On April 30, 1934, CCC Veterans Company 1826 (198 men) arrived in Williams, coming from camp F-12 near Douglas. (Some of the men were said to be veterans of the Spanish American War.)[29] Their supervisors were camp Commander Capt. M.R. Eddy, Lt. C.R. Howe, and camp physician Dr. Geo. H. Spiney. Dan C. Best was project superintendent. The Williams News was optimistic that more work would be accomplished, as these enrollees were work experienced. Their work was said to include improving the Bill Williams Circle Road, improving the JD Dam Road and constructing Kennedy Dam.[30] The latter was located twenty-four miles south of Williams and was the first recreational lake built by the CCC in the area. It was to be 625 acre feet behind a 30'-high earthen dam. Five thousand yards of dirt were to be moved. The Williams News editorialized: "It is hoped that Kennedy Dam will be but the first of many to be constructed in this area."[31] It was completed in late June.[32] After a visit by the Army in April, it was announced the Army would lease space in the Community Hall for a CCC district headquarters. Personnel were to include Capt. Paolo Sperati.[33]

During June, enrollees were working on many projects. They were clearing the Kennedy Dam Reservoir area of trees and boulders, and they graded, re-capped and drained the road to the JD Dam. The Loop Road was getting extensive work, including ditching and installation of "many big culverts." At Summit, Bear, and Hitt Springs, enrollees walled up the springs and installed piping and fencing to keep out livestock. At Summit Spring, twelve water troughs were installed.[34] In mid-June, enrollees fought a forest fire southwest of Kendrick Peak.[35] Also during June, work began on developing water tanks or reservoirs. These may have combined CCC labor with NRA funding.[36] Sand Flat, DT, and Pine Creek Tanks were nearly completed. The next project was said to be digging a barrow pit at Three Mile Lake.[37]

In early July, the Williams News announced the town was the recipient of a $120,000 PWA water grant. It was said the grant involved the Forest Service and CCC cooperating in building the road and clearing the dam area for the Dog Town project.[38] The Phoenix newspaper stated the National Forest had pledged CCC cooperation even with the installation of the pipeline.[39] A week later, the forest supervisor was quoted as saying if County Engineer Wright would survey the road to the Dog Town site, he would commit a CCC crew to begin work "at once."[40]

Camp F-28 had their first inspection on July 14, 1934, by Special Investigator James C. Reddoch. He noted the development of five springs as well as six miles of truck trail construction; seven miles of road maintenance; seventeen miles of telephone line maintenance; 500 acres of fire hazard reduction; 1,050 acres of timber stand improvement; and 4,600 acres of rodent control.[41]

On July 18, Williams was treated to a talk by politically powerful Postmaster General James A. Farley at the Sultana Theater. The day before, Farley had met with Grand Canyon Superintendent Miner Tillotson, Governor Moeur, and others. Regarding the CCC, Farley said: "Lads, coming fresh from school, found themselves in a world destitute of employment.... The problem was to keep these new arrivals in the field of citizenship from swelling the ranks of the unemployed and starting life as vagrants and drifters. So we sent them to the woods." Sending money home aims at preserving people's pride to make mortgage payments, etc. "There is no process by which we can indicate the greatest gain of all—the gain in public morale."[42] The CCC was an alternative to the dole and "its purpose was more to save the self-respect of the men ... than to save timber."[43]

On July 27, the Williams News (page 3) announced that Capt. Eddy was being transferred and the new camp commanding officer was Capt. Nichols. In August, the Kennedy Dam was completed, measuring 225' in length and 37' in height. As there was no water supply nearby, the spike camp men were transported daily twenty miles from camp. The city lent the use of a new Caterpillar, which was frequently used for three shifts. It was finished in thirty-seven days and took 725 man days.[44]

On August 31, Company 1826 reported 171 enrollees (from all five of the 8th Corps states, with most from Arizona and 10 African American veterans). In late September, the Williams Rotary Club and guests met with Company 1826 to hear speakers, including Congresswoman Isabella S. Greenway. She defended the New Deal relief programs, saying that without them the country would have had a revolution by now. Project Superintendent Best summarized the work of the camp: an average of 135 enrollees were at work daily. In addition to Kennedy Dam and the spring development, they had completed 15.2 miles of road building, 100,000 acres rodent control, and 1,650 acres of timber stand improvement.[45] During the month of October, the CCC camp prepared for travel to their winter location at SP-5, Papago Park, leaving on October 27. The night before they left they hosted a Halloween party.[46]

By the end of the Third Enrollment Period, Company 1826 had completed a great deal in a short time. Researcher Patrick Putt credits the company with building the Mount Kendrick lookout cabin; however, it was actually erected in 1911.[47] Putt credits the CCC with the construction of the Camp Clover ranger station and four associated buildings. During this period, the *Williams News* reported on CCC activities frequently. Mysteriously, no mention is made of the CCC doing any building during this time nor is the construction of Camp Clover reported. As Putt's documentation is from a NIRA report, it is possible that the buildings were PWA funded, with the CCC contributing the unskilled labor.[48]

The year in Williams ended on an unfortunate note for Grand Canyon enrollee Frank Flask. Flask, homesick for his Ohio home, stole a car at Grand Canyon, but by the time he reached Route 66 at Williams the sheriff had set up a roadblock. Flask drove around the roadblock, the sheriff pursued him and fired his revolver at Flask, and Flask stopped and was arrested.[49] Fortunately, such extreme criminal behavior in the CCC was uncommon.[50]

1935

On January 4, the Williams Town Council held a public meeting to discuss applying again for CCC camps. Forest Supervisor Walter G. Mann attended and was optimistic for two camps for Williams. However, he advised he had been told by the Forest Service Regional Office that there would be less road work and more emphasis on recreation this time. Mann detailed a list of eight major CCC projects, including fencing around White Horse Lake; improving and extending the Bill Williams trails to connect with the Benham Trail, as well as building three shelters; a recreational lake at Hells Canyon; improving the road from White Horse Lake to Crescent Lake; and a road from Sycamore Point to JD Dam.[51] However, a funding stalemate in Congress postponed CCC decisions till April.

On May 3, the town newspaper announced there would only be one CCC camp.[52] On May 16, Company 1838 arrived at JD Dam (nine miles south of town) from Camp DP-30 at Madera Canyon outside Tucson, totaling 230 men.[53] When Williams had no active CCC camps, Superintendent Mann, in January and May, along with staff, was inspecting CCC work in Arizona.[54] The hopes for extensive recreational work were diminished with a survey of the damage caused to the South Road. There were frequent rock slides and plugged culverts. Enrollees went right to work on the Pine Flat to rim section of the road.[55]

In June, Forest Supervisor Mann and the camp commander spoke to the Williams Rotary Club. Their program started with musical selections from the enrollee group, Oklahoma Blues Boys. Mann said that the South Road would be widened to 20', capped with cinders on gravel, and the drainage improved. Five or six 18'-wide concrete bridges were being installed. Sturdy cattle guards were also being installed. They expected to complete the White Horse Dam by August 1, with two shifts hauling one hundred truckloads of dirt daily. Project Superintendent Best explained that the leak at Kennedy Dam was from cracks in bedrock, and that they would try to patch the cracks by dynamiting and then filling with clay as had been done at Lake Mary.[56]

On June 30, Company 1838 reported a total of 217 enrollees (10 from Texas and the rest from Arizona, with 1 African American). They were supervised by two Army officers and an Army doctor.

In early July, Williams got two FERA-funded transient camps. These portable camps of fifty men had five supervisors. One of their projects was constructing a landing field.[57] In late July, the Kaibab Forest was advised they would have a twenty-man PWA crew to do work like the CCC. They would be doing water development at Spring Valley and the Callender Ranger Station, working on the Bill Williams Trail and boundary fence erection.[58] A forty-man CCC crew was working the Williams-Perkinsville Road, a large crew was at the White Horse Reservoir site clearing debris, and others were building fences, doing reforestation, and eradicating prairie dogs.[59] It is unclear when Company 1838 left Williams, but the company is reported in Texas on August 17, 1935.[60] In late October, much of the CCC road work was washed away in torrential rains, with the worst damage in the Pine Flat area.[61]

1936

In late January, Forest Supervisor Mann told the Williams Rotary Club that he had included the West Cataract Dam in his request for CCC projects. If it was built, it would result in a seventy-acre pleasure lake.[62] On April 30, Company 2833 arrived at F-28 from Topock along with sixty new enrollees from Fort

Worth. (A week before, Lt. G. H. Fruebel and six men had arrived in Williams to get the camp ready.) Their commanding officer was Lt. William E. Cheatham. Don C. Best was again project superintendent. Their work was to include the Perkinsville Road, road and trail maintenance, and fire lookout construction.[63] In a lengthy article in the Williams newspaper, Tracy W. Rice detailed the CCC program. He said during the previous three seasons in the Kaibab the CCC camp spent 1,156 man days fighting fires. CCC recreation work was to include Kennedy Dam (Antelope Lake); White Horse Dam; building fireplaces, restrooms, and tables one mile west of the Williams campground; and Sycamore Rim campground improvements, including fireplaces, tables, and sanitary.[64]

In early May, the forest supervisor spoke to the Rotary Club about the CCC. He noted that that season CCC companies were generally 160 enrollees, rather than 200 as during previous seasons, resulting in just 100–120 men actually working in the field. He outlined fifteen major work programs, including maintaining the telephone line from JD Dam to MC Ranch; maintaining the Bill Williams Mountain horse trails; building the road to White Horse Lake; building a lookout cabin on Bill Williams Mountain; performing spring work at Buck, Lockett, and Summit; improving the timber stand; developing water at Camp Clover; constructing fences; controlling insect pests; and finishing the Perkinsville Road to the Mogollon Rim. The latter job would be two months long, involving eight to ten miles of the road.[65]

The following week, fifty enrollees assisted in fighting a fire at Forty Nine Mile Hill.[66] Later in the month, enrollees began the recreation development at White Horse, including ten fire pits and picnic tables.[67] At the same time, Project Superintendent Best transferred to the Prescott National Forest, and Frank Hanna took his place.

Special Investigator A. W. Stockman inspected the camp on June 26 and reported "a splendid spirit of cooperation." He said the camp had responded to thirty-one fires in the last week.[68] On June 30, the camp reported 155 enrollees (81 from Oklahoma, 61 from Texas, 12 from Arizona, and 1 from New Mexico). Two Army officers, one Army doctor, and an educational advisor were the supervisors.

On July 3, the camp reported the road to the Volunteer Mountain tower completed, including a road circling the top.[69] The following week, over sixty enrollees joined sixty-six enrollees from the Coconino National Forest battling an eight-hundred-acre fire at Jackson Hill east of Garland Prairie.[70] On July 17, a crew of ten left for the Grand Canyon to stay temporarily with Company 847 while they constructed a new 80'-high fire tower and two-room cabin at Grandview. The new tower was to replace an "old windmill tower." Sixty men were working the Perkinsville Road, twenty-three were doing timber stand improvement, and twenty-five were working the White Horse Lake recreation project.[71] The same day, the Williams newspaper (page 8) reported the camp on constant fire duty responding to twenty-five lightning fires in one day. A week later, the newspaper reported that double shifts of bulldozers and jackhammers were working the Perkinsville Road. Foreman Ed Radebaugh was in charge of the Grandview Fire Tower construction, where foundations were set and tower erection underway.[72] The Grandview project was scheduled to be completed by September.[73]

Figure 19. Grandview Lookout Cabin, circa 1935. Courtesy Grand Canyon National Park Museum Collection, #346967.

On July 31, Project Superintendent Hanna spoke to the Rotary Club and enrollees supplied music. He reported a total of 155 enrollees and said that the "company won't tolerate slackers or sticky fingers."[74]

On September 17, work started on the JD Dam–White Horse Road project.[75] On September 22, enrollees and supervisors posed for photos for the Phoenix District *Official Annual*. Lt. William E. Cheatham was camp commander, Lt. John B. Whiting was the exchange officer, Dr. F. S. Spearman was the camp surgeon, and Louis Puente Jr. was the educational advisor.[76] On September 30, the camp newspaper summarized the work projects since the beginning of the season: Perkinsville Road (2,128 man days); timber stand improvement (719); fence construction and maintenance (696); Bill Williams fire lookout cabin construction (247); Grandview lookout tower construction (183); White Horse Lake campground development and JD Dam campground improvements (428); firefighting (953); spring development (67); and telephone line maintenance (30).[77]

On October 1, it was reported that of the 127 men in camp, 52 had signed up to return home. A new travelling library arrived at camp. Educational Advisor Puente was making arrangements for men wanting to finish high school to attend Flagstaff High.[78] On October 15, the *Williams News* (page 5) reported the CCC-constructed picnic grounds had been dedicated. On October 22, Mr. Hanna of the camp reported to the Rotary Club on the progress of the Perkinsville Road. He said that additional signage was completed on the Sycamore Rim drive and work completed on the White Horse recreation area. He said enrollees had remodeled the JD Dam recreation area and had begun the road between JD Dam and White Horse. Buck Spring was cemented and piped to the troughs.[79]

Enrollees finally finished the Perkinsville Road, but were not to be present for the official dedication on November 8, as they were transferred to the Grand Canyon Desert View (NP-4) camp on October 22. The ceremony was attended by 250 and included speeches by Grand Canyon National Park Superintendent Tillotson, Forest Service representatives Kimball and Mann, and Prescott Forest Supervisor Frank Grubb.[80] Community leaders were hopeful that the new road would bring tourists to the area from the Verde Valley and even farther south.

1937

The possibility of a camp for Williams did not look good in early 1937. In April, Forest Supervisor Mann said there would be no camp at Williams, but that the Flagstaff CCC camp would have a spike camp at Spring Valley.[81] However, in early July, Mann announced that a CCC company was coming to JD Dam. They arrived on July 23 with a total of 150 officers and enrollees. Their work was to be erecting a lookout tower and cabin on Bill Williams Mountain, fencing the White Horse Lake recreation area, road building and maintenance, and timber stand improvement.[82] It appears this was Company 2848. (None of the newspapers state the company number. As the Williams enrollees arrived and departed in between the biannual location and strength reports, the company number has been calculated by their destination and date when they left Williams.) According to researcher Putt, the main camp was at JD Dam, but some were stationed at a spike camp at the Spring Valley Ranger Station. He says the latter group was doing forest cleanup, fighting fires, and building roads and trails. Many of the roads were said to follow old railroad grades.[83]

In September, local newspapers reported the construction of the Bill Williams Lookout Tower. The tower was to be 50' high, and materials for the tower were being hauled to the top by two-wheeled cart. It was reported that even the 16' and 18' steel parts for the tower were being hauled by this cart.[84]

In October, the *Northern Yavapai Record* (Ash Fork) reported the enrollees were erecting two stone forest boundary markers. One was on US 66 between Williams and Ash Fork, and the other was on the Williams–Grand Canyon Highway. It was said the stone was native malapai rock.[85] It appears Company 2848 departed Williams on October 23, 1937, arriving the same day at F-30, Madera Canyon. In just a short period of time, Company 2848 finished the lookout and the White Horse Lake fence; erected 105 temporary check dams; made 486 acres of range improvements; and spent 668 man days making truck trails.[86]

1938

During April, the forest supervisor spoke to the Rotary Club, saying that it was very likely Williams would have a summer CCC camp. He outlined his eleven proposed projects for the camp. They included Bill Williams Lookout living quarters; the Volunteer Mountain Fire Lookout; a range fence at Spring Valley (eight miles); road maintenance, including the Perkinsville Road; spring development at Buck Springs and Lockett Springs; trail maintenance; wildlife management; and timber stand improvement (five hundred acres).[87] The first enrollees of Company 3346 were an advance group of fifty. The rest of the men were to arrive later. Of this first group, some went to JD Dam to work on the Perkinsville Road and others went to the thirty-man Spring Valley spike camp to do road maintenance and fight fires.[88]

On May 19, the *Williams News* (page 1) reported the Forest Service was repairing the Bill Williams Mountain Loop Road, and some of the workers were CCC enrollees. On May 26, the newspaper reported the arrival of 135 more enrollees. Lt. Leo Conley was the company commander, who stated more men were arriving on July 1.[89] However, in late June, it was announced many of the new enrollees would be transferred out and replaced later.[90] On July 21, it was announced only sixty enrollees remained, but a new full contingent was to arrive in early August.[91] Not all the CCC boys had left, for the local newspaper reported on July 28 the CCC ball team had blanked the city team, 9–0.

On August 4, the Williams newspaper reported the arrival of the full company to the greetings of community leaders and the high school band.[92] On August 11, the newspaper reported that the company commanding officer, Lt. Conley, accidently shot himself with his .45 revolver and was found some distance from camp.[93] He was reported back at Williams a week later by the *Coconino Sun*. In August, Forest Supervisor Mann reported work was progressing on the Perkinsville Road and enrollees were doing timber stand improvement (removing inferior trees) at Dog Town Wash Reservoir. They were also maintaining the Bill Williams Loop Road, completing the lookout cabin construction, and cleaning the campgrounds.[94]

In September, the *Williams News* announced Company 3346 would be moving south around October 20.[95] Researcher Putt calls this three-month period one of the most productive during the CCC era. In addition to projects already mentioned, he lists 139 man days of firefighting; rebuilding of four miles of the Bill Williams Trail; 3,800 acres of rodent control; installation of four Forest Service portal signs; installation of water troughs at Buck Springs; improvement of turkey habitat at Hitt Spring; and erection of almost 12.5 miles of fence.[96] On October 13, the local newspaper reported nearly all the work done on the Perkinsville Road, but the camp destined to move to Safford in a week.[97] Company 3346 arrived officially on October 22, 1938, at Camp F-41, Noon Creek, south of Safford.

1939

In January, Forest Supervisor Mann outlined future Forest Service recreational projects. He listed more recreational development on Bill Williams Mountain, as well as making the Bill Williams Mountain area a game preserve. He listed more than a dozen possible projects, including a White Horse Lake boat pier and sand beach and a pipeline from Big Springs to White Horse.[98] Even before Company 3348 arrived at Williams, their projects were laid out for readers of the local newspaper. At White Horse Lake, plans called for toilets, landing dock, pier, and beach improvement. Fence construction was planned for Spring Valley and the Benham Plot and other areas. Volunteer Mountain was scheduled for a cabin and fence work. Spring development was planned for Newman Springs and Elk Springs. Slate Mountain was listed for a seven-mile telephone line. Truck trail maintenance was planned for Spring Valley (sixty miles), Williams District (fifty miles), and the Challender District (one hundred miles). Also planned were truck trail and foot trail maintenance, forest stand improvement, fighting forest fires, fire pre-suppression, general cleanup, Oak Tank Turkey Sanctuary, and other wildlife activities.[99] Thirty-eight members were scheduled for arrival on April 29 and the rest in May. The same newspaper announced that Vic Sandberg had arrived at the Forest Service office, where he would be in charge of relief, CCC, and WPA work.

The main group of Company 3348 arrived in Williams officially on May 14 and returned to the JD Dam camp. They were coming from Camp F-64 at Pena Blanca near Nogales. According to the *Williams News*, 150 men arrived, with 40 going to the Spring Valley spike camp, where their work was to include firefighting, fence construction, and road maintenance.[100] On June 30, the official enrollee count showed just 74 enrollees (all but 2 from Pennsylvania). Supervisors were listed as two Army officers, a contract physician, and an educational advisor.

On July 20, the newspaper reported that a one-hundred-acre forest fire near the railroad tracks west of Parks was brought under control by 65 men including the CCC.[101] The following week the newspaper reported that 110 enrollees did a three-day acclimation under the supervision of Commanding Officer Lt. Albert Runser and Educational Advisor Doinee Ravello. The camp technical services staff did a two-day training, including safety practices, proper tool handling, thorough forest fire training, and matching enrollee aptitudes to jobs.[102]

On August 24, the *Williams News* announced that work on the Perkinsville Road was to start, with WPA labor working the section from Williams to the Coleman Lake junction and the CCC resurfacing the section south of there.[103] Company 3348 was destined to leave and return to F-64 in southern Arizona. According to researcher Putt, at the end of their tour, they improved campgrounds at Bill Williams Mountain, JD Lake, Sycamore Rim, and White Horse Lake. Putt reports they constructed campgrounds at Parks, Garland Prairie Vista, and the Lava River Campground north of Bellemont.[104] However, the *Williams News* reported the latter campground constructed "all by FERA labor," so CCC participation is unclear.[105] In addition, the newspaper reported the CCC had made progress on Pine Flat–JD Dam–Sycamore Road; spent 350 man days firefighting; did seventy-five miles of forest road improvement; made spring improvements; constructed six miles of new range fence; constructed seven miles of new telephone lines, including one connecting the Spring Valley Ranger Station and Slate Mountain; planted forty thousand seedlings on the old Johnson burn south of Bellemont; and pruned and thinned two hundred acres of pines.[106] Former enrollee Andrew Bobby, in an oral history interview, remembers making check dams and pruning trees during this time.[107] It is possible that the enrollees constructed the Volunteer Mountain Lookout in 1939. Researcher Putt says the CCC did the construction in 1938; however, Forest Service records indicate 1939 as its construction date.[108] Company 3348 returned officially to F-64 on October 21, 1939.

1940

On February 29, 1940, the *Williams News* reported the beginning of construction on the Moqui Ranger Station located in present-day Tusayan, Arizona. The possibility of a modern ranger station near the Grand Canyon had been in the news in Flagstaff and Williams, off and on, since 1936. However, the question of who built the complex of six rustic buildings still remains a mystery.[109] The National Register (Item No. 93000521) attributes them to the CCC based upon an oral history interview with a former CCC enrollee who says he was stationed at Grand Canyon and participated in their construction. The former enrollee is deceased. A look through many GCNP records, such as monthly reports of the superintendent, CCC camp inspection reports from both Williams and Grand Canyon, and frequent 1940 news articles in the *Williams News*, has resulted in no mention of the Moqui as CCC work. However, a February 16, 1940, *Coconino Sun* article (page 3) is titled: "WPA Men Start Work in the Kaibab." And a 1940 photo of the construction shows signs with the logo "USA/DANGER/WPA." It is this writer's belief that the Moqui complex must be called New Deal, with WPA construction and possible involvement of the CCC.

Figure 20. Moqui Ranger Station under Construction, June 1940. Courtesy Kaibab National Forest.

On April 27, an advance unit of Company 3348 arrived at Williams to get the F-28, JD Dam camp ready. The man body of men, some 140, arrived officially on May 5, 1940, coming from F-64, Pena Blanca, Arizona.[110] Their work was to be timber stand improvement; water development; reforestation; road and trail construction and maintenance; fence building; and recreation area improvements. On May 29, Special Investigator M. J. Bowen visited camp and noted jobs such as road and telephone line construction, reservoir work, and construction of a twenty-thousand-gallon concrete tank: "The camp is in splendid condition."[111]

On May 30, Company 3348 reported 159 enrollees (all but 3 from Pennsylvania). Camp supervisors were two Army officers, a contract physician, and an educational advisor. On June 30, the camp count was just 83, and on July 31, it jumped back up 197 (still almost all from Pennsylvania).

During June, the company spent 205 man days fighting fires. In July, a new commander arrived, Lt. Gregorio P. Martinez Jr. Franklin G. Hanna was again the project superintendent. The *Williams News* reported that in the first six months the average Company 3348 enrollee gained 11.5 pounds. Average enrollee age was 19 and average schooling level was 9th grade.[112] On July 13, 116 new enrollees arrived and did their three-day orientation and vaccinations. Work projects were at Big Springs, Oak Tank, and the road between Pine Flats and JD Dam. Twenty enrollees went to the Spring Valley Ranger Station spike camp, where a new building was being erected and work included building a road to the top of Slate Mountain.[113] According to former F-28 enrollee Merle Timblin, one of the camp projects was painting signs and campground equipment such as trash cans and picnic tables.[114]

On July 28, nearly one hundred enrollees were to visit the Grand Canyon, and the camp ball team was to play the Grand Canyon CCC. Two enrollees were to be sent to Phoenix for lifeguard training in order to monitor swimmers at White Horse Lake. Of the enrollees in camp, just 10% had finished high school; most left school "for economic reasons."[115]

In early August, it was noted there were eleven lightning fires burning at once in Spring Valley. The camp educational program included a dancing class for beginners, and the dance steps included rhumba and the Lindy Hop.[116] Every morning the men had non-combat training that included calisthenics.[117] On August 8, Harry H. Lutz, 54, from Pennsylvania, camp mess steward, died of a heart attack.[118]

The enrollees were developing a close relationship with the town. "The Central Drug is one of the most popular spots with the boys here in camp." The Lone Star Shop was donating magazines and newspapers to the camp, and the Sultana Buffet had donated over one hundred records for the camp phonograph.[119] A short time later, the camp was told they were leaving in October. "The town has been home to us," wrote one enrollee. Everyone has "been fine to us." It will "be hard to depart." We are "not anxious to leave."[120]

The last count of Company 3348 at F-28 showed 190 enrollees (all but 2 from Pennsylvania). Supervisors were two Army officers, a contract physician, a per diem physician, and an educational advisor. On October 12, 127 men started for their next camp, S-208, at Stryker, Montana. Two small groups were going to Winslow, and foreman Homer Moody and 10 men were to remain briefly at F-28 and then go to Nogales to form the nucleus of a new camp of enrollees.[121] According to researcher Putt, the company put in 10,751 man days, improving six springs, installing 1.5 miles of fencing, erecting three forest monuments, and building one landing dock and pier. A short time after arriving in Montana, enrollee J. Manusov wrote the *Williams News* to say their Montana camp was "an enrollee's dream of paradise, but the friendly atmosphere of the townsfolk of Williams, with whom we were friends, can never be forgotten…. We shall miss the coffee at Central Drug, our friends, and the girls we left behind."[122]

The CCC did not return to the Williams JD Dam camp. The country went to war, and for a time, CCC buildings and rolling equipment were to be used in case of mass evacuations.[123] It is unclear what ultimately happened to the F-28 buildings and much of the equipment. Typically, the Army and Navy put them to the war effort. Because the CCC companies were no longer the ever-present firefighters, some of those resources were converted to firefighting. At the Kaibab National Forest, seven CCC trucks were given to the Forest Service for fighting fires.[124] But the CCC and the New Deal were to have a lasting effect on the Kaibab. The economy of Williams was changing from grazing and timber to tourism. The CCC-built trails, roads, picnic areas, and lakes were a great help to that change. None of those recreational "improvements could have been developed as quickly or at such a bargain to the community without the labors of the CCC."[125]

Unless noted otherwise, any reference to the number of enrollees in a company, the location of the company, or company supervisors are from U.S. War Department, Location and Strength of CCC Companies, 1933–1942, NARAMD RG 35 530/65/22/04/05.

1. Connie Reid in her *History of the North Canyon Creek Fish Dams* correctly states that CCC involvement in North Canyon is unproven.
2. Audretsch, *Shaping the Park and Saving the Boys*, 51–57, 72.
3. Putt, *South Kaibab National Forest*, 176.
4. "340 Reforestation Workers Arrive Today," *Williams News*, May 26, 1933, 1, 5.
5. Moose et al., *People and Places of the Old Kaibab*, 52–53.
6. Rice, "Work of CCC Camp Adjacent to Williams," *Williams News*, May 1, 1936, 5.
7. Moose, "Memoirs of Clyde P. Moose," 43.
8. "Local News," *Williams News*, July 28, 1933, 5.
9. "Bellemont Forest Camp Entertains," *Coconino Sun*, August 11, 1933, 7.
10. *Happy Days*, September 16, 1933, 12; *Happy Days*, September 16, 1933, 14.
11. "Tusayan Camps to Be Moved Far to South," *Williams News*, October 6, 1933, 1.
12. "Personals," *Williams News*, October 13, 1933, 2; "Bellemont Briefs," *Williams News*, October 20, 1933, 4.
13. "CCC Contingent En Route to Camp," *Phoenix Gazette*, October 30, 1933, 1.
14. "Bellemont Briefs," *Williams News*, November 3, 1933, 6. "Civilian Conservation Corps Eighth Corps Area, Status Record of CCC Camps Authorized Since Inception of the Program up to … December 31, 1941 … Compiled by Office of Liaison Officer, CCC Fort Sam Houston…," NARACO BLM CCC Directories RG 49 Entry 33, 34 Box 132.
15. Examples include June 12, 1936, through October 15, 1936, and July 11, 1949, through October 10, 1940.
16. "Government Employment Camp near Here," *Williams News*, April 7, 1933, 1, 3.
17. "Road South Made Unemployment Project," *Williams News*, April 14, 1933, 1, 6.
18. "C. of C. Pleased over So. Road," *Williams News*, April 28, 1933, 1.
19. "340 Reforestation Workers Arrive Today," *Williams News*, May 26, 1933, 1, 5.
20. "Reforestation Camp Moves to Barney Flat," *Williams News*, June 2, 1933, 1, 5.
21. "Rotarians Told of CCC Program," *Williams News*, July 14, 1933, 1, 6.
22. "Veterans News and Whipple Items," *Prescott Evening Courier*, September 11, 1933, 8, and September 18, 1933, 2; Arizona Death Records, State File No. 339, Registered No. 186-H.
23. "Fish Dams Included in CCC Program," *Williams News*, September 22, 1933, 1, 2.
24. "CCC Boys Are Good Entertainers," *Williams News*, September 29, 1933, 6; "CCC Camp Terminates Enlistment Period," *Williams News*, September 29, 1933, 1, 6.
25. Putt, *South Kaibab National Forest*, 177.
26. "Farewell Given at Camp Boyce," *Williams News*, November 3, 1933, 1. Early in the CCC program, camps were encouraged to adopt local names, and F-28 and C. E. Boyce, the "daddy" of Williams, were chosen. Perhaps this naming system was confusing, since within a few years it was no longer popular.
27. "End of Unemployment Here Seen in President's New Work Order," *Williams News*, November 17, 1933, 1, 6.

28. Putt, *South Kaibab National Forest*, 177.
29. "Camp Opened by CCC Men," *Arizona Republic*, May 3, 1934, 2.
30. "CCC Company Now at Camp Boyce," *Williams News*, May 4, 1934, 1, 5.
31. "CCC Workers to Build Kennedy Dam Soon," *Williams News*, June 1, 1934, 1, 8; "Construction Started on Kennedy Dam," *Williams News*, June 8, 1934, 1; "A Start in the Right Direction," *Williams News*, June 8, 1934, 4.
32. Putt, *South Kaibab National Forest*, 178.
33. "Wms. Chosen for CCC District Headquarters," *Williams News*, June 15, 1934, 1.
34. "CCC Work Program Going Smoothly," *Williams News*, June 29, 1934, 1.
35. "Forest Fire Burns over 200 Acres," *Williams News*, June 15, 1934, 1.
36. Putt, *South Kaibab National Forest*, 179.
37. "Forest Service Engaged in Water Development," *Williams News*, June 29, 1934, 2.
38. "Waterworks Loan of $120,000 Approved," *Williams News*, July 6, 1934, 1, 8.
39. "Williams Moves for Reservoir," *Arizona Republic*, July 10, 1934, 2.
40. "Road to Dog Town Site Chosen Saturday July Seventh," *Williams News*, July 13, 1934, 1.
41. U.S. CCC, Camp Inspection Reports, NARAMD RG 35/530/65/23/04 Entry 115 (PI #11) Box 8.
42. "Flock from Far and Wide to Hear General Farley Talk," *Williams News*, July 20, 1934, 1, 7.
43. "Farley Is Welcomed to the County," *Coconino Sun*, July 20, 1934, 1, 2.
44. "Kennedy Dam Project Is Completed," *Williams News*, August 24, 1934, 1.
45. "Varied Program at Rotary-CCC," *Williams News*, September 28, 1934, 1, 8.
46. "Camp F-28-A Bids Williams Farewell," *Williams News*, October 26, 1934, 1.
47. Margaret Hangan, e-mail message to author, August 3, 2012.
48. Putt, *South Kaibab National Forest*, 179. See Camp Clover, National Register of Historic Places Registration Form Site Number AR-03-07-01-1008, Item No. 93000520.
49. "Officer's Bullets Halt Dash of Homesick Youth," *Williams News*, December 21, 1934, 1.
50. For a detailed look at misbehaving in the CCC at Grand Canyon, see Audretsch, *Shaping the Park and Saving the Boys*, 82–83.
51. "Williams to Ask for Two 3-C Camps," *Williams News*, January 4, 1935, 1; "Wms. May Get 2 More Recreational Lakes," *Williams News*, January 11, 1935, 1, 8.
52. "Williams to Get One CCC Camp," *Williams News*, May 5, 1935, 1.
53. "CCC Arrive on Thurs. Morning," *Williams News*, May 17, 1935, 1.
54. "CCC Does Excellent Work on Play Camps," *Williams News*, May 17, 1935, 8.
55. "CCC Camp Starts Work on South Road," *Williams News*, May 31, 1935, 1.
56. "South Road to Be Made 20 Feet Wide," *Williams News*, June 21, 1935, 1, 5.
57. "Mobile US Transient Camp to Construct Landing Fields," *Arizona Republic*, July 2, 1935, 5; "CCC to Take Transients," *Arizona Republic*, August 13, 1935, 4.
58. "Kaibab Forest Work to Be Started Soon," *Prescott Evening Courier*, August 5, 1945, 5.
59. "Kaibab to Receive Labor under Setup," *Williams News*, July 26, 1935, 1.
60. See www.ccclegacy.org/camps-texas.htm
61. Putt, *South Kaibab National Forest*, 181.
62. "West Cataract Dam May Be Built This Yr.," *Williams News*, January 31, 1936, 1, 4.
63. "First Contingent of CCC Workers Arrived Today," *Williams News*, April 24, 1936, 1.
64. Tracy W. Rice, "Work of CCC Camp Adjacent to Williams," *Williams News*, May 1, 1936, 5.
65. "Extensive Work Program for CCC Camp," *Williams News*, May 8, 1936, 1, 8.
66. "Camp Fire Results in Damaging Forest Blaze," *Williams News*, May 15, 1936, 1.
67. "Development Started at White Horse," *Williams News*, May 29, 1936, 1.
68. U.S. CCC, Camp Inspection Reports, NARAMD RG 35/530/65/23/04 Entry 115 (PI #11) Box 8.
69. "Volunteer Mountain Road Is Finished," *Williams News*, July 3, 1936, 1.
70. "Forest Fire Burns 8 Hundred Acres," *Williams News*, July 10, 1936, 1.
71. "Kaibab Forest to Erect New Tower," *Williams News*, July 17, 1936, 5.
72. Roger Zuniga, "CCC Current Camp Chatter," *Williams News*, July 24, 1936, 5.
73. Audretsch, *Shaping the Park and Saving the Boys*, 72.
74. "CCC Gives Program at Rotary Lunch," *Williams News*, July 31, 1936, 1, 8.
75. *Williams News*, September 17, 1936, 2.
76. U.S. CCC, Phoenix District, *Official Annual, 1936, Phoenix District, 8th Corps Area, Civilian Conservation Corps* ([Baton Rouge, LA?]: Direct Advertising Co., 1936), 82–83. GCNPMC Cat. #70738.

77. *Kaibab Kalendar,* October 1936, Fiche MN #1669, CRL Newspapers.
78. Mel Alsbury, "Currente Calamo Camp F-28-A," *Williams News,* October 1, 1936, 2.
79. "Rotarians Given Report CCC's Summer Work," *Williams News,* October 22, 1936, 4.
80. "15 Years Effort Ended in Triumph," *Williams News,* November 12, 1936, 1, 5; "Williams–Verde Valley Dist. Highway Dedicated," *Williams News,* November 12, 1936, 1, 8.
81. "Camp Boyce Remains Vacant This Summer," *Williams News,* April 27, 1937, 1.
82. "CCC Camp Now Assured for Wms.," *Williams News,* July 8, 1937, 1; "CCC Camp Is Now on Grounds," *Williams News,* July 29, 1937, 3.
83. Putt, *South Kaibab National Forest,* 182–183.
84. "Construction of Bill Williams Tower Begun," *Northern Yavapai Record* (Ash Fork), September 24, 1937, 2.
85. "Kaibab Erecting Stone Markers," *Northern Yavapai Record* (Ash Fork), October 4, 1937, 3.
86. Putt, *South Kaibab National Forest,* 183.
87. "Rotarians Hear about the Proposed Forest Projects," *Williams News,* April 28, 1938, 1, 8.
88. "CCC Boys to Arrive in Williams Saturday," *Williams News,* May 12, 1938, 1; Putt, *South Kaibab National Forest,* 183.
89. "135 CCC Boys Arrive at Camp near Williams," *Williams News,* May 26, 1938, 1.
90. "Shift of Local CCC Camp Is Announced," *Williams News,* June 30, 1938, 1.
91. "Proposed CCC Camp Change Set for Aug. 1st," *Williams News,* July 21, 1938, 1.
92. "Full CCC Camp Arrives on Tues. from Pa.," *Williams News,* August 4, 1938, 1.
93. "Conley Is Shot by Own Pistol," *Williams News,* August 11, 1938, 1.
94. "Drainage Structures Being Built on S. Road," *Williams News,* August 25, 1938, 1.
95. "CCC Camp to Move in Few Weeks," *Williams News,* September 22, 1938, 1.
96. Putt, *South Kaibab National Forest,* 184.
97. "CCC Camp to Move on the Twentieth," *Williams News,* October 13, 1938, 1.
98. Other projects listed were roads to the Sycamore Canyon Rim from Pine Flat and White Horse Lake; a few small camping developments along US Route 66; a foot of Kendrick Mountain campground; a road across Bull Basin on Kendrick Mountain; reconstruction of the road around Bill Williams Mountain; developing water for turkeys; and the Cataract Dam construction. Walter G. Mann, "Plan Recreational Area about Bill Wms.," *Williams News,* January 12, 1939, 1, 6.
99. "First CCC Boys to Arrive April 29," *Williams News,* April 27, 1939, 1.
100. "Main Body of CCC Camp Arrives Here," *Williams News,* May 18, 1939, 4.
101. "Fire Burns over 100 Acres of Grass Land," *Williams News,* July 20, 1939, 4.
102. Victor O. Sandberg, "CCC Recruits Undergo Training Period," *Williams News,* July 27, 1939, 5.
103. "Work on South Road to Start September First," *Williams News,* August 24, 1939, 1.
104. Putt, *South Kaibab National Forest,* 187.
105. Victor O. Sandberg, "Kaibab Forest Picnic Area Is Completed," *Williams News,* June 8, 1939, 1.
106. "Kaibab CCC Camp to Move Oct 24th," *Williams News,* October 12, 1939, 2.
107. Andrew Bobby, interview by Teri Cleeland, June 15, 1991, Kaibab National Forest, Williams, AZ.
108. Putt, *South Kaibab National Forest,* 183; Margaret Hangan, e-mail message to author, August 7, 2012.
109. For a detailed account of the Moqui Ranger Station construction and the puzzle of who built it, see Audretsch, *Shaping the Park and Saving the Boys,* 108.
110. "Advance Unit of 3-C's to Arrive on Saturday," *Williams News,* April 25, 1940, 1; "140 CCC Men Arrive Sunday," *Williams News,* May 9, 1940, 1.
111. U.S. CCC, Camp Inspection Reports, NARAMD RG 35/530/65/23/04 Box 6 Entry 115 (PI #11) Box 8.
112. J. Manusov, "F-28-A Camp Jottings," *Williams News,* July 8, 1940, 3.
113. J. Manusov, "Life in a Tent," *Williams News,* July 18, 1940, 5.
114. Merle Timblin, telephone conversation with author, August 18, 2012.
115. J. Manusov, "Life in a Tent," *Williams News,* July 25, 1940, 6.
116. J. Manusov, "Life in a Tent," *Williams News,* August 1, 1940, 1, 2.
117. J. Manusov, "Life in a Tent," *Williams News,* August 8, 1940, 2.
118. J. Manusov, "Life in a Tent," *Williams News,* August 15, 1940, 6; Arizona Death Notices, State File No. 60, Registrar's No. 17.
119. J. Manusov, "Life in a Tent," *Williams News,* September 12, 1940, 5.
120. J. Manusov, "Life in a Tent," *Williams News,* September 19, 1940, 6.
121. "Camp F28 (3348) to Be Abandoned," *Williams News,* October 10, 1940, 1.

122. Putt, *South Kaibab National Forest*, 187. Not all towns were as friendly to outsiders as Williams was. Andrew Bobby, CCC enrollee in Williams during the summer of 1939, was also stationed at Nogales and Pinetop. In a June 15, 1991, oral history interview done for the Kaibab National Forest, he said that in Pinetop people would not talk to enrollees, the girls were not allowed to talk to them, and it was very difficult to get a ride there hitchhiking. While at F-28, Bobby had a girlfriend in town and frequently traveled to Flagstaff and the Grand Canyon by hitchhiking. Williams was the friendliest town he was stationed in.
123. "CCC Camps to Be Evacuee Centers," *Williams News,* January 1, 1942, 2.
124. "Kaibab Conditioning Fire Trucks," *Williams News,* April 30, 1942, 2.
125. Putt, *South Kaibab National Forest*, 189.

CHAPTER 7

Prescott National Forest

THIS AUTHOR WAS NOT ABLE to locate any CCC work records of the Prescott National Forest in federal or state archives. So, nearly all we know about their work is from newspaper articles and camp inspection reports. As a result, this account of the CCC work in Prescott National Forest is necessarily incomplete.

The *Prescott Evening Courier* reported regularly about CCC work in Yavapai County, as well as CCC admissions and discharges at the Fort Whipple Veterans Hospital. The latter was the only federally funded facility for enrollees with serious injuries in northern Arizona. CCC admissions appear to have been significant at Fort Whipple, sometimes totaling as many as 12% of the total hospital admissions. The *Evening Courier* was editorially very much pro-CCC. During the nine-year CCC period, this author found nine editorials that appear to be of local creation. On April 6, 1933, even before any CCC camps were located in the state and the legislation was only a week old, the newspaper defended the CCC against critics. "Everyone should praise the president for his effective efforts toward an abatement of want ... delay is fatal to a starving man."[1] In November 1934, the newspaper noted the local economy benefited from the CCC. A few enrollees, they reported, had got into trouble, but "hundreds of others who toe the mark and are developing into strong manhood ... learning some particular vocation, providing support for their families, and performing work in which the public ... benefits. Indeed, there can be no cheaper or better social insurance than the CCC."[2]

In 1936, the newspaper defended the CCC against possible budget cuts: "Anyone who proposes to trim the federal budget by abolishing the forest army ought seriously to consider first how much it will cost the nation 50 years hence to abandon the CCC now."[3] In another 1936 editorial about the CCC educational program, the newspaper praised the work of teaching illiterate boys to read and write. The CCC was "amplifying democracy." "Here is an activity which is every bit as important as the forest conservation work, if not more so."[4] On April 7, 1937, the newspaper supported FDR's hopes for a permanent CCC. And in 1939, after reviewing the CCC sixth annual report, the newspaper declared the CCC "record is impressive and reveals fully how valuable a service this organization has given to the country. It has more than fulfilled its original promise and stands brilliantly outlined against our economic situation as an important contributing source. Let the good work go on."[5]

1933

Just a week after the CCC legislation was signed by the president, Prescott National Forest Assistant Supervisor L. J. Putsch was speaking about the program to the Prescott Kiwanis.[6] Two weeks later, the county was notified three CCC camps were coming to Yavapai County.[7] A week after that, the Forest Service was asking for bids on trucks for the CCC.[8] The following week, Groom Creek, Crown King, and Walnut Creek were stated to be the camp locations.[9] The same day, Forest Supervisor Frank Grubb was meeting with Major Pearl Thomas of Fort Sam Houston to look over camp locations.[10] The following week, Grubb was assisting in the intake of LEM applications, renting trucks, and hiring a clerical worker.[11] By May 22, Army staff was inspecting camp locations, some of the LEMs were being hired, and Grubb announced the Groom Creek and Walnut Creek camps would be "open soon."[12] Days before the first enrollees were to arrive, Forest Service staff were digging a well for the Walnut Creek camp (F-20). A water line was laid to the Groom Creek camp (F-18). Skeleton crews or Army cadre were setting up the camps. Forty-six LEMs were hired.[13]

The first arrivals were 107 enrollees from Fort Huachuca. Another 92 came from Yuma County on May 30, and 93 Yavapai County enrollees were to arrive on May 31.[14] By May 31, each camp was said to have 193 enrollees, but with supervisors and Army staff the total was 212 for each camp. F-18 was staffed by Company 820 and F-20 by Company 822.[15] F-18 was officially occupied on May 28 and F-20 on May 29.

On June 6 and 7, the local newspaper reported the Groom Creek enrollees had fought forest fires. On June 9, the Assistant Forest Supervisor spoke to the Prescott Rotary and summarized CCC work. He said major projects were twig blight eradication, road and trail building, tree thinning, and erosion control. The road from Hassayampa Trail to Quartz Mountain was started. However, two enrollees had already been discharged: one for inciting mutiny and the other for drunkenness."[16] Forest Supervisor Putsch reported Walnut Creek camp projects: reconstructing the

Camp Wood Road, and a spike camp at the Double-O range was doing prairie dog eradication, fence building, building stock tanks, and trail work.[17] On June 26, Forest Supervisor Grubb and Ranger C. E. McDuff were reported to be going to the Walnut Creek Ranger Station to locate a range fence to be built by CCC. A forest fire near Route 89 was extinguished by the Groom Creek CCC.[18] On June 27, the *Prescott Evening Courier* reported the county might get a CCC veterans camp. Water was being tested for a possible camp near Thumb Butte, but it might be known as Mingus Mountain.[19] On June 29, it was reported Groom Creek enrollees were sinking a well for the Thumb Butte camp. At the Walnut Creek Ranger Station, fourteen enrollees and twenty horses and mules were finishing a protective levee and were going to be building stock tanks.[20]

On July 6, Aldo Leopold, regional consulting forester, in charge of CCC erosion control work, arrived for a few days to inspect projects contemplated on the Prescott.[21] On July 12, 191 veterans arrived by special train from Oklahoma. The first group included 13 African American men. These Company 1823V men had already completed two weeks of conditioning while in Oklahoma. They went by truck from Prescott to Camp F-19, Thumb Butte.[22] Two days later, equipment for the removal of twig blight arrived at F-19.

On August 2, the Prescott newspaper summarized the CCC work. The Groom Creek camp had constructed .75 mile of the Quartz Mountain Road; were re-shaping the Senator Highway; had cleared 700 acres of twig blight; had built a new barn at Spruce Mountain Lookout; were half-done with the Mount Union Lookout; and had fought six forest fires. The Thumb Butte camp had constructed .2 mile of the Thumb Butte Road; constructed 1.75 miles of telephone line; done 11.5 acres of timber stand improvement; done trail work on Quartz Mountain Road and the Indian Creek trail; and performed 20 acres of timber stand improvement. The Walnut Creek camp had improved the Camp Wood Road; done Cottonwood Mountain trail work; began the Williamson Valley–Hyde Creek drift fence; prepared the Prescott–Walnut Creek telephone line; completed the Walnut Creek Ranger Station protective levee and completed the new stock tank; and done prairie dog eradication north of the ranger station.[23]

The August 4 *Prescott Evening Courier* reported that Capt. E. B. Jolley was the Groom Creek medical officer. A few days later, it reported that the two shallow wells (12′ and 23′) at the Thumb Butte camp had gone dry, and the camp was purchasing four thousand to five thousand gallons of water daily from the city.[24] In August, the Walnut Creek camp was poisoning prairie dogs in the area south of the Iron Mine divide three miles from the Double O Ranch on Turkey Creek.[25]

On August 19, the Prescott newspaper reported that Walnut Creek enrollee George Marable was near death after being shot at a private residence where he had allegedly gone to steal alcohol. Marable and two other enrollees were said to have taken a CCC truck on official business, but instead went drinking. Marable (also spelled Marrable) was alleged to have a past history of thefts in Yuma and was a suspect in Walnut Camp thefts. He was taken to the Fort Whipple Veterans Hospital, where he convalesced for some weeks.[26] Marable's condition gradually improved; however, the September 24 newspaper reported "Marable Faces Cripple's Life." It is unclear if he was charged for any legal infractions. R. B. Allison, his alleged assailant, was bound over for trial on assault charges, but his fate is unknown.

On August 25, the Groom Creek camp had treated 1,300 acres for twig blight.[27] The Walnut Creek camp was contemplating a new spike camp for fence construction, possibly near the sawmill on Camp Wood Road.[28] On August 31, Camp F-18 (Company 820) reported 180 Arizona enrollees (with 1 African American), with four Army officers (including a medical officer) and four Army enlisted men. Camp F-19 (Company 1823V) reported a total of 173 men (nearly all from Oklahoma, with 16 African Americans). Their supervisors were four Army officers (including a medical officer) and three enlisted men. Camp F-20 (Company 822) had a total of 187 enrollees (all from Arizona, with 2 African Americans). Their supervisors were four Army officers (including a medical officer) and two enlisted men.

On September 6, the *Prescott Evening Courier* editorialized "Aid Needed in Fight to Save Trees," saying more help was needed eradicating twig blight. They reported that the Yavapai County Chamber of Commerce and the Public Welfare Board had requested more CCC aid. Five days later, the newspaper reported the city police court looked like "CCC Day," as two Grand Canyon area enrollees, a Thumb Butte enrollee, and a Groom Creek enrollee were charged with intoxication. In September, the newspaper announced 160 PWA men would also be doing twig blight eradication.[29] Also in September, it announced two of the Prescott camps would be moving for the winter. The Walnut Creek enrollees were going to Turkey Creek, and the Groom Creek men were going to Verde No. 1 at the junction of the Verde River and Oak Creek. The digging of wells for both camps had begun.[30] On September 29, Capt. Wiley Adams, the Thumb Butte camp commanding officer, charged he had broken a crime ring at the camp that was stealing blankets, clothing, and shoes and reselling them in Prescott. He said some would be discharged when their present enlistment ended.[31]

On September 30, Camp F-18 (Company 820) reported 131 Arizona enrollees. Camp F-19 (Company 1823V) reported a total of 91 men (nearly all from Oklahoma, with 5 African Americans). Camp F-20 (Company 822) had a total of 155 enrollees (all from Arizona, with 2 African Americans).

In early October, it was announced that Company 1823V would be moving to Texas about December 1.[32] A few days later, Forest Supervisor Grubb said 370 men were engaged in twig blight control: 250 NRA, 100 Groom Creek camp, and 20 Thumb Butte camp.[33] The next day, the Prescott newspaper reported Grubb, medical officer Major Williams, and Lieutenant Nelson of Flagstaff were inspecting the Turkey Creek area for CCC camp sites.[34] On October 17, the newspaper announced the county was looking for 100 young men to sign up for CCC work. Miss Grace M. Sparkes, official of the County Welfare Board, was quoted: "Due to the fact that the Grand Canyon camp men come in contact with tourists from all parts of the world, higher qualifications for these men are required than for other camps in the country."[35] The prospective enrollees were to be given a physical exam at the Fort Whipple Veterans Hospital and then go by train to the canyon. On October 23, the newspaper reported 88 men left to the "crack CCC camp at the Grand Canyon."[36] On October 25 and 26, the newspaper reported officials were still inspecting Turkey Creek as a possible site for the Walnut Creek enrollees to move to for the winter. A Mayer citizens group offered to lease land there for the CCC camp, leaving the decision up in the air.[37] On October 30, the new camp site was approved on leased land near Mayer.[38]

On October 31, Camp F-18 (Company 820) reported 203 enrollees (nearly all from Arizona and 20 from Texas). Camp F-19 (Company 1823V) reported a total of 193 men (from Oklahoma, Texas, and Arizona, with 9 African Americans). Camp F-20 (Company 822) had a total of 200 enrollees (nearly all from Arizona, with 5 African Americans).

Twig blight work was proceeding well, and on November 4, the Prescott newspaper reported the Groom Creek camp had completed over five thousand acres. On November 16, the newspaper reported that Forest Supervisor Grubb and Ranger McDuff were going to the Walnut Grove district to look into the possibility of stock tanks to be built by CCC.[39] On November 28, Groom Creek (F-18) CCC equipment was being moved to Verde No. 1 (F-39), where preliminary work project plans were fences, erosion control, and road work.[40]

On November 30, Camp F-18 (Company 820) reported 196 enrollees (nearly all from Arizona, with 18 from Texas and 3 African Americans). Camp F-19 (Company 1823V) reported a total of 170 men (from Oklahoma, Texas, and Arizona, with 9 African Americans). Camp F-20 (Company 822) had a total of 188 enrollees (nearly all from Arizona, with 6 African Americans).

On December 1, Company 1823V enrollees and staff boarded a train for Camp S-26 at Camp Abilene, Texas.[41] During their stay in Arizona, Company 1823V enrollees had been frequently in the newspaper for run-ins with the law. The December 4 newspaper reported that the Police Court during November "floated" twenty-two men to Captain Adams, 1823V company commander, and seven were still serving time in jail, six had been turned over to county authorities, seven had received suspended sentences, and fifteen paid fines totaling $201.

On December 4, Company 822 moved from Walnut Creek (F-20) to Mayer (F-33), and Company 820 moved from Groom Creek (F-18) to Verde No. 1 (F-39). On December 7, Supervisor Grubb reported one hundred enrollees were working on the new Paradise-Verde Dam. Eighteen Mayer camp men were returning to the Double-O Water Tank project southeast of Seligman started by the Walnut Creek camp, and three hundred CWA men were doing twig blight work.[42] On December 11, the newspaper reported some of the Mayer enrollees were "building corrals six miles out."[43]

1934

On January 13, Rangers McDuff and W. G. Koogler from the Forest Service Regional Office were at the Mayer CCC camp to inspect the work on the Shew Stock Tank on Hassayampa River near Walnut Grove.[44] Other Mayer projects were the cut-off to Crown King from Black Canyon Road to Cleator (sixty enrollees); the Pine Flat Stock Tank (twenty-two enrollees); and soil erosion control work (fifty enrollees).[45]

On January 31, Camp F-33, Mayer (Company 822) reported 188 enrollees (all but 4 from Arizona, with 5 African Americans). Camp F-39, Verde No. 1 (Company 820) reported 197 enrollees (all but 15 from Texas, with 4 African Americans).

In early February, the Prescott newspaper reported the Mayer CCC camp was expected to finish the Cedar Canyon Earth Tank west of Mayer by February 15 and was doing erosion control work on Mayer Flats and road work between Black Canyon Highway and Cleator.[46] On February 10, the Mayer camp reported 250 people at a recent CCC dance. Music was by Leonard Ross and the Rhythm Rustlers.[47] On March 20, the newspaper reported Forest Supervisor Grubb was working on CCC work programs for three camps starting about May 15. He expected camps at Thumb Butte, Groom Creek, and Lynx Creek, with the main work to be twig blight control.[48]

On April 9, the Mayer camp had nearly finished building the bridge across Turkey Creek between Black Canyon Highway and Crown King.[49] On April 24, the Yavapai County Chamber of Commerce sponsored a party for five area CCC camps (Sedona, Mayer, Beaver Creek, Verde No. 1, and Cottonwood) and guests at Verde No. 1. The program included a baseball game, a concert, a singing program, an open-air concert, speeches, and a dance. Attendance was said to be large.⁵⁰ On the same day, the Prescott newspaper reported on the area CCC work, quoting Forest Supervisor Grubb: the Verde Valley camps since July 1933 had completed 8,000 acres of twig blight eradication; 40,320 acres of prairie dog eradication; 47 miles of fence; sixteen cattleguards; ten stock tanks; 37,000 check dams; 745 acres of erosion control; 40.5 miles of road construction; 13 miles of trails construction; four bridges; two lookout towers; and 6 miles of telephone line construction.⁵¹

Figure 21. Increasing Height Check Dam Hayfield Draw, Work by Verde Camp, 1934. Photograph by F. L. Kirby. Courtesy U.S. Forest Service, Southwestern Regional Office, #288162.

On May 1, Company 820 moved back to F-18, Groom Creek; Company 822 moved back to F-19, Thumb Butte; and Company 860 moved from F-32, Clarkdale, in the Coconino National Forest to F-62, Lynx Creek, a new Prescott camp. On May 15, the Prescott newspaper reported that Groom Creek enrollees were staffing Spruce Mountain Lookout.⁵² On May 21, the *Arizona Republic* reported 150 CCC enrollees from Groom Creek and Lynx Creek near Crown King were in the Bradshaw Mountains fighting fires. On May 22, the same newspaper reported that 336 CCC men from Thumb Butte, Lynx Creek, and Groom Creek were fighting a Prescott National Forest fire.

On June 2, the Prescott newspaper reported the death of Lynx Creek laborer Rufus L. Thomas, 30, in an auto accident on June 1.⁵³ On June 12, it reported a CCC spike camp for tanking that was established north of Jerome by the Groom Creek camp.⁵⁴ On July 5, two of the vacant F-39, Verde No. 1, buildings were reported consumed by fire.⁵⁵

Special Investigator James C. Reddoch inspected F-18, Groom Creek, and noted no serious problems on July 14. Their work was listed as twig blight eradication and water tank construction.⁵⁶ Reddoch inspected F-19, Thumb Butte, the same day and noted the work to be twig blight eradication, road construction, and rodent control. His report noted: "Neither the 'Camp Spark' nor any other Communistic publications being received."⁵⁷ He also inspected F-62, Lynx Creek, and reported work to be twig blight eradication, road and cattle guard construction, recreations sets, and telephone line construction.⁵⁸

On August 15, Forest Supervisor Grubb was inspecting CCC work of a .75-mile road from Middleton to the Swastika Mine.⁵⁹ On August 23, Capt. John S. Mulligan took over as Groom Creek commanding officer, replacing Capt. George Bergfield, who was returning to civilian life. Capt. William G. Kneeland was the new commander at the Lynx Creek camp, replacing Capt. Fred Calkins, who also was returning to civilian life.⁶⁰ The following day, the Prescott newspaper reported that NIRA crews were finishing recreation improvements such as picnic tables and toilets at the Indian Creek recreation area where the CCC had earlier built erosion control walls. The CCC was completing similar improvements at Wolf Creek as well as a gravity water system.⁶¹

On August 31, Camp F-18, Groom Creek (Company 820) reported 185 enrollees (32 from Texas and 153 from Arizona, with 6 African Americans). Camp F-19, Thumb Butte (Company 822) reported 141 enrollees (83 from Arizona and 58 from Texas, with 13 African Americans). Camp F-62, Lynx Creek (Company 860) reported 152 enrollees (124 from Arizona and 28 from Texas, with 11 African Americans).

On September 5, the *Prescott Evening Courier* reported a "CCC crew has just finished construction of a stock tank at Jack Stanley's Coyote ranch in Lonesome Valley and is moving to King's canyon to build another."⁶² Less than three weeks later, the newspaper reported: "A 60-foot steel lookout tower for Mingus mountain is due to arrive here toward the end of this week. It will be erected by a CCC crew from Lynx Creek and will replace an obsolete 30' wooden tower there has been in use a number of years."⁶³ On September 28, the newspaper reported Forest Supervisor Grubb and Lynx Creek Project Superintendent Cecil Overstreet were inspecting the work of the Lynx Creek spike camp at Mingus Mountain. The projects were the construction of the recreation area and its surrounding fence and a lookout tower.⁶⁴

In early October, the *Prescott Evening Courier* reported that a CCC camp would be located at the Johnson Wash Ranger Station that winter to improve parks, put in public wells, clean underbrush, and develop water as needed.⁶⁵ In mid-October, Forest Service rangers and two CCC twig blight crews brought

Figure 22. Juniper Crib Check Dams, by Walnut Creek CCC Camp F-20-A, 1933. Photograph by W. G. Koogler. Courtesy U.S. Forest Service, Southwestern Regional Office, #283278.

a fire under control north of the Golden Eagle Mine.66 The same day, the newspaper reported that more than half the city arrests in September were members of the CCC and transient camps.67 On October 29, Company 822 moved from Thumb Butte (F-19) to Mayer (F-33).

On October 31, Camp F-18, Groom Creek (Company 820) reported 198 enrollees (23 from Texas and 175 from Arizona, with 7 African Americans). Camp supervisors were four Army officers, including a medical officer and an educational advisor. Camp F-33, Mayer (Company 822) reported 174 enrollees (91 from Arizona and 83 from Texas, with 16 African Americans). Camp supervisors were three Army officers, including a medical officer. Camp F-62, Lynx Creek (Company 860) reported 177 enrollees (87 from Arizona and 90 from Texas, with 10 African Americans). Camp supervisors were three Army officers, including a medical officer.

On November 5, Company 820 moved from Groom Creek to Verde No. 1 (F-39), and Company 860 left Lynx Creek for the Coconino NF (F-32), Clarkdale. By November 8, the new 60' steel fire tower on Mingus Mountain was finished by the Lynx Creek camp.68 On November 9, the Mayer camp was said to be less than two weeks away from completing the road in Camp Wood, cutting grades from 15% to 6% over the divide. When the Mayer enrollees finished, they were to be transferred to Crazy Basin to complete the road unfinished from last summer from the Black Canyon Highway to Crown King.69 On November 12, the Mayer camp had 190 enrollees, but 65 were at spike camps at Thumb Butte and the Camp Wood Road. Their work was said to include building and rebuilding roads, erecting fences, and erosion control work.70 In November, the Forest Service indicated the development of recreational facilities at Powell Springs near Cherry was to be a priority project for CCC Camp Verde No. 1. Plans called for ten fireplaces, concrete tables, toilets, and a well.71 On November 30, the Forest Service announced the Mayer camp enrollees would begin work in a week on the Crown King Ranger Station and outbuilding. The latter was to be frame construction, with the ranger station to be five rooms of stone.72

According to the December 1934 *Tiger Rag*, the camp newspaper of Verde No. 1, the camp's work was to be fences, including the Lang Excluded Area and Wolf Creek area fences. The work of the winter camp was mainly soil erosion control dams, cattle tanks, and building roads and trails.73 On December 15, at the Cleator spike camp of F-33, Mayer, Thomas A. Spencer, 40, died of a heart attack.74 On December 22, the Prescott newspaper reported Elbert Malone, an enrollee at NP-3 at the bottom of Grand Canyon, was brought out of the canyon by mule litter, then sent by ambulance from the canyon to the Fort Whipple Veterans Hospital for treatment of appendicitis.75

1935

January did not begin on a positive note, as enrollee Edward W. Rucker, 18, died at Fort Whipple Veterans Hospital. He had been hospitalized for fifteen days and died from pneumonia and other complications.

On January 31, Company 820 at Verde No. 1 (F-39) reported 193 enrollees (152 from Arizona and 41 from Texas, with 7 African Americans). Company 822 at Mayer (F-33) reported 183 (114 from Arizona and 69 from Texas, with 13 African Americans).

On February 19, the Prescott newspaper reported erosion control work by the CCC near Mayer and south of Cottonwood using five thousand plants from the CCC unit at Boyce Thompson Arboretum.76 According to the January 1935 *Tiger Rag*, after completion of the Black Canyon fence, the Cherry Creek fence work would begin. After that, work on fences around the Forest Preserve near Ash Fork would begin when a spike camp was established.77

On March 9, Special Investigator Reddoch visited Verde No. 1 and noted work projects in road construction, trails, fences, reservoirs, and erosion control.78 On March 12, Reddoch inspected the Mayer camp and found no major problems. He summarized the work as road construction and maintenance, bridge construction, stock tank construction, erosion control, and ranger station construction.[79] On April 16, the Prescott newspaper reported that Ranger John C. McNelty and a group of Mayer enrollees had put out a fifteen-acre lightning fire southwest of Bolada.[80]

With the arrival of summer weather, Prescott National Forest welcomed three CCC companies. On May 15, Company 820 returned to Camp F-18, Groom Creek. On May 19, Company 822 returned to F-19, Thumb Butte, and Company 860 went to F-62, Lynx Creek. On May 17, the Prescott newspaper reported that CCC boys were manning Spruce Mountain Lookout.

On June 12, Jack W. Burnett, 19, an F-18 enrollee from Texas, died at Beaumont Hospital in El Paso.[81] The cause of his death and reason for being in El Paso is unknown.

On June 30, Company 820, Groom Creek (F-18, 7 miles southeast of Prescott) reported 196 enrollees (almost evenly divided between those from Arizona and from Texas, with 1 African American). Thumb Butte Company 822 (F-19, 4.5 miles west of Prescott) reported 191 enrollees (168 from Arizona and the remainder from Texas, with 9 African Americans). Lynx Creek Company 860 (F-62, 12.9 miles southeast of Prescott) reported 183 enrollees (131 from Texas and the rest from Arizona, with 6 African Americans).

On July 1, the Phoenix newspaper reported that a 320-acre fire near Bolada was contained by two hundred enrollees called in from three camps.[82] On July 9, the *Prescott Evening Courier* (page 2) reported that a CCC foreman was being treated for a burned foot after he and six enrollees put out a small forest fire. They had been called away from their job poisoning prairie dogs. Just three days later, the Phoenix newspaper reported William H. Jahnke, Thumb Butte enrollee, fell about twenty feet while working and was admitted to the Fort Whipple Veterans Hospital (he may have been doing twig blight eradication.).[83]

About this time, Prescott was one of three host cities for a nine-game, two-day CCC baseball tournament. Teams involved included Petrified Forest, Kingman, Mormon Lake, Schultz Pass, and Indian Gardens.[84] In mid-July, 115 Groom Creek and Thumb Butte enrollees with National Forest officers were reported fighting twelve lightning-caused fires.[85] During July and August, the Prescott camps fought numerous small forest fires, which are typical during the Arizona monsoon season.

On August 24, the Prescott newspaper reported a "grand and glorious program" when the county chamber of commerce brought a program of music and artists to the Lynx Creek camp.[86] At the end of this month, two enrollees (one from Groom Creek) were admitted to the Fort Whipple Veterans Hospital for injuries after falling from trees, apparently doing twig blight work.[87]

In early September, E. R. Seivers, a regional Forest Service engineer from Albuquerque, arrived with two enrollees "to begin locating and checking up on lookout towers and other triangulation points" with the assistance of four Thumb Butte enrollees, with work estimated at one month.[88] On September 14, Thumb Butte enrollee Gordon Ford, 18, reported to the camp physician with acute tonsillitis. He was transferred to the Fort Whipple Veterans Hospital immediately. His condition worsened, and he died of pneumonia on October 5, 1935.[89]

On October 3, the *Prescott Evening Courier* reported on CCC work, stating that thirty thousand acres were affected by blight. Two hundred enrollees from all three area camps were doing eradication work. The Groom Creek had a spike camp of twenty-three converting the old narrow gauge railroad ten miles out of Jerome into an auto road and building two stock tanks, including one on the Perkins Cattle Company range. At Indian Creek, a spike camp of twenty was improving the recreation area with toilets and garbage pits. The Thumb Butte work included prairie dog eradication in the north part of Walnut Creek south of Seligman. The Crown King spike camp was building the ranger station barn and improving the road between Crown King and the Black Canyon Highway. The Lynx Creek camp had a Mingus Mountain crew of twenty doing recreational improvements, reconstructing the telephone line to Mingus Mountain Lookout, and doing maintenance work on the tower cabin. Their principal job was reported to be a dirt dam at the mountaintop.[90] On October 21, F-62, Lynx Creek was shut down for the winter. The destination of Company 860 is uncertain. On October 22, Company 820 vacated F-18, Groom Creek; its destination is also unknown.

On November 3, Company 822 moved from Thumb Butte back to F-33, Mayer.[91] Special Investigator Reddoch inspected Company 822 and found no major problems on November 19. He summarized their work as road construction and maintenance, fence construction, spring development, and stock tank construction.[92]

In December, the Prescott newspaper reported that the National Forest would be using occupants of the transient camps for twig blight eradication, doing work similar to the CCC. The initial four transient camps (including Prescott) started with 250 men working; eventually, the Prescott camp housed, fed, and worked a total of 600 men.[93]

On December 16, enrollee Thomas A. Spencer, 40, of the Cleator (or Crazy Basin) spike camp died after drinking a pint of alcohol. Death was due to acute dilatation of the heart, according to Medical Corps officer Lt. E. B. Jolley.[94]

In December 1935, Company 822's camp newspaper summarized the work projects, saying the camp had spike camps in three locations. At Crown King, enrollees were constructing buildings and doing landscaping, digging a 35′ well, and putting in pipelines. Road work on the Senator–Horsethief Road was to follow. At Cleator, an average of forty-five men were rebuilding the old Crown King Railroad into a motor road. The work involved large fills and concrete bridges with a Caterpillar, a power-controlled grader, and several compressors and jackhammers. At Thumb Butte, enrollees completed the Indian Creek Recreation Area and started building the Granite Basin Road and improving the Willow Creek Ranger Station.[95] On December 31, Company 822, Mayer, reported 184 enrollees (51 from Texas and the rest from Arizona, with 12 African Americans).

1936

On January 18, the *Prescott Evening Courier* (page two) reported eight Mayer camp enrollees were attending Prescott Business College, going to night classes three days a week. Also in January, the newspaper reported on fire losses by the Prescott National Forest. Acreage burnt in 1935 was 356 acres, compared to the 1934 loss of 1,103 acres. Much of the reduction was credited to CCC firefighting efforts.[96] J. C. Nave, Prescott National Forest Supervisor, was inspecting CCC work in January, including the Cleator to Crown King Road.[97]

On February 15, the Prescott newspaper (page 3) reported that Mayer Army Commander Lt. John Janak was being replaced by Capt. Scott Duncan. On March 30, the newspaper reported (page 3) that Duncan was being transferred to Petrified Forest and being replaced by Lt. X. C. Nemeck. During April, Dr. Jolley was reported as joining the staff of the Jerome Phelps Dodge Hospital and no longer a member of the CCC.[98]

During April, the Prescott National Forest reported the three-year summary of local CCC work. Supervisor Nave stated that the twig blight eradication was "the most important activity" of the camps. He said the blight was first recorded in 1917, and so far 24,000 acres had been treated. The six local camps had constructed six miles of telephone line and reconditioned five miles. They had constructed new fire lookout towers at Mingus Mountain, Towers Mountain, and Mount Union, replacing obsolete wooden ones. Recreational development had occurred through spike camps at Wolf Creek, Indian Creek, and Mingus Mountain. Winter work included erosion control, treating 800 acres with 3,190 dams. Two springs had been developed, sixty-one miles of fence erected, and six stock tanks constructed. Road work included sixty-four miles constructed, with eight new bridges, and five miles repaired, including the Crown King and Horse Thief Basin Roads as well as eight miles of the road to Camp Wood. The Crown King Ranger Station was developed. Recreation development was completed at Powell Springs at Cherry, and a total of ninety forest fires were fought.[99] The Mayer CCC camp was to remain through the summer, with projects including twig blight eradication and road construction near Crown King.[100]

Figure 23. New Crown King Ranger Station Dwelling Built by the CCC, 1936. Photograph by R. H. Lewis. Courtesy U.S. Forest Service, Southwestern Regional Office, #360419.

In late April, work began on a new CCC camp site at the Fairgrounds, including moving out the transient camp. Equipment housed there would be moved to the Wolf Creek transient camp.[101] Fairgrounds buildings used for the transient camp were said to be modified for CCC enrollees, as 160 enrollees from Yuma were expected soon.[102]

On May 5, Company 835 arrived from BR-13, Yuma, to F-19 (Fairgrounds, formerly Thumb Butte camp) and consisted of 157 officers and men.[103] On May 16, Company 2855 left F-46, Stockton Pass, near Willcox and arrived at F-62, Lynx Creek. The same day, Company 2870 left F-47, Turkey Creek, near Willcox and arrived at F-18, Groom Creek. Just three days before their arrival, the Prescott newspaper (page 2) reported that soon 925 men would be doing twig blight work. A total of eight CCC camps were to join the fight in the Coconino, Prescott, Tonto, and Sitgreaves National Forests.[104] In the Prescott hopes were high. "We're at last heading off the blight," said Assistant Forest Supervisor McNelty. They anticipated 750 enrollees treating 30,000 acres by fall. The Lynx Creek, Fairgrounds, and Groom Creek camps were almost exclusively doing blight work. The Mayer camp would have spike camps at Lynx Creek and Horse Thief Basin doing recreational improvements.[105]

Special Investigator A. W. Stockman inspected F-33, Mayer, on June 12. "Enrollees seemed a happy lot," he wrote. "At other camps I had enrollees ask me whether it would be possible to be transferred to 'Mayer Camp.'" Stockman credited much of the positive atmosphere to the Mayer community, about 200, who extended hospitality to enrollees in every way. Enrollees used the community swimming pool freely and kept it clean. In the prevailing spirit, a number of enrollees on their Saturday day off repaired the town main street. The company had a spike camp at Horsethief Basin, thirty-nine miles away.[106]

Stockman inspected the Fairgrounds camp (F-19) on June 16 and summarized its work as twig blight eradication, truck trail construction, public campground development, and fire suppression work. Its buildings were still in the process of rehabilitation from the previous use as a transient camp. Some of the former stables were being converted to CCC use. Its barracks was a building 40 x 240'. Morale was "enthusiastic."[107]

The following day, Stockman inspected the Groom Creek camp (F-18), where he noted cooperation between all company members. Enrollees were living in thirty-five pyramid tents, along with some frame buildings. Work was twig blight eradication (ten thousand acres) and fire pre-suppression and suppression.[108]

He inspected F-62, Lynx Creek, on June 18 and reported "splendid" cooperation between the Army and the Forest Service. The enrollees were also living in pyramid tents on platforms, with some wooden buildings for purposes such as storerooms, latrine, workshops, and the kitchen. He reported their work as twig blight eradication (twenty thousand acres) and fire pre-suppression and suppression. He reported 169 enrollees in camp and another 63 in a spike camp at the same site. He noted complaints that enrollees wanted more than one weekly liberty trip to Prescott and that water conservation did not allow as many showers as they wanted.[109]

On June 24, the Prescott newspaper had a lengthy article about three men who were formerly enrollees but were now leaders at F-19, Fairgrounds. The company commander was Lt. George W. Tyson, who enrolled on November 8, 1934. The camp project superintendent, John C. Britt, first enrolled at Prescott on January 3, 1934. The camp educational advisor, Robert M. Wallace, enrolled at Fort Huachuca on October 22, 1933. "If the enrollee has the ability and is willing to apply himself, the sky is the limit," said Wallace.[110] Details of the Fairgrounds camp were revealed in another lengthy article in the same newspaper. Their main work was twig blight eradication along White Spar Road. A group of twenty-five enrollees would soon finish road construction on the Granite Basin Road and then do recreational work in the Prescott National Forest. The enrollees were proud of their recreation hall with many taxidermy specimens.[111]

July was positive for the Fairgrounds camp, as the Prescott newspaper reported on July 20 that they won the regional baseball championship by beating NP-4, Grand Canyon. The same month, the camp newspaper reported on work accomplished, stating that their recreation area work included Mingus Mountain, Wolf Creek, Indian Creek, Cherry Creek, Granite Basin, and Horse Thief Basin.[112] On July 17, the Prescott newspaper reported a small group of WPA men were starting work on the Granite Basin Dam.[113]

Enrollee work was praised in an August newspaper article featuring Project Superintendent C. B. Morrill. After three and a quarter years, enrollee accomplishments included construction of 40 miles of road (including 3.5 miles into Granite Basin and 1 mile into the Indian Creek recreational area); construction of eleven bridges (two were 115' long and 40' high); construction of four recreational areas; building of seven stock tanks; development of fifteen wells and springs; construction of 100 miles of fence; and extinguishment of 250 fires. "Crown King ranger station, consisting of dwelling, office and barn, built of stone, and the well and water system, were all constructed by the CCC. This is considered one of the finest ranger stations in the country." He revealed that a large part of four thousand acres of twig blight had been treated as much as four times.[114]

In September, the Fairgrounds camp newspaper reported that over one thousand acres had been treated for twig blight during the month. Enrollees were working on the Granite Basin Road and the Groom Creek Cut-off Road.[115] Also in September, the local newspaper interviewed F-19 Educational Advisor Jason Greer. The article listed the educational courses offered, both general and occupational. Recreational trips included a five-truck convoy to Grand Canyon, and many sports were offered. The library had over five hundred books, lectures and religious talks were held weekly, and individual guidance and counseling was offered.[116]

The *Official Annual* in September listed Company 2870 (F-18) supervisors as Lt. Stanley L. Stewart, commanding officer; Lt. S. M. Walker, exchange officer; Lt. Edward M. Lipan, camp surgeon; and Dan C. Best, project superintendent. Company 835 (F-19) supervisors were Lt. Richard F. Hardin, commanding officer; Lt. William T. Brian, second in command; Lt. David Epstein, camp surgeon; Robert M. Wallace, educational advisor; and C. B. Merrill, project superintendent. Company 822 (F-33) supervisors were Lt. Francis L. Nemeck, commander; Lt. Stanley J. Reed, exchange officer; Dr. Bayard Neff, camp surgeon; Milton C. Haffa, educational advisor; and James Cheek, project superintendent. Company 2855 (F-62) supervisors were Lt. Philip J. Mehle, commanding officer; Lt. Willis J. McNabb, exchange officer; Lt. Harvey C. Baldwin, camp surgeon; Jack A. Thompson, educational advisor; and J. P. Sweet, project superintendent.[117]

The October 1 *Phoenix Evening Courier* reported the Fairgrounds (F-19) baseball team ended the season as Phoenix District champ with a 21-5 record. Orders for CCC companies to move were reported in early October, with only the Mayer camp to remain through the winter, where it was to work on recreational areas at Horse Thief Basin and Granite Basin, building roads, and doing Mayer-area range improvements.[118] On October 29, Company 2855 moved from F-62, Lynx Creek, to F-46, Stockton Pass, and Company 2870 moved from F-18, Groom Creek, to F-49, Turkey Creek. Company 835 (F-19, Fairgrounds) moved to BR-23, Yuma, on November 2, 1936.

In November, the Forest Service regional forester reported that twig blight in the Prescott National Forest had grown from 5,500 acres in 1917 to over 50,000 acres in the ponderosa in 1936. So far, enrollees had treated over 40,000 acres in the Prescott. He was quoted optimistically as saying the blight was "slowly but surely giving way before the efforts of hundreds of CCC boys."[119] At the end of the year, the Mayer camp had only forty men in camp, as many enrollees were on leave for the holidays.

1937

January 1937 began one of the worst winters northern Arizona had ever seen. Unprecedented heavy snow stranded people, with the CCC frequently coming to their rescue. (See chapter 1, *CCC to The Rescue!*). In Yavapai County, the Mayer camp pitched in to feed grain to quail. Initially, enrollees put out two thousand pounds of grain at 110 locations in mid-January. A week later, the *Prescott Evening Courier* reported they were distributing seven thousand pounds of grain, enough to keep sixty enrollees busy for a week.[120] The Mayer boys were also plowing the roads of snow.[121] In early February, the Prescott newspaper reported the water line to Mayer from Grapevine Springs had burst for two miles and that CCC camp officers offered the owner of the waterworks twenty-five CCC boys to assist with the burst pipes.[122]

By March, snows had diminished enough to begin the summer season work planning. J. C. Nave, forest supervisor, inspected three new wooden buildings under construction at Horse Thief Basin, a future spike camp of the Mayer camp.[123] By March 18, the Prescott newspaper reported enrollees were doing twig blight eradication work. On March 31, the public was invited to a CCC anniversary party at Horse Thief Basin, where the Mayer camp was hosting a barbecue. The county chamber of commerce was sponsoring a touraide, with the Forest Service supplying two mechanics at the tour rear for minor car repairs.[124] The April 4 barbecue was a huge success, with five hundred attending and three hundred coming via the touraide.[125]

Figure 24. Shelter on Horsethief Basin Campground, 1937. Photograph by R. King. Courtesy U.S. Forest Service, Southwestern Regional Office, #349804.

In late April, Foxworth-Galbraith Lumber Co. received the contract for lumber to rehab the CCC camps at F-19, Thumb Butte; F-18, Groom Creek; and F-62, Lynx Creek, that were to be occupied in the summer.[126] About the same time, an advance contingent of three truckloads of enrollees arrived to prepare the camps for the arrival of enrollees expected in mid-May.[127] On Sunday, May 16, the first enrollees arrived via a special Santa Fe train. Company 2847 departed camp F-64, Pena Blanca, and occupied F-18, Groom Creek, and Company 2861 departed camp SP-6, Manville Wells, and occupied F-62, Lynx Creek. On May 22, Company 822 moved from the Mayer camp to F-19, Thumb Butte. Just two days after the Thumb Butte enrollees arrived in camp, they were putting out a small forest fire, and one hundred Groom Creek enrollees were doing twig blight work.[128] Later in the month, Thumb Butte men began erosion control work at Iron Springs. That work was mainly building small check dams in deep gullies and planting trees and grasses later.[129]

On June 30, F-19, Thumb Butte (Company 822) reported 151 enrollees (125 from Arizona and the rest from Texas and Oklahoma, with 14 African Americans). F-18, Groom Creek (Company 2847) reported 151 enrollees (122 from Texas and the rest from Arizona and Oklahoma, with 1 African American). F-62, Lynx Creek (Company 2861) reported 134 enrollees (72 from Texas, 29 from Arizona, 18 from Oklahoma, and 15 from New Mexico).

By July, with the monsoon thunderstorms in full swing, the Horse Thief spike camp and Groom Creek enrollees were reported putting out many forest fires.[130] Special Investigator Stockman was at Thumb Butte (F-19) on July 17 and reported morale as "superior" and the commanding officer "outstanding." He noted there were seventy-four enrollees at the Horse Thief spike camp, where they frequently responded to forest fires. He reported there were fourteen African American enrollees and reported no friction between them and the white enrollees. Apparently, this camp was typical of the times, as he reported: "The colored enrollees are grouped in their own tents, mess tables, and also on the work job."[131] (See chapter 3 sidebar, *Diversity in the CCC*.)

Stockman next went to Groom Creek (F-18) where he reported (via an attached letter) that the Eagle-Picher Mining & Smelting Co. wrote that twenty-three boys had been hired and they were "far better" than the typical inexperienced applicant, as their training and discipline made a good showing. Stockman attached another letter to his report indicating on June 4 an enrollee fell twenty-five feet while doing twig blight eradication and was now at the Fort Whipple Veterans Hospital. He said that if he lived he might be paralyzed from the waist down for life. Stockman said he was told there was an average of two falling accidents per week. The letter indicated the work was generally thirty to one hundred feet above ground. Stockman's letter had a tone of deep concern about the climbing work. He recommended a number of additional safety measures, including replacing leather-soled shoes with composition ones.[132]

The next day, Stockman went to F-62, Lynx Creek, where he noted the water supply was not dependable. He said that if there was not rain in the next six days they would have to haul water. He summarized their work as fire suppression, pre-suppression, and twig blight (11,000 acres). He wrote the camp "is administered in a superior way," noting Capt. Benjamin F. Rose was the commanding officer. He called D. H. Whitlow, the project superintendent, "very cooperative." He reported he was impressed with the contract physician, noting a very clean infirmary.[133]

On July 24, the Prescott National Forest added another camp with the arrival of Company 1840 from SCS-1, Duncan, to the F-39, Verde No. 1 camp (fourteen miles southeast of Clarkdale). In early August, Forest Supervisor Nave said that Camp F-39 would soon establish a Mingus Mountain spike camp to improve the road from Route 79 to the summit recreation area. He said after completion of the summit road a road from the summit to Allen Springs would be started. He expected that to take one year.[134] The Groom Creek and Thumb Butte camps continued fighting fires in August. Late in the month, the local newspaper reported that the Thumb Butte camp was short on water and was hauling it from Prescott. In August, the Lynx Creek camp newspaper reported that since their arrival in May 1937, twig blight work had covered 316 areas, 80,967 trees were treated and pruned, and 6,217 man days had been worked.[135]

Unfortunately, the eradication, or control, of twig blight was dangerous work. The cover of the September 1937 issue of the Company 2847 (Groom Creek) camp newspaper *Pine Needle* was titled: "In Memoriam: Porter H. Gilliam of Texas." Gilliam was pruning twig blight from trees near Goldwater Dam when he fell, necessitating hospitalization in the Fort Whipple Veterans Hospital. He was transferred to the Station Hospital, Fort Sam Houston, Texas, where he died September 1, 1937. He must have been well liked, as the camp newspaper read: "His ever ready smile and winning personality will ever remain a fond memory in the hearts of his fellow enrollees."[136]

On September 18, the Lynx Creek camp held a "Constitution Anniversary" get-together with guests including Capt. T. W. Tway, sub-district commander; Lt. Elmer L. Gladow, company commander; Dr. W. M. Hubbard, camp surgeon; D. G. Revello, educational advisor; and Doyle Whitlow, project superintendent.[137] On September 20, the *Prescott Evening Courier* reported (page 2) that Company 2847 was to be disbanded and evacuated on September 30. In October, Company 2861 was to move out of Lynx Creek on October 23, and Company 822 was to move from Thumb Butte to the Fairgrounds camp on October 31.[138] Unfortunately, we know little of CCC work the remainder of the year.

On December 31, 1937, Camp F-19, Fairgrounds (Company 822) reported 161 enrollees (from Arizona, Texas, Oklahoma, and New Mexico, with 6 African Americans). Their supervisors were three Army officers, an educational advisor, and a per diem contract physician. Camp F-39, Verde No. 1 (Company 1840) reported 167 enrollees (two-thirds from Texas). Their supervisors were two Army officers, a contract physician, and an educational advisor.

1938

The year began on a tragic note with the death of Fairgrounds enrollee Antonio P. Rodriguez, 20, of Jerome on January 14. Rodriguez was run over by a train in the Prescott Yards. There were no witnesses.[139]

In January, the Prescott newspaper ran two stories about the low number of forest fires nationally and in the local forest. The year 1937 was said to be, in terms of recorded burns and man-caused fires, the lowest since 1906. "Much assistance has been rendered by the CCC not only in improving communication and transportation systems on the forests, but in helping fight the fires which occur." In the Prescott National Forest, it was the lowest number of fires in five years, and the CCC was named as one reason for this. No fire in 1937 burned more than twenty-four hours.[140]

In January, the *Prescott Evening Courier* reported that the Verde CCC camp was trying new plants in dike and ditch construction erosion control work.[141] In March, it was learned that F-39, Verde No. 1, would be discontinued in May.[142] In April, Verde No. 1 replaced three thousand feet of telephone line along the Verde River that had been washed out in a flood the month before.[143] Camp F-19, Fairgrounds, announced they would have their fifth anniversary celebration on April 3, with a motorcade going to three area recreation sites at Wolf Creek, Indian Creek, and Granite Basin. The agenda included a barbecue, sports, and a dance. The new Granite Basin recreation area was just finished, including picnic tables, benches, fireplaces, a year-round water system, toilets, garbage pits, and ample trailer park room.[144] The celebration was quite a success, with seventy-seven vehicles in the motorcade and 1,310 plates served. Forest Supervisor Nave summarized the five years of CCC work in the forest. So far, 44 miles of roads had been constructed and six recreation areas developed. A total of 150 forest fires were fought; 1,130 acres received erosion control work (gullies plugged, spreaders, and dikes); and 29,000 acres of prairie dog eradication were completed. Forty water projects were completed (stock tanks, springs, wells, and earthen dams); 191 miles of range fence were constructed; and 40,000 acres of twig blight control was completed, often for a second or third time. Nave estimated the total value to the National Forest at $850,000.[145]

On May 9, the local newspaper reported that the Fairgrounds camp would send twenty-four enrollees to the Horse Thief Basin spike camp for the summer. On May 22, the Verde No. 1 camp (F-39) was closed down, and Company 1840 enrollees were either discharged or were moved to Groom Creek.[146] One hundred twenty-five of the Verde enrollees moved to Groom Creek along with the Army officers, the camp physician, and the project superintendent.[147] In early June, Ranger George Mutz of Yeager Canyon Ranger Station said the CCC was making many improvements at the Mingus Mountain recreation area.[148] At the end of June, two F-18, Groom Creek, enrollees were patrolling the roads and cautioning picnickers of fire danger.[149]

On June 30, F-19, Fairgrounds (Company 822) reported 207 enrollees (96 from Arizona, 98 from Texas, and the rest from Oklahoma and New Mexico, with 9 African Americans). There was no report for F-18, Groom Creek.

On July 26, the Prescott newspaper reported Forest Supervisor Nave saying the Granite Basin Dam was "approved as a CCC project." It was to be an arched concrete structure 25′ high and 400′ long. Work was to begin in fifteen to twenty days.[150]

By early September, the CCC was at work on the dam hauling rock and sand for the concrete and finishing up the Granite Trail that went up the mountain.[151] At the same time, the F-18, Groom Creek, camp newspaper reported that the Drake and Verde spike camps would return to the main camp in about two weeks and about the same time a new spike camp would be established at Barrel Springs.[152] Three and a half weeks later, the camp newspaper reported the Mingus Mountain road work was almost finished. Enrollees were doing road work near Mt. Union and fence lines.[153] During mid-October, enrollees were cleaning up the Mayer camp area and buildings, and on October 25, Company 3320 moved from Groom Creek to Mayer, F-33. Unfortunately, little is known of the CCC projects through the rest of the year.

On December 31, 1938, F-19, Fairgrounds (Company 822) reported 165 enrollees (nearly all from Texas and Arizona, with 12 African Americans). Camp F-33, Mayer (Company 3320) reported 89 men (all but 5 from Pennsylvania).

1939

CCC work began in January on the Sainte Agathe ski course in the Indian Creek area. When completed by summer, plans called for three ski runs, a toboggan run, probably an ice skating rink, and a three-hundred-car parking lot. The longest run was nearly a mile. The championship ski runs were laid out by C. E. Long.[154] Also during January, Forest Supervisor Nave and Jack Orr, staff specialist, visited the CCC camps and investigated the road improvements on Senator Highway into Crown King and the new road from Mingus Mountain to Jerome.[155] In January, the F-18, Mayer, camp newspaper reported the current projects as landscaping at Granite Basin and the Tonto Ranger Station; Granite Basin Dam; Thumb Butte Road; and boundary fencing. Lots of work remained at the Willow Creek Ranger Station and cleanup at the Indian Creek ski run.[156] In February, projects were erosion dams, road building, and construction of watering troughs to be placed at springs.[157]

Special Investigator Stockman visited the Fairgrounds camp on March 22 and called their labor "splendid work."[158] The following day, Stockman was at the Mayer camp and reported it to be one of the cleanest camps he had seen. He reported the commanding officer doing "splendid work." Mayer had two spike camps: Mingus Mountain (thirty-two miles distant), with forty-five men, and Barrel Springs (eighteen miles distant), with thirty-five men.[159]

In March, the camp newspaper reported projects as the Granite Basin Dam, blasting the boundary fence post holes, Thumb Butte Road, and odd jobs at the Willow Creek Ranger

Station.[160] In early April, the *Prescott Evening Courier* announced that a new camp was to be established a half mile west of the Walnut Creek Ranger Station, with Company 3320 to move there from Mayer upon completion of the camp.[161] By mid-April, F-19, Fairgrounds, enrollees were pouring concrete at the Granite Basin Dam.[162] During April, the Forest Service staff was training all the enrollees in firefighting, fire prevention, and enrollee safety. Apparently, this was the first year that the training was compulsory.[163] On April 24, Oliver B. Wright, 54, a CCC foreman, died at Mercy Hospital after being struck by a boom at the Granite Basin Dam project.[164]

In May, the camp newspaper reported on work projects. Enrollees were removing all traces of the Groom Creek camp, pouring concrete at the Granite Basin Dam, working on the Thumb Butte Road, and erecting the Burnt Ranch boundary fence.[165] On June 30, Company 3320 moved officially from F-33, Mayer, to the new F-79, Walnut Creek, camp (43.6 miles northwest of Prescott).

On June 30, F-79, Walnut Creek reported 77 enrollees (all but 4 from Pennsylvania). F-19, Fairgrounds (Company 822) reported 173 enrollees (all but 21 from Arizona, with 5 African Americans).

During June and July, enrollees frequently fought forest fires, with a fire near Bolada requiring 235 workers, including all the enrollees from both camps.[166] In September, the F-19, Fairgrounds, camp newspaper reported the Granite Basin Dam was 85% complete. The Barrel Spring spike camp was doing Senator Road work, and a few men were at the old Horse Thief Basin spike camp working on the Crown King Road.[167]

In early November, the Prescott newspaper summarized CCC jobs and future projects. During the past summer, the Walnut Creek camp had nearly completed a steel bridge construction across Walnut Creek above the J.R. Williams Ranch; constructed a number of game study plots; done erosion control work on the south fork of Walnut Creek; painted the Walnut Creek Ranger Station; constructed one mile (of twelve) of the Walnut Creek to Camp Wood road; and begun construction of the Mammoth Cave Road. During the past enrollment period, the Fairgrounds camp had completed the Granite Basin dam; reconstructed two miles of the old Senator Highway (when completed it would open a direct route from Prescott to Crown King); completed construction of the Thumb Butte road connecting it to the Copper Basin Road, thus completing the loop; completed eight miles of range fence; done numerous spring developments; and reconstructed six miles of telephone line between Iron Springs and the Tonto Ranger Station. For the winter, the Mayer camp would use the Mingus Mountain spike camp to work on the road to Triangulation Point on Mingus Mountain; work on the ski run and other recreation improvements on Mingus Mountain; complete the surfacing of Sycamore Road; construct stock tanks; develop springs; construct forest boundary fences; construct game study plots; and construct a lake at Crystal Springs. For the next period, the Fairgrounds camp would finish the Indian Creek ski run parking lot and shelter; construct additional recreational facilities at Indian Creek, Wolf Creek, and Thumb Butte; do erosion control work above Granite Basin Dam; install a water system in the Granite Basin summer home area; construct fifteen miles of range fence; develop springs; erect road and trail signs, and maintain roads.[168]

On November 11, Company 3320 moved from F-79, Walnut Creek, to F-33, Mayer. In December, the F-19, Fairgrounds, camp newspaper noted work was progressing on the ski area run, shelter, and parking lot. Fence work was in the Copper Basin country, and telephone line construction was near Iron Springs.[169]

On December 31, the F19, Fairgrounds, camp (Company 822) reported 166 enrollees (94 from Texas, 71 from Arizona, and 1 from Oklahoma). This was the first time Company 822 did not have African American enrollees, defying the 1935 national ban on integrated companies. (See chapter 3 sidebar, *Diversity in the CCC.*) The F-33, Mayer, camp (Company 3320) reported 102 enrollees (98 from Pennsylvania).

1940

January started on a positive note for the Fairgrounds camp, as they were entertained with orchestral selections by the local WPA cultural arts group.[170] The Fairgrounds boys were working on a 400'-long toboggan run at the ski area, where they had completed six ski runs. Fence and telephone line work were progressing. Enrollees were working out of the Barrel Spring spike camp.[171] At the Mayer camp, Saturday night CCC dances continued through the winter, often attracting many ranchers as well as Mayer and Humboldt residents.[172]

In January and February, the Fairgrounds camp reported 231 and 225 enrollees (almost evenly divided between those from Texas and from Arizona). The Mayer camp reported 205 and 201 enrollees (nearly all from Pennsylvania).

During February, the Fairgrounds camp reported the Indian Creek ski run work nearly completed. Granite Basin erosion control work continued as well as work on the O9R telephone line.[173]

In March and April, the Mayer camp reported just 155 enrollees, while the Fairgrounds camp reported 150 and 220 enrollees for the same months. On April 15, the *Prescott Evening Courier* reported that two thousand people had attended the dedication of the CCC-built Granite Basin Dam. There were many speakers, including Forest Supervisor Nave, Lt. Kenneth S. Cox of the Fairgrounds camp, and Lt. Albert V. Bruni of the Mayer camp. The 10.5-acre lake was for recreation, and stocking of fish in it was anticipated. The dedication activities included music and a barbecue by the Kiwanis.[174]

Figure 25. Granite Basin Dam, 1940. Photograph by C.W. McKenzie. Courtesy U.S. Forest Service, Southwestern Regional Office, #406079.

The Fairgrounds camp in April reported the cutting of infested trees along Copper Basin and Thumb Butte Roads; fence construction around the Granite Basin watershed; Granite Basin erosion control; recreation area work; and connection of the O9R telephone line to the Willow Creek Ranger Station and completion of it to Iron Springs.[175] Also in April, the Mayer camp reported the Sycamore Ranger Station would be finished soon, and the power line stock tank was finished.[176]

On May 31, F-19, Fairgrounds, reported 219 enrollees (two-thirds from Arizona, including one veteran, and one-third from Texas). The Mayer camp reported 153 enrollees (all but 4 from Pennsylvania). In early June, Company 3320 was working out of the Barrel Springs spike camp.[177] On June 8, a group of ten enrollees were on their way into Prescott and, upon passing Mercy Hospital, noticed smoke. They immediately stopped and brought out all the patients to safety.[178]

Special Investigator M. J. Bowen visited the Fairgrounds camp on June 11 and noted that desertions were very high, which seemed true of all the 8th Corps camps. He inspected the new reservoir and called it "very good work."[179] Bowen visited the Mayer camp the next day and summarized the work program as road and fence construction, spring development, and campground development. The camp administration was "doing well." Mess and morale were "good." He did make suggestions to improve the lunches that were sent out to enrollees working in the field.[180] On June 29, Company 3320 moved from Mayer camp to F-79, Walnut Creek. On June 30, F-19, Fairgrounds (Company 822) reported 172 enrollees, and F-79, Walnut Creek (Company 3320) reported just 65 enrollees.

Granite Lake must have been some sight, as Special Investigator Bowen was quoted as saying it was the "best project in the nation."[181] Unfortunately, we know very little of CCC work during the remainder of 1940, as most of the newspaper articles for this time period are of baseball games, crime reports, fire reports, and the like. For the three-month period from July 31 to September 30, F-19, Fairgrounds (Company 822) reported 224, 222, and 153 enrollees (generally with two-thirds from Arizona, including one veteran, and one-third from Texas). For the same period, F-79, Walnut Creek (Company 3320) reported 211, 205, and 199 enrollees (all but a few from Pennsylvania).

On October 17, a truck with seventeen enrollees overturned two miles north of Walnut Creek on the Prescott-Seligman highway, and Philadelphia enrollee Charles James Mellor, 18, was killed. The death was ruled accidental.[182]

On October 31, F-19, Fairgrounds, reported 223 enrollees, and F-79, Walnut Creek, reported 205 enrollees. On November 1, the Prescott newspaper reported Regional Forester Frank C. W. Pooler and Forest Supervisor Nave were inspecting the CCC camp at Walnut Creek, the spike camps at Barrel Springs and Mingus Mountain, and the work at Horse Thief Basin. On November 15, Company 3320 moved from Walnut Creek to F-33, Mayer.[183] On December 7, the Prescott newspaper reported the Mayer CCC Thanksgiving dance was attended by a large crowd. The music was provided by a Victrola just purchased by the O.K. Café.[184]

On November 30 and December 31, F-19, Fairgrounds (Company 822) reported 202 and 155 enrollees, and F-33, Mayer (Company 3320) reported 204 and 68 enrollees. Typically the end-of-the-year count was low, as many enrollees were on leave.

1941

Like the previous six months, we know very little of the CCC work for this year. In mid-January, the CCC was credited as being a major player in the lighting of the Mingus Mountain ski area.[185]

On the national level, it was announced that enrollees, who previously did not participate in outright military training, would now be doing close-order drill, but without weapons.[186]

On January 31 and February 28, F-19, Fairgrounds (Company 822) reported 186 and 176 enrollees (80% of the enrollees from Arizona and the rest from Texas, with 1 veteran). F-33, Mayer (Company 3320) reported 195 and 192 enrollees (nearly all from Pennsylvania).

At the end of March, the Fairgrounds camp invited the community to an open house emphasizing "vocational opportunities" in the CCC. The CCC was also stressing the importance to National Defense. "Training and camp life provide many short cuts to military preparedness in learning to live and work together, improving health, and learning discipline."[187]

At the Fairgrounds camp, radio training was featured.[188] Company Commander Lt. Gerald Post reported the 8th anniversary open house would feature work exhibits explaining timber stand improvement, insect eradication, and forest fire suppression and prevention. There were to be educational work displays including a radio display. The woodworking and photography shops would be up for inspection, and the entire camp would be open to visitors.[189]

In early April, Fairgrounds enrollees began work on improvements at the Granite Creek recreation area, including the construction of fireplaces, picnic tables, and sanitation facilities.[190] At the end of April and May, F-19, Fairgrounds (Company 822) reported 136 and 177 enrollees (with 1 veteran), while F-33, Mayer (Company 3320) reported 180 and 177 enrollees. In May, the *Prescott Evening Courier* reported that the Mayer camp was to disband in June, with officers and enrollees transferring to other camps or taking discharges and the camp formally closed on June 21.[191]

Special Investigator Bowen visited the Fairgrounds camp on June 18 and reported work to be timber stand improvement, campground development, and road construction and maintenance. He said the camp was making "very good progress."[192]

On June 24, Company 822 moved from the Fairgrounds camp to F-80, Flagstaff, and on June 28, Company 1826, a veterans company, moved from South Mountain Park at Phoenix to the Fairgrounds camp. Company 1826V had been formed very early on and served in many places throughout the state, including F-28 at Williams. It was also unusual in that they continued to have an integrated company long after Washington's ban; when they arrived in Prescott, they were the only Arizona company that was still integrated.

On June 30, they reported 138 enrollees (men from five 8th Corps states, with most from Arizona and New Mexico and 12 African Americans). On July 31, they reported 192 men (with 12 African Americans). Their reported numbers dropped to 182 on August 31, went to 202 on November 30, and at the end of the year were 185, with 12 African Americans. At that time, they reported that most men were from Arizona and New Mexico. Their supervisors were an Army officer, a contract physician, and an educational advisor. Little is known of their work until they disbanded in 1942.

1942

F-19, Fairgrounds (Company 1826V) reported 159 enrollees on January 31 and 157 on March 31, with 12 African Americans. By this time, the number of Arizona camps was decreasing dramatically, with just nine camps statewide on March 31. On April 30, the camp reported 137 men, and the last War Department report on May 31 had only five companies statewide, with Company 1826V reporting 171 men, with 10 African Americans. It is unclear when they disbanded. Nationwide, all enrollees were discharged by September 30, 1942. It is likely they disbanded by July 24, 1942, as a newspaper article on that date stated that all Arizona CCC camps were now under the U.S. Army Engineers.[193]

The Fairgrounds camp buildings were apparently the property of the local fairgrounds association and likely reverted back to them. The Mayer camp buildings became the custody of the Forest Service in 1941. However, the buildings came under Army authority in 1942 and were used for a short time as a center for Japanese Americans relocated under the U.S. War Relocation Authority.[194] The Mayer buildings appear to be the only CCC camp nationwide used for this purpose, and that was short-lived. Two hundred forty-five Japanese Americans were housed at the "Mayer Assembly Center" from May 7 to June 2, 1942.[195]

Unless noted otherwise, any reference to the number of enrollees in a company, the location of the company, or company supervisors are from U.S. War Department, Location and Strength of CCC Companies, 1933–1942, NARAMD RG 35 530/65/22/04/05.

1. "Criticism of the Roosevelt Relief Plan," *Prescott Evening Courier*, April 6, 1933, 4.
2. "The CCC Comes in for Praise," *Prescott Evening Courier*, November 2, 1934, 12.
3. "Conservation Force a Vital 'Army,'" *Prescott Evening Courier*, April 17, 1936, 14.
4. "The CCC's Other Side Is Cheering One," *Prescott Evening Courier*, October 1, 1936, 4.

5. "Accomplishments of the CCC," *Prescott Evening Courier*, July 12, 1939, 4.
6. "Putsch Speaks on Forestation," *Prescott Evening Courier*, April 6, 1933, 7.
7. "Three Camps in Prescott Area," *Prescott Evening Courier*, April 21, 1933, 1.
8. "16 Reforestation Trucks Wanted," *Prescott Evening Courier*, April 26, 1933, 3.
9. "Yavapai Gets 3 Forest Groups," *Prescott Evening Courier*, May 3, 1933, 1.
10. "Get Ready for Forest Forces," *Prescott Evening Courier*, May 3, 1933, 7.
11. "Forest Service to Rent Trucks," *Prescott Evening Courier*, May 13, 1933, 5.
12. "Brief Items in the Daily Life of Prescott," *Prescott Evening Courier*, May 22, 1933, 3.
13. "Forest Groups Due Tomorrow," *Prescott Evening Courier*, May 27, 1933, 1, 7.
14. "Forest Camps Are Filling Up," *Prescott Evening Courier*, May 30, 1933, 1, 3.
15. "Last of Forest Men in Tonight," *Prescott Evening Courier*, May 31, 1933, 1, 7.
16. "Rotary Told of Forest Activity," *Prescott Evening Courier*, June 9, 1933, 1, 7.
17. "Reforestation Idea Explained," *Prescott Evening Courier*, June 19, 1933, 1, 2.
18. "Brief Items in the Daily Life of Prescott," *Prescott Evening Courier*, June 26, 1933, 3.
19. "May Establish Camp for Vets," *Prescott Evening Courier*, June 27, 1933, 1.
20. "Brief Items in the Daily Life of Prescott," *Prescott Evening Courier*, June 29, 1933, 3.
21. "Brief Items in the Daily Life of Prescott," *Prescott Evening Courier*, July 6, 1933, 3.
22. "Oklahoma Vets Here for Camp," *Prescott Evening Courier*, July 12, 1933, 1, 3.
23. "Progress Made on Forest Told," *Prescott Evening Courier*, August 2, 1933, 1, 2.
24. "Thumb Butte Forest Camp Wells Go Dry," *Prescott Evening Courier*, August 8, 1933, 3.
25. "Prairie Dogs Onslaught Target," (Jerome) *Verde Copper News*, August 18, 1933, 4.
26. "Camp Worker Is Near to Death ... Shot after Alleged Robbery," *Prescott Evening Courier*, August 19, 1933, 1, 7.
27. "Pine Tree Twig Blight Told Of," *Prescott Evening Courier*, August 25, 1933, 6.
28. "Brief Items in the Daily Life of Prescott," *Prescott Evening Courier*, August 28, 1933, 8.
29. "6 CCC Camps to Move to Verde," *Prescott Evening Courier*, September 22, 1933, 1.
30. "Sites Selected for Two Camps," *Prescott Evening Courier*, September 27, 1933, 1.
31. "CCC Officer to Check Thievery," *Prescott Evening Courier*, September 29, 1933, 1, 6.
32. "Butte Camp Is Going to TX," *Prescott Evening Courier*, October 5, 1933, 1, 6.
33. "Brief Items in the Daily Life of Prescott," *Prescott Evening Courier*, October 11, 1933, 3.
34. "Brief Items in the Daily Life of Prescott," *Prescott Evening Courier*, October 12, 1933, 2.
35. "Want Recruits for CCC Camp," *Prescott Evening Courier*, October 17, 1933, 1, 7.
36. "88 Men Go to Grand Canyon," *Prescott Evening Courier*, October 23, 1933, 1.
37. "Camp Site Location to Be Decided Soon," *Prescott Evening Courier*, October 25, 1933, 2; "CCC Camp Gets Counter-Order," *Prescott Evening Courier*, October 26, 1933, 1, 3.
38. "Brief Items in the Daily Life of Prescott," *Prescott Evening Courier*, October 30, 1933, 3.
39. "Brief Items in the Daily Life of Prescott," *Prescott Evening Courier*, November 16, 1933, 3.
40. "Brief Items in the Daily Life of Prescott," *Prescott Evening Courier*, November 28, 1933, 3.
41. "Army CCC Staff May Move Here," *Prescott Evening Courier*, December 2, 1933, 1, 3; U.S. War Department, Location and Strength of CCC Companies, 1933–1942, NARAMD RG 35 530/65/22/04/05.
42. "To Use 100 Men on Erosion Job," *Prescott Evening Courier*, December 7, 1933, 7.
43. "Mayer Notes," *Prescott Evening Courier*, December 11, 1933, 7.
44. "Brief Items in the Daily Life of Prescott," *Prescott Evening Courier*, January 13, 1934, 3.
45. "Brief Items in the Daily Life of Prescott," *Prescott Evening Courier*, January 15, 1934, 2.
46. "Brief Items in the Daily Life of Prescott," *Prescott Evening Courier*, February 6, 1934, 3.
47. "CCC Dance Is Big Success," *Prescott Evening Courier*, February 10, 1934, 3.
48. "Brief Items in the Daily Life of Prescott," *Prescott Evening Courier*, March 20, 1934, 3.
49. "Brief Items in the Daily Life of Prescott," *Prescott Evening Courier*, April 9, 1934, 7.
50. Grace M. Sparkes, "5 CCC Camps to Have Big Party," *Prescott Evening Courier*, April 13, 1934, 1, 4.
51. "Grubb Reports CCC Camp Work," *Prescott Evening Courier*, April 24, 1934, 1, 6.
52. "Brief Items in the Daily Life of Prescott," *Prescott Evening Courier*, May 15, 1934, 3.

53. "CCC Man Killed in Road Mishap," *Prescott Evening Courier,* June 2, 1934, 1, 8; Arizona Death Records, State File No. 341, Registered No. 353-H.
54. "Brief Items in the Daily Life of Prescott," *Prescott Evening Courier,* June 12, 1934, 2.
55. "Yavapai CCC Buildings Burn," *Arizona Republic,* July 5, 1934, 8.
56. U.S. CCC, Camp Inspection Reports, NARAMD RG 35/530/65/23/04 Entry 115 (PI #11) Box 8.
57. Ibid. Radical publications such as *Champion of Youth* and *Spark* were strictly forbidden by CCC authorities. See Melzer, *Coming of Age,* 109.
58. U.S. CCC, Camp Inspection Reports, NARAMD RG 35/530/65/23/04 Entry 115 (PI #11) Box 8.
59. "Brief Items in the Daily Life of Prescott," *Prescott Evening Courier,* August 15, 1934, 2.
60. "Brief Items in the Daily Life of Prescott," *Prescott Evening Courier,* August 23, 1934, 2.
61. "Finish Improvements in Recreational Area," *Prescott Evening Courier,* August 24, 1934, 2.
62. "Brief Items in the Daily Life of Prescott," *Prescott Evening Courier,* September 5, 1934, 2.
63. "Brief Items in the Daily Life of Prescott," *Prescott Evening Courier,* September 24, 1934, 2.
64. "Brief Items in the Daily Life of Prescott," *Prescott Evening Courier,* September 28, 1934, 2.
65. "Cherry Items," *Prescott Evening Courier,* October 8, 1934, 8.
66. "20-Acre Forest Fire Rages near Prescott," *Prescott Evening Courier,* October 17, 1934, 3.
67. "Transient and CCC Arrests Are in Lead," *Prescott Evening Courier,* October 17, 1934, 5.
68. "Brief Items in the Daily Life of Prescott," *Prescott Evening Courier,* November 8, 1934, 2.
69. "Local News," *Prescott Evening Courier,* November 9, 1934, 2.
70. "Mayer Notes," *Prescott Evening Courier,* November 12, 1934, 6.
71. "Forest Men Finish Recreational Plans," *Prescott Evening Courier,* November 22, 1934, 2; "Cherry Items," *Prescott Evening Courier,* November 24, 1934, 2.
72. "Crown King Ranger's House Soon to Start," *Prescott Evening Courier,* November 30, 1934, 3.
73. Fiche MN #0517, CRL Newspapers.
74. "Brief Items in the Daily Life of Prescott," *Prescott Evening Courier,* December 17, 1934, 2; Arizona Death Records, State File 519, Registered No. 597-H.
75. "Fort Whipple," *Prescott Evening Courier,* December 22, 1934, 5. This appears to be a not uncommon Grand Canyon occurrence.
76. "Forest Service Obtains Plants," *Prescott Evening Courier,* February 19, 1935, 1, 3.
77. Fiche MN #0517, CRL Newspapers.
78. U.S. CCC, Camp Inspection Reports, NARAMD RG 35/530/65/23/04 Entry 115 (PI #11) Box 9.
79. Ibid.
80. "15-Acre Fire on This Forest Is Reported," *Prescott Evening Courier,* April 16, 1935, 3.
81. U.S. CCC, Camp Inspection Reports, NARAMD RG 35/530/65/23/04 Entry 115 (PI #11) Box 9; "CCC Worker Dies," *El Paso Herald Post,* June 13, 1935; Texas Death Index #27872.
82. "Prescott Forest Fire Is Subdued," *Arizona Republic,* July 1, 1935, 1.
83. "Fall from Tree Hurts CCC Lad," *Arizona Republic,* July 12, 1935, 10.
84. "CCC Ball Tournament Billed This Week-End," *Prescott Evening Courier,* July 10, 1935, 5.
85. "12 Lightning Fires Started on Forest," *Prescott Evening Courier,* July 15, 1935, 8.
86. Grace M. Sparkes, "Program Given Lynx Creek CCC," *Prescott Evening Courier,* August 24, 1935, 3. A similar program was given for the Groom Creek enrollees in September.
87. "Fort Whipple," *Prescott Evening Courier,* August 30, 1935, 5.
88. "Brief Items in the Daily Life of Prescott," *Prescott Evening Courier,* September 5, 1935, 2.
89. U.S. CCC, Camp Inspection Reports, NARAMD RG 35/530/65/23/04 Entry 115 (PI #11) Box 9; Arizona Death Records, State File No. 399, Registered No. 3[?]7 B.
90. "Make Headway on Twig Blight," *Prescott Evening Courier,* October 3, 1935, 3.
91. U.S. CCC, "CCC Camps Occupied During Ninth Period" June 1, 1937. NARACO RG 79 8NS-079-94-139 79-58A-014 Box 153.
92. U.S. CCC, Camp Inspection Reports, NARAMD RG 35/530/65/23/04 Entry 115 (PI #11) Box 9.
93. "250 Transients Will Start Work on Forest," *Prescott Evening Courier,* December 13, 1935, 5; "Transient Camp Is Closed Down," *Prescott Evening Courier,* December 28, 1935, 2.
94. "Memo regarding death of Thomas Spencer," U.S. CCC, Camp Inspection Reports, NARAMD RG 35/530/65/23/04 Entry 115 (PI #11) Box 9; Arizona Death Records, State File No. 519, Registered No. 419-H.
95. *Turkey Creek Gobbler,* December 1935, Fiche MN #0519, CRL Newspapers.
96. "Tells of Fires on This Forest," *Prescott Evening Courier,* January 20, 1936, 8.

97. "Brief Items in the Daily Life of Prescott," *Prescott Evening Courier,* January 22, 1936, 2.
98. "Dr. E.B. Jolly Will Join Hospital Staff," *Prescott Evening Courier,* April 10, 1936, 2.
99. "Local Forest Officials View Work of CCC in Three Years," *Prescott Evening Courier,* April 16, 1936, 3.
100. "Three C Camp to Remain at Mayer," *Prescott Evening Courier,* April 16, 1936, 2.
101. "CCC Camp Sites Are Considered," *Prescott Evening Courier,* April 29, 1936, 1, 2.
102. "Fairgrounds Chosen for CCC Camp Site," *Prescott Evening Courier,* May 1, 1936, 8.
103. "CCC Enrollees Reach Prescott," *Arizona Republic,* May 6, 1936, sect. 2, 1.
104. "Experimental Work with Blight Is Done," *Prescott Evening Courier,* May 15, 1936, 10.
105. "CCC Heading off Blight on Forest," *Prescott Evening Courier,* May 23, 1936, 8.
106. U.S. CCC, Camp Inspection Reports, NARAMD RG 35/530/65/23/04 Entry 115 (PI #11) Box 9.
107. Ibid., Box 8.
108. Ibid., Box 8.
109. Ibid., Box 9.
110. "Climb of Three Enrollees at Prescott CCC Camp Is Disclosed," *Prescott Evening Courier,* June 24, 1936, 2.
111. "One Hundred Sixty-Seven Men Now At Fair Grounds CCC Camp," *Prescott Evening Courier,* June 24, 1936, 5.
112. *Broadcaster,* July 15, 1936, Fiche MN #0529, CRL Newspapers.
113. "Plan Work at Granite Basin," *Prescott Evening Courier,* July 17, 1936, 2.
114. "3C Boys Here Given Praise," *Prescott Evening Courier,* August 29, 1936, 1, 8.
115. *Broadcaster,* September 1, 1936, Fiche MN #0529, CRL Newspapers.
116. "CCC Education Program Broad," *Prescott Evening Courier,* September 26, 1936, 7.
117. U.S. CCC, Phoenix District, *Official Annual, 1936, Phoenix District, 8 Corps Area, Civilian Conservation Corps* ([Baton Rouge, LA?]: Direct Advertising Co., 1936), 28–29, 32–33, 34–35, 38–39. GCNPMC Cat. #70738.
118. "CCC Camps Get Moving Orders," *Prescott Evening Courier,* October 8, 1936, 8.
119. "CCC Boys Do Good Work on Twig Blight," *Williams News,* November 19, 1936, 6.
120. "Mayer CCC Puts Out Quail Grain," *Prescott Evening Courier,* January 14, 1937, 8; "Quail Are Fed Tons of Grain," *Prescott Evening Courier,* January 21, 1937, 1, 8.
121. "Mayer," *Prescott Evening Courier,* January 26, 1937, 5.
122. "Mayer," *Prescott Evening Courier,* February 9, 1937, 8.
123. "Brief Items in the Daily Life of Prescott," *Prescott Evening Courier,* March 4, 1937, 2.
124. "Public Invited to Visit Camps," *Prescott Evening Courier,* March 31, 1937, 3.
125. "Touraide Marred by One Accident," *Prescott Evening Courier,* April 5, 1937, 8.
126. "Brief Items in the Daily Life of Prescott," *Prescott Evening Courier,* April 27, 1937, 2.
127. "Camps Are Prepared for CCC Enrollees," *Arizona Republic,* May 5, 1937, sect. 2, 1.
128. "Brief Items in the Daily Life of Prescott," *Prescott Evening Courier,* May 18, 1937, 2.
129. "CCC Is Doing Work on Erosion Control," *Prescott Evening Courier,* May 26, 1937, 2; "Soil Erosion Project Is Started at Iron Springs," *Williams News,* June 3, 1937, 5.
130. "Lookouts Have Busy Time Fighting Fires," *Prescott Evening Courier,* July 16, 1937, 2; "CCC Crew Puts Out Small Forest Fire," *Prescott Evening Courier,* July 22, 1937, 3; "Lightning Starts Five Forest Fires," *Prescott Evening Courier,* July 24, 1937, 8; "Forest Fire Burns over Timbered Area," *Prescott Evening Courier,* July 28, 1937, 8.
131. U.S. CCC, Camp Inspection Reports, NARAMD RG 35/530/65/23/04 Entry 115 (PI #11) Box 8.
132. Ibid., Box 8.
133. Ibid., Box 9.
134. "CCC Boys Will Work on Road up Mingus," *Prescott Evening Courier,* August 4, 1937, 3.
135. *Dreamer,* August, 1937, Fiche MN #1696, CRL Newspapers.
136. Fiche MN #1682, CRL Newspapers. According to Texas Death Records, his full name was Nathaniel Porter Gilliam, and he was 18.
137. *Society:* "Camp F-62-A Observes Constitution Anniversary," *Prescott Evening Courier,* September 18, 1937, 9.
138. "Thumb Butte Camp Is Going to Fairgrounds," *Prescott Evening Courier,* September 28, 1937, 2.
139. "Train Wheels Kill CCC Boy," *Prescott Evening Courier,* January 15, 1938, 1, 8; Arizona Death Records, State File No. 506, Registered No. 20-S.
140. "Forests Report Low Fire Record," *Prescott Evening Courier,* January 21, 1938, 12; "Forest Fire Loss Least in 5 Years," *Prescott Evening Courier,* January 26, 1938, 2.
141. "New Plants Tried by Forest Service," *Prescott Evening Courier,* January 31, 1938, 2.
142. "County Will Lose Cottonwood CCC," *Prescott Evening Courier,* March 18, 1938, 14.
143. *The Conservator,* April 20, 1938, Fiche MN #1172, CRL Newspapers.
144. "CCC Barbecue Outing April 3," *Prescott Evening Courier,* March 21, 1938, 3.

145. "Big Crowd at CCC Barbecue," *Prescott Evening Courier,* April 4, 1938, 2.
146. U.S. War Department, "Location and Strength of CCC Companies, June 30, 1938," shows only F-19 at the Prescott NF. However, U.S. CCC, Camp Directories 1933–1942, Records of the CCC, Entry 13, NARAMD RG 35 530/65/11/1, shows F-18 occupied during the Eleventh Enrollment Period, but not occupied during the Twelfth Enrollment Period.
147. "125 CCC Move to Groom Creek," *Prescott Evening Courier,* May 24, 1938, 3; "Civilian Conservation Corps Eighth Corps Area, Status Record of CCC Camps Authorized Since Inception of the Program up to … December 31, 1941 … Compiled by Office of Liaison Officer, CCC Fort Sam Houston…," NARACO BLM CCC Directories RG 49 Entry 33, 34 Box 132. Seven of the buildings were turned over to the FS for administrative use, and the rest went to the Army and FS for CCC use.
148. "Brief Items in the Daily Life of Prescott," *Prescott Evening Courier,* June 3, 1938, 2.
149. "Brief Items in the Daily Life of Prescott," *Prescott Evening Courier,* June 27, 1938, 3.
150. "Brief Items in the Daily Life of Prescott," *Prescott Evening Courier,* July 26, 1938, 3.
151. "Brief Items in the Daily Life of Prescott," *Prescott Evening Courier,* September 2, 1938, 3 and September 7, 1938, 3.
152. *Tenderfoot,* September 3, 1938, Fiche MN #1818, CRL Newspapers.
153. *Tenderfoot,* September 28, 1938, Fiche MN #1818, CRL Newspapers.
154. "Work Started on Ski Course," *Prescott Evening Courier,* January 20, 1939, 3.
155. "Brief Items in the Daily Life of Prescott," *Prescott Evening Courier,* January 19, 1939, 3.
156. *Pine Croft News,* January 25, 1939, Fiche MN #0519, CRL Newspapers.
157. *Pine Croft News,* February 25, 1939, Fiche MN #0519, CRL Newspapers.
158. U.S. CCC, Camp Inspection Reports, NARAMD RG 35/530/65/23/04 Entry 115 (PI #11) Box 8.
159. Ibid., Box 9.
160. *Pine Croft News,* March 25, 1939, Fiche MN #0519, CRL Newspapers.
161. "Walnut Creek to Be Site of New Camp," *Prescott Evening Courier,* April 7, 1939, 3.
162. "Pouring Cement at Granite Basin Dam," *Prescott Evening Courier,* April 18, 1939, 3.
163. "Fighting of Fire Is Practiced by CCC," *Prescott Evening Courier,* April 24, 1939, 3.
164. "Injuries Fatal to O. B. Wright," *Prescott Evening Courier,* April 27, 1939, 3.
165. *Pine Croft News,* May 25, 1939, Fiche MN #0519, CRL Newspapers.
166. "235 Men Fight Forest Fire Blaze," *Prescott Evening Courier,* July 13, 1939, 1, 8.
167. *Pine Croft News,* September, 1939, Fiche MN #0519, CRL Newspapers.
168. "Walnut Creek CCC Camp to Be Moved to Mayer District," *Prescott Evening Courier,* November 10, 1939, 7.
169. *Pine Croft News,* December 1939, Fiche MN #0519, CRL Newspapers.
170. "WPA Group Presents Camp Entertainment," *Prescott Evening Courier,* January 12, 1940, 2.
171. *Pine Croft News,* January 1940, Fiche MN #0519, CRL Newspapers.
172. "Mayer," *Prescott Evening Courier,* January 27, 1940, 7.
173. *Pine Croft News,* February 1940, Fiche MN #0519, CRL Newspapers.
174. "Crowd Attends Dam Dedication," *Prescott Evening Courier,* April 15, 1940, 2.
175. *Pine Croft News,* April, 1940, Fiche MN #0519, CRL Newspapers.
176. *Pennzonian,* April 26, 1940, Fiche MN #1818, CRL Newspapers.
177. *Pennzonian,* June 7, 1940, Fiche MN #1818, CRL Newspapers.
178. Letter from Mercy Hospital with Company 822 records, U.S. CCC, Camp Inspection Reports, NARAMD RG 35/530/65/23/04 Entry 115 (PI #11) Box 8.
179. U.S. CCC, Camp Inspection Reports, NARAMD RG 35/530/65/23/04 Entry 115 (PI #11) Box 8.
180. Ibid., Box 9.
181. "Granite Basin Lake Is a Beautiful Sight," *Prescott Evening Courier,* July 1, 1940, 4.
182. "Crash Fatal to CCC Youth," *Prescott Evening Courier,* October 18, 1940, 1, 8; "Death of CCC Boy Accident," *Prescott Evening Courier,* October 19, 1940, 3.
183. "Brief Items in the Daily Life of Prescott," *Prescott Evening Courier,* November 1, 1940, 2.
184. "Mayer," *Prescott Evening Courier,* December 7, 1940, 6.
185. Ed Long, "Prescott Ski Area Lighted," *Prescott Evening Courier,* January 16, 1941, 3.
186. "CCC Enrollees Learn Close Order Drill," *Prescott Evening Courier,* January 17, 1941, 1.
187. "CCC Activity Program Wide," *Prescott Evening Courier,* March 28, 1941, 3.
188. "CCC Training Radio Experts," *Prescott Evening Courier,* March 31, 1941, 3.

189. "Complete Plan for CCC Event," *Prescott Evening Courier,* April 3, 1941, 3.
190. "Brief Items in the Daily Life of Prescott," *Prescott Evening Courier,* April 4, 1941, 3.
191. "Will Disband CCC Company," *Prescott Evening Courier,* May 27, 1941, 2; "Civilian Conservation Corps Eighth Corps Area, Status Record of CCC Camps Authorized Since Inception of the Program up to ... December 31, 1941 ... Compiled by Office of Liaison Officer, CCC Fort Sam Houston...," NARACO BLM CCC Directories RG 49 Entry 33, 34 Box 132. When a camp was abandoned and expected to be re-occupied, Army practice was to assign a caretaker to guard the property.
192. U.S. CCC, Camp Inspection Reports, NARAMD RG 35/530/65/23/04 Entry 115 (PI #11) Box 8.
193. "Army Takes Over Nearby CCC Location," *Coconino Sun,* July 24, 1942, 1.
194. "Army to Use Two Arizona Sites for Japanese," *Coconino Sun,* April 10, 1942, 1.
195. Jeffrey F. Burton et al. *Confinement and Ethnicity: An Overview of World War II Japanese American Relocation Sites* (DOI, Western Archeological and Conservation Center, 1999), part 4, chapter 16, 2.

CHAPTER 8

Division of Grazing Camps, Yavapai County
The Division of Grazing and the CCC: An Overview

WHEN THE CCC BEGAN, AGENCIES such as the Forest Service and the National Park Service had been in existence for some years. They had already instituted some centralized planning and setting of development standards and plans, so they were well poised to take immediate advantage of the CCC program. However, the Division of Grazing (DG) of the Department of Interior was not established until July 17, 1934, to administer the Taylor Grazing Act of June 28, 1934, "the first law ever passed by Congress to regulate grazing on the public domain."[1] Decades of overgrazing had resulted in "the gradual destruction of the grass cover and the spread of desert." The act's intent was to save stockmen from "wildcatters, from overproduction, and from each other" by controlling "grazing on the public range."[2]

But objectives of the law, such as "orderly use of the range," were not meaningful until CCC labor was introduced. The Division of Grazing was quick to put the CCC to work on its objectives. The first DG camps were established in April 1935, and eventually CCC camps were established in the fifty-eight grazing districts of the ten participating western states.[3] By June 1936, the CCC had forty-five camps in ten western states. CCC Director Robert Fechner said the grazing lands have been "so-over-grazed that many years will be required to accomplish satisfactory rehabilitation."[4] When stockmen met in Washington, D.C., in July 1936, they were urging additional CCC range protection camps and further range policing.[5] At the same time, the huge pool of CCC labor began surveying and mapping the vast western grazing lands. In Arizona and New Mexico, their goal was 84,000,000 acres.[6] Approximately 142 million acres were administered by DG, and by the end of the New Deal, over eleven million head of livestock had grazed federal lands.[7]

CCC projects were carried out after the work was suggested and approved by local DG advisory boards. Major areas of CCC work included surveys of range lands; water projects, such as spring development and water reservoir construction; construction of stock trails and stock driveways; construction of fences and corrals; erosion control; flood control; eradication of poisonous weeds; rodent control; reduction of predatory animals; drought relief; cricket control; and emergency work in flood, fire, and downed aircraft. "In 1 short year ... range rehabilitation" has advanced "in some sections from 10 to 20 years."[8] In Arizona, the participation of the CCC in the implementation of the Taylor Grazing Act must be called nothing less than critical to the speedy implementation of the act as well as the completion of an astounding number of projects, frequently of lasting quality.

Congress Junction (DG-47)
1935

The first indications Yavapai County was getting Division of Grazing CCC camps was a Prescott newspaper article reporting two camps in the southern part of the county. The Congress Junction camp was said to be on the James Reese Ranch, 3.5 miles west of Route 89 on the Congress Junction–Hillside Road.[9] (The camp is variously called the Date Creek camp and the Kirkland camp. To lessen confusion, Congress Junction is used throughout this study.) A later newspaper article said the camp was located at Bill Seliger's ranch, with Ray E. Pringle as construction foreman.[10] It was also described as located 12 miles west of Congress Junction.[11] It was not in an organized grazing district. By July 21, the *Arizona Republic* reported the camp was under construction by a crew of twenty-five.[12]

DG-47 was officially occupied on August 17, 1935, by Company 2854. Lt. Knute Hansson was reported to be the commanding officer.[13] Ensign Edward Carlson brought a cadre of fourteen Thumb Butte Company 822 men on August 17. On August 20, one hundred new enrollees arrived from Amarillo, and on August 21, seventy-nine arrived from Fort Worth.[14]

In early October, local stockmen were invited to a meeting at the camp to discuss the camp's projects. Ernest Carleton was reported to be the project superintendent of the 187-man camp. They were already improving the road from the Arrowhead Service station on Route 89 to the Date Creek station.[15] Forty-three ranches were represented on the committee, and they recommended a stock drive from Congress Junction to Skull Valley. There was also interest in stock tanks and wells.[16]

In mid-October, DG-47 was to participate in a Prescott CCC athletic meet along with Forest Service camps. Baseball, track, boxing, wrestling, ping-pong, horseshoes, and other sports were scheduled, according to Dori Hjalmarson, the state CCC educational director.[17] Later in the month, Carleton spoke to Kiwanis and emphasized his new enrollees were generally good. However, some were having problems adjusting to the new surroundings. He quoted a homesick boy: "I came from around Amarillo, where you can look in every direction as far as the eye can see. But here we are in this little old hole and the mountains around about are just a-squishin me." Carleton said he counseled the boy at length, yet he was AWOL the following day. Four of the boys could not write their names, and some did not want to wear shoes. He gave much credit to LEMs for teaching the enrollees heavy equipment operation, how to mind their clothing, and in general how to "watch out for themselves."[18]

November began on a positive note, as a number of Wickenburg groups entertained the camp.[19] CCC Inspector James C. Reddoch inspected the camp on November 18 and noted that the present work was road construction and betterment, but that after January they would start well drilling, spring development, and stock tank construction.[20] At Thanksgiving time, the camp was reported to have 195 enrollees, leaders, and staff (most from Texas, with 25 from Arizona and 12 from Oklahoma).[21]

In early December, the camp began work on the New Octave Road where a spike camp was set up. The new cut-off road was said to be opening soon.[22] On December 2, the Prescott newspaper reported that Miss Sharlot M. Hall gave an entertaining program on pioneer life to the camp.[23] Nine days later, the newspaper featured an AP dispatch stating: "389 CCC Camps to Shut up on Jan. 1."[24] It was not until early January that newspaper readers learned that the two Yavapai County DG camps would be retained until at least April 1.[25] At the end of the year, DG-47 had 170 white enrollees (139 from Texas and the remainder from Arizona and Oklahoma).

1936

During the first half of the year, there is little information about the camp's work. At the end of January, the camp's commanding officer, Lieutenant Hansson, was transferred to Phoenix, leaving John A. Mehlhon in charge.[26] In February, project superintendents from the six area CCC camps were called to Phoenix to meet with Grazing Inspector John W. Johnson to plan for the spring work.[27] In March came word that DG-47 might be disbanded in April.[28] In April, Company 2854 was ordered to Elk Springs, Colorado.[29] It is not known exactly when they departed Congress Junction. They are recorded as arriving at DG-1, Elk Springs, on May 6, 1936. DG-47 is recorded as unoccupied during the Seventh Enrollment Period (April 1, 1936 to September 30, 1936) in the DOI CCC camp directory.[30]

In early October, newspapers announced an increase in CCC camps, including the re-occupation of DG-47.[31] The camp was officially occupied on October 16 by Company 852. They previously worked at SCS-2, Pima, Arizona. Work began on October 19 with two projects: Sunflower Flats Erosion Project and Camp Trail. The former covered 1,400 acres of grazing lands, constructing diversion dams, percolators, spreaders, and rock and brush gully plugs. The Camp Trail work consisted of maintenance and improvements, including eighteen major crossings. Construction of the 4-mile-long Date Creek Trail began on November 16, involving both reconstruction and maintenance.[32]

On the same day, Inspector E. W. Samuell arrived for a three-day inspection. He noted company strength at 181, but that much of the equipment was run down and needed painting. The camp was scrupulously clean and the enrollees "contented." The commanding officer, Capt. D. L. Ray, "was very capable." "The mess was good." The educational advisor "appears to be very good." Earl Alcott, the project superintendent, is "capable," and in a short while, "everything will be running properly." Regarding the planned work projects, he called the 600–man day Cottonwood Trail project "wisely chosen and will do much good." He concluded: "I believe this will be one of our best camps."[33]

Work on the Cottonwood Trail, about 3 miles long, started November 25. Heavy rock deposits that involved "excessive blasting" and bad weather meant intermittent work on this project. Samuell returned for a two-day inspection on December 1 to just 149 enrollees and camp morale that was "very low." Reasons for this seemed to be the new camp location and a commanding officer who "seems too hard on enrollees." Samuell asserted that "the work program does not appeal to many stockmen as much of the work is the Sunflower Flats Erosion impacts only a few stockmen."[34] He returned two weeks later and reported: "Morale of the enrolled men [is] rather low. Don't like the distance from town. Should work out alright." The Army: "Seems to be cooperating and a fair mess." The Sunflower Flats Erosion Projects were good work. The Camp Trail is in "first class shape." The Cottonwood Trail, which led to the Billingsley Ranch, replaces a terrible road, he reported.[35] On December 31, the camp had 142 men from five different 8th Corps states.

1937

On January 28, 1937, the camp began work on the Congress Flats Erosion Area. "The area was chosen because of the unusually fine opportunity to concentrate on the principals [sic] of water spreading and flood irrigation." During the heavy winter snows, the camp was active in feeding of wildlife.36 In March, an area grazing district was voted in. It was hoped that would result in the two county DG camps continuing. However, it appeared that both camps would be moved after April 1. There was some hope the camps would return in the fall.37 Unfortunately, little is known of the camp's work the rest of the year. The camp was officially abandoned on May 2, 1937.38 Company 852 traveled to DG-51, Rock Springs, Texas.

Yava (DG-8)
1935

DG-8 was said to be located at the Wayne Ritter Ranch near Yava, otherwise known as the Henry Ritter Ranch39 and sixteen miles west of Kirkland.40 Also called the Thompson Valley, Kirkland, and Hillside camps, the Army reported it occupied on October 24, 1935, by Company 2541. Little is known of the early history of the camp. Company 2541 was located previously at F-401, Salmon, Idaho, on June 25, 1935. Special Investigator Reddoch visited the camp on November 18 and noted that the only work authorized then was road betterment.41 According to the camp newspaper, 190 new enrollees from West Virginia arrived in camp on November 24.42 In early December, J. L. Gay and M. B Quimby were said to be the superintendents at the new camp.43 On December 31, the *Arizona Republic* reported that Company 2541 was to be replaced by Company 1849 by June 30.44 At year's end, the camp had 186 enrollees (160 from West Virginia and the rest from Arizona and Texas). Camp managers included an Army captain and first lieutenant, a contract physician, and an educational advisor.

1936

The Prescott newspaper announced 185 West Virginia enrollees were leaving on January 5 to be replaced by 50 enrollees from BR-17 Parker Dam.45 Company 1849 arrived in camp on January 13, 1936. The *Prescott Evening Courier* reported that the camp was to be retained in the area until at least April 1.46

On March 6, the local newspaper reported the camp hosted a large gathering of sheepmen, goatmen, and cattlemen discussing fencing of a sheep drive and Taylor Grazing Act possibilities.47 In early March, the camp had a formal dedication for the recently completed Reagan Truck Trail. The truck trail lay two miles north of Yava and opened up the mesa country. Other camp projects were the Mule Shoe Ranch to S H Ranch 7-mile-long truck trail that was nearing completion, re-vetment and bank protection of the Yava bridge, road widening at Lawler Hill of Hillside Road, maintenance of the 6-mile-long Kirkland–Hillside Road, and a 12-mile-long telephone line.48

Figure 26. Typical Raising a Phone Line Pole, CCC Company 819, 1936. Courtesy Grand Canyon National Park Museum Collection #9254.

On April 11, the Phoenix newspaper announced Dr. E. B. Jolley, Hillside camp CCC physician, was going to Jerome as physician at the Phelps Dodge Hospital. Jolley has been a CCC medical officer for four years.49

Special Investigator A. W. Stockman visited the camp on June 13 and pronounced it "is ably administered." He summarized some of the work: Yava Bridge soil erosion; Chilson Fence, 23 miles long; Yava stock tank of 3 acres; Pike Cutoff Truck Trail, 6 miles; Sunflower Flats erosion, 640 acres; and the S. H. Truck Trail, 8 miles just completed. He also included in his report a long list of substantial contributions of materials by companies and ranchers, such as 3,000 pounds of cement by Chilton & Son; 24 miles of wire by Chilson; 35 miles of wire by Jack Sparks; 625 pounds of powder by the Humboldt Mine; and Hillside telephone line materials by Ray Cowden, Chilson, Satitite, Darnell, and Rice.50 On June 23, Special Investigator Samuell noted the camp had 172 enrollees. He reported "everything in good shape" and the "mess is probably the best of any camp we have in this district."51 On June 30, Company 1849 had 168 enrollees (from Arizona, Colorado, Texas, Oklahoma, and New Mexico, with 1 African American).

Inspector Samuell returned on July 15 and reported 162 enrollees. He observed that the Army and camp technical services worked in "complete harmony." The educational program was very good, and all the foremen were teaching courses. A new twenty-five-man spike camp was ready for occupancy and called "a credit to [the] base camp." It was located thirty-eight miles west of the main camp and was constructing the Wild Horse Basin Truck Trail. The Colburn Truck Trail was nearing completion, and the 24-mile-long Chilson Fence was one week from completion. The twelve-acre Yava stock tank was finished. The Cowden Springs development was started, with ranchers supplying materials. The Sun Flower Flats soil erosion work was "good looking."[52] On July 21, the Phoenix newspaper reported the dedication of the CCC-constructed Yava Dam.[53]

On August 31, enrollee Clarence Melton, 19, of Oklahoma, was killed in a truck accident. Melton was riding on the back of the flatbed truck, the truck slid into a ditch, and Melton was crushed under the truck. The truck driver was convicted and given a ninety-day jail term for reckless driving.[54]

In about September 1936, Lt. Ralph T. Smith was commanding officer, Lt. Richard C. Corbyn was exchange officer, Edward T. Wolf was camp surgeon, Troy W. Cocke was educational advisor, and Edward M. Joyce was project superintendent.[55]

On October 13, Samuell inspected the camp for three days and reported camp strength at only 74. He advised: "Army: Gives 100 per cent cooperation and feeds well." He reported the rodent control project going well, with average catches of seventy-five gophers per day. Enrollees were trapping as many as one hundred gophers per day, with 220 traps on a four-acre plot. All other jobs reported on were rated satisfactory or higher. Lt. Ralph T. Smith was the commanding officer, E. M. Joyce was the project superintendent, and Troy W. Cocke was the educational advisor.[56]

On November 2, the Prescott newspaper had a lengthy illustrated article about DG CCC work. It included details of the work projects and future projects. Project superintendent Joyce reported that DG-8 communicated with Phoenix via a new $5,000 radio. "Communication with side camps on isolated sections of the range is by carrier pigeons," he said.[57]

On November 18, Samuell inspected for two days and reported 164 enrollees. Regarding morale he said: "The men all seem satisfied. No complaints." Of the Army he wrote: "This is still a show camp for the Phoenix District." One local stockman was quoted as saying the CCC fences were the "best fences he had ever seen." Regarding the Date Creek cutoff, the work was satisfactory, but there was much powder work due to hard granite. He wrote: "This will be a great benefit to the community when completed because the traffic is heavy and lots of ore trucks travelling the crocked narrow road that is being cutoff makes it dangerous." "The Wild Horse Basin Truck Trail is a beautiful job."[58]

On December 23, the Prescott newspaper reported the stockmen of the county voted by two out of three to form a grazing district in southwest Yavapai County. The article quoted Ed Jamieson, president of the Mohave County Livestock Association, saying that in the event that Yavapai stockmen did not desire a grazing district "we in Mohave county are going to get your CCC camps; in fact, we have already asked that they be moved into our district." Grazing districts were said to be popular in Mohave. Removal of CCC camps from the county would be a serious blow to the livestock industry, reported the article.[59]

A week later, the newspaper detailed the camp's gopher control work. County agricultural agent E. S. Turville authored the piece, saying about 22,400 acres had been covered so far and he estimated 150,000 gophers would be removed. He said enrollees started at Wagoner and moved west through Walnut Grove. The plan was to work Skull Valley and thence the Kirkland district west along the valley. He said each boy covered about 5 acres daily.[60] On December 31, Company 1849 had 147 white enrollees (most from Oklahoma, Texas, and New Mexico).

1937

The blizzard that impacted northern Arizona, southern Utah, and Nevada also impacted Yavapai County. In the Yava area, snow ranged from 14" to 3'. Most camp work was curtailed, and enrollees focused on the rescue of stranded people and the relief of wildlife. The camp used tractors and blades, working both day and night, to relieve snow-bound ranchers. "In one case where no other means was available we transported a supply of groceries on a tractor by night over a snow bound area to an isolated camp in the mountains occupied by some fifteen people who were entirely out of food, arriving there we found a woman seriously ill and succeeded in getting her out by hooking the tractor onto the husband's car and literally dragging it over the surface of the snow until we arrived at a cleared road." In another case, they saved a goat rancher from losing his entire herd by clearing his road so he could transport hay and grain to the starving animals.[61] The camp's project superintendent, E. M. Joyce, and the Prescott Fish and Game Association purchased tons of grain for the starving quail. Enrollees also brought incapacitated birds into camp, cared for them, and released them later. Many songbirds were also saved by the feeding. It was estimated that those efforts saved 50% of the quail.[62]

The life of the camp was extended a bit when the grazing district was approved. The local newspaper said that both county grazing camps would not be moved at least until the next enrollment period began in April.[63] Inspector Samuell visited the camp on March 31 and noted camp strength was 159, with 9 LEMs. He reported that the local stockmen were disappointed the camp was leaving. The company had produced "a friendly feeling." The Wild Horse Basin spike camp was moving back to the main camp, leaving 78% of the truck trail completed. He noted the "basin people are very disappointed that this couldn't have been completed but appreciate the work that has been done."[64] The 8th Period narrative report noted this truck trail work was impeded substantially by the heavy snows and then by the very wet ground afterwards. Unfortunately, this report is all the information we have about the company work in 1937.

At Hillside, the camp completed a community corral that included partitions and a branding chute and two cement water troughs. Also at Hillside was a telephone line connecting the CCC camp to Hillside and the Hillside Cattle Company. At Cowden Springs, development included digging down 20′ and constructing a rubble masonry wall, which allowed the water to flow to a cement storage tank and water troughs. The rodent control work was done by foreman S. E. Barber and a crew of ten enrollees. As many as four thousand pocket gophers per square mile were trapped.

The 4.5-mile-long Colburn Truck Trail was completed. It was a link between the county highway between Kirkland and Yava with the S.H. Truck Trail and Pikes Cut-Off. The 2.5-mile-long Date Creek Cut-Off Truck Trail required substantial blasting and construction of culverts. The Nichols Truck Trail was reported less than a mile long leading from the county highway to the Nichols Ranch. Work was started, but it is uncertain if it was completed.[65] In addition to the Yava stock tank completed in 1936, the camp completed several other reservoirs and tanks, both large and small.[66]

On April 10, the local newspaper announced the Yava camp was to be abandoned, but there was hope for a later re-occupancy.[67] DG-8 was officially abandoned on May 2, 1937.[68] It was not re-occupied. Company 1849 arrived at DG-65, Massadona, Colorado, on May 4.

Unless noted otherwise, any reference to the number of enrollees in a company, the location of the company, or company supervisors are from U.S. War Department, Location and Strength of CCC Companies, 1933–1942, NARAMD RG 35 530/65/22/04/05.

1. U.S. Civilian Conservation Corps, *Annual Report of the Director of Emergency Conservation Work, Fiscal Year Ending June 30, 1936*, 42.
2. Schlesinger, *Age of Roosevelt*, 345.
3. Wirth, *Civilian Conservation Corps of the United States Department of the Interior, March 1933 to June 30, 1943*, 33.
4. "Tells Work of Grazing Camps," *Prescott Evening Courier*, June 13, 1936, 2.
5. "Stock Leaders Tell Ickes of Grazing Needs," *Arizona Republic*, July 10, 1936, 1, 8.
6. "CCC Enrollees under Grazing Division Will Map Vast Area," *Prescott Evening Courier*, July 10, 1936, 10.
7. Lowitt, *New Deal and the West*, 67.
8. U.S. CCC, *Annual Report of the Director of Emergency Conservation Work, Fiscal Year Ending June 30, 1936*, 43. See also Wirth, *Civilian Conservation Corps of the United States Department of the Interior, March 1933 to June 30, 1943*, 33–35.
9. "Select 2 More CCC Camp Sites," *Prescott Evening Courier*, May 29, 1935, 1, 3.
10. "Congress Junction," *Prescott Evening Courier*, July 29, 1935, 4.
11. U.S. BLM (Bureau of Grazing), CCC Correspondence Relating to the Establishment and Administration of the Camp Work Program, 1935–39, General Correspondence, Records of the Bureau of Land Management (Bureau of Grazing), NARACO RG 47 File Entry 2 Box 6.
12. "CCC Building Work Is Started," *Arizona Republic*, July 21, 1935, sect. 2, 2.
13. "Congress Junction," *Prescott Evening Courier*, September 2, 1935, 6.
14. *Prescott Evening Courier*, November 27, 1935, 2.
15. "Stockmen to Meet at Date Creek CCC Camp," *Prescott Evening Courier*, October 5, 1935, 8.
16. "Stock Drive Proposed to Congress Junction," *Prescott Evening Courier*, October 9, 1935, 7.
17. "CCC Athletic Meet Scheduled," *Arizona Republic*, October 12, 1935, sect. 2, 2.
18. "CCC Leader Talks before Kiwanians," *Prescott Evening Courier*, October 24, 1935, 2.
19. *Arizona Republic*, November 2, 1935, 6.
20. U.S. CCC, Camp Inspection Reports, NARAMD RG 35/530/65/23/04 Entry 115 (PI #11) Box 10.
21. "CCC Will Have Loaded Tables," *Prescott Evening Courier*, November 27, 1935, 2.
22. *Date Creek Rattler*, November 25, 1935 and December 16, 1935, Fiche MN #1689, CRL Newspapers.
23. "Tells Boys about Date Creek Camp" *Prescott Evening Courier*, December 2, 1935, 9.

24. See also "Arizona to Lose Six CCC Companies by January 16," *Arizona Republic,* December 31, 1935, 2. The state's only "colored" CCC camp at Fort Huachuca was one of the six. This company, 2871, composed largely of Texas enrollees, was the state's only African American company.
25. *Prescott Evening Courier,* January 4, 1936, 2; per a telegram from Congresswoman Greenway to Grace Sparkes, the chamber of commerce secretary.
26. "Congress Junction," *Prescott Evening Courier,* January 29, 1936, 2.
27. "Federal Range Work Discussed," *Arizona Republic,* February 22, 1936, 7.
28. "CCC to Disband 21 State Camps," *Arizona Republic,* March 20, 1936, 8.
29. *Date Creek Rattler,* April 11, 1936, Fiche MN #1689, CRL Newspapers.
30. U.S. Department of the Interior, CCC, "Directory of All CCC Camps Supervised by the Technical Agencies of the Department of the Interior since Inception of the CCC Program" (Dec. 31 1940), NARACO BLM(GS) CCC Directories RG 49 Entry 34, 35 Box 133.
31. "CCC to Add Nearly 500," *Arizona Republic,* October 2, 1936, sect. 2, 5.
32. U.S. BLM, Grazing, "Narrative Report of Camp Accomplishments, DG47A Eighth Period," Narrative Reports of Individual CCC Camps, 1936–1938, NARACO, RG 49/15/6/7/4/1 Box 6 Entry 19 (PI #11) Box 75.
33. U.S. BLM, Camp Inspection Reports, 1938–1942, NARACO RG 49 Entry 20 Box 86.
34. Ibid.
35. Ibid.
36. U.S. BLM, Grazing. "Narrative Report of Camp Accomplishments, DG47A Eighth Period," Narrative Reports of Individual CCC Camps, 1936–1938, NARACO, RG 49/15/6/7/4/1 Box 6 Entry 19 (PI #11) Box 75.
37. "May Forestall Two DG Camp Transfers," *Prescott Evening Courier,* March 19, 1937, 2; "Says DG Camps Will Be Moved," *Prescott Evening Courier,* April 10, 1937, 2.
38. "Civilian Conservation Corps Eighth Corps Area, Status Record of CCC Camps Authorized Since Inception of the Program up to … December 31, 1941 … Compiled by Office of Liaison Officer, CCC Fort Sam Houston…," NARACO BLM CCC Directories RG 49 Entry 33, 34 Box 132.
39. "Select 2 More CCC Camp Sites," *Prescott Evening Courier,* May 29, 1935, 1, 3.
40. U.S. BLM (Bureau of Grazing), CCC Correspondence Relating to the Establishment and Administration of the Camp Work Program 1935–39, General Correspondence, Records of the Bureau of Land Management (Bureau of Grazing), NARACO RG 47 File Entry 2 Box 6.
41. U.S. BLM, Camp Inspection Reports, 1938–1942, NARACO RG 49 Entry 20 Box 86.
42. *Depression Cure,* November 28, 1935, Fiche MN #1412, CRL Newspapers.
43. *Prescott Evening Courier,* December 3, 1935, 2.
44. "Arizona to Lose Six CCC Companies by January 16," *Arizona Republic,* December 31, 1935, 2.
45. *Prescott Evening Courier,* January 3, 1936, 2.
46. *Prescott Evening Courier,* January 4, 1936, 2.
47. "Kirkland," *Prescott Evening Courier,* March 6, 1936, 13.
48. "Open Truck Trail with Ceremonies," *Prescott Evening Courier,* March 9, 1936, 3.
49. "CCC Camp Physician Gets Hospital Post," *Arizona Republic,* April 11, 1936, sect. 2, 1.
50. U.S. CCC, Camp Inspection Reports, NARAMD RG 35/530/65/23/04 Entry 115 (PI #11) Box 10 .
51. U.S. BLM, Camp Inspection Reports, 1938–1942, NARACO RG 49 Entry 20 Box 84.
52. Ibid.
53. "New Yava Dam Dedication Held," *Arizona Republic,* July 21, 1936, 10.
54. "Inquest into Death of CCC Boy Slated," *Prescott Evening Courier,* September 1, 1936, 3; "CCC Truck Driver Gets 90-Day Term," *Prescott Evening Courier,* September 3, 1936, 6; Arizona Death Records, State File No. 442, Registered No. 302-J.
55. U.S. CCC, Phoenix District, *Official Annual, 1936, Phoenix District, 8th Corps Area, Civilian Conservation Corps* ([Baton Rouge, LA?]: Direct Advertising Co., 1936), 24–25. GCNPMC Cat. #70738.
56. U.S. BLM, Camp Inspection Reports, 1938–1942, NARACO RG 49 Entry 20 Box 84.
57. *Prescott Evening Courier,* November 2, 1936, 4.
58. U.S. BLM, Camp Inspection Reports, 1938–1942, NARACO RG 49 Entry 20 Box 84.
59. "Mohave after Yavapai Camps," *Prescott Evening Courier,* December 23, 1936, 1, 3.
60. E. S. Turville, "CCC Boys Carry on Gopher War," *Prescott Evening Courier,* December 30, 1936, 6.
61. U.S. BLM, Grazing, "Narrative Report of Camp Accomplishments, DG8A Eighth Period," Narrative Reports of Individual CCC Camps, 1936–1938. NARACO, RG 49/15/6/7/4/1 Box 6 Entry 19 (PI #11) Box 74.
62. Ibid.; "Quail Are Fed Tons of Grain," *Prescott Evening Courier,* January 21, 1937, 1, 8. Six thousand pounds of grain were distributed, and sixty enrollees worked on this project for nearly a week.

63. "May Forestall Two DG Camp Transfers," *Prescott Evening Courier,* March 19, 1937, 2.
64. U.S. BLM, Camp Inspection Reports, 1938–1942, NARACO RG 49 Entry 20 Box 84.
65. U.S. BLM, Grazing, "Narrative Report of Camp Accomplishments, DG8A Eighth Period," Narrative Reports of Individual CCC Camps, 1936–1938. NARACO, RG 49/15/6/7/4/1 Box 6 Entry 19 (PI #11) Box 74.
66. U.S. CCC, "Resume of CCC Program," December 30, 1938, BLM (GS) CCC Work Program Correspondence, 1938–39, NARACO RG 49 Entry 4 Box 13, page 46.
67. "Says DG Camps Will Be Moved," *Prescott Evening Courier,* April 10, 1937, 2.
68. "Civilian Conservation Corps Eighth Corps Area, Status Record of CCC Camps Authorized Since Inception of the Program up to … December 31, 1941 … Compiled by Office of Liaison Officer, CCC Fort Sam Houston…," NARACO BLM CCC Directories RG 49 Entry 33, 34 Box 132.

CHAPTER 9

Camp Newspapers

ALMOST FROM THE BEGINNING OF the CCC in 1933, individual camps published mimeographed and sometimes printed newspapers. Although today much of their content appears quaint, even naïve, they open for us a clear window into the minds of the CCC boys and their leaders.

The typical CCC boy in an Arizona camp was often from a farm or small town in Arizona, Texas, Oklahoma, Colorado, or New Mexico. Later, some enrollees were shipped to Arizona from Pennsylvania and nearby states. Sometimes these Eastern boys were from large cities such as Philadelphia and Pittsburgh. If he was lucky, he had finished high school. Most likely he had never had a paying job. He probably did not have a driver's license.

A Big Job

Nationally, the first camp newspapers appeared in mid-April 1933. On May 20, the first issue of *Happy Days*, a national weekly CCC tabloid, appeared. By July 1933, *Happy Days* was publishing five hundred thousand copies weekly.[1] At the end of the CCC in 1942, well over five thousand camp newspapers appeared, published by nearly three thousand CCC companies.[2] Nationwide, by 1937, 80 percent of CCC companies had a local camp newspaper.[3] *Happy Days* promoted the publication of local camp newspapers in a number of ways. They reprinted stories from camp newspapers, and they offered to critique any camp newspaper that submitted a sample for analysis and then printed a review along with a rating from one to five stars.[4]

Of the forty-four companies in this study, newspapers have survived from twenty-five companies. The typical camp newspaper was from four to twenty pages long and was usually a monthly. Often the newspapers were produced as part of a journalism class taught by the camp's educational advisor.[5] At Grand Canyon, Robert Ashe, educational advisor to Camp 819, described putting out the monthly newspaper as "quite a job." Often, one enrollee, frequently titled the assistant educational advisor, was used full-time for the newspaper work.[6]

The CCC newspapers varied in quality. Some companies were able to establish a close relationship with the local town newspaper. The latter might print the actual camp newspaper or run a regular CCC column in their pages.[7] Frequently their names changed. When a camp moved to another location, a newspaper might cease publication. Sometimes the newspaper's staff was discharged, seriously affecting the publication. But even with all these variables, the newspapers remain a diary and often a history of the company.[8] And importantly, says CCC historian Richard Melzer of New Mexico: "Camp newspapers reinforced CCC values and life lessons…. If a main purpose of the CCC was to help mold loyal, hard-working, cooperative Americans, CCC newspapers helped set the mold with words of instruction surrounded by words and images of diversion."[9]

Northern Arizona's camp newspapers followed the national norm. Their titles varied from the prosaic to the unusual and the exotic, even to the suggestive. Company 311 of Flagstaff published *The Eight-Holer* in 1939, no doubt referring to their latrine. Company 2541 of Hillside published *Depression Cure*. For a short time, Pipe Spring's Company 2557 newspaper was called *See See See News*. Topock's Company 2833, located on the Arizona-California state line, published the *Calizonian*. Prescott's Company 3320, composed of many Pennsylvanians, was titled *Pennzonian*. By far, northern Arizona camp newspaper titles were commonplace, such as *Pipe Post* (Pipe Spring); *Petrified Log*, *Kaibab Kalendar* (Williams); *Date Creek Rattler*, *Dreamer* (Lynx Creek); and *The Conservator* (Clarkdale).

The newspapers were distributed to company staff and enrollees. They were sometimes mailed to a boy's local town newspaper and family members. Occasionally, material was "borrowed" from other camp newspapers or *Happy Days*. But it appears much of their material was original. The content of the camp newspapers in this study fits into three broad categories: entertainment, information, and editorial.

Newspapers as Entertainment

A typical northern Arizona newspaper frequently had cartoons featuring enrollees and leaders. Much of the newspaper humor consisted of short jokes. Like typical young men, the subjects of the jokes were often what was on their minds—girls, money, and jobs. And often the names in the jokes appear to be actual camp enrollees.

The "Jokes" column of the Double Springs, Company 863's *Big Tree Breeze* had this exchange:

Allen Garret: Peaches, if you were out with a girl who didn't smoke, drink, or pet, what would you do to show her a good time?

Peaches: I'd teach her to smoke, drink, and pet.[10]

The Flagstaff, Company 821's *Echo of the Peaks* "Laughs" page had this witty story:

I'm sorry, said Flowers, who hoped to get away with it, but I haven't any money to pay for that meal.

That's all right, said the cashier. We'll write your name on the wall and you can pay next time you come in.

Don't do that. Everybody who comes in here will see it.

Oh, no, they won't. Your overcoat will be hanging over it.[11]

The Double Springs, Company 863's *Lakeside Mirror* contained this exchange:

Lieut.: If you discovered you had $10.00 in your pocket right now, what would you do?

Fuller: I'd try to find out whose pants they were.[12]

From time to time the humor was not the young males' typical subjects. Congress Junction, Company 2854's "Grab-a-Grin" page contained this:

Curley Myers: This rope is to catch cows with, mam [sic].

Sweet Young Easterner: How interesting Mr. Myers, but what do you use for bait?[13]

The September 1937 *Dreamer* (F-62, Company 2861) "Humor Page" contained this:

Chongo—What's my temperature, Doctor?

Cox—Hundred and three.

Chongo—What's the world's record?[14]

Double Springs, Company 863's *Big Tree Breeze* "Smiles" page had this:

Alfonso Perez: I don't believe no woman could be so fat.

Nick Portillo: What yer reading now Little Alfonso?

Perez: Why, this newspaper tells about an English woman that lost two thousand pounds.[15]

Round Valley, Arizona's Company 2865 *Camp News* had this cute witticism:

Teacher: "What is a cannibal Jimmy?"

Jimmy: "I don't know."

Teacher: "Well, if you ate your mother and father what would you be?"

Jimmy: "An orphan."[16]

Northern Arizona camp newspapers infrequently "borrowed" from nearby camp newspapers. This joke, out of Company 863's *Big Tree Breeze,* was noted in other camp newspapers at least three other times, and each time the names were changed:

Where did you get that sheep, Red? asked Mr. Hosford.

Out on the Mesa, replied Red Morgan.

What are you going to do with her?

I'm going to make a pet out of her.

Where are you going to keep her? asked the inquisitive Mr. Hosford.

I'm going to keep her there in our tent, was the curt reply.

How about the awful stink?

Oh she'll have to get used to that.[17]

From time to time a newspaper would feature song lyrics. Original poetry appeared in many newspapers. Generally, the poems were editorial in nature, emphasizing positive themes, a "can do" attitude and the like. This original bit of poetry is from the Hualapai Mountain Park, Company 830's *Wallapai Tiger*:

NO GOLDBRICK, THIS

Here's to a worker
Who's never a shirker.
He's a go-getter from the start.
He's been a swell friend,
Whose staunchness knows no end.
He's a pal after my own heart.[18]

But once in a while poems were strictly entertaining in nature. The Petrified Forest National Monument, Company 831's *Petrified Log* printed this:

Ambitions in the CCC

To sleep all day
To leave your bed unmade
To get out of sweeping
To sneak out of Saturday clean-up
To work up suction with the cooks[19]

On occasion, camp newspapers would have poetry that was surprising. (For a short sampling of more CCC camp newspaper poetry and song, see Appendix 3.) Philip Teague authored this poem that appeared in Company 2863's *Denim Doings*:

Sylvia
Dark-eyed maiden
Of the forest,
Look upon me;
As I tell thee
Of my love.
O, Bright Rainbow

Of the shadows,
May we ever
Be together
In the summers
Yet to come![20]

Wilburn T. Whitlock of Company 1837 in Kingman wrote his song "Your Lament":

Where are you now? Where did you go
After we said goodbye?
Where are you dear? I want you so
Here as the moon rises high.
One little word, ghost in the moonlight
Oh, tell me, why was it spoken?
One little word, haunting a June night.
Mocking a heart that is broken.
Where are you now? Are you alone?
Are you unfettered and free?
My heart is calling—"You are my own."
Forgive—and wait for me.[21]

Reading the camp newspapers gives a glimpse into a time when nicknames, at least among men, seem to be much more common than today. The newspapers also reflect some of the unique slang of the CCC. Nicknames for the organization included *Tree Army, Tree Troopers,* and *Tree Monkeys*. A wheelbarrow was often a *sand wagon,* and the enrollee who pushed it was a *truck driver.* The camp's educational advisor was *prof* or *brains*. Common foods often had their special names: toast was *shingles,* sliced peaches were *gold fish,* and prunes were *army strawberries*. Since the evening meal for the boys required them to dress in a regulation uniform, one's black tie was a *meal ticket*.[22]

Many of the most popular slang terms are no longer recognized by most. A *goldbricker* was a loafer. *Hooey* meant nonsense. A *crud* was a boy who was slovenly. A *peavie* was a rookie. When chow was served, those who lined up for seconds or thirds were *wolves*. And if you did not roll your own cigarettes but bought them in a pack, you smoked *tailormades*.[23]

A Source of Information

The informational aspects of camp newspapers were many. From time to time, national news stories were included. "Comings and Goings" columns helped enrollees keep up on men who were being discharged as well as new company members. News items on "Infirmary News," evening movie fare, new company jobs, and new books and magazines in the camp library were no doubt important, and occasionally a dance or lecture was announced.

From time to time, the "news" was a mix of gossip, even innuendo. One issue of the Company 863 newspaper was titled "The Mudsplasher" and another page was "Beaver Clippins."[24] The Pipe Springs newspaper speculated that enrollees Floyd Higehock and Andy Worley were going to sign up for an additional six months, as the girls in Kanab had "inveighed the two into town every week end."[25]

The September 8, 1934, F-6, Double Springs *Big Tree Breeze* reported: "Ford Caulkins and Roland Byers were caught red-handed behind Spearman's Store the other night attacking a couple of quarts of harmless, weak-looking milk." The case was thrown out of court. "If the fluid was 'whitemule,' its kicks would have been strong enough to protect itself."[26]

From time to time, northern Arizona newspapers had articles dealing with the history of the CCC company and local community history. *Echo of the Peaks* told of the first enrollees arriving at the new company area where "there were no buildings, no company street, no headquarters—in fact, the only thing to see in Camp now is … one little lonesome water faucet."[27] News of what was happening to the company pet, articles about good hygiene, and advertisements for services offered by other enrollees appeared from time to time. A few of the newspapers had crossword puzzles.

During the Thanksgiving and Christmas holidays, the dinner menus were always featured. Contests were sometimes announced, such as "The Best Barracks" or "Reading Library Books Tally," frequently awarding the winner with cigarettes. Camp newspapers often announced educational opportunities. Many courses were listed in the newspapers, with occupational classes the most popular, followed by remedial and craft classes. An especially well-read section of the camp newspaper was the results of recent camp sports competitions. At least eleven sports were mentioned in the Grand Canyon newspapers, with baseball, boxing, volleyball, billiards, and football appearing to be the most popular.[28]

Safety was a frequent topic. "Riding on (truck) fender, bumpers, running boards and cab top will be prohibited," declared the *Hualpai Echo*.[29] Another frequent topic was updating the reader on progress on a particular job or project. The Company 821 newspaper, in an article titled "Porky Crew at Work," explained in detail the rationale for killing porcupines as well as the specifics of the poison baits used. It noted that 530 porcupines were shot near Flagstaff in a two-month period.[30] Patriotic essays were also common fare.

Page of Dirt

This guy Murray must be quite a popular man back home considering the fan mail he gets.

What's wrong Fallon, why didn't you send the pillow case to the girl you intended it for?

Who is the fellow who put Home Sweet Home on a mat and then reenrolled? How about it Bixler?

Will the Columbia guys ever come out of it? Never mind, men you'll be home with your sweethearts some time.

They say if you stay here long enough you'll get just like "Bloomers".

What did Roman think he was, trying to give himself a baldy? Wise up, pal, you're no contortionist, try to borrow 20¢.

Whistle it Peterlan and make yourself understood.

Hey, Chink! You're supposed to take your shoes off when you go to bed.

Take that important look off your face Hopie, you're only a truck driver.

Who's the guy that is always complaining about the food and the last one to leave the table? Maybe Moffitt could answer that one.

Look out fellows, here comes the boy with the large biceps. Oh, hello, Harry.

They say that every time Big Stoop feels a breeze he reaches for a blanket.

Hey, Mr. Finn wanted a good driver, not you "Fats".

Who was the guy from barrack No. 2 that was mistaken for a barrel the other night?

If Rose didn't write to Parise who would inspire him?

Moe might not be aware of it but we, (the entire barracks), hope he gets to make it to town Saturday night.

Pegula says he is going to be a hermit for the next six months. Does he have a reason? It must be love.

Figure 27. "Page of Dirt" from Forest Desert, Company 3342 Newspaper, September 1, 1939. Courtesy Petrified Forest National Park Museum Collection #5193.

Editorials

Nearly every newspaper issue had an editorial. The editorials were frequently original, literate, and, sometimes, passionate and sincere. Company 863's newspaper opined that CCC camps "have largely eliminated the threat that enforced idleness brought to the spiritual and moral stability of many of the men … most of the men leaving are better citizens and better prepared to cope with the world then when they enrolled."[31] Company 2847's masthead declared: "With or without offense to friend or foe, I sketch your camp life exactly, exactly as I go."[32] Congress Junction, Company 2854 declared their policy as "1 – To Give a Thought, 2 – To Give a Laugh, 3 – To Print the Newsworthy, (4 – To Print Bigger and Better Rumors – This issue only!)."[33]

Many of the newspaper editorials emphasized a positive "can do" attitude. The Company 3342 newspaper editorialized: "Whether you have moved a step forward to success, or remained stationary by disregarding all the advantages of the CCC, was entirely in your hands."[34] Company 831's commander Lt. Louis M. Linxwiller reminisced that he had "only praise" for the last year in camp. "Let your achievements of 1935 be merely stepping stones to even greater things in 1936."[35] When Company 831 was departing Petrified Forest, Superintendent Charles J. Smith praised the company work saying: "You have been a credit to your organization and your country. Boys, we'll be missing you."[36] Company 3342, in a very personal editorial, praised enrollee Robert Perry for progressing from digging ditches to moving up in more responsible jobs, brushing up on his high school typing and shorthand, and then landing a $1,620-a-year camp clerical position.[37]

Another feature of *Happy Days* and camp newspapers was the almost reverential treatment of President Franklin Delano Roosevelt. Frequently, camp newspapers contained drawings of FDR.[38] In the July 1, 1936, *Voice of the Pack* (Company 847, Grand Canyon), Foreman Walter V. Martin wrote that FDR through the CCC "visioned the poor and needy, with a younger generation and gave them hope and an opportunity to help support their love ones. Thousands of undernourished Americans … began to take a new pulse beat, color in their once pallid faces, and luster in their eyes. They had found a new freedom … They were developing and hardening a once lifeless body and thanking [FDR]." In a short piece titled "CCC Game Hunter," Kingman's *Wallapai Tiger* stated: "The editors rise to remark that Andy Miller's trapping of animals is not so hot, when you consider that Franklin D. Roosevelt drove the wolves from millions of doorsteps."[39]

---

1. Cornebise, *The CCC Chronicles*, 66. For an example of a *Happy Days* front page, see Audretsch, *Shaping the Park and Saving the Boys*, 46.
2. Cornebise, 25.
3. Ibid., 43. The most complete collection of CCC camp newspapers is housed at the Center for Research Libraries (CRL), and many of those are available on microfiche.
4. See *Happy Days*, February 22, 1936, 14; April 18, 1936, 14; and June 20, 1936, 18, for comments about the Kingman camp's *Hualapai Echo*.
5. Cornebise, *The CCC Chronicles*, 2.
6. Robert Ashe, oral history interview, August 18, 1995, 4, GCNPMC.
7. The *Williams News* (summers of 1936 and 1940) and the Kingman *Mohave County Miner* (1935 through 1937) are excellent examples of these cooperative CCC columns. The St. George, Utah, *Washington County Times*, which reported on the camp serving the Arizona Strip, appears to have given the most detailed coverage of CCC camps. It covered the St. George camp, almost always weekly, from 1935 to 1939. It also carried columns regarding other nearby camps such as those at Zion National Park.
8. Cornebise, *The CCC Chronicles*, 23.
9. Melzer, *Coming of Age*, 108–109.
10. July 27, 1934, Civilian Conservation Corps Newsletters, Serials Collection, AHSLA.
11. September 12, 1934, Civilian Conservation Corps Newsletters, Serials Collection, AHSLA.
12. June 14, 1935, Civilian Conservation Corps Newsletters, Serials Collection, AHSLA.
13. March 23, 1936, Fiche MN #1689, CRL Newspapers.
14. Fiche MN #1696, CRL Newspapers.
15. October 19, 1934, Civilian Conservation Corps Newsletters, Serials Collection, AHSLA.
16. March 31, 1937, Civilian Conservation Corps Newsletters, Serials Collection, AHSLA.
17. October 19, 1934, Civilian Conservation Corps Newsletters, Serials Collection, AHSLA.
18. August 8, 1934. It should be noted that the Wallapai Tiger is a very bothersome area insect.
19. April, 1936, Fiche MN #0526, CRL Newspapers.
20. October, 1940, Fiche MN #1698, CRL Newspapers.
21. *Happy Days*, February 17, 1940, 16.
22. Davidson, "C.C.C. Chatter," 210–211.
23. Danner, "C.C.C. Slang," 212–213.
24. *The Lone Beaver*, March 31, 1937, Civilian Conservation Corps Newsletters, Serials Collection, AHSLA.

25. *Pipe Post,* February 9, 1936, Fiche MN #1423, CRL Newspapers.
26. Civilian Conservation Corps Newsletters, Serials Collection AHSLA.
27. May 25, 1934, Civilian Conservation Corps Newsletters, Serials Collection, AHSLA.
28. Other Grand Canyon sports were track, tennis, golf, ping-pong, horseshoes, and croquet.
29. September, 1937, Fiche MN #1171, CRL Newspapers.
30. *Echo of the Peaks*, June 8, 1934, Civilian Conservation Corps Newsletters, Serials Collection, AHSLA.
31. "Some People's Opinion of Us," *Big Tree Breeze,* July 14, 1934, Civilian Conservation Corps Newsletters, Serials Collection, AHSLA.
32. *Pine Needle,* July, 1937, Fiche MN #1682, CRL Newspapers.
33. *Date Creek Rattler,* January 13, 1936, Fiche #MN 1689, CRL Newspapers.
34. *Forest and Desert,* June 8, 1940, Fiche MN #1831, CRL Newspapers.
35. *Petrified Log,* December, 1935, Fiche MN #0526, CRL Newspapers.
36. *Petrified Log,* April, 1936, Fiche MN #0526, CRL Newspapers.
37. *Forest and Desert,* October 1, 1939, Fiche MN #1831, CRL Newspapers.
38. An excellent example is the front page of Kingman's Company 2865's *Camp News,* March 31, 1937, Civilian Conservation Corps Newsletters, Serials Collection, AHSLA.
39. August 8, 1934, Civilian Conservation Corps Newsletters, Serials Collection, AHSLA.

CHAPTER 10

John A. Thompson Ranch (SCS-27)

Soil Conservation Service and the CCC: An Overview

THE U.S. SOIL CONSERVATION SERVICE (first in the Department of Interior, then the Department of Agriculture) was made permanent by the Congressional Soil Conservation Act of April 27, 1935. It was the direct result of the Dust Bowl droughts and flooding of 1934–1935. The act authorized the establishment of soil conservation districts that could offer farmers a variety of programs. Work projects might be on private land, with the landowner supplying the materials and the WPA or CCC contributing the labor.[1] In Arizona, typically the CCC "constructed dikes, installed wire and brush percolators to trap sediments, plowed furrows, built dams, terraced hillsides, and straightened creeks. They also built truck trails and replanted overgrazed vegetation."[2] In Arizona, while the Forest Service had the largest number of CCC camps, the SCS had the third-largest number.

SCS-27
1940

SCS-27 was short-lived, and since it was some distance from any town, there are limited newspaper accounts of camp activity. Unfortunately, only limited information was located in archives. Company 2863 officially arrived at the John A. Thompson Ranch (Long Meadow, twenty-two miles northwest of Prescott) on July 20, 1940. It was previously at SCS-24, the A Kimble Ranch area near Rucker Canyon.

On July 31, 1940, the company reported 193 white enrollees (176 from Texas, 16 from Arizona, including 1 veteran, and 1 from New Mexico). The supervisors were two Army officers, a contract physician, and an educational advisor.

According to the Prescott newspaper, the camp was located at Williamson, Arizona. Capt. Robert Yount was the commanding officer, and C.P. Hook was the project superintendent.[3] The camp newspaper was titled *Denim Doings*, and it was one of few camp newspapers in northern Arizona that had articles in both English and Spanish.[4]

From August 31 to September 30, the number of enrollees dropped from 187 to 98, which is typical of the end of an enrollment period. On October 31, the camp count jumped back up to 192 (127 from Texas, 64 from Arizona, and 1 from New Mexico). The end-of-the-year count was 148 (95 from Texas, 52 from Arizona, and 1 from New Mexico). Company 2863 apparently departed SCS-27, as they are next noted to be back at SCS-24, Rucker Canyon on January 31.

1941

Company 2863 returned to SCS-27 on May 17, 1941, with their May 31 count showing 156 enrollees (91 from Texas, 64 from Arizona, and 1 from New Mexico). The *Prescott Evening Courier* reported their return, stating that they were to continue soil and moisture conservation work on the John A. Thompson Ranch and the Lloyd C. Lakin farm while work was to start on the Cecil White Ranch in Upper Skull Valley.[5]

Special Investigator M. J. Bowen inspected the camp on June 19 and noted that the buildings were new and portable and power was coming from three 5kw units. He noted that athletic equipment was lacking and that many of the enrollees were Catholic and wanted to attend services in Prescott. He said trucks were to arrive in the future to make that possible. He reported that there had been 176 enrollees leaving at the end of their enrollment, with 34 honorable discharges, 18 dishonorable discharges, 1 administrative discharge, and 17 dismissals. (The number of other-than-honorable discharges appears to be a bit high, but in light of the availability of many defense jobs by 1941 and the camp's isolation, those numbers appear to not be unusual.) Bowen reported the camp morale was poor, with many men asking to be transferred out. The mess was poor, apparently due to inexperienced staff and lack of fresh eggs and produce. Work projects were said to be check dams, jetties, water spreaders, etc. Bowen reported work progress was lacking due to poor lunches and lower camp strength. He apparently thought the camp situation serious enough that he sent a letter to CCC Assistant Director C. H. Kenlan in Washington detailing the camp situation. Bowen noted that the day he was there the Army Sub-district Commander Lt. Murray was in camp the same day and promised to send experienced mess staff immediately from a nearby camp that was shutting down. He also promised trucks immediately for the religious services on Sundays and new athletic equipment.

In light of all the deficiencies, Bowen asked to be sent back to re-inspect soon.[6] He filed a "follow-up report" on July 3 reporting morale as "improving." The mess was improved after two experienced mess staff were assigned to camp. New athletic equipment was purchased, and trucks were now taking the

Figure 28. Typical CCC Tank Construction, Deer Tank No. 1, Grand Canyon National Park, Company 819, 1933. Courtesy Grand Canyon National Park Museum Collection #29861.

Catholic enrollees to town for Sunday services.[7]

Camp strength from June 30 to August 30 jumped from 122 to 180. On August 31, D. S. Baird was the commanding officer, James W. Dorsey was the subaltern, and William Mileusnich was the educational advisor.[8] By October 31, the total enrollees had dropped to 131 (90 from Arizona and 41 from Texas). At that time, there were considerable changes in camp supervisors, with Harold E. Sias as commanding officer, L. W. Doson as educational advisor, and Louie McGavic as project superintendent. By November 30, a new commanding officer was noted as Earl McMimimy.[9]

On December 15, the Prescott newspaper reported that the camp was to remain, according to a telegram from Congressman John R. Murdock.[10] At the end of the year, the camp had 111 enrollees (85 from Arizona and the rest from Texas). Supervisors were two Army officers and an educational advisor. No physician was noted.

1942

Company 2863 reported 67 enrollees on January 31 and 56 on February 28 (39 from Arizona, including 1 veteran, and the rest from Texas). There are no reports on the company after this, and it appears it was disbanded during March 1942.

Unless noted otherwise, any reference to the number of enrollees in a company, the location of the company, or company supervisors are from U.S. War Department, Location and Strength of CCC Companies, 1933–1942, NARAMD RG 35 530/65/22/04/05.

1. Olson, *Historical Dictionary of the New Deal*, 466.

2. Collins, *New Deal in Arizona*, 223.

3. "CCC Camp to Move July 20," *Prescott Evening Courier*, July 3, 1940, 3.

4. September 1940, Fiche MN #1698, CRL Newspapers.

5. "CCC Williamson Valley Move Set," *Prescott Evening Courier*, May 20, 1941, 3.

6. U.S. CCC, Camp Inspection Reports, NARAMD RG 35/530/65/23/5 Box 12.

7. Ibid.

8. U.S. SCS, "Minutes of Monthly Safety Meeting–August Camp SCS A-27," Records of the SCS, Arizona Office, Consolidated Records of the CCC Camps in AZ, 1936–1942, NARACA RG 114 Box 1.

9. U.S. SCS, "Minutes of Monthly Safety Meeting–October 31st, 1941, Camp SCS A-27"; U.S. SCS, "Minutes of Monthly Safety Meeting–November 31st, 1941, Camp SCS A-27," ibid.

10. "CCC Camp Remains," *Prescott Evening Courier*, December 15, 1941, 3.

CHAPTER 11

Parker Dam (BR-17, BR-18, FWS-1)

CCC ASSISTANCE TO BUREAU OF RECLAMATION and Fish and Wildlife Service projects was a very small part of the overall Arizona CCC work. In addition, all three of these camps were short-lived.

BR-17 (Parker Dam)

Company 1849 officially arrived at Camp BR-17 (5.4 miles north of Topock) on November 6, 1935. Arrival of the Company was announced earlier in the *Mohave County Miner*, indicating they were previously at Silver City, New Mexico.[1]

Three weeks after their arrival, Special Investigator James C. Reddoch inspected the camp and reported their work was to be the clearing of brush in the area of the future reservoir. (This work was said to be "physically demanding" and "involved felling trees, then piling and burning them." Heavy equipment such as bulldozers was sometimes used to augment the hand labor.)[2] He reported that 1st Lt. Ralph T. Smith was the commanding officer. He noted the water well was being chlorinated, as it was contaminated, and a new well was being dug. He reported that Lieutenant Smith had told him that recently twenty-five enrollees had complained about the food.[3] Apparently, the clearing of brush ceased on December 31, 1935.[4]

At the end of the year, Company 1849 had 173 enrollees (99 from New Mexico, with 1 African American, 66 from Texas, and 8 from Arizona). Their supervisors included an Army physician and an educational advisor. The camp was officially abandoned on January 12, 1936, with the buildings salvaged for four other CCC camps.[5] Company 1849 transferred to DG-8, Hillside, Arizona.[6]

BR-18 (Upper Parker Dam)

Company 2833 officially arrived at Camp BR-18 (5.4 miles north of Topock) on November 6, 1935, and was organized at High Rolls, New Mexico. They were inspected by Special Investigator Reddoch on December 3, 1935, and were noted to be clearing river banks.[7] On December 31, they reported a total of 180 white enrollees (154 from Texas and 13 from both Arizona and New Mexico). They reported an Army commanding officer and a contract physician.

Their February 7 camp newspaper, *The Calizonian*, reported Lt. Wm. E. Cheatham as commanding officer, Maj. Guy O. Squire as contract physician, Louis Puente Jr. as educational advisor, and R. C. Link as project superintendent. The camp newspaper also reported that of the twenty-five thousand acres that needed to be cleared they had cleared twenty-five acres. The newspaper reported that enrollees recently had a tour of the impressive dam construction work. The enrollees on the tour were scared by arriving just after a terrible fire at a two-story men's dormitory that killed eleven men. Some of the charred bodies were still in sight when the enrollees arrived. The newspaper reported the camp had built a baseball diamond, fielded a team, and already played the Needles team. The nine-page newspaper reported on the camp educational program (thirteen classes), included an official roster of enrollee names, and had nearly a page of jokes.[8] In the March *Happy Days*, the CCC newspaper reported the camp was contemplating forming a drama club.[9]

Although BR-18 was occupied for only a short time, two controversies developed that would take a great deal of time for Special Investigator Reddoch. The first controversy started on February 10, 1936, when Roscoe Stephens of Kingman alleged BR-18 Project Superintendent Link had said that "he didn't want any Washington appointed foremen" and that Link had endangered eighty enrollees by putting them into an unsafe firefighting situation. Through the month of March, Reddoch investigated, ultimately involving CCC Assistant Director James McEntee. In a March 3 letter to McEntee, Reddoch reported that Stephens had been fired from his foreman position by Link for being drunk on duty. In the letter, he stated Link "is far above the average Camp Superintendent" and that Lt. Cheatham reported Stephens was indeed drunk when discharged. He also enclosed other letters detailing the former foreman's drunkenness at work. There was no truth to the allegation of endangering enrollees at the forest fire. But Link indeed did refer to some foreman as "political foremen." On March 31, McEntee wrote Arizona Congresswoman Isabella Greenway. The letter said none of the charges of Stephens against Link can be substantiated, including animosity "to those who were appointed through political endorsements." Nor did Link endanger "enrollees in connection with their fighting a forest fire." The investigation was complete, with no foundation for any further action. "Evidence clearly indicates that Stephens was under the influence of liquor on numerous occasions."[10] It is unclear to this writer if Stephens indeed was a political appointee beholden to Congresswoman Greenway or if Stephens had involved Greenway after the fact.

Not long after the Stephens incident, G. O. Shirley, the camp contract physician, wrote a letter with multiple allegations regarding the commanding officer and camp administration. He alleged that on at least one occasion a radical enrollee had yelled that the American flag should be hauled down and the red flag put up in its place, and the enrollee was not disciplined. He alleged that the BR-18 camp officers were eating better food than the enrollees and that food invoices had been falsified. Reddoch investigated and wrote Charles H. Taylor, assistant director of Emergency Work in Washington, on May 22, 1936. He could find no evidence regarding the alleged incident of an enrollee calling for the raising of the red flag. He said that there were some instances of officers on occasions getting better food than enrollees, but not any more often than in other camps. He did establish that Lieutenant Cheatham did on occasions take fruit home with him, but this was "negligible." Reddoch did establish that on occasions Cheatham did falsify a food bill such as mutton being substituted for beef and the like. Reddoch said that Cheatham realized he "has been indiscreet and careless, and has exercised very poor judgment" in falsifying records of what was bought. Reddoch reported that he does "not believe the Government has suffered any loss" or that Cheatham "has personally profited." On June 7, Reddoch wrote John M. Gibbs, CCC special agent, "It is my opinion that Dr. Shirley very much exaggerated the true conditions at camp BR-18. Dr. Shirley is overly suspicious since he has made charges against all Camp Commanders he has served."[11]

BR-18 and BR-17 cleared a total of 574 acres for the reservoir and maintained 7.5 miles of road.[12] BR-18 was officially abandoned by Company 2833 on April 20, 1936. The buildings were salvaged by the Army and moved to BR-74 at Yuma.[13] Company 2833 moved to F-28, Williams, Arizona.

FWS-1

During July 1941, a fifty-man contingent from the Yuma BR-74 camp arrived in Kingman with the mission of constructing the camp buildings.[14] Like the Parker Dam predecessors, this camp too would be short-lived. Unfortunately, little records were found dealing with their work projects.

FWS-1 (nineteen miles west of Parker, AZ) was officially occupied on September 14, 1941, by Company 3840. Earlier, on August 31, Company 3840 was reported at SCS-26, Flux Canyon, Arizona.

On September 30, the camp reported 180 enrollees (about 30% from Arizona and nearly all the rest from Texas). Supervisors were an Army commanding officer, a contract physician, and an educational advisor. From October 31 to December 31, camp strength varied between 110 and 126 (most enrollees were from Texas and Arizona, with one Oklahoma veteran). Once the United States was on a war footing, camp strength fell. In January 1942, Company 3840 had only 67 enrollees; at the end of February, it had 81.

On March 18, Special Investigator M. J. Bowen inspected the camp. He reported work to include road and campground construction, seeding, construction of the Army camp and guard stations, and the Indian Service building program. As the Army controlled the area security enrollees were "much restricted." Camp conditions were said to be fair. The mess, which was unsatisfactory in the past, was improving under a new commanding officer. There were no subversive activities. Morale was fair. Every two weeks there was a liberty trip to Blythe or Needles, California. As the camp chaplain was Protestant and most of the enrollees were Spanish Americans, Catholic Bowen recommended getting a contract Catholic chaplain.[15]

One detailed narrative report from this camp survives and gives a picture of its work for that quarter, including construction of the checking station for the BR construction camp area and construction of the cantonment for the 368th Infantry. The latter project included site landscaping, installation of water lines, and construction of a bath house, kitchen, and latrine. Other completed work included construction of a portable boat house; general cleanup; improvement of the CCC camp, including roads and garage facilities; power line construction; construction of a footpath and stairway to the guard speed boats; and beginning work on a 4,100′ truck trail. Work was begun on the warehouse fence and on the manufacture of bricks for the service building. Work would start on the planting of seeds for aquatic foods in the Bill Williams area. Installation of two drop inlets (with two more begun) was completed as a cooperative project with the USIS Colorado River Indian Irrigation Project. Future work included the maintenance of the road to the Japanese Reception Center. The report estimated one year of work on the "Japanese project," "including roads, fences, irrigation ditches, irrigation structures, leveling land, flood control, dams, etc."[16]

Camp FWS-1 continued to the very end of the CCC, reporting 108 enrollees on March 31 and 48 on April 30. The last War Department report of the CCC for Arizona on May 31, 1942, showed just five camps for the state with Company 3840 reporting 74 enrollees (8 from Texas and 33 from both Arizona and New Mexico). A short time later on July 2, Congress voted to no longer fund the CCC, but to fund its termination. By September 1942, all enrollees nationwide had been discharged.[17] It is unclear when FWS-1 was officially disbanded.

Figure 29. Shovel and Truck Working on Bill Williams Truck Trail, FWS-1, 1942; Shovel Is Enrollee-Operated. Courtesy NARAMD, RG 22/150/03/01/01 Box 3.

Unless noted otherwise, any reference to the number of enrollees in a company, the location of the company, or company supervisors are from U.S. War Department, Location and Strength of CCC Companies, 1933-1942, NARAMD RG 35 530/65/22/04/05.

1. "Two CCC Camps Transferred to Topock District," *Mohave County Miner,* October 18, 1935, 4.
2. Pfaff, *The Bureau of Reclamation's Civilian Conservation Corps Legacy,* 26.
3. U.S. CCC, Camp Inspection Reports, NARAMD RG 35/530/65/23/04 Entry 115 (PI #11) Box 7.
4. Pfaff, *The Bureau of Reclamation's Civilian Conservation Corps Legacy,* A-91.
5. "Civilian Conservation Corps Eighth Corps Area, Status Record of CCC Camps Authorized Since Inception of the Program up to ... December 31, 1941 ... Compiled by Office of Liaison Officer, CCC Fort Sam Houston...," NARACO BLM CCC Directories RG 49 Entry 33, 34 Box 132.
6. "Topock News," *Mohave County Miner,* January 17, 1935, 7.
7. U.S. CCC, Camp Inspection Reports, NARAMD RG 35/530/65/23/04 Entry 115 (PI #11) Box 7.
8. U.S. Bureau of Reclamation, CCC Activities, 1935–37, NARACO RG 115 Entry 21 Box 16.
9. March 14, 1936, 7.
10. U.S. CCC, Camp Inspection Reports, NARAMD RG 35/530/65/23/04 Entry 115 (PI #11) Box 7.
11. Ibid.
12. Pfaff, *The Bureau of Reclamation's Civilian Conservation Corps Legacy,* A-91.
13. "Civilian Conservation Corps Eighth Corps Area, Status Record of CCC Camps Authorized Since Inception of the Program up to ... December 31, 1941 ... Compiled by Office of Liaison Officer, CCC Fort Sam Houston...," NARACO BLM CCC Directories RG 49 Entry 33, 34 Box 132.
14. "50 Man Contingent from Yuma CCC Moved to Kingman," *Mohave County Miner,* July 3, 1941, 10.
15. U.S. CCC, Camp Inspection Reports, NARAMD RG 35/530/65/23/04 Entry 115 (PI #11) Box 10.
16. US DOI, Fish and Wildlife Service, "Narrative Report for Quarter Ending March 31, 1942, FWS-1-A," Records of the F&WS, Records of the CCC, NARAMD RG 22/150/03/01/01 Entry 193 Box 3.
17. Audretsch, *Shaping the Park and Saving the Boys,* "The CCC Had Become Outmoded," 68.

Sidebar:
Health and Safety in the CCC

During the first and second CCC enrollment periods (April 5, 1933–March 31, 1934), the number of enrollee deaths alarmed the program's leaders. In April 1934, a formal safety program was launched. Throughout the CCC program, safety was always a major concern, with its death and accident statistics comparing favorably to Army and civilian accident and death statistics.[1] Perhaps an indicator of the importance the Army attached to health and safety is the fact that the War Department's 1937 *Civilian Conservation Corps Regulations* allotted 35 pages to medical, sanitation, hygiene, etc., topics out of 153 pages of text.

The company commander was ultimately responsible for all medical issues. Other key personnel involved in safety education and setting safe work environments were the other military officers, the camp educational advisor, the project superintendent, and the camp physician or camp surgeon. The latter, if he took his job seriously, could play a key role in preventing sickness, injuries, and deaths.

One camp physician who appears to have taken his job seriously was Dr. Walter E. Whalen, camp surgeon at

DG-45, St. George, Utah. He explained that even before the camp was established a safe and adequate camp water supply must be found. When a camp is established, there must be adequate sewage, septic tanks, grease traps, and latrines. He and the company commander would inspect the mess and kitchen, supply rooms, refrigerators, dishes, pots and pans, supply rooms, bath houses, and latrines. Food was inspected upon delivery, and food handlers were to be inspected frequently.[2]

A 1937 newspaper article (apparently an 8th Corps Army news release) emphasized the preventative role of the camp physician. He must guard the camp water supply and periodically send water samples in for chemical analysis. He should check the daily menus, monitor water drainage and garbage disposal, keep an eye on the camp kitchen, and supervise the camp infirmary. The article notes that the 8th Corps had 144 Army medical officers and 128 civilian doctors. Each CCC district had fifteen ambulances distributed through the district. Army dental teams travelled thorough the 8th Corps area, with the goal of visiting every camp each six months.[3]

Within a few years of the Army's emphasis on safety and accident prevention, the CCC death rate began to drop. By the end of the program in 1942, the rate was lower than in the general male population of the same age range. The *Final Report* of the agency claimed that "between 3,500 and 4,000 men" are "now healthy who would have been dead under the usual expected mortality."[4]

What accounts for this enviable safety record? The vigilance of the military and the technical agency supervisors appears to be the most important factor. The inspections by the very independent CCC special investigators surely saved many lives. Of course, each company was required to have a physician, and ambulances were frequently available or located at the camp. Louis Purvis, a former enrollee of Grand Canyon CCC Company 818, wrote that there was "very little work" for the CCC hospital at Phantom Ranch at the bottom of the canyon. He ascribed this to three factors: the excellent medical staff, the safety-conscious military, and the "safety-strict" work supervisors.[5]

1. See Audretsch, "Safety, Deaths and Accidents," in *Shaping the Park and Saving the Boys*, 73–75.

2. "St. George Camp by Dr. Walter E. Whalen, Camp Surgeon," *Washington County News,* June 18, 1935, 5.

3. "CCC Objectives Are Broadened to Make Program More Useful," *Prescott Evening Courier,* December 15, 1937, 10.

4. U.S. Federal Security Agency, *Final Report of the Director of the Civilian Conservation Corps*, 58.

5. Purvis, *Ace in the Hole,* 72, 76.

CHAPTER 12

Hualapai Mountain Park, Kingman (SP-8, SP-9, CP-2)
State Parks and the CCC: A Short Overview

THE NATIONAL PARK SERVICE WAS requested to supervise CCC work in non-federal park areas such as state, county, and municipal parks. Under the program, NPS staff such as landscape architects and engineers assisted the CCC in the design and construction of eight hundred state parks.[1] Nationwide, a majority of the parks the NPS assisted "had no State park system or organization."[2] In Arizona, the NPS assisted in the development of parks such as South Mountain and Papago in Phoenix, Colossal Cave in Vail, Randolph in Tucson, and Hualapai in Mohave County.[3]

1933

In northern Arizona, Kingman and Mohave County were the most proactive of all in lobbying for the CCC. And once the boys arrived, Mohave County groups were the most vigorous to involve them in local social activities. From the very beginning of the CCC, the Kingman *Mohave County Miner* frequently reported about CCC activities, often with a positive spin. Kingman-area boys enrolled in the CCC at the beginning and wrote home from Flagstaff of having "a dandy time" with "plenty of work, plenty of fun, and lots of good things to eat."[4] Later in 1933, county representatives wrote Congresswoman Isabella Greenway recommending the CCC build a road to the Hualapai Mountains.[5] (However, not until mid-1934 did Mohave County officials apply successfully for a local CCC company.) In an article on the front page of the October 6, 1933, issue, the newspaper urged boys to enroll saying: "It would be a great thing for the boys to make the winter a little easier on their parents or family." On the front page of the November 10 newspaper was an article about a Winslow boy in jail for CCC desertion. The newspaper explained: "Boys who get homesick may possibly get a furlough … The camps are excellent and the work is light, compared with other work, and they got sufficient pay to cover the necessities of the family, as well as their own." The December 8 newspaper told of five Kingman boys from the Verde CCC camp visiting home for Thanksgiving, saying "they are well treated" and "have comfortable quarters."

1934

On February 16, the *Mohave County Miner* noted on the front page that the county supervisors had applied for two CCC camps for work at "the present Boy Scout camp." NPS Inspector Don R. Hull advised the supervisors that an adequate water supply was needed. The application had a lengthy list of projects, including firebreaks, roadside clearing, trail clearing, lookout houses, firefighting and facilities, general cleanup, trail building, public water systems, insect and rodent control, erosion control, tree and plant disease control, and bridges and guard rails.

On March 16, again on the front page, the *Mohave County Miner* noted that two six-month camps were initially approved for the "Wallapai Mt. Camps," pending Army engineer site inspection. One week later, the newspaper, in a lengthy front page article, noted that two camps were assured for April for "a permanent summer resort." The article indicated that a telegram from Arizona Senator Carl Hayden pronounced "splendid work" by county commissioners and the chamber of commerce committee. One week later, the newspaper declared on page one, "Army Officers Approve CCC Camp Sites Wednesday" and "Government Visitors Enthusiastic over Findings at Site in Wallapai Mountains."

Those approving the site included Captain P. H. Sperati, Major R. P. Williams, Lt. D. H. Nelson, and Inspector Hull. They "were profuse in their praise for the location and the need and possibilities of a great deal of work." They inspected the county hospital. The county had already been working on the road and the spring. A crew was to follow soon to install a telephone line and develop the spring further.

On April 20, thirty CCC men arrived in three trucks. However, the following week the newspaper noted that the water supply at the summit was uncertain and the camp site was being moved from the big saddle north of the American Flag mining camp to the old Davis Ranch area, with water to come from the Dean Mine.[6] During May, the *Mohave County Miner* reported the installation of a water line as well as debate over adequate water for a second camp. On June 1, on the front page, the *Mohave County Miner* proclaimed, "Water for 2nd CCC Camp Is Now Certain." The chamber of commerce directors had voted to underwrite the cost of the additional water to be purchased at $50 per month from the owners of the

Windmill property. The same issue, on the front page, reported that the lumber and equipment was being hauled in and the first full contingent of enrollees was to arrive June 10.

Company 830, consisting of white enrollees from Texas and Arizona, arrived officially on June 10, 1934, to staff SP-8 (apparently located at Live Oak Basin near the Dean Mine). On June 15, one of the Kingman churches sponsored a dance for the new enrollees.[7] On June 22, the *Mohave County Miner*, on the front page, announced "46 Structures in CCC Camp" and that construction was nearing completion and enrollees were already doing trail and road construction.[8] The same newspaper front page reported that the Kingman baseball team beat the CCC team, but a re-match a week later left the CCC as winners. And on page five, James B. Neal of company 830 wrote, "Nothing [is] to be feared of these boys."

Figure 30. Hualapai Mountain Park CCC Camp SP-8?, September 1934. Courtesy NARAMD, RG 79/150/35/17/07 Box 5.

In June, Company 830 dug out a small spring, improving its flow from a mere seep to 1,400 gallons per day. They also built a tool house, did surveys, constructed fire breaks, re-constructed the truck trail into camp, excavated for the foundation of a ranger station, and constructed .4 mile of trail from the picnic area to Aspen Spring.[9]

On July 3, Company 874, consisting initially of about 100 enrollees, arrived from Papago Park in Phoenix. They were to occupy SP-9, located at the "Windmill" site on Big Sandy Road.[10] On page 2 of the same newspaper, the editorial proclaimed, "Let's Keep Our CCC Boys and Let's Get Some More." Good work had been done so far, and a county park in Kingman was proposed. A week later, the *Mohave County Miner* noted the CCC company officers were welcomed at the chamber of commerce luncheon and told the chamber was "ready to serve them in any way possible."[11]

During July, the Company 830 baseball team, the Wallapai Tigers, played the Oatman and Valentine CCC-ID teams. Also in July, Company 830 constructed 1.6 miles of 50'-wide fire break, cleared 2.8 miles of the planned road, completed 1.6 miles of the Aspen Springs Trail, constructed a blacksmith shop, constructed a temporary powder house, began work on expanding Aspen Spring, and completed surveys of 15.6 miles of roads and trails.

The camp investigated the need for rodent control, poison plant control, and forest insect control, but found no need for these actions.[12]

During August, Company 874 fielded their baseball team, playing the Kingman town team and Company 830. On August 17, the *Mohave County Miner* (page 7) asked citizens to donate old magazines for the CCC boys by leaving them at the newspaper office. During this month, Company 874 did roadside and trailside clearing; road construction; worked on the Aspen Spring Trail, including blasting with dynamite; dug out a large area for a storage tank at Aspen Spring; and built small check dams and bridges in conjunction with the trail work.[13] Apparently, during August there was a concern about the CCC companies staying through the winter. Company 830's camp newspaper reported the "Kingman Chamber of Commerce & other organizations [are] trying to keep CCC camp there for coming winter. Chamber has sent a rep to San Francisco to intercede."[14] On August 31, Company 830 (SP-8) had 168 white enrollees (109 from Texas and 59 from Arizona) and Company 876 (SP-9) had 152 white enrollees (all from Arizona).

Figure 31. Hualapai Mountain Park CCC Camp SP-9, Company 874, August 1934. Courtesy Mohave Museum of History and Arts, #9981.

During September and October, Company 830 (SP-8) completed four miles of the 14′-wide road into the park. With the exception of a small air compressor, all the road work was done with hand tools, such as picks, shovels and wheelbarrows. They also did roadside and trailside clearing, cleared fire breaks, cleared about fifty acres of trees infected by mistletoe, and constructed trails. The ranger station was also completed.[15]

During September and October, Company 874 (SP-9) did trailside and roadside cleanup; carried out trail construction; installed a water system, including a ten-thousand-gallon tank to the picnic area; constructed eight picnic shelters and one trailside shelter; constructed five stone fireplaces and eight wooden benches at the picnic area; and cleared about fifteen acres of dead materials surrounding the picnic area, ranger station, and lookout house. The latter, 18 x 30′, was also completed by the enrollees. They also did trail work, constructed campground latrines, and completed the work at Aspen Spring.[16] According to the *Mohave County Miner*, the CCC completed the trail to Aspen Spring as well as one to Potato Patch.[17]

The completion of the ranger station was celebrated by a ceremony attended by numerous townspeople. The chamber of commerce underwrote the celebration, which included two orchestras, boxing matches, picnic lunches, speeches, and games.[18] According to the *Mohave County Miner*, over seven hundred people attended. (The newspaper noted the road and recreation hall were not yet finished.)[19]

Unfortunately, both companies were set to leave Kingman soon. But not before the local newspaper stated the two camps "have enlivened the town to such an extent that they will surely be missed, and their place in the community will be hard to fill…. Citizens owe a great deal to the officers and men of the two camps."[20] Frank Toohey, acting project superintendent of SP-8, wrote: "It was a very quite [sic] and sad crowd of boys that pulled out of the station at Kingman. Most of the inhabitants of the town were at the station to bid the boys good bye…. They are good boys and will be missed in Kingman."[21] Company 874 (SP-9) left Kingman officially on October 25, and Company 830 (SP-8) left on October 26.[22] On October 31, Company 830 was located at camp F-12, Rucker Canyon, near Douglas, and Company 874 was at SP-3, South Mountain Park. The CCC would return, but this would be the only time two companies were located here.

1935

Less than two months after the CCC left Kingman, the local newspaper editorialized that the community should begin to plan for the CCC for the summer of 1935.[23] In January, the *Mohave County Miner* reported the chamber of commerce and the county supervisors were planning, and ultimately, they made formal application for CCC assistance with Hualapai Mountain Park and developing the park property north of the hospital.[24] In April, the county was notified by telegram a camp was assured. The new location had a plentiful water supply and was to be near the Lawe Ranch below the recreation camp.[25] In June, the Army advertised for bids on rigid wooden buildings; Jerome Lumber Company got the bid, and by late in the month, construction was being rushed. Forty-plus local men were employed in the camp construction.[26] On July 1, 1935, Company 1837 officially occupied SP-8, coming by convoy and train from SP-6, Manville Wells State Park, near Tucson.[27] Capt. E. L. Hinton was in command, with 207 enrollees arriving.[28]

Although the enrollees arrived on July 1, the construction of the camp buildings was not completed until July 31. Apparently, the lack of planning before the camp set-up resulted in the lack of formal work projects being approved when the men got to camp. Project Superintendent Frank Toohey reported enrollee morale "at a low ebb." Toohey also reported little of a "spirit of good fellowship between the Army and the D.I. personnel that has at all times in the past been manifest." Enrollees were busy constructing a fire break around camp as well as roads into camp. Toohey reported that water was coming from Wheeler Springs, approximately .25 mile from camp, and American Flag mine, approximately 1.5 miles away. He called the water supply "sufficient."[29] However, the first inspection by the CCC special investigator on July 14 noted the water supply was diminishing.[30] Tragedy struck camp on July 12 with the death of Jeff P. Thomason, 58, of Sunglow, Arizona, said to be an enrollee.[31] The uncertain water situation plagued the camp until November when some of the water line was replaced and the pipe was wrapped with roofing paper to deter freezing. It was not until the October-November camp narrative report that an adequate supply of nine thousand daily was reported.

Morale improved greatly during August and September. Project Superintendent Toohey attributed that improvement to the selection of a new educational advisor (Earl A. Campbell) and the new commanding officer who "both have shown an interest in the welfare of the boys." Army personnel were said to be cooperative in "every manner." Toohey said that outside groups such as the Rotary Club were providing entertainment for the boys. The camp boxing team was "second to none."[32] The *Mohave County Miner* reported the camp baseball team playing Kingman, the Valentine CCC-ID team, and the Fort Mohave Transient Camp team.

In August 1935, the *Mohave County Miner* began a program of printing news columns of the area CCC camps written by the camp newspaper editors. Although the columns were irregular, the practice lasted for two years. SP-8's column was called *CCC News* and was authored first by Samuel Moreno and later by Ray Salazar.

Once the camp baseball team finished the season with ten wins and seven losses, a basketball team was organized.[33] Considerable detail is lacking regarding the camp work projects for this period. Besides realignment of the park road, the company buried below ground the Aspen Springs pipeline that was installed aboveground and subject to freezing.[34] Considerable work was done on the park road during October, eliminating many of the dangerous places. Enrollees also worked the picnic area and parking lot.[35] The October-November narrative report noted that several enrollees recently transferred to the camp were unable to adjust to the prevailing conditions, so a few left. The new project superintendent, H. E. Dalton, noted that buildings to house trucks and other equipment were completed.[36] Special Investigator James C. Reddoch inspected the camp on November 27 and noted nothing lacking. He remarked: "Merchandising conducted by Eddie York, enrollee, is one of the best Educational Projects SP-8 has. York has five boys working for him" in town and other camps selling men's clothing apparel.[37] The November 29 *Mohave County Miner* (page 3) noted a telephone line was being installed from the camp to town.

In mid-December, the *Mohave County Miner* reported on the camp's successful educational program. 100% of the enrollees were said to be participating.[38] The newspaper reported a detailed list of projects, including a new water system, fire breaks, new driveways, community building alterations, a wide trail to Potato Patch, parking areas, and new storage garages.[39] At year's end, Company 1837 reported 160 enrollees (138 from Arizona, 15 from Oklahoma, and 7 from Texas). Supervisors included two Army officers and a contract physician.

1936

Early in the year, the December-January narrative report noted the arrival of a new commanding officer. Apparently this was 1st Lt. William K. Ringgold, who is noted as C.O. in the *Official Annual ... 1936, Phoenix District, 8th Corps Area, CCC*.[40] This publication also noted 2nd Lt. Edgar C. Roberts as exchange officer and Dr. B. H. Burnett as camp surgeon. Construction of fire breaks, bank sloping, reduction of fire hazards, parking area work, trail construction, and construction of guard rails and culverts were some of the projects listed in the bi-monthly report. The wet weather at high elevation necessitated significant labor in diverting water away from parking areas and buildings.[41]

On February 28, Richard D. Silas, a regional NPS inspector, complimented the park, saying no Arizona park "can be so completely and perfectly classed as a real state park."[42] The February-March narrative report detailed the additional labor needed to deal with the snow at the camp elevation. Nearly 3½' of snow fell in late March, so the bulldozer and all the enrollees were used to keep the road open to camp. The snow also slowed projects, such as the Aspen Spring work; eventually, work there was halted till the snow melted. Other work included setting the poles and stringing four miles of telephone line, sign making, re-construction of fireplaces, and construction of fire breaks and trails. The report called morale "very good" in spite of the fact "it is necessary to go 18 miles to practice baseball and basketball."

Attached to this bi-monthly report was Educational Advisor Campbell's report for the Sixth Enrollment Period (October 1, 1935 to March, 31, 1936). 100% enrollee participation was reported. Thirteen vocational courses were being taught by ten instructors (foremen and enrollees). On-the-job instruction averaged ninety-nine enrollees. Forty-four men were taking academic courses, including eight for basic literacy and twenty-four for sixth through eighth grade.[43] Attached to this report was a supplementary narrative report that lists other work, including construction of a ten-bay equipment and blacksmith shop made from materials from the abandoned summer camps; construction of a total of 10.5 miles of telephone line so far; landscaping the picnic area; obliteration of undesirable roads, dumps, trails, and borrow pits; and parking lot construction.[44]

By the end of March, the *Mohave County Miner* noted that an average of fifty-five men were working on the telephone line, with the poles coming from Greenhorn Canyon.[45] The line was completed by April 10.[46] On June 10, the camp newspaper, *Hualapai Echo*, reported that Educational Advisor Campbell was organizing a camp orchestra, which included banjo, violin, guitar, and Spanish guitar. The camp canteen was averaging sales of over $1,300 per month, with candy and cigarettes totaling 59% of sales. Men were now being assigned to fire duty.[47]

Special Investigator A. W. Stockman visited the camp on June 23 and wrote: "I never have seen any better arranged nor maintained barracks than at this camp."[48] Unfortunately, our knowledge of work projects is limited as few detailed reports were found in archives by this author. On June 30, Company 1837 had 174 enrollees (80 from Texas, 69 from Arizona, 24 from Oklahoma, and 1 from Colorado).

July began with an eight-day visit from the NPS associate landscape architect to the park. He reported: This was "my first comprehensive study of this beautiful mountain park area, it was necessary to completely review past and present ECW projects." He stated the "remodeling of the Boy Scout Lodge will be accomplished and several rental cabins built, which are badly needed."[49]

On July 12, the Phoenix *Arizona Republic* printed a long article, including photos of the CCC work at Hualapai Mountain

Park. In addition to the work outlined above, the article listed "artistic iron work on doors and shutters."⁵⁰ During July, Company 1837 combined their baseball team with the Round Valley Company 2865 boys' team and beat teams in Kingman and Chloride. On August 4, the *Hualapai Echo* reported a fly camp of three enrollees doing surveying work was operating at Potato Patch. It was also reported that as part of a cooperative program with Western U.S. colleges and universities, Francis Gebby, an engineering junior at the University of Arizona, was in camp for the summer gaining practical experience.⁵¹

On August 14, the Kingman newspaper had a lengthy article on a recent inspection of the camp by Special Investigator Stockman. It is unclear if this was the June 23 inspection or another. The camp was given a "superior" rating, and Stockman was quoted as saying he had "never seen any better arranged nor maintained barracks." He praised the "conscientious effort" to comply with all safety regulations.⁵²

Figure 32. Rock Culvert Construction Hualapai Mountain Park, circa 1936. Courtesy NARAMD, RG 79/150/35/17/07 Box 5.

On September 11, the *Mohave County Miner* reported the camp had finished seventeen campground fireplaces, the Aspen Spring tunnel was nearly complete, and the uninhabitable cabins at Old Settler's Potato Patch had been razed.⁵³ During October, the *Mohave County Miner* announced that plans were moving forward for cabins at the park with the arrival of NPS staff, including architect James Meason. It was said that the park board plans called for some forty cabins and a fifty-thousand-gallon water storage reservoir.⁵⁴ At year's end, Company 1837 had 157 enrollees (99 from Oklahoma, 33 from Arizona, 24 from Texas, and 1 from Colorado).

1937

January did not start well for the SP-8. Four feet of snow on the ground by the first week in January forced the evacuation of more than one hundred enrollees to the Round Valley CCC camp.⁵⁵ This was the beginning of the most severe winter anyone could remember. A January-February narrative report indicated the fifty-thousand-gallon reservoir was nearly complete; all the Alpine Shelters in the picnic area were complete; the sign and marker program was underway; and the furniture for community building was 20% complete.⁵⁶ In spite of their own difficulties, the enrollees donated the "substantial sum" of $40 to the Ohio-Mississippi flood relief effort.⁵⁷

From February 20 to March 20, the severe weather kept any jobs from being completed. During this period, 5,000 man days were devoted exclusively to road maintenance, including the clearing of snow.⁵⁸ In mid-March, local chamber of commerce officials were assured that Camp SP-8 would remain for the next enrollment period.⁵⁹

During April and May, Cabin No. 1 was set to be finished by June 1, and four cabins were "well on the way to completion."⁶⁰ By early April, snow had melted enough that both CCC camps held an anniversary party attended by many locals.⁶¹ On April 30, the *Mohave County Miner* reported the formation of a Diamond League, to include the Hualapai and Round Valley CCC camps, Oatman, Chloride, Needles, and Kingman.⁶² During May, three enrollees were working as park guides.⁶³

A May-June narrative report listed the following jobs as completed: fencing, a pipeline,

Figure 33. Overnight Cabin Recently Completed at Hualpai Mountain County Park, SP-8, 1937. Courtesy NARAMD, RG 79/150/35/7/7 Box 16.

a cattle guard and entrance effect, a table and bench, campground development, spring and water hole, and parking area.[64] On June 25, the *Mohave County Miner* reported on the inspection visit of NPS Inspector Richard Sias. He reported that future park development, including new cottages, landscaping, trails, and road construction, had been approved. Four cottages were said to be under construction, with two to be approved soon.[65] The official June 30 count for Company 1837 reported 149 white enrollees (106 from Oklahoma, 29 from Arizona, 13 from Texas, and 1 from Colorado).

Regrettably, minimal information was located on work projects during this period besides road work. A July-August narrative report said: "The community building area … has been transformed form an unsightly and very badly scarred sector into a beautiful, naturalistic park development."[66] The report also contained photos of three of the completed cabins. An August-September narrative report indicated that one of the Swiss-Alpine–style picnic shelters was nearly complete. It reported that they went over plans for a new-type cabin that was cheaper.[67] An October-November narrative report said three Alpine Shelters were completed and two were about 50% completed. They were called "excellent craftsmanship."[68] A December narrative report summarized the work so far, saying the "construction of the overnight cabins is of high quality, and their modified Swiss Chalet type of architecture fits nicely in the landscape."[69]

The *Mohave County Miner* had three articles about the large number of appendectomies from both the Hualapai Mountain and Round Valley camps. By early December, it was estimated that thirty-four boys had been hospitalized since September for this procedure.[70] On December 31, the company had 151 enrollees (120 from Texas, and the rest from Arizona, Colorado, or Oklahoma).

1938

The first information we have about this new year is not until March, when the Kingman newspaper reported the camp was inviting the community to their anniversary celebration on April 3. Guests could attend guided tours, including the recently completed fifty-thousand-gallon concrete reservoir and four new cabins. New projects were said to include new trails to the mountaintop and new and larger picnic shelters.[71] On April 8, the *Mohave County Miner* proclaimed: "More Cabins Planned for Hualapai Park; Four Cabins, Reservoir and Sewer Line Are Nearly Complete Now." Planning teams from the NPS and CCC were said to be in the park.[72] The March-April issue of the camp newspaper noted that a chicken coop was being erected for three hundred recently purchased chicks. The CCC dentist visit was proclaimed: "Dentist's Visit Causes Woe among Enrollees."[73]

In early June, the *Mohave County Miner* reported that eight cabins were available for rent and eleven more were planned for the next six months. The new sewage disposal system was to ready by July 4.[74] A generator was taking the place of the hauling of ice for the mess hall.[75] Along with the Round Valley camp, a combined CCC baseball team was fielded in June, but was beat by the Kingman team on June 19 by a score of 8 to 5.[76] On June 30, a total of 238 enrollees were reported (142 from Oklahoma, 67 from Texas, 1 from Colorado, and 28 from Arizona).

In September, good progress was reported on the new comfort station construction.[77] Also in September, the *Mohave County Miner* reported, "CCC Will Build Softball Field in Hualapai Park."[78] Special Investigator Stockman filed a report on October 20 listing serious difficulties at the camp. He heard some enrollee complaints about food and credited some of that to many of the cooks being in training. However, he indicated food deliveries were often late and speculated that the lateness and lower quality of food were the result of the camp having to accept the low bid. He stated bluntly that the water supply was inadequate. Enrollees were only allowed one shower per week. He stated the situation was serious and merited an investigation. He heard enrollee complaints that there was only one liberty trip to town each week. Although he reported the camp administration appeared satisfactory, he wondered why there were not more Spanish-speaking supervisors, with 85% of the enrollees Spanish speaking.[79] Stockman returned on November 14 and reported that the Army had boosted water capacity from seven thousand to ten thousand gallons by the construction of new facilities. Eggs were now being ordered in smaller quantities from a new egg company, so there was no spoilage.[80]

During November, a new concrete basketball court was completed.[81] On December 31, the camp had 149 enrollees (133 from Arizona and the rest from Texas, except for 1 Oklahoma veteran). The camp showed no subordinate Army officer, only the commanding officer, something Stockman had reported in his October inspection.

1939

Records for the camp during this year are very sketchy. The *Mohave County Miner* reported a CCC basketball team during the winter months. The camp baseball team played frequently during the summer. No information about the camp's work activities was found in the *Mohave County Miner*. On June 30, Company 1837 reported 145 enrollees (all but 2 from Arizona). Only one Army officer was reported.

Apparently, a decision was made during the summer to close down SP-8 during the winter. The *Mohave County Miner* reported the VFW went on record opposing the seasonal camp closing.[82] Two weeks later, the *Miner* reported that Senator Hayden indicated the camp was closing September 30. A week later, the newspaper reported the camp shutdown was delayed until November in order to finish current projects.[83] Ultimately, Company 1837 moved on October 20 and was officially reported at Tucson Mountain Park (Manville Wells) on October 21.

1940

On March 14, the *Mohave County Miner* reported that the CCC camp at Hualapai Mountain Park would be re-established. On April 25, the newspaper reported that forty men were being sent ahead from Tucson to ready the Hualapai camp for re-occupation. On May 19, Company 1837 returned. However, the camp designation changed from SP-8 to CP-2. The camp had its last inspection by a special investigator when M. J. Bowen visited on June 4. He noted that the buildings were in need of work and the library of 1,600 volumes had "very active use."[84]

Shortly after returning, Company 1837 was reported fighting a fire near the Producers Mine.[85] Unfortunately, this author found no records of their 1940 work projects. During their final tenure at CP-2, enrollee counts varied during June through October from 130 to 199, always with over 90% from Arizona and usually most of the remainder from Texas. For the first time in county history, a call for Mohave County boys to join the CCC went begging. No applicants were reported.[86]

With war going on in Europe and Asia, jobs in U.S. defense industries were more and more common. On October 31, the *Mohave County Miner* reported the camp was to leave, having completed all the planned work, and it was likely the camp would not return. CP-2 was officially abandoned on November 3, 1940, and Company 1837 returned to Tucson.[87] Ultimately, the buildings were disassembled and moved to CCC camps throughout the state. In February, the *Mohave County Miner* reported a crew of thirty men (apparently from Veterans Company 1826 at South Mountain Park) had started the six-week dismantling project.[88]

Unless noted otherwise, any reference to the number of enrollees in a company, the location of the company, or company supervisors are from U.S. War Department, Location and Strength of CCC Companies, 1933 3–1942, NARAMD RG 35 530/65/22/04/05.

1. U.S. Federal Security Agency, *Final Report of the Director of the CCC*, 43.
2. Wirth, *Civilian Conservation Corps of the United States Department of the Interior*, 30.
3. Paige, *Civilian Conservation Corps and the National Park Service*, Appendix C-1.
4. "Letters Home from Camps Tell of the Many Activities," *Mohave County Miner*, July 14, 1933, 1, 8.
5. "Recommends That CCC Build Road to Wallapai Mts.," *Mohave County Miner*, October 6, 1933, 1.
6. "Water Supply for Wallapai Camps Considered Uncertain," *Mohave County Miner*, April 27, 1934, 1.
7. *Mohave County Miner*, June 15, 1934, 1.
8. Photos of the camp show nearly all the structures were tents, with only a few wooden structures. Typically, the wooden structures would be the kitchen and bathing facilities.
9. "Narrative Report, Camp SP-8-A, Wallapai Mountains, June 1934," Project Reports on CCC Projects in State and Local Parks, 1933–1937, NARAMD RG 79/150/35/17/07 Entry 95 (PI #166) Box 5.
10. "Second Contingent of CCC Arrived in Kingman Tuesday," *Mohave County Miner*, July 6, 1934, 1.
11. "Chamber Welcomes CCC Officers at Thursday Luncheon," *Mohave County Miner*, July 6, 1934, 1.
12. "Narrative Report, Camp SP-8-A, Wallapai Mountains, July 1934," Project Reports on CCC Projects in State and Local Parks, 1933–1937, NARAMD RG 79/150/35/17/07 Entry 95 (PI #166) Box 5.
13. "Picture Supplement to Narrative Report for the Month of August from Camp SP-9-A," Project Reports on CCC Projects in State and Local Parks, 1933–1937, NARAMD RG 79/150/35/17/07 Entry 95 (PI #166) Box 5.
14. *Wallapai Tiger*, vol. 1, no. 1, August 8, 1934, Civilian Conservation Corps Newsletters, Serials Collection, AHSLA.
15. "Pictures of Work Scenes of Projects, Camp SP-8-A, September 1934," and "Narrative Report, Camp SP-8-A, Wallapai Mountains, October 1934," Project Reports on CCC Projects in State and Local Parks, 1933–1937, NARAMD RG 79/150/35/17/07 Entry 95 (PI #166) Box 5.
16. "Narrative Report, Camp SP-9-A, Wallapai Mountains, October 1934," Project Reports on CCC Projects in State and Local Parks, 1933–1937, ibid; "Supplementary Narrative Report, March 31, 1937, Camp SP-8-A," Project Reports on CCC Projects in State and Local Parks, 1933–1937, ibid.
17. "Splendid Results Shown by CCC Workers in Park Areas of the Wallapai Mountains," *Mohave County Miner*, September 21, 1934, 1, 10.

18. "Entire County to Join in Mt. Park Dedication," *Mohave County Miner*, October 19, 1934, 1, 10.
19. *Mohave County Miner*, October 26, 1934, 1, 8.
20. "Last of CCC Boys Are Leaving Tonight," *Mohave County Miner*, October 26, 1934, 6.
21. "Narrative Report, Camp SP-8-A, Wallapai Mountains, October 1934," Project Reports on CCC Projects in State and Local Parks, 1933–1937, NARAMD RG 79/150/35/17/07 Entry 95 (PI #166) Box 5.
22. "Civilian Conservation Corps Eighth Corps Area, Status Record of CCC Camps Authorized Since Inception of the Program up to … December 31, 1941 … Compiled by Office of Liaison Officer, CCC Fort Sam Houston…," BLM CCC Directories, NARACO RG 49 Entry 33, 34 Box 132.
23. "Let's Get Ready for the CCC Camps," *Mohave County Miner*, December 7, 1934, 2.
24. "Plans for Return of CCC Camp Are Now Under Way," *Mohave County Miner*, January 11, 1935, 1; "A Formal Bid for CCC Camp Is Now Filed," *Mohave County Miner*, January 25, 1935, 1.
25. "CCC Camp for Hualapai Mts. Now Assured," *Mohave County Miner*, April 26, 1935, 1; "Site Chosen for First CCC Camp in Hualapai Mountain Park Area," *Mohave County Miner*, May 24, 1935, 1
26. *Mohave County Miner*, June 7, June 21, and June 28, 1935, 1.
27. "235 Men Arrive for CCC Camp in County Park on Hualapais," *Mohave County Miner*, July 5, 1935, 1.
28. "Corps Moves to New Camp," *Arizona Republic*, July 6, 1935, sect. 2, 1.
29. "Narrative Report, June-July 1935, Camp SP-8-A," Project Reports on CCC Projects in State and Local Parks, 1933–1937, NARAMD RG 79/150/35/17/07 Entry 95 (PI #166) Box 5.
30. U.S. CCC, Camp Inspection Reports, NARAMD RG 35/530/65/23/04 Entry 115 (PI #11) Box 7.
31. Arizona Death Records, State File No. 286, Registered No. 56. His surname was incorrectly spelled Thompson in the latter as well as in the local paper. See "CCC Worker Dies in Camp Friday Night," *Mohave County Miner*, July 19, 1935, 5.
32. "Narrative Report, Aug.-Sept. 1935, Camp SP-8-A," Project Reports on CCC Projects in State and Local Parks, 1933–1937, NARAMD RG 79/150/35/17/07 Entry 95 (PI #166) Box 5.
33. Samuel Moreno, "Hualapai Echo CCC No. 1837," *Mohave County Miner*, October 18, 1935, 8.
34. "Photographic Report Oct. 1, 1935, Camp SP-8-A," Project Reports on CCC Projects in State and Local Parks, 1933–1937, NARAMD RG 79/150/35/17/07 Entry 95 (PI #166) Box 5.
35. "Hualapai Park Road Greatly Improved Now," *Mohave County Miner*, November 1, 1935, 1.
36. "Narrative Report, Oct.-Nov. 1935, Camp SP-8-A," Project Reports on CCC Projects in State and Local Parks, 1933–1937, NARAMD RG 79/150/35/17/07 Entry 95 (PI #166) Box 5.
37. U.S. CCC, Camp Inspection Reports, NARAMD RG 35/530/65/23/04 Entry 115 (PI #11) Box 7.
38. "Vocational School Established at CCC Camp in Hualapais," *Mohave County Miner*, December 13, 1935, 1, 6.
39. "Many Improvements Made in Hualapai Park," *Mohave County Miner*, December 13, 1935, 3.
40. U.S. CCC, Phoenix District, *Official Annual, 1936, Phoenix District, 8th Corps Area, Civilian Conservation Corps* ([Baton Rouge, LA?]: Direct Advertising Co., 1936), 53. GCNPMC Cat. #70738.
41. "Narrative Report, Dec.–Jan. (January 31, 1936), Camp SP-8-A," Project Reports on CCC Projects in State and Local Parks, 1933–1937, NARAMD RG 79/150/35/17/07 Entry 95 (PI #166) Box 5.
42. *Mohave County Miner*, February 28, 1936, 1, 12.
43. "Narrative Report, February–March (March 31, 1936), Camp SP-8-A," Project Reports on CCC Projects in State and Local Parks, 1933–1937, NARAMD RG 79/150/35/17/07 Entry 95 (PI #166) Box 5.
44. "Supplementary Narrative Report, March 31, 1937, Camp SP-8-A," Project Reports on CCC Projects in State and Local Parks, 1933–1937, ibid.
45. Ray Salazar, "Hualapai Mountain CCC Camp News," *Mohave County Miner*, March 27, 1936, 8.
46. Ray Salazar, "Hualapai Mountain CCC Camp News," *Mohave County Miner*, April 10, 1936, 13.
47. *Hualapai Echo*, vol. I–VIII, June 10, 1936, Records of the NPS, SW Regional Office, NARACO RG 79 8NS-79-92-223 38/18/3:1-39/4/6:4 Box 142.
48. U.S. CCC, Camp Inspection Reports, NARAMD RG 35/530/65/23/04 Entry 115 (PI #11) Box 7.
49. U.S. NPS, Branch of Plans and Design, Monthly Narrative Reports, 1936–38, NARAMD RG 79/150/35/7/7 Box 5.
50. "Rugged Hualapai Park Is Noted for Scenery," *Arizona Republic,* July 12, 1936, 7.
51. *Hualapai Echo*, vol. I–X, August 4, 1936, Records of the NPS, SW Regional Office, NARACO RG 79 8NS-79-92-223 38/18/3:1-39/4/6:4 Box 142. See also "Students Enroll for Forest Work," *Arizona Republic,* July 21, 1936, 5.
52. "Hualapai CCC Camp Given a High Rating," *Mohave County Miner*, August 14, 1936, 2, 6.

53. Ray Salazar, "Hualapai Mountain CCC Camp News," *Mohave County Miner*, September 11, 1936, 8.
54. "Architect Assigned to CCC Camp in Hualapais to Make Drawings for New Cabins," *Mohave County Miner*, October 30, 1936, 1.
55. "110 Hualapai CCC Boys Are Moved to Round Valley Camp," *Mohave County Miner*, January 8, 1937, 1.
56. Clinton F. Rose, "Jan. 21 to Feb. 20, 1937 Monthly Narrative Report to Chief Architect," U.S. NPS, Branch of Plans and Design, Monthly Narrative Reports, 1936–38, NARAMD RG 79/150/35/7/7 Box 16, 4.
57. *Mohave County Miner*, February 12, 1937, 5.
58. Clinton F. Rose, "Feb. 20 to March 20, 1937 Report of Associate of Landscape Architect Clinton F. Rose," U.S. NPS, Branch of Plans and Design, Monthly Narrative Reports, 1936–38, NARAMD RG 79/150/35/7/7 Box 15.
59. "CCC Camp for a Longer Period Now Assured," *Mohave County Miner*, March 19, 1937, 1, 12.
60. Clinton F. Rose, "April 21 to May 20, 1937 Report of Associate of Landscape Architect Clinton F. Rose," U.S. NPS, Branch of Plans and Design, Monthly Narrative Reports, 1936–38, NARAMD RG 79/150/35/7/7 Box 15.
61. "Mohaveites Are CCC Guests at Birthday Party," *Mohave County Miner*, April 9, 1937, 1.
62. *Mohave County Miner*, April 30, 1937, 1.
63. *Hualapai Echo*, vol. II, no. VI, May 30, 1937, Fiche MN #1171, CRL Newspapers.
64. Clinton F. Rose, "May 21 to June 20, 1937 Monthly Narrative Report to Chief Architect," U.S. NPS, Branch of Plans and Design, Monthly Narrative Reports, 1936–38, NARAMD RG 79/150/35/7/7 Box 16, 13.
65. *Mohave County Miner*, June 25, 1937, 1, 6.
66. Clinton F. Rose, "July 21 to Aug. 20, 1937 Monthly Narrative Report to Chief Architect," U.S. NPS, Branch of Plans and Design, Monthly Narrative Reports, 1936–38, NARAMD RG 79/150/35/7/7 Box 16, 4.
67. Clinton F. Rose, "Aug. 21 to Sept. 20, 1937 Monthly Narrative Report to Chief Architect," U.S. NPS, Branch of Plans and Design, Monthly Narrative Reports, 1936–38, NARAMD RG 79/150/35/7/7 Box 16.
68. Clinton F. Rose, "Oct. 21 to Nov. 20, 1937 Monthly Narrative Report to Chief Architect," U.S. NPS, Branch of Plans and Design, Monthly Narrative Reports, 1936–38, NARAMD RG 79/150/35/7/7 Box 8, 16.
69. U.S. NPS, Branch of Plans and Design, "December 1937 Monthly Narrative Report to Chief Architect by H. H. Cornell," Monthly Narrative Reports, 1936–38, NARAMD RG 79/150/35/7/7 Box 16.
70. "Eleven Added to Appendectomy List," *Mohave County Miner*, December 10, 1937, 1.
71. "Hualapai Mountain CCC Camp to Hold Open House April 3," *Mohave County Miner*, March 25, 1938, 1.
72. *Mohave County Miner*, April 8, 1938, 1, 12.
73. *Hualapai Echo*, vol. III–III, March–April 1938, Records of the NPS, SW Regional Office, NARACO RG 79 8NS-79-92-223 38/18/3:1-39/4/6:4 Box 142.
74. *Mohave County Miner*, June 3, 1938, 1.
75. *Hualapai Echo*, vol. III, no. V, June–July 1938, Fiche MN #1171, CRL Newspapers.
76. *Mohave County Miner*, June 24, 1938, 7.
77. U.S. NPS, Branch of Plans and Design, "September 1938 Monthly Narrative Report to Chief Architect by H. H. Cornell," Monthly Narrative Reports, 1936–38, NARAMD RG 79/150/35/7/7 Box 16.
78. *Mohave County Miner*, September 30, 1938, 1.
79. U.S. CCC, Camp Inspection Reports, NARAMD RG 35/530/65/23/04 Entry 115 (PI #11) Box 7.
80. U.S. CCC, Camp Inspection Reports, NARAMD RG 35/530/65/23/04 Entry 115 (PI #11) Box 7.
81. *Hualpai Eagle*, vol. 1, no. 2, Thanksgiving, 1938, Fiche MN #1171, CRL Newspapers.
82. *Mohave County Miner*, August 25, 1939, 1.
83. "CCC Camp Will Finish Work in Mountain Park," *Mohave County Miner*, September 15, 1939, 1.
84. U.S. CCC, Camp Inspection Reports, NARAMD RG 35/530/65/23/04 Entry 115 (PI #11) Box 7.
85. *Happy Days,* June 8, 1940, 1.
86. "County Fails CCC Enlistment Quota," *Mohave County Miner*, October 24, 1940, 3.
87. "Civilian Conservation Corps Eighth Corps Area, Status Record of CCC Camps Authorized Since Inception of the Program up to … December 31, 1941 … Compiled by Office of Liaison Officer, CCC Fort Sam Houston…," BLM CCC Directories, NARACO RG 49 Entry 33, 34 Box 132.
88. "Hualapai Camp Being Removed," *Mohave County Miner*, February 6, 1941, 5.

Sidebar:
Camp Controversy

If anyone in the CCC organization deserved the label "straight shooter," it was Special Investigator A. W. Stockman. Stockman was independent, honest, candid, frequently outspoken, and not easily misled. Along with E. W. Samuell, James C. Reddoch, M. J. Bowen, and later Hamilton Draper, these men completed hundreds of independent CCC camp inspections in northern Arizona from 1936 through 1942.

The job of the special investigators appears to be twofold. They made regular camp inspections, guided by an inspection manual, examining enrollee safety and morale. Their reports included comments, and often suggestions, on camp sanitation and water supply, clothing, storage of hazardous materials such as gasoline and explosives, operation of motor vehicles, safety programs, educational programs, and the camp's supervisory personnel. Camp inspection reports frequently had comments about the existence of Communistic activities, adequacy of religious services, recreational activities, first aid training, reports of AWOLs, machinery safeguards, adequacy of the Army mess, and the cooperation (or lack of) between the Army and the technical agencies. For a young enrollee, during his first time away from home, the special investigator might be his only recourse from an overly strict supervisor or unsafe work condition.

Operating like a present-day inspector general, special investigators were ordered to special situations such as the death of an enrollee, an allegation of impropriety, and an enrollee writing a complaining letter to a VIP or to Robert Fechner, CCC director, in Washington, D.C. Special investigators did not have the power to dismiss or discipline CCC, technical agency, and Army staff. But their recommendations were frequently taken very seriously, even to the extent of the Army district commander simultaneously investigating alongside the special investigator.

In April 1939, Stockman received one of his most demanding problems—a petition from fifty-four enrollees from Hualapai Mountain Park Company 1837. The signers of the petition, calling themselves "the American boys of Co. 1837," were "very displeased with the mexicans [sic] (Spanish Americans) boys of this company." (See Figures 34 and 35.) Their complaints included the charge that the Spanish-speaking enrollees got drunk, insulted American girls, and did the same to camp visitors. They charged that the camp educational advisor was a "drunkard" and favored the Spanish-speaking enrollees. They asked that the American enrollees and Spanish American enrollees "be in separate camps" and that Stockman visit the camp and interview enrollees.

Stockman went to the camp and held separate meetings with the English-speaking and Spanish-speaking enrollees. He wrote shorthand accounts of each meeting. In his detailed report, Stockman summarized the complaints of the English-speaking boys: favoritism to Spanish-speaking enrollees; dominance of camp activities by the Spanish-speaking enrollees; speaking in a foreign language; Spanish-speaking enrollees acting negatively in Kingman; the educational advisor was a drunk and a gambler; unsatisfactory food and athletic equipment. The Spanish-speaking enrollees charged that they were unfairly restricted in Kingman and asked to be able to go on liberty trips to Oatman where there were considerable Spanish-speaking people. Stockman summarized: "The majority of complaints, particularly with regard to ill treatment from other enrollees, have emanated from English speaking enrollees."

Along with the Army Sub-district Commander Capt. Thomas D. Tway, Stockman spent days investigating the complaints of both the English-speaking and Spanish-speaking enrollees. Stockman and Tway interviewed Kingman business owners, deputies, and community leaders. Upon his return, Stockman held meetings with each group and wrote a detailed report to CCC Assistant Director James J. McEntee dated June 11, 1939. Segregation was not the answer, reported Stockman. The town of Kingman did restrict Spanish-speaking enrollees. However, the road to Oatman was unsafe for an Army vehicle, so liberty trips there were not possible. He reported that he and Captain Tway could find no difference in the actions of English- and Spanish-speaking enrollees while in Kingman. They were unable to identify the incident of the white girl being harassed by the Mexican enrollee. Stockman reported the frequent speaking of Spanish had been corrected by limiting that to barracks areas. Athletic equipment complaints were being corrected. "In my opinion, and that of practically all others, the mess is unsatisfactory, the mess sergeant incapable and his temperament unsuited for necessary dealings with enrollees." He was to be replaced immediately. District Headquarters announced corrective measures regarding Educational Advisor Campbell. (He recognized he was indiscreet by drinking when leading Kingman liberty trips.)

Stockman finished his report with a statement, a bit cryptic sounding, that he was approached by one of the English-speaking enrollees privately. This enrollee, who wished to remain anonymous, alleged that five white enrollees were the ringleaders of the complaining group and that many of the other enrollees feared reprisals by the ringleaders.[1]

---

1. U.S. CCC, Camp Inspection Reports, NARAMD RG 35/530/65/23/04 Entry 115 (PI #11) Box 7.

Inclosure No. 3

XXXXX
CCC Co. 1837, Camp SP-8-A
Kingman, Arizona
April 26, 1939

Mr. Stockman
Office of Director
Washington, D. C.

Dear Sir:

    We the American boys of Co. 1837 are very displeased with the mexicans (Spanish Americans) boys of this company. We have only two barracks of American Boys and four barracks of the mexicans. There is exactly one hundred and eight mexicans in this Co. out of 196 enrollees.

    There has been and is hard feelings between the two races and it seems that there always will be if conditions that exist now continue to exist. in the near future. When we go to town the mexican boys ruin our reputation by getting drunk, and running down the girls of our race, and not only that but it is the same in camp whenever we have visitors.

    We also have an educational adviser who is nothing but a drunkard and favors only the mexicans and as he has been in the town of Kingman some time he runs down the boys to the townspeople and has been heard to state that we the white boys are roughnecks and etc.

    We the American boys of Company 1837 and not only of this Co. but other companys in the eighth corps area believe that the American boys and the mexicans (Spanish Americans, as our Commanding Officer would have us call them) should be in seperate camps.

    If this could be arranged where we could be seperated, I am sure there would be better understanding , better co-operation, and am sure that there would be better Companies.

    We would very much appreciate it if you would visit this Co. and interview some of the boys and find xxxxour statements true. We the American boys (The under Signed) would very much appreciate it if you would please help us in this matter.

[Signatures:]
Jack Wesley Rankins
John N. Westfall asst. Ldw.
J. W. Bryan - asst ldr
William Stoney
Malyn L. Rark
John R. Williams
David Terrell
George Acker
Robert C Davis
Rob Kimbrell
Irving Stewart
Curtis Goodely
Delbert W Martindell
Manuel Westfall
Richard M. Stuck
Thurman E. White

Figure 34. Petition Dated April 16, 1939, SP-8. Courtesy NARAMD, RG 35/530/65/23/04 Entry 115 (PI #11) Box 7.

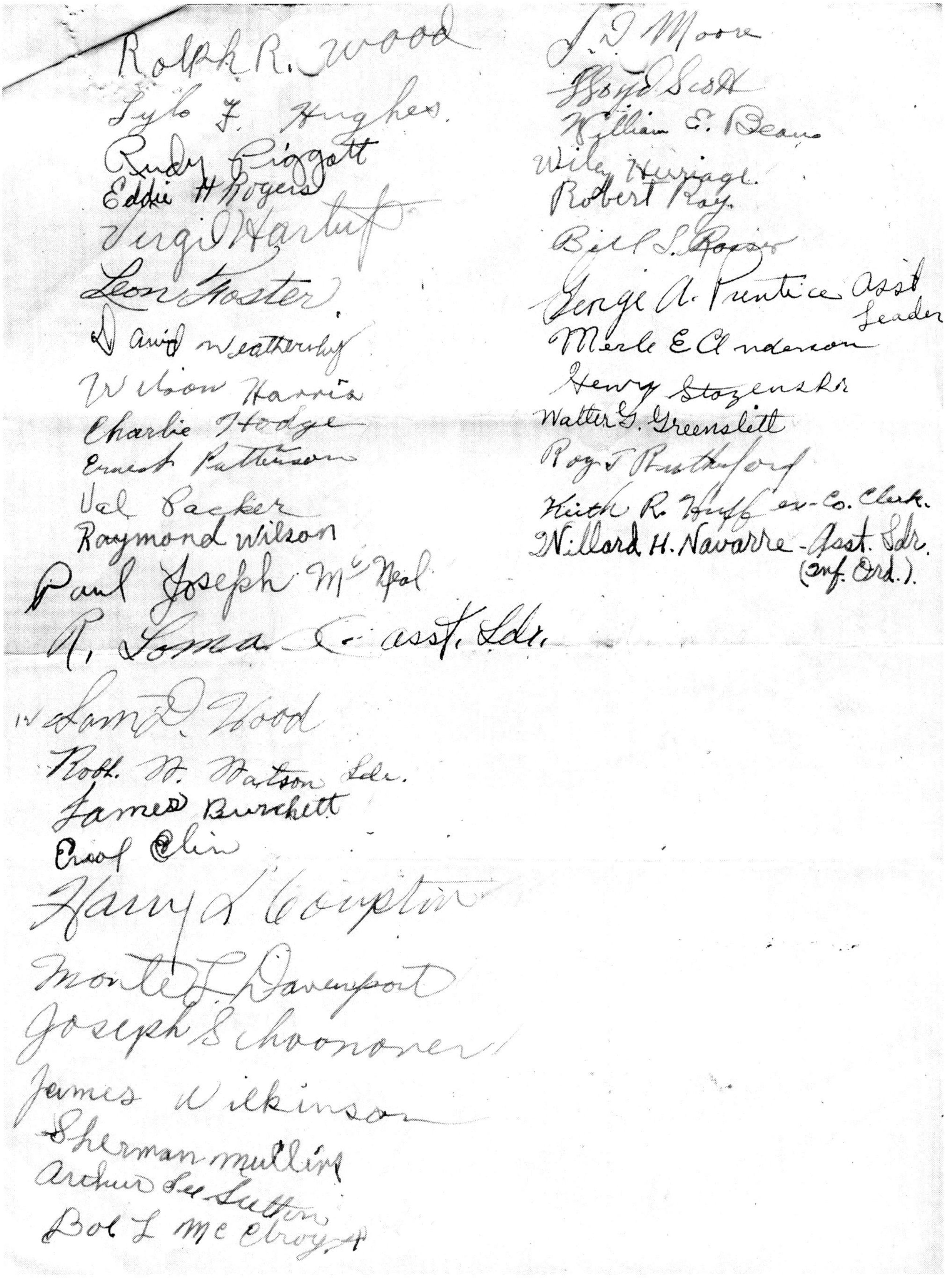

Ralph R. Wood
Lylo F. Hughes
Rudy Piggott
Eddie H Rogers
Virgil Hartut
Leon Foster
David Weatherly
Wilson Harris
Charlie Hodge
Ernest Patterson
Val Packer
Raymond Wilson
Paul Joseph McNeal
R. Toma — asst. Ldr.

Sam D. Wood
Robt. H. Watson Ldr.
James Burchett
Enoof Olin
Harry L Compton
Monte L Davenport
Joseph Schoonover
James Wilkinson
Sherman Mullins
Archur Lee Sutton
Bob L McElroy

S. D. Moore
Lloyd Scott
William E. Bean
Wiley Hisinger
Robert Ray
Bill S. Rosser
George A. Prentice Asst Leader
Merle E Anderson
Henry Stozenski
Walter G. Greenslett
Roy T Rutherford
Keith R. Huff ex-Co. Clerk
Willard H. Navarre - Asst. Sdr.
(Inf. Ord.)

Figure 35. Petition Dated April 16, 1939, SP-8, continued. Courtesy NARAMD, RG 35/530/65/23/04 Entry 115 (PI #11) Box 7.

CHAPTER 13

Round Valley (DG-46)

1935

THE FIRST INDICATION OF THE placement of a Division of Grazing camp in Mohave County occurred in May 1935 when a telegram from Congresswoman Isabella S. Greenway indicated the county was scheduled for seven CCC companies, including two DG camps.[1] On May 31, the Kingman newspaper, in a front page article, reported that several hundred acres of land in the Round Valley area were being leased for the camp. The camp was said to be "right where the Cofer Ranch is now [in 1982]."[2] The camp was to be located on land leased by the Division of Grazing, and the first project was to be a well for the camp.[3] On July 26, again on the front page, the newspaper reported that fifteen (train) car loads of materials had arrived for the Round Valley camp assembly. Company 2865 arrived in the area on August 21, 1935, with a staff that included a Navy ensign as commander, an Army subaltern, a contract physician, and an educational advisor. The camp was located 26.8 miles southeast of Kingman. The project superintendent was J. R. Sallenger. The first men were apparently from Texas. While the camp was being occupied, the water well was still being drilled.[4] While the Kingman newspaper gave the CCC camp extensive coverage, and there were frequent camp inspections, only a few narrative work reports have survived for DG-46. So, this account is surely incomplete.

By September, the camp was repairing the road to Big Sandy.[5] In October, they had received seven new two-ton Reo trucks and were planning work on the road to Hackberry as well as building a drift fence starting at Cane Springs Ranch. The Kingman newspaper noted they were "progressing splendidly" with their work on the Round Valley–Kingman Road.[6]

During October, the Kingman newspaper began to carry frequent columns about the CCC camps, apparently written by enrollees. The column written about the Round Valley camp was said to be authored by Priest C. High. The October 25 column told of the camp work, which up to that point was road work, post cutting, and fencing. It also mentioned that Assistant Educational Advisor Richard Gibson had classes of fourteen enrollees in first and second grades, eight in third grade, twenty-four in the typing class, and one in bookkeeping.[7] In the same issue, the camp was lauded for the Big Sandy Road improvement, which consisted of straightening curves, cutting brush alongside the road, and drainage work. The article stated, "The people of Mohave county … should be very appreciative of the good work."[8]

During November, Round Valley had its share of inspections. Early in the month, John Deeds, assistant grazing director, visited and said the camp was "doing fine work." About the same time, Daniel Bromley, grazing engineer, visited.[9] Late in the month, CCC Special Investigator James C. Reddoch visited.[10] No problems were noted. The local newspaper trumpeted the camp work with the headline: "Free Water Supply: Wells, Windmills and Tanks to Be Installed without Cost to Stockmen by CCC Camps under Taylor Grazing Act." The article explained that one well rig was now at the Round Valley camp, and the camp had the necessary tents, etc., for fly camps to undertake projects in the county once the county committee geologist approved the projects.[11] A week later, the Round Valley camp was again featured on the front page with these words: "Sandy Road Now in Best Condition since Construction." "At no time in the history of the Sandy highway has it been in or near its present excellent condition," said the newspaper.[12]

In December, the newspaper reported that a larger educational program had begun since the arrival of Educational Advisor Charles Hollinger. Dr. F. E. Walthall was the new camp doctor.[13]

At year's end, the camp had 172 enrollees (139 from Texas and the rest from Arizona and Oklahoma). There were no African American enrollees noted in the Army reports.

1936

January found DG-46 doing mostly road construction, with crews working on the road from Round Valley to Wikieup. One crew was building an extensive rock wall where Knight Creek curved. Another crew was cutting brush alongside the road south of Trout Creek.[14] The Trout Creek crew even attended a Saturday night dance along with the Round Valley CCC camp orchestra.[15] At month's end, the camp powder house was said to be nearing completion.[16] During January, eight miles of road work on the Kingman–Round Valley–Wikieup road were completed.[17]

By February, the camp basketball team was playing games in Kingman. During this month, the camp completed six more

Figure 36. Company 2865, Camp DG-46A, Round Valley, March 1936. Courtesy Mohave Museum of History and Arts, #4647.

miles of road construction. Carpenters were building spike camp buildings for Trout Creek, and a twenty-five-man spike camp for the Francis Creek Truck Trail was in the making. Silent films were replaced with talkies, and the *Rin Tin Tin* movie was a huge success.[18] During April, the 28-mile-long Round Valley–Wikieup road was completed, thus finishing the Kingman to Wikieup work. The Little Sandy soil erosion control project was progressing slowly.[19]

During early May, work was progressing on expanding the Bacon Stock Tank, and more than thirty enrollees visited Boulder Dam and Lake Mead.[20] Also in early May, twenty-four enrollees moved to the Francis Creek spike camp. In 1982, this spike camp was said to be "between the Cofer place and the Bartmus place right by the Bolo Cattle Company."[21] Two men were at a side camp at the Bacon Stock Tank to guard the equipment and horses of the half-finished project. The Little Sandy soil erosion control project was said to consist of 2,500 acres of velocity checks, gulley plugs, and brush plugs. This work was done chiefly with rock and stone, but work coming up was to include woven wire check dams, burlap sack dams, and wire and brush spreader fences. An average of four enrollees daily were learning surveying for the Round Valley–Hackberry Truck Trail.[22] The camp baseball team was hot, scoring five victories in mid-May, including wins over Wikieup (twice), Company 1837 (Hualapai Mountain Park), Kingman, and Oatman.[23]

Early June found some of the enrollees fighting a fire near the Democrat Mine. A poisonous plant eradication project for two hundred acres of rattle weed was started.[24] Later in June, the camp began the Cofer Fence project, reportedly six miles in length.[25]

On June 22, CCC Special Investigator A. W. Stockman inspected Round Valley and filed a very favorable report. He called the camp "a splendid one," particularly in light of its isolated location. The two military commanders (commanding officer Ensign Edmund L. Engel and executive officer 2nd Lt. W. S. Schlotzhauer Jr.) were "conscientious, alert, and possessed with initiative." Project Superintendent Sallenger "wants to be especially cooperative." Cooperation between the Army and technical staff "seems splendid." Stockman reported the Army sub-district commander "is untiring and cooperative" and wants to make all district camps "outstanding." Stockman noted that nineteen enrollees started an "incipient food strike": four were discharged, and the commanding officer ultimately prevailed on the rest to return to work. Apparently, these enrollees were trying to get discharged rather than remain in camp. He noted that the mess sergeant and cooks were young and experienced, but that there were problems with the lunches. Some new training for the mess sergeant was planned. Camp morale was good. There were liberty parties to Kingman every Saturday and Sunday, as well as Saturday night dances at Wikieup and some special recreation trips. Stockman was not able to visit the Francis Creek spike camp, but understood it to be "a model type."[26] Apparently, the camp educational classes included things such as leathercraft, as the company took top honors at a Kingman craft show.[27] At the end of the month, enrollees had completed one mile of the Round Valley–Hackberry Truck Trail, six miles of the Francis Creek Truck Trail, and seven thousand acres of Little Sandy soil erosion control.[28] On June 30, DG-46 had 149 men (most from Texas).

On July 7, 1936, CCC Special Investigator E. W. Samuell inspected the camp and noted "everything is [in] exceptionally good shape." He pronounced the Francis Creek spike camp the "cleanest and neatest side camp I have visited." The Little Sandy soil erosion control project was "very neat work."[29] A few days later, the Kingman newspaper announced, "Round Valley CCC to Build Side Camp in Hualapai Valley." The article noted that the Caterpillar was being operated twenty-four hours a day using four operators.[30] On July 31, the newspaper reported that the Hualapai Valley spike camp going up would have fifty men and its most likely project would be the 32-mile-long Hualapai Truck Trail. The Caterpillar crew was working a double shift on the Round Valley–Hackberry Truck Trail.[31] The same newspaper issue mentioned that 150 Sandy Valley residents had signed a petition to the Division of Grazing in Washington, D.C., commending Company 2865, DG-46, "for very excellent work and efforts."[32] A week later, the newspaper said that the Little Sandy soil erosion control project was now 10% done at 10,000-plus acres, involving 6,838 man days.[33]

On August 21, the camp celebrated its first anniversary with a party, including music and boxing. One hundred people attended. Approval was granted for two Hualapai Valley spike camp projects: the 32-mile-long Hualapai Truck Trail and the Hualapai Valley Soil Erosion Project No. 1.[34] On September 4, the local newspaper reported 7.5 miles had been completed on the Francis Creek Truck Trail so far and two thousand more acres done on the Little Sandy soil erosion control project.[35] In about September, Ensign Edmund L. Engel was commanding officer; 2nd Lt. Ernest L. Kirkland was exchange officer; Dr. Claude E. Putnam was camp surgeon; E. Leeds Gulick was educational officer; and J. R. Sallenger was project superintendent.[36]

In early October, the CCC well rig returned from Chloride, where it had been working for "a couple of weeks."[37] The following week, the newspaper reported that Andrew Baker of Kingman was the new LEM and blacksmith and an Army mess sergeant was visiting to improve the camp mess.[38] Three new company projects were approved: Neal Spring, Upshaw Well, and the Antelope Fence (two miles enclosing three stock tanks at Little Sandy Wash).[39] Investigator Samuell visited the camp on October 16 and pronounced the "base camp in very competent hands," the Hualapai Valley spike camp to be a "dandy camp," and the Francis Creek spike camp "well in hand." He reported the new mess sergeant had "straightened things out."[40] At the end of October, two new projects were approved: Moss Spring and the Lookout Truck Trail (twenty miles of road improvement).[41] At the same time, ninety new Oklahoma enrollees arrived to bring the camp back to full strength. The Cofer Fence project was hitting lots of rugged land and rock. The Hualapai side camp was working on the Hualapai Valley No. 1 soil erosion project and had almost finished with the Neal Spring project.[42]

On November 20, the camp sponsored a night of entertainment at Mohave Union High School. The 6-mile-long Berry Truck Trail project was approved, and the 5-mile-long Round Valley–Hackberry Truck Trail was completed.[43] Special Investigator Samuell filed a report the same day, saying that he had talked with area stockmen as well as Kingman residents and concluded "CCC Boys [were] admitted to homes and social affairs which proves the[ir] high regard" in the community. This is one of our best camps and the work program is the best balanced and the stockmen seem the most appreciative." He reported the Francis Creek Truck Trail and the Neal Spring project were completed, and the Kingman Road was 42% complete, but the Cofer Fence was proving to be a "tough job." He checked on some finished projects and found the Antelope Stock Tank filled and the Bacon Stock Tank filled and ran over, with the spillway working perfectly. He said both spike camps were "far ahead" in "neatness, cleanliness and in morale."[44] By mid-December, the Wilson Fence project was being surveyed.[45] At year's end, the camp had 152 enrollees (89 from Oklahoma, 47 from Texas, and 16 from Arizona).

1937

Across northern Arizona, the snows fell like few had ever seen. (See chapter 1, *CCC to the Rescue!*) At the Hualapai Mountain CCC camp, 4′ of snow forced the temporary movement of many of the enrollees to Round Valley until the road to their camp could be re-opened.[46] In addition, heavy snow forced most of the Francis Creek spike camp men back to the main camp.[47] It seems likely that it was not possible to do much of the scheduled camp work. But, like other CCC camps that had a Caterpillar, they went to the rescue of stranded ranchers. Enrollees rescued the Day family in the Francis Creek area, and they took out twenty-six people from the Democrat Mine area who had been stranded for two weeks.[48]

Figure 37. DG-46 Emergency Work, 1937, Democrat Mine Road, Twenty-Six Stranded for Twenty Days. Courtesy U.S. BLM, Kingman Field Office.

On February 19, the *Mohave County Miner* reported that the Kingman–Round Valley Road erosion project had begun. "Range examiner Floyd Allen and his detached crew of enrollees from DG-44A, Fredonia, AZ, are now stationed at this camp to do range survey work in this grazing district."[49] In late February, enrollees J. D. Blair and John Phillips were reported heading to San Diego for a baseball tryout.[50] The camp basketball team competed throughout February and March, frequently traveling to Kingman, and finished the season with three wins and three losses.[51] During March, the camp announced an open house for April 4, the completion of the preliminary survey of the Wilson Fence project, and the installation of a electric generator at the Hualapai Valley spike camp.[52] The March 31 camp newspaper noted that area stockmen had proposed seventy miles of new fence projects for the CCC, including the Mullen and Gaddis Fences; that a root cellar had been added to the kitchen facilities; and that a group of twenty-nine boys recently had crossed Red Lake, gone to a spring, and then climbed to the top of the mountain.[53]

The April 1, 1937, narrative report offers more details of the camp's work up to that time. Ten miles of the Kingman–Round Valley Road were re-worked. Six miles of the Hackberry–Round Valley Road were completed. "This road when completed will have the stockmen of the lower Sandy river, a more direct route to the town of Hackberry, their shipping point, reducing the cost of marketing their stock." Enrollees added 3,200 acres to the Little Sandy soil erosion control project. The Upshaw Well was drilled to 150 feet, but water had not been struck yet. The Wilson Fence (dividing the T. R. Wilson and Bud Odle allotments) was almost complete. Substantial time was spent in rescuing marooned miners and ranchers and clearing roads. The Hualapai Valley spike camp completed 2,500 acres of soil erosion control work. The Neal Spring development increased the water supply by 50%, so 1,500 head could then be watered. Six miles of the Francis Creek Truck Trail had been completed. When completed, this route was touted as giving Francis Creek residents a direct route to Kingman. Other work included the Cofer Fence.[54] On April 30, the Kingman newspaper announced the formation of a new baseball league that included the Round Valley and Hualapai Valley CCC camps and local teams from Kingman, Oatman, Chloride, and Needles.

On May 13, Special Investigator Samuell inspected the camp again along with Army Sub-district Commander Captain Hastings.[55] Samuell noted camp strength to be 158, including 12 LEMs. He rated the main camp and Hualapai Valley spike camp as "the best he had ever seen," with much credit due to the new commanding officer, Lt. James Younts, "for the way he has built up the morale." He noted the following projects in the report: Francis Creek Truck Trail–59% complete; Round Valley–Hackberry Truck Trail–39% complete; Cofer Fence–51% complete; Kingman Road–42% complete; Antelope Fence–43% complete; Upshaw Well–complete; and Valley Spring–75% complete.[56] The Kingman newspaper (May 14, 1937, page 10) noted that Lt. Donald Ratliff of the Army Dental Corps and his assistant were visiting camps doing enrollee dental exams.

On June 2, the camp experienced its first death with the passing of Kelsey Young, 20, of Oklahoma at the Kingman hospital from pneumonia.[57] On June 18, the newspaper announced Round Valley had established its third spike camp, located fourteen miles northwest of Peach Springs. The new side camp was called Buck and Doe and had been established to cut fence posts.[58] On June 30, DG-46, Company 2865 had 147 men (107 from Oklahoma and the rest from Arizona and Texas).

Figure 38. Buck and Doe Spike Camp, 1937. Courtesy NARACO, RG 49/15/C/6/1 Box 62.

Special Investigator Samuell visited the camp on July 1 and noted all three spike camps were "very clean." He noted some work progress: Francis Creek Truck Trail–65% complete; Round Valley–Hackberry Truck Trail–completed; Antelope Fence–completed; and Hualapai Valley Rodent Control–just started. The camp was absent an educational advisor, so Samuell emphasized the camp technical staff had to do more educational work.[59] Later in the month, J. V. Lloyd, Grand Canyon National Park deputy superintendent, along with Captain Hastings visited Round Valley. Lloyd was interested in their spike camp operations. Drilling on the Neal Well project was starting at the same time.[60]

In early August, the Hualapai Valley spike camp was temporarily shut down so the men could work on the Francis Creek

Figure 39. DG-46 Dam, circa 1937. Courtesy U.S. BLM, Kingman Field Office.

Truck Trail.⁶¹

On August 18, Investigator Samuell filed an inspection report indicating company strength was only 120. Work on the Cofer Fence was going slowly because of rock, and the Hualapai rodent control project was delayed. Other projects mentioned were Gaddis Fence, Berry Truck Trail, Berry Tank, Neal Well, the Buck and Doe Range Survey, Little Sandy Erosion, Francis Creek Truck Trail, Kingman Round Valley Erosion, Hualapai Soil Erosion, Hualapai Truck Trail, and Wilson Fence.⁶²

On September 3, the Kingman newspaper noted the Round Valley second-anniversary party, with a picture show and dance. A chaperoned bus had been available to bring ladies from Kingman.⁶³

Figure 40. DG-46 Sloping a Cut on Round Valley–Hackberry Truck Trail, 1937. Courtesy NARACO, RG 49/15/C/6/1 Box 62.

On September 22, Samuell inspected again, noting only 110 enrollees. He also noted that many projects were delayed. Cofer Fence was 92% complete. Other projects listed on the report included Little Sandy Soil Erosion, Mullen Fence, Neal Well, Hualapai Valley Rodent Control, Hualapai Valley Range Survey, Francis Creek Truck Trail, Kingman Round Valley Soil Erosion, Hualapai Truck Trail, Wilson Fence, Gaddis Fence, and Berry Tank.⁶⁴ A detailed narrative report for the Ninth Enrollment Period (April 1–September 30, 1937) offers details and photographs of the work. The Round Valley–Hackberry Truck Trail was completed, saving Round Valley ranchers thirty-two miles over the former route. The Berry Truck Trail was completed, offering ranchers a shorter route to Hackberry. Francis Creek Truck Trail improvements were completed, and ranchers had given it a "great deal of favorable comment." The Antelope Fence, which surrounded two stock tanks, was completed. The Cofer Fence, which fenced the division between the Arizona Livestock Company and Clyde Cofer, was completed. The latter individual was said to control over 18,000 head of sheep, cattle, and horses. The rodent control program continued, with a crew of twenty-five eliminating kangaroo rats, antelope squirrels, round-tailed squirrels, and pocket gophers. Valley Spring was developed and flowed five gallons per minute. That project included blasting a new line to the storage tank. Post cutting for some eighty miles of fence continued at the Buck and Doe spike camp.⁶⁵

On October 1, the Kingman newspaper announced, "Population of CCC Camps Is Cut One Half." Budget cutting in Washington was hitting Round Valley, with fifty-four Round Valley enrollees being discharged and fifteen Round Valley enrollees going to Topock to tear down the CCC camp, as men there were being sent to Yuma.⁶⁶ Throughout the rest of the year, the only news of Round Valley was a series of articles about the explosion of appendectomies at the Round Valley and Hualapai Mountain camps.⁶⁷ At year's end, the camp had 183 enrollees.

Figure 41. Fifty Posts, One Hundred Stays Per Shift by These Two Enrollees, DG-46, 1937. Courtesy NARACO, RG 49/15/C/6/1 Box 62.

1938

Little is known about work the Round Valley CCC camp did the first six months of the year. The view today is a bit confusing for this period, as the War Department location and strength reports for June 30, 1938, list no camp for Round Valley. However, the local newspaper lists a number of camp social and athletic activities during April, May, and June.

On July 12, a new CCC company, Company 340, composed mostly of enrollees from Pennsylvania, occupied Round Valley, replacing Company 2865.[68] On August 29, Special Investigator Samuell visited the camp and posted a inspection letter reporting that projects were "not progressing as fast as we would like due to the new enrollees being from Pennsylvania, most of them from the streets of Philadelphia, and it will take them some time for them to realize that they must work and that their work must be good." The Arizona Livestock Fence Section B was almost half-complete. The Gist Cattle Guard on the Wikieup Road was good, except it was too high. He said the Bartemus Fence needed to be re-worked.[69]

He returned on October 1 to an improved work situation. The Arizona Livestock Fence (Project #4652) was "finished yesterday and was exceptionally well built." The Trout Creek Corral (Project #4663) "looks good so far." The earlier difficulties encountered building the Bartemus Fence (Project #4650) had been corrected, but the project still had problems. Rodent control (Project #4648) was satisfactory, and post cutting (Project #4637) was moving faster, with good posts and stays.[70]

On October 21, the Kingman newspaper published a laudatory article about the improvements the CCC camps were making in the area grazing districts. The Round Valley Camp DG-46 was said to have constructed eighty miles of fences and reconstructed eighty miles of roads; erected five stock tanks; treated fifty thousand acres for kangaroo rats; and developed several wells and springs.[71]

Special Investigator A. W. Stockman filed a report on the same day, leaving us with a mixed picture. There were many enrollee complaints about the food, but the commander wanted to correct them. Liberty trips to town were limited, and the enrollees wanted more. He said enrollees were being charged $.50 per month for a movie program, but the films were old. Stockman reported he had many similar complaints about such compulsory movie programs and had reported them. Most of the enrollees were Pennsylvania city boys, and despite the complaints, morale was good "and I understand it is improving steadily." Both of the camp Army officers were from the East and "appear capable, conscientious and anxious to meet the requirements and high standards of their District Commander and objectives of the CCC Director." The Buck and Doe spike camp had twenty-seven men. There were water shortages at times due to well machinery that was old and that needed to be replaced, he concluded.[72]

On October 29, the camp hosted a dance, with the Hualapai CCC camp orchestra and chaperoned transportation for the Kingman girls.[73] Special Investigator Samuell inspected the camp and its projects for four days in mid-November and found most things in order. The Walters Fence (Project #4661) was said to be a good fence and just a week away from completion. He was very unhappy with the Bartemus Fence (Project #4649) in the Granite Mountains and the Mickle[74] Fence (Project #4667) east of the Hackberry Road for being "miserably crooked." Attached to his report was a letter to DG-46 Project Superintendent J. R. Sallenger saying the "camp engineer should not spend a day in camp till the fences were corrected."[75] The camp ended the year with just 82 enrollees (78 from Pennsylvania and the rest from Arizona).

1939

Although the Kingman newspaper did little reporting of the camp in the first half of the year, frequent inspections help give a reasonable look at its major work projects. On January

24, Special Investigator Samuell filed a report of four days of inspection. Construction had begun at the Rock Creek spike camp. The Bartemus Fence had only three weeks remaining to completion; however, travel time to and from the job totaled five hours each day! The Mickle Fence had forty-five men on the job, and 9.5 miles had been completed. The Walters-Cauthen Fence in the Peacock Mountains (Project #4662) was nearly complete. Bishop Tank (Project #4670) had fifty men doing hand labor.[76]

Samuell's mid-February report noted a number of jobs were progressing slowly due to snow. The Mickle Fence work was said to be "good work." The Yeast Fence (Project #4673) had just started out of the Hualapai spike camp. The base camp still had water problems.[77]

On March 22, Samuell reported the Rock Creek spike camp had just opened, with barracks from the old Hualapai spike camp. Besides ongoing jobs, he noted the Yeast-Neal Fence out of the Hualapai spike camp. He noted that the camp educational program was rated highest or second-highest in the state by the Army.[78]

On April 10, Samuell inspected for four days and noted low morale due to the orders to move the main camp. Five fence projects were in progress, and the Bartemus Fence was scheduled for completion in a week. The Bishop Tank was nearing completion.[79]

On May 5, the Kingman newspaper reported the Round Valley camp was moving to a new location site three miles southwest of town, northeast of the Lewis Dairy.[80] The May 25–27 inspection noted the Rock Creek spike camp was "neat and orderly," and twenty-one of its men were working the Duncan-Herridge Fence. The Hualapai spike camp had thirty men and was in good condition. The Buck and Doe spike camp had thirty-one men and was neat and orderly. Samuell noted the following fence projects: Clifford-Neal, Neal, Neal-Tucker, Brown, Clifford-Marshall, and Yeast.[81] DG-46 had an impressive work record. Besides the projects noted above, they were also said to have constructed telephone lines, corrals, and holding traps.[82]

Round Valley was officially abandoned June 5, 1939 and Company 2865 appears to have disbanded.[83] On June 23, the *Mohave County Miner* (page 1) reported the CCC was to put in four miles of fence around town, with the county furnishing the materials. Enrollees and staff were moved to DG-133 in Kingman. This author has not been able to find specific reasons for the abandonment of DG-46 and its movement to the DG-133 site. Was it the problems with the water supply referred to by the special investigators?

Unless noted otherwise, any reference to the number of enrollees in a company, the location of the company, or company supervisors are from U.S. War Department, Location and Strength of CCC Companies, 1933–1942, NARAMD RG 35 530/65/22/04/05.

1. "Seven Camps Scheduled for Mohave County," *Mohave County Miner*, May 10, 1935, 1, 8.
2. *Trails, Rails and Tales*, 219.
3. "Grazing Project Wins Approval," *Arizona Republic*, June 2, 1935, sect. 2, 2. It was assumed that when the camp was abandoned, the well, windmill, and pumping plant would be left for public use.
4. "CCC News," *Mohave County Miner*, August 30, 1935, 4.
5. "Round Valley CCC Camp Repairing Road to Big Sandy," *Mohave County Miner*, September 20, 1935, 1.
6. "New Road to Hackberry Is CCC Camp Plan," *Mohave County Miner*, October 11, 1935, 1.
7. "Round Valley CCC Camp by Priest C. High," *Mohave County Miner*, October 25, 1935, 3.
8. "Round Valley Crews Rush Sandy Road Improvement," *Mohave County Miner*, October 25, 1935, 7.
9. "Round Valley CCC Camp by Priest C. High," *Mohave County Miner*, November 15, 1935, 4.
10. U.S. CCC, Camp Inspection Reports, NARAMD RG 35/530/65/23/04 Entry 115 (PI #11) Box 10.
11. *Mohave County Miner*, November 22, 1935, 1.
12. *Mohave County Miner*, November 29, 1935, 1.
13. "Round Valley CCC Camp by Priest C. High," *Mohave County Miner*, December 20, 1935, 11.
14. "Round Valley CCC Camp by Priest C. High," *Mohave County Miner*, January 24, 1936, 6.
15. "Big Sandy News," *Mohave County Miner*, January 17, 1936, 6.
16. "Round Valley CCC Camp by Mike Kowal," *Mohave County Miner*, January 31, 1936, 6.
17. "Round Valley CCC Camp by Mike Kowal," *Mohave County Miner*, February 7, 1936, 6.
18. "Round Valley CCC Camp by Mike Kowal," *Mohave County Miner*, March 6, 1936, 9.
19. "Round Valley CCC Camp by Mike Kowal," *Mohave County Miner*, April 17, 1936, 11.
20. "Round Valley CCC Camp by Mike Kowal," *Mohave County Miner*, May 1, 1936, 7.
21. *Trails, Rails and Tales*, 219.
22. "Round Valley CCC Camp by Mike Kowal," *Mohave County Miner*, May 8, 1936, 2.
23. "Round Valley CCC Camp by Mike Kowal," *Mohave County Miner*, May 22, 1936, 8.

24. "Round Valley CCC Boys Halt Forest Fire in Hualapais," *Mohave County Miner,* June 5, 1936, 4.
25. "Round Valley CCC Camp to Start First Fence Project," *Mohave County Miner,* June 26, 1936, 3.
26. U.S. CCC, Camp Inspection Reports, NARAMD RG 35/530/65/23/04 Entry 115 (PI #11) Box 10.
27. *Happy Days,* June 27, 1936, 20.
28. "Round Valley CCC Camp by Mike Kowal," *Mohave County Miner,* July 3, 1936, 10.
29. U.S. BLM, Camp Inspection Reports, 1938–1942, NARACO RG 49 Entry 20 Box 86.
30. *Mohave County Miner,* July 10, 1936, 6.
31. "Round Valley CCC Camp by Mike Kowal," *Mohave County Miner,* July 31, 1936, 6.
32. *Mohave County Miner,* July 31, 1936, 9.
33. "Round Valley CCC Camp by Mike Kowal," *Mohave County Miner,* August 7, 1936, 8.
34. "Round Valley CCC Camp by Mike Kowal," *Mohave County Miner,* August 28, 1936, 7.
35. "Round Valley CCC Camp by Mike Kowal," *Mohave County Miner,* September 4, 1936, 2.
36. U.S. CCC, Phoenix District, *Official Annual, 1936, Phoenix District, 8th Corps Area, Civilian Conservation Corps* ([Baton Rouge, LA?]: Direct Advertising Co., 1936), 46–47. GCNPMC Cat. #70738.
37. *Mohave County Miner,* October 2, 1936, 2.
38. "Round Valley CCC Camp," *Mohave County Miner,* October 9, 1936, 10.
39. "Round Valley CCC Camp," *Mohave County Miner,* October 16, 1936, 5.
40. U.S. BLM, Camp Inspection Reports, 1938–1942, NARACO RG 49 Entry 20 Box 86.
41. "Round Valley CCC Camp," *Mohave County Miner,* October 30, 1936, 2.
42. "90 New CCC Boys Arrive at Round Valley Camp 23d," *Mohave County Miner,* October 30, 1936, 10.
43. "CCC Sponsors Entertainment, Dance Tonight," *Mohave County Miner,* November 20, 1936, 10.
44. U.S. BLM, Camp Inspection Reports, 1938–1942, NARACO RG 49 Entry 20 Box 86.
45. "Round Valley CCC Camp," *Mohave County Miner,* December 11, 1936, 10.
46. "110 Hualapai CCC Boys Are Moved to Round Valley Camp," *Mohave County Miner,* January 8, 1937, 1.
47. "Round Valley CCC Camp," *Mohave County Miner,* January 15, 1937, 5.
48. "CCC Boys Rescue Marooned Family," *Mohave County Miner,* February 5, 1937, 1. Photos in the collection of the Kingman BLM District Office indicate the CCC opened roads to the Cofer and Bartamus Ranches.
49. "Round Valley CCC Camp," *Mohave County Miner,* February 19, 1937, 11.
50. "Two CCC Boys to Try Out with San Diego Ball Team," *Mohave County Miner,* February 26, 1937, 1. Their successfulness was not reported.
51. "Round Valley CCC Camp," *Mohave County Miner,* March 12, 1937, 8.
52. "Round Valley CCC Camp," *Mohave County Miner,* March 19, 1937, 10.
53. *Division of Grazing News,* March 31, 1937, Civilian Conservation Corps Newsletters, Serials Collection AHSLA.
54. BLM, Grazing, "ECW Narrative Report, Camp DG46A," Narrative Reports of Individual CCC Camps, 1936–1938, NARACO, RG 49/15/6/7/4/1 Box 6 Entry 19 (PI #11) Box 75.
55. No doubt this is George D. Hastings, who was Grand Canyon Company 818 Army staff and later Grand Canyon Army sub-district commander. See Audretsch, *Shaping the Park and Saving the Boys,* 35, 55, 73.
56. U.S. BLM, Camp Inspection Reports, 1938–1942, NARACO RG 49 Entry 20 Box 86.
57. "CCC Boy Dies at Mohave Hospital" *Mohave County Miner,* June 4, 1937, 1; Arizona Death Records, State File No. 312, Registered No. 37.
58. "Round Valley CCC Camp," *Mohave County Miner,* June 18, 1937, 7.
59. U.S. BLM, Camp Inspection Reports, 1938–1942, NARACO RG 49 Entry 20 Box 86.
60. "Round Valley CCC Camp," *Mohave County Miner,* July 23, 1937, 3.
61. "Round Valley CCC Camp," *Mohave County Miner,* August 6, 1937, 8.
62. U.S. BLM, Camp Inspection Reports, 1938–1942, NARACO RG 49 Entry 20 Box 86.
63. "Round Valley CCC Camp Celebrates Birthday Tonight," *Mohave County Miner,* September 3, 1937, 1.
64. U.S. BLM, Camp Inspection Reports, 1938–1942, NARACO RG 49 Entry 20 Box 86.
65. U.S. BLM, Grazing, "Ninth Period Illustrated Narrative Report, Camp DG-46-A," Narrative Reports of Individual CCC Camps, 1936–1938, NARACO, RG 49/15/6/7/4/1 Box 6 Entry 19 (PI #11) Box 75.
66. *Mohave County Miner,* October 1, 1937, 1.
67. "Blame Diet for CCC Appendicitis Epidemic," *Prescott Evening Courier,* December 16, 1937, 1. The AP article from Kingman reported eighteen appendectomies at Round Valley and Wallapai in the previous two weeks, with no deaths but with some physicians blaming excessive protein in the diet.

68. "CCC Camps Are Both Filled to 200 Man Quota," *Mohave County Miner,* July 15, 1938, 1.
69. U.S. BLM, Camp Inspection Reports, 1938–1942, NARACO RG 49 Entry 20 Box 86.
70. Ibid.
71. "CCC Grazing Camp Has Greatly Improved Ranges and Roads in County's Great Grazing Districts," *Mohave County Miner,* October 21, 1938, sect. 4, 10.
72. U.S. CCC, Camp Inspection Reports, NARAMD RG 35/530/65/23/04 Entry 115 (PI #11) Box 10.
73. "Round Valley CCC to Be Dance Hosts," *Mohave County Miner,* October 28, 1938, 6.
74. Mickle is also spelled Mickel in the CCC records, but Mickle appears to be the more likely spelling. Dan Messersmith, e-mail message to author, July 11, 2012, regarding a search of data in the Mohave Museum of History and Arts.
75. U.S. BLM, Camp Inspection Reports, 1938–1942, NARACO RG 49 Entry 20 Box 86.
76. Ibid.
77. Ibid.
78. Ibid.
79. Ibid.
80. "Round Valley 3C Camp Moving to Kingman Canyon," *Mohave County Miner,* May 5, 1939, 1.
81. U.S. BLM, Camp Inspection Reports, 1938–1942, NARACO RG 49 Entry 20 Box 86.
82. U.S. CCC, "Resume of CCC Program," December 30, 1938, BLM (GS) CCC Work Program Correspondence, 1938–39, NARACO RG 49 Entry 4 Box 13, page 47.
83. "Civilian Conservation Corps Eighth Corps Area, Status Record of CCC Camps Authorized Since Inception of the Program up to … December 31, 1941 … Compiled by Office of Liaison Officer, CCC Fort Sam Houston…," NARACO BLM CCC Directories RG 49 Entry 33, 34 Box 132.

CHAPTER 14

Kingman (DG-133 and G-133)[1]

1939

ON MAY 5, THE KINGMAN NEWSPAPER reported the Round Valley camp was moving to a new location three miles southwest of town, northeast of the Lewis Dairy.[2] DG-133 was occupied on June 5 by Pennsylvania enrollees of Company 340. On June 30, the camp only had 29 men. According to the Kingman newspaper, 151 area enrollees had just mustered out to Pennsylvania, but replacements were coming in soon.[3]

CCC Special Investigator E. W. Samuell inspected the camp in early July and noted a number of shortcomings, including the work of the mechanic. All of the new enrollees had not yet arrived.[4] Samuell's August 3–5 report noted the new men had arrived and appeared to be of higher quality than previous enrollees. Merle B. Quimby was the camp's project superintendent. New camp buildings had arrived, and construction was to begin soon. A carpenter was to be hired to rush the buildings. His report listed comments on the supervisors, including a suggestion to let the mechanic go. The regular educational program had started. The Rock Creek spike camp, twenty-three miles away, was to be closed temporarily, with the tools, etc., moved to the main camp. The Hualapai spike camp was open and would have men soon. The Buck and Doe spike camp had been opened on August 3 with twenty-five men. New barracks and a kitchen, etc., were to be added soon so that the spike camp could expand to sixty enrollees, as it would need to supply posts to DG-133 and DG-109 (Arlington).

Work projects included the Hackberry Holding Pasture, engaging fifty enrollees, which was slated to be finished soon, with the enrollees assigned to the Herridge Fence project. The Mickle Fence had just started, with twenty-one enrollees working on the project. The Logadon-Duncan Fence had twenty-two men but was "tough going."[5] On September 15, the Kingman newspaper noted that seven of the camp enrollees were hurt near Hackberry when their truck hit a guardrail and overturned. None were seriously injured.[6]

On October 21, CCC Special Investigator Hamilton Draper inspected for three days and reported unsanitary conditions at the Buck and Doe spike camp. The post cutting crew there had increased from thirty-six to forty-eight. The posts were good quality, but their production goal was doubtful because of scattered timber, rough trails, and inexperienced enrollees. It was likely to close December 1 due to snow. The Round Valley spike camp was being prepared for occupancy soon. Work projects included the 3-mile-long Duncan-Herridge Fence (Project #4668), just started with twenty-six men. The Duncan-Herridge Fence (Project #4669) had twenty-six men at work, was 90% complete, and was a "very good job." The camp had no resident doctor, so a physician from Kingman was called when needed.[7]

Draper returned for a four-day inspection on November 15 and reported all the problems noted on the October report had been corrected. Post cutting at the Buck and Doe spike camp had increased slightly, but the camp would close down about December 16. Work projects included the Clack-Logsden-McNair and the Clack-Logsden-Arizona Livestock Fences; the Clack Fence, just started with twenty-eight men; and the Big Sandy Road Cattle Guard, just started. He noted the Duncan-Herridge Fence (Project #4668) was completed through very rough country and was a "very good job." The Wall Cattle Guard was said to need changes.[8]

Draper's December 6–7 report noted the county was supplying materials for five cattle guards and that the Old Highway 66 Cattle Guard had been started. The Clack-Logsden-McNair Fence, one mile from Kingman, was being finished and was "very good." Hualapai Tank No. 1 on the Arizona Livestock Company allotment had been started. The Clack Fence was just completed, but had taken longer than planned, as one mile done by a previous foreman had to be re-done.[9] At the end of the year, G-133, Company 340, had 85 enrollees (all from Pennsylvania except 2 from Arizona). Camp overseers included two Army officers, a contract physician, and an educational advisor.

1940

January 23–25 was the first of many inspections of the year. Special Investigator Samuell noted that there was "great improvement in this camp," but the new Pennsylvania enrollees "appear to be weak and undernourished and it will take some time for them to come out of it." The "best safety program that I have seen anywhere was held while I was at this camp." He said the educational program "works particularly well." Work projects he noted were the Bonelli-Searchlight Fence, just started at Boulder Dam Highway two miles north of the Pleasant Valley Service Station; the Bonelli-Epperson Fence running east from the Dam Highway with twenty-six men and 2.5 miles nearly completed; and a fence running west from the Dam Highway. All fence work was "very satisfactory." The Antelope spike camp had twenty-six men working, but the work was slow, as "very few of these Philadelphia boys know how to handle tools." The Hualapai spike camp had twenty-six men completing the salvage of the camp. Engineer Thompson and three boys were completing a survey of the Bonelli Fences next to the Pete Bozart Fence.[10]

Draper returned for a two-day inspection on February 20, reporting that general camp conditions "have improved." The educational program was good, but he expected improvements. The safety program was "the best," and an attached letter to the report from grazier John Ray Painter to Quimby dated March 9 stated that the safety program originated in the camp was "now being used in all the camps in the Region. Much favorable comment has been received on this program from the Washington Office." Some of the work projects were the Town Fence and Slaughter House Cattle Guards, which were started. The Gist-Cornwall Fence had twenty-six men from the Round Valley spike camp working, and it was "very good." The Antelope spike camp had twenty-five men erecting three barracks, a mess hall and kitchen, and foremen's quarters. The buildings, with a sixty-man capacity, were to be ready soon. The Hualapai Tank No. 1 project had three men working two shifts with the "Cat," and they were moving about 250 yards of dirt a day; Draper noted it "will be an excellent reservoir when completed." Five miles of the Bonelli-Searchlight Fence (three hours driving time each day) had been completed, with fifty men at work on it, and their work was "A-1." The Bonelli-Epperson Fence, thirty-five miles from camp, had twenty-five men at work and was "up to standard in every respect."[11] At the end of February, camp strength stood at 200 enrollees.

March was a busy month at G-133. Samuell inspected for two days beginning March 20, and except for the mechanic, the "camp is in the best condition I have ever seen it in." The work program was the "best we have ever had in this camp," and there was plenty of future work on hand. Twenty-one men had just started the Bonelli-Yeast Fence. The Duncan-Herridge Fence No. 3 was started March 20 with nineteen men. The Town Fence and five cattle guards had just been finished. The Bonelli-Searchlight Fence had 7 of its 13 miles completed, with twenty-seven enrollees on the job. The Bonelli-Epperson Fence had 10 of 26 miles completed, with twenty-seven men working. The Duncan-Logsden Drift Fence had just started. The Arizona Livestock Tank No. 1 was nearing completion at 18' deep and was "very good work." According to Samuell, the Antelope spike camp would need additional buildings. The Buck and Doe spike camp was being prepared for re-occupancy, but two extra buildings were needed. The Round Valley spike camp was being closed, and arrangements were being made for a spike camp at Wikieup.[12]

On March 28, the Kingman newspaper outlined the past and future camp work. Project Superintendent Quimby was quoted as saying two more years of projects remained. The camp had 201 enrollees and had already constructed 150 miles of fence. Four out of five tanks had been completed. Future side camps would be at Big Sandy near Wikieup and at Yucca. Enrollees at the Buck and Doe spike camp near Milkweed Springs had already cut thirty thousand fence posts. The 6-mile-long Bonelli-Searchlight Fence was just finished, and the City Fence was close to completion. The Cane Springs spike camp was moving to Antelope Springs east of Dolan Springs. It then had thirty-five men, who were erecting the camp, and then their number would go to sixty. The camp obtained water from a 1.5-mile-long pipeline, and there would be an electric plant to supply lights to all buildings.[13] According to the camp newspaper, the Antelope Springs spike camp "is situated in the midst of the dense Joshua forest which is inspiring in itself."[14]

Samuell's next inspection in April was two days long, but the report was short. He reported that the next fence project was to be the Bonelli-Ray-Hall Fence.[15] During May, the camp was involved in fighting four forest fires.[16] The May 23 issue of the *Mohave County Miner* (page 9) touted the camp newspaper with an article titled, "Excellent Paper Is Published by CCC Camp at Kingman."

In late May, Draper inspected the camp for three days, with his report emphasizing work projects. The McConnico Corral, four miles south of camp, was 40% done, with twenty enrollees working on the project. The Santa Fe Railway was supplying materials for the project, and Draper called the workmanship "very good." The Logsdon-Duncan Fence (Project #133-42) was eight miles from camp, but rough roads made the drive one hour long, and it was slated to be completed in a week. The Bonelli-Searchlight Fence (Project #133-36) had twenty-four men working its west end. The work was judged as very good, but going slowly due to rough ground. The Neal-Yeast Fence (Project #4673) had about two miles finished by the Antelope spike camp. He noted the fence project had started out of the old Hualapai spike camp and been suspended one year ago. He called it "excellent" work. Twenty-nine Buck and Doe spike camp enrollees were cutting posts. The Hualapai Tank No. 1 was getting "finishing touches" and looked to be an "excellent job."[17]

Draper returned for a three-day inspection June 11 and noted both spike camps had to be closed on June 19, as 120 enrollees were returning to the East and new men would not arrive in July. Work projects included the completion of the Logsdon-Duncan Fence; modification of the McConnico Corral; completion of the Bonelli-Searchlight Fence, which was "very well constructed"; completion of another 1.5 miles of the Neal-Yeast Fence; and the completion of the Hualapai Tank No. 1, with the "Cat" crew moving to Bishop Tank.[18] Between the end of March and May 31, camp strength dropped from 176 to 165. However, on June 30, just 48 enrollees were in camp.

On July 14, over 200 new enrollees arrived in Kingman and 159 Pennsylvania enrollees went to G-133. An article in the *Mohave County Miner* noted that about 45 new men would be sent to the Buck and Doe spike camp and 60 to Antelope Spring spike camp. Post cutting, a fence project in the Sacramento Valley, and a ten–acre feet tank near Long Mountain were said to be current projects. A shortwave radio was being installed at camp and side camps, which would include communication with Phoenix.[19] The newspaper reported the camp had fought a brush fire in the Cerbat Mountains six miles southwest of Mt. Tipton.[20]

Inspector Samuell visited the camp for two days on July 31 and noted both spike camps were not yet occupied due to all the new enrollees. Work projects included the Hualapai Reservoir No. 1, which was just completed. He noted that it stood 31′ from the top of the dam to the bottom. Three crews totaling eighty-one men were working the Bonelli-Epperson Fence, with one crew building a truck trail. Fourteen miles of fence were completed, with twelve to go. The camp had no lost time accidents since their safety program started, except for three hernia cases.[21] The end-of-July camp strength was 206 enrollees (nearly all from Pennsylvania).

On August 1, all the new men finished a four-day orientation course to camp life and training in the correct handling of tools. Their first projects were said to include building an arbor and a water cooling system. Their educational courses were said to include photography, music, leathercraft, leader training, fence construction, carpentry, cement, surveying, and mechanics.[22] In early August, the *Mohave County Miner* reported that six enrollees were sent to fight a forest fire and forty-four men were off to the Buck and Doe spike camp for fence post cutting.[23]

Samuell was in camp on September 4–5 for a two-day inspection. He noted Army Sub-district Commander Hastings was in camp and complimented the project superintendent on both spike camps. Forty-five enrollees were at the Buck and Doe spike camp, but post cutting was down to two hundred posts per day as enrollees were constructing a truck trail to get to new trees. A crew of four enrollees was surveying under the camp engineer's supervision. Work projects included the Bonelli-Epperson Fence (thirty-seven miles from camp), which had 9 miles to go out of a total of 26. He noted that the west-end crew of this project "must shoot every hole." Thirty-five enrollees had only two weeks to go on the Truxton Canyon Agency Fence located east of Red Lake. Twelve enrollees were reconstructing the camp road that washed out on September 3.[24]

Draper inspected September 21–22 and noted that thirty men were at Buck and Doe spike camp, but looking for new territory for posts. Other work projects were the Bonelli-Epperson Fence, rated as "very good"; the Neal-Yeast and Truxton Agency Fences out of the Antelope Spring spike camp, with both rated "good work"; and the McConnico Corrals, Scales, and Loading Chutes, rated as "very well constructed." He reported that two shifts of 7–8 men were to start rushing the Trout Creek Corral project in order to finish before cattle loading on October 5.[25]

The problem of finding enough posts to cut was solved in early October by the leasing of some school sections of land.[26] Draper inspected for three days in late October and noted post cutting and fence work. The Bonelli-Ray-Hall Fence, seven miles from the Antelope Springs spike camp, was "good work." The Trout Creek Scales and Corral improvements were nearly complete and a "nice job."[27]

Samuell inspected November 6–8 and reported the Army had given the camp an excellent rating. The Buck and Doe spike camp had thirty-five men and was in the "best shape I have ever seen the side camp." He called the supply of posts "a great showing," indicating 12,000 line posts, 25,000 stays, 350 corral posts, and 1,200 panel posts were ready for use. The Bonelli-Yeast Fence was over half-done, and an end-of-month completion was anticipated. The Neal-Yeast fence was within three miles of completion. The Bonelli-Epperson Fence would likely take to the end of the following month.[28]

From August through November, camp strength varied between 200 and 186. However, many men were coming to the end of their enrollments. Less than 60 were left in camp when 123 left camp on December 1. Replacements numbering some 160 were expected on January 10.[29]

In mid-December, the Kingman newspaper reported the camp foremen were undergoing national defense training.[30] Just before Christmas, Samuell inspected for two days. He reported the Antelope Springs spike camp had twelve men doing cattle guard work. Two trucks were hauling posts for the Miller-Wall Fence.[31] At the end of the year, G-133, Company 340, had 58 enrollees (54 from Pennsylvania and 4 from Arizona).

1941

On January 13, Samuell inspected the camp for four days. Fifty-eight men were in camp awaiting the arrival of the new enrollees. Work projects mentioned included the Bonelli-Epperson Fence, where the "Cat" was making a truck trail. He reported the Bonelli-Epperson Fence No. 2 was almost impossible to reach and recommended a change in the cooperative agreement. The Antelope Springs spike camp had eight enrollees, with four constructing buildings. The Bonelli-Searchlight Fence had three cattle guards being poured.[32] On January 22, 142 new enrollees from Pennsylvania were set to arrive.[33] The following week, the camp entertained the local business and professional men's club. The camp was said to have good well water and electric lights and power.[34] The month ended on a negative note, with 2 Pennsylvania enrollees sentenced to prison for auto theft.[35] On January 31, the camp had 198 enrollees (all but 3 from Pennsylvania).

The camp was inspected by Samuell on February 18–20. Ongoing work projects included twenty-nine men working on the Herridge-Smith and Potter Fence, with 3 miles completed and less than 1 mile to go. He predicted it would be completed at the end of the month. Twenty-nine men were working the Bonelli-Epperson Fence, with sections in the middle and ends yet to be completed. "The extreme ends I believe should be done by other than enrollees." Twenty-nine enrollees were on the Bonelli-Yeast Fence project, with 5 miles completed out of 6.[36] (This was the last BLM inspection located. As inspection reports after this date were very infrequent, the record of work after this date is incomplete.)

The February 27 *Mohave County Miner* had a lengthy article about the grazing work of the CCC stating that "one of the greatest aids to proper supervision of local ranges by federal grazing service has been the work performed" by the CCC in last six years. Work completed included more than two hundred miles of boundary fence, with about twenty cattle guards; six stock watering tanks; about ten thousand acres treated for rodents in the Big Sandy; more than one hundred miles of roads and stock shipping corrals at Trout Creek and McConnico; substantial fence work by the Antelope Springs spike camp near historic White Hills; and one hundred thousand fence posts cut by the seasonal Buck and Doe spike camp.[37] Corrals were also constructed at Louise, and loading shoots were to be constructed at Yucca and Hackberry.[38] On February 28, the camp had 188 enrollees (including 2 Arizona veterans).

In early March, the Kingman newspaper announced that the camp was holding a military drill competition on Saturday and the public was invited.[39] In early April, the camp held an anniversary dinner, inviting all locals. It was reportedly well attended. The camp softball team beat the local team 7–6.[40]

CCC Special Inspector M. J. Bowen inspected the camp May 16 and reported the "camp [is] in splendid condition." Morale was good and the officers were doing very well. Cooperation was excellent. The mess was good. However, a very great nuisance was "the large herds of cattle that roam through the camp grounds, drink all the water in the fire barrels, and committing other very great nuisance." He recommended the construction of a fence around camp. He summarized the work completed, but did not indicate for what time period: 101 miles of fencing; 39,300 cedar posts; 108,000 cedar stays; twenty cattle guards; three corrals; one stock reservoir; twelve brush fires extinguished; one thousand pounds of seeds collected; fifty miles of truck trail; and one mile of telephone line.[41]

The May 22 issue of the Kingman newspaper reported the camp was addressed by American Legion spokesmen on the topic of Americanism.[42] On May 29, the newspaper noted that enrollees were posting warnings along the main highways regarding range fires.[43] On May 31, the camp had 170 enrollees (nearly all from Pennsylvania and 2 Arizona veterans). On June 12, the Kingman newspaper reported the CCC had sent twenty boys to successfully fight a 640-acre fire near the Producers Mine.

The same day, the newspaper reported 127 Pennsylvania enrollees were returning home.[44] A week later, the newspaper announced that Company 340 was moving to Montana. They were being replaced by Company 4812, which arrived from Nogales on June 25. On June 30, G-133, Company 4812, had 104 enrollees (over 90% from Texas). Fifty enrollees from BR-74, Yuma, and other companies that were being disbanded were transferred to G-133.[45] From July through September, company strength varied between 150 and 159 enrollees. By the end of the year, G-133 had only 110 men (80% from Texas and the rest from Arizona).

1942

At the beginning of the year, G-133, like many other CCC camps, was suffering from a lack of acceptable enrollees. With the American economy rapidly converting to a war economy, many higher-paying jobs were available in defense industries. Also, more and more young men were being drafted into the military. On January 31, the camp had only 67 enrollees (most from Texas), while the February count showed only 31. On February 12, the Kingman newspaper reported enrollees were clearing ground for the VFW firing range.[46] Bowen inspected the camp for two days beginning March 19, and he noted "very good" camp administration, an "excellent" mess, and "excellent" morale. However, desertions were high.[47] At the end of April, the camp had 66 enrollees.

Camp G-133 was officially closed May 13, 1942.[48] The following day, the *Mohave County Miner* summarized the camp's previous three years of work as follows: construction of 129 miles of fence, thirty-two cattle guards, and three shipping corrals, using 27,000 fence posts; completion of two reservoirs and one pumping station; extinguishing of fifteen range fires;

collection of 2.75 tons of flare seed; rodent control on 300 acres; and construction of 17.5 miles of truck trails.[49]

Unless noted otherwise, any reference to the number of enrollees in a company, the location of the company, or company supervisors are from U.S. War Department, Location and Strength of CCC Companies, 1933–1942, NARAMD RG 35 530/65/22/04/05.

1. The abbreviation change from DG to G occurred when the name Division of Grazing was changed to Grazing Service in late 1939. In 1946, the name changed again to Bureau of Land Management.
2. "Round Valley 3C Camp Moving to Kingman Canyon," *Mohave County Miner,* May 5, 1939, 1. The War Department location and strength reports located the new camp 4.3 miles southwest of the railhead.
3. "151 CCC Boys to Leave Today, More Coming in 2 Weeks," *Mohave County Miner,* June 23, 1939, 1.
4. U.S. BLM, Camp Inspection Reports, 1938–1942, NARACO RG 49 Entry 20 Box 86.
5. Ibid.
6. "Seven Boys from Local CCC Camp Injured in Auto Wreck near Hackberry Last Friday," *Mohave County Miner,* September 15, 1939, 1, 8.
7. U.S. BLM, Camp Inspection Reports, 1938–1942, NARACO RG 49 Entry 20 Box 86. The dirty spike camp resulted in John Ray Painter, acting regional grazier, writing Project Superintendent Quimby on November 10 stating: "If we do not maintain these side camps properly, the Army will close them." (Letter attached to inspection report.)
8. Ibid.
9. Ibid.
10. Ibid.
11. Ibid.
12. Ibid.
13. "Two Years' Work Remains on CCC Projects Here," *Mohave County Miner,* March 28, 1940, 7.
14. *The Cattle Guard News,* March, 1940, Fiche MN #0181, CRL Newspapers.
15. U.S. BLM, Camp Inspection Reports, 1938–1942, NARACO RG 49 Entry 20 Box 86.
16. *The Cattle Guard News,* June 15, 1940, Fiche MN #0181, CRL Newspapers.
17. U.S. BLM, Camp Inspection Reports, 1938–1942, NARACO RG 49 Entry 20 Box 86.
18. Ibid.
19. "223 Enrollees Arrived Sun. for CCC Camp Here," *Mohave County Miner,* July 18, 1940, 1, 14.
20. "CCC Boys Beat Brush Fire in Cerbats Monday," *Mohave County Miner,* July 25, 1940, 1.
21. U.S. BLM, Camp Inspection Reports, 1938–1942, NARACO RG 49 Entry 20 Box 86.
22. "Enrollees Complete Orientation Period, Start Regular Work and Vocational Education Program," *Mohave County Miner,* August 1, 1940, 3.
23. "CCC Boys Put Out Brush Fire, Reopen Reservation Camp," *Mohave County Miner,* August 8, 1940, 1.
24. U.S. BLM, Camp Inspection Reports, 1938–1942, NARACO RG 49 Entry 20 Box 86.
25. Ibid.
26. Painter to Quimby, 4 October 1940, ibid.
27. U.S. BLM, Camp Inspection Reports, 1938–1942, NARACO RG 49 Entry 20 Box 86.
28. Ibid.
29. "123 CCC Boys Left Sunday for Pennsylvania," *Mohave County Miner,* December 5, 1940, 1.
30. "Local CC Now Trains Foremen," *Mohave County Miner,* December 12, 1940, 12.
31. U.S. BLM, Camp Inspection Reports, 1938–1942, NARACO RG 49 Entry 20 Box 86.
32. Ibid.
33. "142 CCC Boys Will Arrive in Kingman Monday," *Mohave County Miner,* January 16, 1941, 1.
34. "Civilian Conservation Corps Camp at McConnico Is Host to Kingman Business and Professional Men," *Mohave County Miner,* January 23, 1941, 10.
35. "Fifty Mile Ride Lands Two Boys in Penitentiary," *Mohave County Miner,* January 30, 1941, 1, 10.
36. U.S. BLM, Camp Inspection Reports, 1938–1942, NARACO RG 49 Entry 20 Box 86.
37. "Civilian Conservation Corp Work Is Big Asset to Local Livestock Growers," *Mohave County Miner,* February 27, 1941, sect. 5, 5.
38. "Four Shipping Pens Constructed by CCC," *Mohave County Miner,* February 27, 1941, sect. 5, 8.
39. "CCC Camp Will Hold Military Drills Sat.," *Mohave County Miner,* March 6, 1941, 1.
40. "CCC Celebration Is Largely Attended," *Mohave County Miner,* April 10, 1941, 1.
41. U.S. CCC, Camp Inspection Reports, NARAMD RG 35/530/65/23/04 Entry 115 (PI #11) Box 10.
42. "Gordon, Mylius Address CC Camp on Americanism," *Mohave County Miner,* May 22, 1941, 4.
43. "CCC Boys Painting Range Fire Warnings," *Mohave County Miner,* May 29, 1941, 3.

44. "Severe Range Fire Threatens Producers Mine," and "Large Group of CCC Enrollees Go Home," *Mohave County Miner,* June 12, 1941, 1, 3.
45. "50 Man Contingent from Yuma CCC Moved to Kingman," *Mohave County Miner,* July 3, 1941, 10.
46. "Work On (VFW) Rifle Range Started," *Mohave County Miner,* February 12, 1942, 3.
47. U.S. CCC, Camp Inspection Reports, NARAMD RG 35/530/65/23/04 Entry 115 (PI #11) Box 10.
48. Per telegram in Records of the BLM (Grazing Service), CCC Camp Histories, 1933–45, NARACO RG 49/Entry 5 Box 22.
49. "Local CCC Camp Closed Wednesday, Has Long Record of Range Services during Three Years of Operation," *Mohave County Miner,* May 14, 1942, 9.

CHAPTER 15

St. George, Utah (DG-45)

CAMP DG-45 WAS INDEED AN anomaly. The camp's work was in the state of Arizona in western Mohave County north of the Colorado River.[1] Even though it was listed as an Arizona camp, it was housed in Utah. It was listed in the Army's 8th Corps reports, but it was under the jurisdiction of Fort Douglas, Utah, in the 9th Corps. Most of its enrollees were from the 5th Corps area of Ohio, West Virginia, Indiana, and Kentucky. All of them were white.

As it turns out, St. George was not the original location for the camp. It was originally set to be located at Black Rock in Arizona. (See chapter 15 sidebar, *Showdown at Black Rock*.) Unlike most CCC camps whose barracks were on public land, the DG-45 barracks were located on private land, with the $25 monthly rent paid by the St. George Chamber of Commerce. But what might appear to be liabilities were not. The camp accomplished significant work, and judging from the local newspaper, the personnel were popular throughout the region. It must be noted that even though the St. George newspaper frequently covered camp activities in detail, many BLM JDR files and *Record Book* entries are missing, so this account of its work is necessarily incomplete.

1935

Company 2558 was organized at Fort Douglas and arrived at their St. George camp on about October 27, 1935.[2] According to a camp inspection report, the camp was "originally occupied by Forest Service in December 1933. DG took over work Oct. 27, 1935."[3] On December 31, the company had 190 enrollees (nearly all from Kentucky). Their leaders were three Reserve Army officers, a full-time contract physician, and an educational advisor. Their commanding officer was Capt. B. H. Bryant, and D. M. Thompson was their technical supervisor. Lester I. Parker from Wolf Hole and Floyd Hallmark and James Bundy from Mt. Trumbull were their first foremen.

Their first ten days were for conditioning. As of November 7, their trucks and heavy road building equipment had not yet arrived.[4] The first priority of the Stockmen's Advisory Council was building an adequate road into the area. "The old existing trail from St. George to Wolf Hole, a distance of thirty miles, was only a trail. It had been used for 75 years by wagons and stock alike but was a narrow, crooked and tortuous route to have to traverse. It usually took two hours to negotiate the thirty miles by automobile.... In wet weather it was almost impassable and made the transportation of supplies for stock a very uncertain proposition."[5]

The local newspaper, the *Washington County News*, announced that the company had started work on improving the Wolf Hole Road on November 12. Although the heavy equipment had not yet arrived, 120 men were said to be improving the road. It was estimated that 10,000 man days were needed to improve the twenty-one miles of road from the state line to Wolf Hole. Grades were said to be 10% or less; however, two sections of 13% and 16% were noted. The new alignment would be close to the existing road, with the greatest deviation to be from the state line to Mokaac Spring.[6] On November 21, the St. George newspaper announced that the company would begin work soon improving Mokaac Spring, including corrals (Project #45-01).[7]

In December, the *Washington County News* reported that the CCC camps at Pipe Spring and St. George were doing projects recommended by the Stockmen's Advisory Council, District No. 1, Arizona, in conjunction with the Taylor Grazing Act. The newspaper article noted that the two camp superintendents were attending the next meeting of this council.[8] By mid-December, the Wolf Hole Road project was progressing, with the arrival of some of the needed equipment. (Up to that point, all work was being done with hand tools.) The 1.5 miles of the road were completed, and six fresnos (horse-drawn scrapers) and one plow were now at work. In addition, a truck-towed grader and one compressor had arrived. They were still awaiting the arrival of heavy equipment.[9] For the first two months of work on the road, an average of 145 men were working every day.[10] Tragedy struck when the local newspaper reported that Kentucky enrollee Archie Engle died of pneumonia.[11] The local newspaper noted during the last two weeks of the year the arrival of camp library books and a pool table, and a big Christmas dinner.

1936

On January 1, an R-5 Caterpillar, a LeTourneau bulldozer, and an Austin #1 pull grader were received and put to work immediately on the Wolf Hole Road.[12] Early January started with the camp in quarantine. (No details were given, and the quarantine was lifted on January 13.) During this time, an Army bacteriologist from the Presidio inspected the camp. Garages for trucks were being constructed at the camp. The boys had their first movie show courtesy of a Hurricane theater. On January 8, a Wolf Hole spike camp under the supervision of Tommy Self was operating for the purpose of cutting poles.[13] In late January, Capt. Fred Klenk was appointed company commander. On Saturdays, Educational Advisor E. A. Anderson was supervising basketball practice for the enrollees at Dixie Junior College in St. George. The Dixie Junior College ladies glee club visited the camp.[14] By the end of February, the camp announced its educational program was progressing nicely, with many practical and academic subjects taught by camp staff as well as by St. George teachers. The camp newspaper was titled *The Outpost*.[15]

Throughout March and April, work continued on the Wolf Hole Road and Mokaac Spring development. At the end of March, 8 miles of road were completed (14′-wide roadbed), with four months expected to completion.[16] In a March 31 narrative report, it was noted that initially none of the enrollees knew how to handle a fresno and many "had no conception of

Figure 42. Mokaac Spring Corral, Pipeline, Storage Tank, Troughs, and Chute, 1936. Courtesy NARACO, RG 49/15/C/6/1 Box 62.

the handling of horses." By March 31, all "were skillful teamsters and good riders."[17] The work at Mokaac Spring apparently continued through the winter. It included digging up the spring and running a pipe nearly .5 mile to a new concrete spring house (capacity 25,000 gallons) near the new corral project. One of the three constructed corrals was 130 x 175′. The corrals included 96′ of concrete water troughs.[18]

The development of the road and spring was seen as a boon to stockmen, as the scarcity of water had stopped development. The spring was on the line of travel from Mount Trumbull and Parashaunt to St. George. DG-45's developments would "afford convenient access to the great grazing region north of the Colorado, and make possible its development in an orderly and consistent manner."[19] The Mokaac Spring development was completed in the spring. Forty thousand sheep and three thousand cattle were said to pass that way each spring and fall.[20]

On June 30, 1936, Company 2558 had 107 enrollees (all but 11 from Ohio, Kentucky, or Indiana). Unfortunately, the documents available for the year's last half do not give a clear picture of all the camp's work projects. On two occasions, the *Washington County News* mistakenly reported that the St. George company was erecting the Fort Pierce Wash Bridge. However, Company 2558 had been initially forbidden from doing work outside Arizona. The bridge was actually completed by a Utah CCC company.[21] This author assumes substantial labor was still devoted to the Wolf Hole Road.[22] It is not clear if there were many other work projects during the remainder of the year. One exception to the "Arizona rule" was emergency work. Company 2558 sent fifty men under Project Superintendent Thompson to fight a large forest fire in the Oak Grove area.[23] The *Washington County News* reported that Arizona CCC enrollees were participating in a range survey.[24]

Much of the reporting of Company 2558 during the rest of the year in the local newspaper was about social events such as camp programs and the camp baseball team. The company recorded its second enrollee death when enrollee Ralph Lewis, 21, was washed away in a flash flood in July.[25] His body was not recovered immediately and was found some distance away.[26] Lewis and two other enrollees had driven a truck into a flooded Atkinville wash.[27] Apparently, the truck got stuck in the wash, and when the flash flood increased from 2′ to 6′ deep, the other enrollees were able to jump successfully from the vehicle, but Lewis was washed away. CCC Special Investigator E. W. Samuell faulted Lewis for violating "instructions given by the foreman not to cross running water," as well as other instructions. Regarding morale, he stated the "boys do pretty well." He recommended that the camp be moved from St. George to nearer Wolf Hole.[28]

In July, the local newspaper reported the camp educational department was putting on one-act plays at the camp. Also in July the camp newspaper reported that Jim Bundy along with camp musicians "Cowboy" Eldridge Blair and Schuyler Maggard "had a gala night" at a Mt. Trumbull dance.[29] In August, the camp glee club was performing for other Utah CCC camps. Also in this month, three Kentucky enrollees were charged with assault after getting in a fight outside a dance pavilion with a local boy. Two received two months in jail. The other enrollee was charged with assaulting a deputy with a deadly weapon by throwing a brick at him. He was to be tried later. It is unclear what his punishment was.[30]

In September, the *Washington County News* reported that the portable buildings for the spike camp were nearly completed.[31] In October, the camp held a first-anniversary party, inviting the community to music, boxing, a ball game, and dinner.[32] At month's end, 86 new men arrived (84 coming directly from Fort Knox, Kentucky, and 2 LEMs from Arizona). The Wolf Hole spike camp was said to have 34 men supervised by Floyd Hallmark. Twenty-two men were taking a typing class at Dixie Junior College.[33]

On November 5, the local newspaper noted that the Wolf Hole spike camp had ten educational courses. On November 26, it reported the camp was under quarantine for spinal meningitis. On December 17, it stated that three enrollees had joined missionaries to do a Christmas program at the nearby Indian reservation. At year's end, Company 2558 had 156 enrollees (about three-quarters from Kentucky).

As early as November 1936, the St. George camp undertook work projects in Utah. The first documented project was the Purgatory Truck Trail (Project #45-30), begun on November 9 and completed on December 19, 1936.[34] This shift away from exclusively Arizona work is unclear at best. JDR records are incomplete, and *Range Improvement Record Book* entries are condensed and sometimes faded. From a practical view, it was likely very difficult to keep all the enrollees busy when the Wolf Hole Road work was so far from camp and the spike camp had limited capacity. Transporting men to this work site surely was uncertain in rain or snow. Was the motivation of the camp supervisors to keep enrollees busy working nearby in Utah rather than risk trouble resulting from enrollee idleness? The motivation is unknown, but this change would result in controversy. (See chapter 15 sidebar, *Showdown at Black Rock*.)

1937

The year began with terrific snowfall and cold in Arizona and southern Utah, and the CCC played a critical role in the rescue efforts. (See chapter 1, *CCC to the Rescue!*) While some of the men were out participating in the rescue efforts, the St. George newspaper reported in January that the camp education committee was meeting to pick courses for the enrollees. Courses that were adopted included vocational agriculture and general carpentry, and it was said that Dixie Junior College was cooperating with the program. The camp glee club was performing in the community, and the camp drama club was performing in camp. The *Washington County News* in an editorial about the CCC being permanent stated, "The CCC has been kept more effectively out of politics than any other recent experiment in human affairs."[35]

On January 25, CCC Special Investigator James C. Reddoch noted that the 28-mile-long truck trail improvement (Wolf Hole Road?) was 25% complete, the 20-mile-long truck trail job was 75% complete, and the stock bridge redecking was 10% complete. He noted the area the company covered in Arizona was three thousand square miles.[36]

During February and March, there were no reports of company work, but the camp basketball team was in the news. During April and May, the big news seemed to be the April 20 smoker the camp hosted, featuring a softball game, music, and boxing.[37] On May 3, the Wolf Hole spike camp was reopened.[38] Gene Carroll's Caterpillar crew was there. Educational Advisor Anderson traveled there teaching classes in Spanish and leathercraft.[39] At the end of June, Captain Vernon Peterson, Fort Douglas district inspector, inspected camp and pronounced the Wolf Hole spike camp "one of the best he has inspected."[40] Company strength stood at 125 (85% from Kentucky).

In early July, the St. George newspaper noted that the camp was progressing on the Wolf Hole Road, with thirty-five enrollees at the spike camp. It noted that James Bundy was the other foreman, and their work was mostly new road construction.[41] On July 23, replacements from the Cleveland, Ohio, area arrived directly from Fort Knox.[42] In August, the *Washington County News* stated the camp would be constructing a road from St. George to Dameron Valley.[43] This project, pushed by the chamber of commerce, appears not to have been adopted.

During September, much of the news from the camp was social and athletic. For its Labor Day celebration, "Dago" Luizzo won the pie eating contest and was awarded $1 and a pie. Other contests included a three-legged race and a wheelbarrow race. *Chan of the Opera* was the "talkie" movie.[44] In late September, forty-five new enrollees arrived from Ohio, Kentucky, and Indiana. New educational classes included typing, taught by Evelyn Cannon of Dixie Junior College; social dancing, taught by Maurine Whipple; and photography, taught by Hugh Watson.[45]

The St. George newspaper noted the Wolf Hole spike camp was inspected in late October and late November. On October 31, the *Range Improvement Record Book* noted $23,108.80 had been expended so far on the Wolf Hole Road (Project #45-02).[46] In December, the *Washington County News* reported that Roy Wright of Moccasin was appointed foreman and that he was in charge of adobe brick manufacture for the new truck and storage garage and blacksmith shop.[47] Santa Claus visited the camp on December 23 and gave each enrollee

Figure 43. 215-Foot Suspension Bridge over Ft. Pierce Wash, 1937. Courtesy NARACO, RG 49/15/C/6/1 Box 62.

"a fine necktie." Enrollees in the neatest barracks were awarded a trip to Boulder Dam. The Dixie Junior College orchestra performed a musical program for the company. Year-end company strength was 151 (117 from Kentucky, 31 from Ohio, and 3 from Indiana).

1938

In mid-January, the St. George newspaper noted the camp was trying a novel way to teach some educational classes. Elementary classes were offered before work for a half hour, four days a week. The newspaper also noted that the Wolf Hole spike camp was down to seventeen enrollees and was awaiting the delivery of powder to finish the Quail Canyon Dugway (Project #45-12). The twenty-enrollee adobe brick crew was producing seven hundred bricks per day.[48] During January, a range survey crew consisting of six enrollees, a supervisor, and a draftsman arrived and began work.[49]

On January 27, Special Investigator Reddoch inspected the camp and this time reported the work area of the camp to be 2,100 square miles. Like his report a year earlier, he noted no morale problems. Reddoch noted that of the 500 man days estimated for the range survey, 335 had been done. He reported that the Apex Reservoir construction (Project #45-09) was nearly complete, with less than 300 man days remaining of the 3,000 estimated. The Eardley-Terry Truck Trail (5,000 man days) was half-complete, and the Virgin Truck Trail construction had completed 3,671 man days of the 5,000 estimated. (All three of these were Utah projects.) He noted a list of thirteen approved projects that had not been started and estimated four years to complete them all. On a less than positive note, Reddoch stated the camp buildings (said to be previously occupied by the Forest Service) had reverted to the private landowner Sherman Lamb in 1934, and that Lamb was charging the chamber of commerce $300 annual rent for the land. Reddoch went on to report he had learned "through a reliable source" that Lamb was not going to renew the lease when it expired on July 1, 1938, and recommended no improvements be made to the buildings.[50]

In February, Foreman Bundy and his Wolf Hole crew had temporarily stopped work on the Little Tank storehouse and were cutting four thousand posts for future corrals. Forty-six new enrollees arrived from Fort Knox, bringing the camp to 189 enrollees, the highest since January 1936.[51] Gene Carroll, machine operator, was returning to Kentucky. A course in truck driving that included operation, maintenance, safety, and laws was the camp's most popular, with about fifty attending.[52] On February 17, the *Washington County News* noted (page 3) that the range survey crew was now working out of the Wolf Hole spike camp.

March events included a new commanding officer, Capt. Q. B. Woolums. A crew of twenty-four started work at Mokaac Spring, rebuilding the spring box, installing a new concrete trough, and revamping the corral chute.[53] Leader Haven Godsey was leading a crew that had started drilling (preparatory to blasting) on the Quail Canyon Dugway.[54] At month's end, Project Superintendent Thompson authored a front page article for the St. George newspaper indicating the CCC had brought $120,000 in spending to the area in the previous twenty months.[55]

On April 7, the camp hosted an estimated 1,500 guests for a CCC anniversary celebration that included an open house, baseball game, races, kids' games, Dixie Junior College band concert, retreat ceremony, and refreshments.[56] During April and May, there was news of the CCC survey crew. Several St. George enrollee survey crews were sent to a special ten-day school in Kingman to learn plant identification and range conditions. It was noted that a six-member survey crew walked south twelve miles to their last job, and when they finished their clothes were in shreds. They were making topographical maps and careful observations of plants, landmarks, and water conditions. The "Cat" crew was repairing the Wolf Hole Road after winter snows and spring rains.[57]

During May and June, the St. George newspaper noted that camp buildings were being re-roofed and a new education building was being constructed. In May, the Littlefield Corral was completed by a crew that apparently had set up a spike camp.[58] Littlefield residents held a special dinner for the boys

Figure 44. Heavy Going on Wolf Hole Road, 1938. Courtesy NARACO, RG 49/15/C/6/1 Box 62.

the night before they returned to the main camp.[59] In early June, the Wolf Hole crew was repairing damage to the Quail Canyon Dugway.[60] On June 30, Company 2558 had 136 men (most from Indiana or Kentucky).

By mid-year 1938, nearly a dozen Utah projects had been completed, and there may have been more. Utah projects completed in 1937 included the Beaver Dam Wash Road (Project #45-03, completed May 22, 1937), Valley Truck Trail (Project #45-05, completed June 18, 1937), Summit Corral (Project #45-07, completed August 14, 1937), and Poison Weed Eradication (Project #45-08, completed October 5, 1937). Projects completed during 1938 included the Virgin Truck Trail (Project #45-06, started June 21, 1937, and completed June 18, 1938); Apex Reservoir (Project #45-09, completed February 7, 1938); Eardley-Terry Cut Off Truck Trail (Project #45-10, completed March 25, 1938); Gould Spring Corral (Project #45-20, started June 1 and completed June 18, 1938); and St. George–Cedar City Stock Divide (Project #45-26, exact completion date uncertain). Then, abruptly, Utah projects stop. Was this the result of Senator Carl Hayden's pressure? (See chapter 15 sidebar, *Showdown at Black Rock*.)

In July, District Grazier Emil Blankenagel, rancher Charles Esplin, and camp engineer P. J. Schiele took an overnight trip into the Arizona Strip, then made plans for the development of Hidden Springs, including piping water 300′ to an existing 30′ concrete tank. They also visited Big Spring.[61] Later in the month, 60 new Ohio enrollees arrived, bringing the company strength to 189. "The new men are adapting themselves to the camp routine in splendid spirit," reported the local newspaper. An air compressor and other equipment arrived from Duncan, Arizona.[62]

From August 1938 to May 1939, frequent inspections by Special Investigator Samuell give a detailed picture of the camp's work. The camp seemed to be a beehive of activities. On August 8, Samuell noted that eighty enrollees were working on the main Wolf Hole Road; ten men from the Wolf Hole spike camp were repairing the side road to Mokaac Corral; fifteen men, apparently at their own side camp, were doing Quail Canyon road construction; ten Wolf Hole spike camp men were working ten miles west cutting posts at the rate of seven hundred to eight hundred per week; and forty men had been sent to Las Vegas to construct a new CCC camp. Company strength was 186.[63]

For the period of August 13 through 18, Samuell noted work toward post cutting areas off the Wolf Hole Road near the Black Rock Trail. Forty men were working on constructing the Stateline Reservoir, all hand labor. He noted that work had begun on a Parashaunt spike camp with the well digging down 15′ and the materials for the camp being hauled from the DG-44, Hack Canyon spike camp.[64] The August 25 *Washington County News,* reported that all men in the main camp as well as the spike camp were working on the Quail Canyon Dugway in order to finish before bad weather arrived.[65]

Apparently, there was some concern on the part of Arizona Strip stockmen about DG-45 shutting down. In a front page story of the September 8, 1938 *Washington County News*, District Grazier Huling E. Ussery, reacting to a petition signed by a large number of stockmen, was quoted as saying the camp would remain in St. George until March 31. Ussery indicated he wanted branch camps established at Parashaunt and Wolf Hole. The same newspaper headlined an enrollee death. Howard L. McBride, 18, of Indiana was crushed when a truck overturned enroute to Wolf Hole.[66]

In early October, the St. George newspaper reported that Mr. Bickley, temporary camp engineer, had a surveying crew readying the Parashaunt Fence (Project #45-46).[67] In mid-month, the newspaper reported that the Wolf Hole spike camp was getting a newer, larger shower house made of adobe brick.[68] The following week, the newspaper reported the arrival of 84 new enrollees from Terre Haute, Indiana, bringing the camp strength to 196. Interestingly, the newspaper reported the Company 2558 men were in three states: 25 at the Wolf Hole and Parashaunt spike camps, 13 at Las Vegas, 5 at Phoenix, and 3 on detached service at Salt Lake City.[69]

From October 31 through November 5, Special Investigator Samuell inspected the camp facilities. He noted that the twenty-five men at the Parashaunt spike camp were working on an allotment division fence and seventy-seven men were working the Quail Canyon Dugway. The State Line Reservoir work had been temporarily halted. His written inspection noted numerous shortcomings.[70] However, at the same time, the local newspaper reported that a Captain Sessions, district inspector, had spent two days inspecting all the camp facilities and said that the Parashaunt spike camp was one of the finest he had seen.[71] In spite of earlier suggestions that the St. George camp buildings not be improved in October and November, the local newspaper noted a bath house addition, remodeling of the kitchen storehouse, and a complete re-wiring of all the camp buildings.

On December 1, the newspaper reported all the enrollees had returned from Las Vegas, bringing camp strength to 145. The following week, the newspaper reported work was progressing rapidly at the Ellis Larson Reservoir.[72] The bottom was said to be cement lined and the reservoir able to hold 63,000 gallons. The same article reported work had begun on a water storage tank and corral near the top of the Quail Canyon Dugway, adding a second watering place for livestock along the thirty miles between Wolf Hole and St. George.[73]

In mid-December, Special Investigator Samuell spent two days inspecting the camp. He noted twenty-six enrollees "making good progress" (all hand labor) on the State Line Reservoir; twenty-five men on the Larson Reservoir, which he said was requiring a 5' diversion dam in the Blackrock Wash; and thirty-eight men working on the Quail Canyon Truck Trail project. He recommended that the Wolf Hole spike camp install a flag and flagpole.[74]

At year's end, Special Investigator Reddoch noted that, against his suggestions, many improvements to the main camp had been made, while the lease with the private landowner had expired and had not been renewed. He noted in his report that he understood Lamb now wanted rent of $1,500 a year, was willing to sell the buildings back to the government for $6,500, and had obtained a lawyer. On December 31, 1938, camp strength stood at 137 (all from Indiana, Kentucky, or Ohio except for 1 from Arizona).

1939

The reports of the CCC in the local newspaper's first issue of the year were mixed for the CCC. The front page proclaimed, "Three Check Artists Plead Guilty to Charges." Two of the bad check wrongdoers were enrollees. The newspaper's supplement told of Special Investigator Reddoch inspecting the camp the previous Friday. He was most interested in the welfare of the enrollees and said he was "well pleased."[75] Mid-month, the newspaper noted that the camp's old stave tank was being replaced by a three-thousand-gallon concrete tank. A Wolf Hole spike camp crew was building a new drift fence.[76] At the end of January, the camp and spike camp's mess and kitchen rated a "superior" from the district military inspector.[77]

In February, considerable snow fell at Wolf Hole, so enrollees were assigned to put new metal roofs on the tents and were improving the electric plant.[78] On February 8, Special Inspector Samuell noted that twenty-six enrollees were finishing up the Larson Reservoir and that it was "one of the best jobs I have seen." Twenty-nine men were working the State Line Reservoir, but work was questionable as they were continually hitting gypsum. Forty enrollees were working the Quail Canyon Truck Trail, but work was slow due to snow. The Hurricane Segregation Fence Project No. 1 (Project #45-40) was slow due to snow.[79]

In March, the St. George newspaper noted the marriage of enrollee and assistant leader Clifford Leach to local girl Marie Prisbrey and their move to Indiana.[80] In mid-March, Samuell made two inspections, finding shortcomings both at the main camp and the Wolf Hole spike camp. At Wolf Hole, he said the boys were "very dissatisfied." The bath house there was failing due to the presence of gypsum in the cement. He found a dirty foreman's barracks, a littered garage, and a number of gas and kerosene safety violations. He returned three days later to find both camps cleaned up. He noted the Larson Reservoir included a 90' concrete dam across Black Rock Wash and that maintenance on the Black Rock Truck Trail had started.[81]

On April 13, the St. George newspaper (page 7) noted that the camp had over five hundred guests for its CCC Anniversary Open House on April 7. The Parashaunt spike camp was being made ready for occupancy, concrete was being poured at the Ellis Larson Reservoir, and eighty-one new enrollees had arrived from Fort Knox. The following week, the newspaper noted (page 7) that Foreman James Bundy and ten men were at the Parashaunt spike camp, installing a new light plant and getting it ready for forty men to arrive on May 1.

In mid-April, Samuell spent three days at the main and side camps. He noted marked improvements, which he attributed to the arrival of Acting Project Superintendent Roy Wright. He noted the camp had been one of the poorest and was now one of the best. The work was "well balanced," the educational program greatly improved, and morale "greatly enhanced." He noted work on the Black Rock Truck Trail was at two shifts, with a third shift being considered.[82]

In early May, the local newspaper noted that a concrete foundation and floor for a new Wolf Hole shower facility was completed. The article noted the Wolf Hole "Cat" crew was working three shifts (twenty-two hours daily) on the Black Rock Road, and "fast progress was being made."[83] The following week, the *Washington County News* reported (page 4) the Ellis Parker Reservoir concrete and fence were finished.

In late May, Samuell spent three days at the camp facilities and noted that the camp's educational program had 100% attendance, with "safety stressed in each class." He noted the Parashaunt spike camp was working on the Mathis Steer Pasture (twenty-eight enrollees). (The 3.6-mile-long Mathis Steer Pasture Fence [Project #45-44, BLMSTG JDR 010172] was started on May 22, 1939, and finished on August 11, 1939, in 1,432 man days [BLMSTG-*RIRB*].) He also noted the latter camp needed fencing to keep cattle out of the camp. The Wolf Hole bath house was just two days from completion. State Line Reservoir was to be completed the following day. Eighteen boys were "making good" on the Quail Canyon Truck Trail, and forty were at work on the Black Rock Truck Trail. He recommended abandonment of the Quail Reservoir project, as it had a gravel base.[84]

During June, clues to work projects are in Samuell's month-end reports. He noted that forty enrollees were working at the site of the new G-135 camp at Short Creek installing water lines. The Parashaunt spike camp completed 1 mile of the 3.5-mile-long Mathis Steer Pasture Fence.[85] He indicated the Wolf Hole spike camp had fifteen men cutting posts.[86] On June 30, 1939, Company 2558 had 136 men (all from Indiana, Ohio, or Kentucky).

On July 1, the camp had twenty-four enrollees and four foremen fighting a two-thousand-acre brush fire near Black Rock Mountain. The *Washington County News* reported that ten square miles of range, one ranch building, and four sheep wagons were saved.[87] The same newspaper article said that 61 new replacements from a Lebanon, Ohio, reception center were expected the week of July 20 to bring camp strength to 195.

Samuell spent three days at camp at month's end and reported forty-three men and the "Cat" were at Short Creek. Twenty-three Parashaunt spike camp men were scheduled to finish the Mathis Steer Pasture Fence on August 20 and then would start on the 7.125-mile-long Parashaunt Segregation Fence. Work continued on the Quail Truck Trail. Wolf Hole men were cutting posts, and the next Wolf Hole project was to be the Atkins Brothers Fence that started two miles east of Poverty Knoll and ran north for five miles.[88]

During August, the abandonment of DG-45 at St. George was announced in the local newspaper. The newspaper indicated that some buildings were being dismantled and moved to Short Creek and that the rest would be moved in the future. The newspaper also reported that having the St. George camp on private land was a problem and the city had agreed to buy the land, but not until the official orders had been given to move. The report mentioned a letter from John Ray Painter, chief grazier, saying a 1940 summer camp was planned for Black Rock.[89]

Even though DG-45 was officially abandoned on August 21, 1939,[90] spike camp work as well as work on the Short Creek main camp continued into November.[91] It appears the abrupt ending of the St. George camp (see chapter 15 sidebar, *Showdown at Black Rock*) left a number of jobs in jeopardy, and decisions were made to complete them.

Samuell visited the area in late August and indicated that forty-one men were dismantling the DG-45 buildings (Project #45-54) satisfactorily. He noted the Parashaunt spike camp had finished the Parashaunt Camp Fence and the Mathis Steer Pasture Fence. Their current projects were a three-man survey crew and twenty-seven men working the Parashaunt Fence. The Wolf Hole spike camp was working the Atkin Brothers Segregation Fence.[92]

In early October, Hamilton Draper inspected and noted that two trucks and five men were hauling DG-45 materials to Short Creek. The Wolf Hole spike camp had six men building a fence surrounding their camp. He noted that Foreman Bundy, with eighteen men, had completed two miles of the Atkin Brothers Segregation Fence. Twenty-six men were working at Short Creek laying the water line to camp.[93] Work was also progressing on the Short Creek Camp Gravel Area (Project #45-53, completed October 31) and the .5-mile-long Short Creek Camp Fence (Project #45-49, completed October 31).[94]

The last camp inspection report in the files is dated October 25–26, 1939, and Samuell reports the salvage of the DG-45 buildings was completed.[95] No mention is made of the Parashaunt spike camp in this or the earlier report. The Wolf Hole spike camp crew had finished the fence surrounding their camp, and 4.5 miles of the Atkin Brothers Segregation Fence were complete, leaving the job close to finished. He called the latter work a "very good job throughout." He said that Project #135-4, consisting of 1,500 fence posts, 2,000 stays, and wire, was completed for Nevada. Was this Parashaunt spike camp work? He noted that the water line for the Short Creek camp was nearly complete, with only 900′ remaining.[96] It appears the Short Creek buildings and infrastructure were finished soon after, but they would wait until April for their official occupancy.

In just a short period, Company 2558 managed to complete an enviable record of accomplishments. Sadly, their stay in St. George had come to an abrupt end. Noteworthy was a huge list of projects for the future. A 1938 camp inspection report listed thirteen projects approved but not yet begun, totaling 67,050 man days![97]

According to a December 30, 1938, CCC report addressed to the Division of Grazing director, the Arizona Strip "is probably the most undeveloped part of the whole country and for that reason it has been necessary to build many trails in order to begin development of the range."[98] Today, "one sees a well developed road and trail system accessing nearly every corner of the region" that was originated by the CCC. This first step was critical to the development of the Arizona Strip. The CCC "development of range projects, soil erosion control, better livestock and resource management showed the government and the people of the Arizona Strip who made a living from it what could be done with an attitude of hard work, determined direction, and cooperation. The CCC set the stage for everything that came after it and set a standard still envied by those of us who are familiar with the work nearly 80 years after they did it."[99]

Unless noted otherwise, any reference to the number of enrollees in a company, the location of the company, or company supervisors are from U.S. War Department, Location and Strength of CCC Companies, 1933–1942, NARAMD RG 35 530/65/22/04/05.

1. It appears that Utah work was allowed beginning November 1, 1936. (See chapter 15 sidebar, *Showdown at Black Rock*.) See also U.S. BLM (Grazing Service), CCC, "Report of the 8th Period, DG-45, March 31, 1938," Narrative Reports of Individual Camps, 1936–1938, NARACO RG 49/15/C/6/1 Box 62.
2. The St. George newspaper states they arrived on November 1, but the location and strength report lists October 27.
3. U.S. CCC, Camp Inspection Reports, NARAMD RG 35/530/65/23/04 Entry 115 PI #11 Box 10.
4. "CCC Camp at St. George Occupied November 1st," *Washington County News*, November 7, 1935, 8.
5. U.S. BLM (Grazing Service), CCC, "Report of the 6th Period, DG-45, March 31, 1936," Narrative Reports of Individual Camps, 1936–1938, NARACO RG 49/15/C/6/1 Box 62.
6. "St. George CCC Camp to Improve Wolf Hole Road," *Washington County News*, November 14, 1935, 1. Mokaac Spring during the CCC period is variously spelled Mokeac and Mociac.
7. "Mociac Spring Work to Be Done by St. George CCC Camp," *Washington County News*, November 21, 1935, 2.
8. "Stockmen's Advisory Council … to Meet Soon," *Washington County News*, December 12, 1935, 1.
9. "Progress Made on Wolf Hole Road," *Washington County News*, December 12, 1935, 1.
10. U.S. BLM (Grazing Service), CCC, "Report of the 6th Period, DG-45, March 31, 1936," Narrative Reports of Individual Camps, 1936–1938, NARACO RG 49/15/C/6/1 Box 62.
11. "St. George Camp Enrollee Dies at Local Hospital," *Washington County News*, December 12, 1935, 1.
12. U.S. BLM (Grazing Service), CCC, "Report of the 6th Period, DG-45, March 31, 1936," Narrative Reports of Individual Camps, 1936–1938, NARACO RG 49/15/C/6/1 Box 62.
13. "St. George CCC Camp," *Washington County News*, January 9, 1936, 1.
14. "St. George CCC Camp," *Washington County News*, January 30, 1936, 5.
15. "St. George Camp Launches General Educational Program," *Washington County News*, February 20, 1936, 1, 4.
16. "Mokiac Spring, Road Project Complete, Is Aid to Stockmen," *Washington County News*, March 26, 1936, 1, suppl. The width was widened to 18′ later. See U.S. BLM (Grazing Service), CCC, "Report of the 10th Period, DG-45, March 31, 1938," Narrative Reports of Individual Camps, 1936–1938, NARACO RG 49/15/C/6/1 Box 62.
17. U.S. BLM (Grazing Service), CCC. Ibid.
18. D. M. Thompson, "Development Work at Mokiac Spring Almost Completed," *Washington County News*, February 27, 1936, 1, 5. This author visited the spring and corral in February 2012, and although the water troughs were not being used, the fences appeared to be quite sturdy.
19. John T. Woodbury, Sr., "Mokeac Spring: Its Development and What It Means," *Washington County News*, August 6, 1936, 1, 10. The spring appears to be the only reliable water source between those grazing areas and St. George. Woodbury also envisaged a system of CCC-constructed feeder roads into the Wolf Hole Road.
20. U.S. BLM (Grazing Service), CCC, "Report of the 10th Period, DG-45, March 31, 1938," Narrative Reports of Individual Camps, 1936–1938, NARACO RG 49/15/C/6/1 Box 62.
21. "Bridge over Port Pierce Wash … Constructed by Camp D.G. 30 …," *Washington County News*, October 22, 1936, 1, 8. According to the "Report of the 8th Period, DG-45, March 31, 1937," Company 2558 built a suspension bridge in the same area before the Cedar City company finished their bridge. See U.S. BLM (Grazing Service), CCC, Narrative Reports of Individual Camps, 1936–1938, NARACO RG 49/15/C/6/1 Box 62.
22. The July 10 camp inspection report by E. W. Samuell reported that all 106 enrollees were working the Wolf Hole Road, with 12 miles completed. He reported that the west half of the Arizona Strip for the CCC "will afford work indefinitely." U.S. BLM, Camp Inspection Reports, 1938–1942, NARACO RG 49 Entry 20 Box 86.
23. "Disastrous Forest Fire Destroys 2000 Acres on Reserve," *Washington County News*, June 25, 1936, 1. Utah CCC companies participating included those from the Leeds, Gunlock, Cedar City, and Duck Creek camps. "D. G.

Boys Fight Fire," *Arizona Strip*, July 4, 1936, Fiche MN #1424, CRL Newspapers.

24. "Range Survey by CCC Enrollees Begins in Ariz.," *Washington County News*, July 6, 1936, 1, 5. See U.S. BLM (Grazing Service), CCC, "Report of the 8th Period, DG-45, March 31, 1937," Narrative Reports of Individual Camps, 1936–1938, NARACO RG 49/15/C/6/1 Box 62, indicating the crew covered forty townships in two and a half months.
25. "CCC Enrollee Loses Life in Flood on Arizona Strip," *Washington County News*, July 16, 1936, 1, 5.
26. "St. George Camp," *Washington County News*, July 23, 1936, 8. The body was found near Mesquite, NV.
27. "Death of Ralph K. Lewis,"*Arizona Strip*, August 6, 1936, Fiche MN #1424, CRL Newspapers.
28. U.S. BLM (Grazing Service), CCC, Narrative Reports of Individual Camps, 1936–1938.
29. "Musicians Go to Mt. Trumbull," *Arizona Strip*, August 6, 1936, Fiche MN # 1424 CRL Newspapers.
30. "CCC Boys Charged with Assault, Given Sentences Today," *Washington County News*, August 27, 1936, 1, 8.
31. "St. George Camp," *Washington County News*, September 10, 1936, 3.
32. *Washington County News*, October 29, 1936, 1, 9.
33. "News of the St. George Camp," *Washington County News*, October 29, 1936, 3. According to the March 31, 1937, "Eighth Period Illustrated Narrative Report," the Wolf Hole spike camp was established on October 1 and located three miles north of Wolf Hole, with thirty-five enrollees and a foreman. All water was hauled from St. George. Kitchen and mess were in tents, and a sod-covered cellar for cool storage was nearby. All tents, including sleeping ones, were said to be floored and walled to 2.5′. See U.S. BLM (Grazing Service), CCC, Narrative Reports of Individual Camps, 1936–1938, NARACO RG 49/15/C/6/1 Box 62.
34. BLMSTG-*RIRB*.
35. January 21, 1937, 4.
36. U.S. CCC, Camp Inspection Reports, NARAMD RG 35/530/65/23/04 Entry 115 PI #11 Box 10.
37. "St. George CCC Camp to Stage 'Smoker' Thursday, April 30," *Washington County News*, April 27, 1937, 1.
38. *Arizona Strip*, May 9, 1937, Fiche MN #1424, CRL Newspapers.
39. "News from the St. George CCC Camp," *Washington County News*, May 27, 1937, suppl.
40. "St. George CCC," *Washington County News*, June 24, 1937, 6.
41. "St. George Camp Reports Progress on Wolf Hole Road," *Washington County News*, July 8, 1937, 1, 4.
42. "St. George CCC Camp," *Washington County News*, July 29, 1937, 5.
43. "Road to Dameron Valley May Be Constructed by St. George CCC Camp–Must Receive Approval of Grazing Board …," *Washington County News*, August 5, 1937, 1, 8.
44. "St. George CCC Camp Observes Labor Day," *Washington County News*, September 9, 1937, 5.
45. "St. George Camp," *Washington County News*, September 23, 1937, 4.
46. BLMSTG-*RIRB*. This appears to be the most expensive project throughout the five Arizona Strip CCC camps.
47. "St. George Camp," *Washington County News*, December 16, 1937, 3.
48. "St. George CCC Camp," *Washington County News*, January 13, 1938, 5.
49. "St. George CCC Camp," *Washington County News*, February 3, 1938, 5.
50. U.S. CCC, Camp Inspection Reports, NARAMD RG 35/530/65/23/04 Entry 115 PI #11 Box 10.
51. "St. George CCC Camp," *Washington County News*, February 3, 1938, 5.
52. "St. George CCC Camp," *Washington County News*, February 10, 1938, 3.
53. "St. George CCC Camp," *Washington County News*, March 3, 1938, 3. The addition of the chute is Project #45-34 and BLMSTG JDR 010136 listed it as completed 8-19-38 and affecting forty thousand sheep.
54. "St. George CCC Camp," *Washington County News*, March 17, 1938, 3.
55. "CCCs Bring $180,000 into County Says Supt. D. M. Thompson," *Washington County News*, March 31, 1938, 1.
56. *Washington County News*, March 24, 1938, 1, and April 7, 1938, 1, 4.
57. "St. George Camp Boys Attend 10-Day School in Kingman, Ariz.," April 14, 1938, 8; "St. George CCC Camp," *Washington County News*, May 5, 1938, 8; Wolf Hole Road Maintenance, Project #45-33, BLMSTG-*RIRB*.
58. This appears to be Project #45-39, BLMSTG-*RIRB*.
59. "St. George CCC Camp," *Washington County News*, May 26, 1938, 6.
60. "St. George CCC Camp," *Washington County News*, June 2, 1938, 4.
61. "St. George CCC Camp," *Washington County News*, July 7, 1938, 4.
62. "St. George CCC Camp," *Washington County News*, July 21, 1938, 3.
63. U.S. BLM (Grazing Service), CCC, Narrative Reports of Individual Camps, 1936–1938, NARACO RG 49/15/C/6/1 Box 62.

64. U.S. BLM (Grazing Service), CCC, Narrative Reports of Individual Camps, 1936–1938, NARACO RG 49/15/C/6/1 Box 62. The local newspaper reported that the Parashaunt spike camp was to be a twenty-five-man operation, to be finished by the end of September, and they would be building a reservoir and cutting posts till winter set in. See "St. George CCC Camp," *Washington County News,* September 15, 1938, 6. The exact location of this spike camp remains uncertain. St. George BLM archeologist John M. Herron pointed out that a reference to the spike camp in BLMSTG JDR 010172 Mathis Steer Pasture placed it south of MacDonald Flat.
65. "St. George CCC Camp," *Washington County News,* August 25, 1938, 6.
66. Utah death certificate 002260363 indicates McBride was 18 and died at about 2:30 p.m., September 2, 1938.
67. "St. George CCC Camp," *Washington County News,* October 6, 1938, 5.
68. "St. George CCC Camp," *Washington County News,* October 13, 1938, 6.
69. "St. George CCC Camp," *Washington County News,* October 20, 1938, 2.
70. U.S. BLM (Grazing Service), CCC, Narrative Reports of Individual Camps, 1936–1938, NARACO RG 49/15/C/6/1 Box 62.
71. "St. George CCC Camp," *Washington County News,* October 27, 1938, 4.
72. Project #45-37, started November 21, 1938, and completed April 28, 1939, BLMSTG-*RIRB.*
73. "St. George CCC Camp," *Washington County News,* December 8, 1938, 5.
74. U.S. BLM (Grazing Service), CCC, Narrative Reports of Individual Camps, 1936–1938, NARACO RG 49/15/C/6/1 Box 62.
75. "St. George CCC Camp," *Washington County News,* January 5, 1939.
76. "St. George CCC Camp," *Washington County News,* January 12, 1939, 4.
77. "St. George CCC Camp," *Washington County News,* January 26, 1939, 4.
78. "St. George CCC Camp," *Washington County News,* February 16, 1939, 7.
79. U.S. BLM, (Grazing Service), CCC, Narrative Reports of Individual Camps, 1936–1938, NARACO RG 49/15/C/6/1 Box 62.
80. "St. George CCC Camp," *Washington County News,* March 9, 1939, 5.
81. U.S. BLM (Grazing Service), CCC, Narrative Reports of Individual Camps, 1936–1938, NARACO RG 49/15/C/6/1 Box 62. Project #45-41 started March 20, 1939, and was completed June 24, 1939, BLMSTG-*RIRB.*
82. Ibid.
83. "St. George CCC Camp," *Washington County News,* May 4, 1939, 10.
84. U.S. BLM (Grazing Service), CCC, Narrative Reports of Individual Camps, 1936–1938, NARACO RG 49/15/C/6/1 Box 62.
85. BLMSTG JDR 010172 was listed as completed 8-11-39 and affecting five hundred cattle. Its initial estimate was 1,000 man days to complete.
86. U.S. BLM (Grazing Service), CCC, Narrative Reports of Individual Camps, 1936–1938, NARACO RG 49/15/C/6/1 Box 62. Post Cutting Project No. 2, Project #45-45, was begun June 22, 1939, and completed December 31, 1940, with 3,087 posts and stays cut, BLMSTG-*RIRB.*
87. "St. George CCC Camp," *Washington County News,* July 20, 1939, 3.
88. U.S. BLM (Grazing Service), CCC, Narrative Reports of Individual Camps, 1936–1938, NARACO RG 49/15/C/6/1 Box 62.
89. "Dismantling Work Starts on St. George CCC Camp This Week," *Washington County News,* August 17, 1939, 1, 10.
90. "CCC 8th Corps Area, Status of CCC Camps Authorized since Inception of the Program up to and Including December 31, 1941," NARACO CCC Directories RG 49 Entry 33, 34 Box 132.
91. See Samuell to the Director, 15 November 1939, NARACO RG 49 Records of the BLM (Grazing Service), CCC, Narrative Reports of Camp Programs, 1940–43, Entry 12, Box 42, where Samuell indicates DG-135 was abandoned November 4, 1939.
92. U.S. BLM (Grazing Service), CCC, Narrative Reports of Individual Camps, 1936–1938, NARACO RG 49/15/C/6/1 Box 62. The Atkin Brothers Segregation Fence, according to BLMSTG JDR 010054, was begun on February 2, 1938, and completed on March 3, 1940; it was 5 miles long and said to affect 6,650 head of livestock.
93. U.S. BLM (Grazing Service), CCC, Narrative Reports of Individual Camps, 1936–1938, NARACO RG 49/15/C/6/1 Box 62. Project #45-55 BLMSTG-*RIRB* indicates work on the water lines and wells began August 16, 1939, and was completed October 31, 1939, with 16,000′ constructed at a cost of $6,069.17.
94. BLMSTG-*RIRB.*
95. Project #45-54 BLMSTG-*RIRB* indicates this was completed October 4, 1939.
96. U.S. BLM (Grazing Service), CCC, Narrative Reports of Individual Camps, 1936–1938, NARACO RG 49/15/C/6/1 Box 62.

97. U.S. CCC, Camp Inspection Reports, NARAMD RG 35/530/65/23/04 Entry 115 PI #11 Box 10. The list included the 42-mile-long Pierces Ferry Truck Trail (22,000 man days), the 13-mile-long Mount Trumbull Truck Trail (13,000 man days), and the 15-mile-long Twist Hills Truck Trail (7,500 man days).
98. U. S. DG, CCC Work Program Correspondence, 1938–1939, NARACO RG 49, Entry 4, Box 13.
99. John M. Herron, e-mail message to author, June 13, 2012.

Sidebar:
Showdown at Black Rock

Camp DG-45 was an anomaly. It was administered by the Army 9th Corps, reported as an 8th Corps camp, composed of men mostly from the 5th Corps, and located on private land. Even though it was located in Utah, nearly all of the camp's work was in Arizona. From the camp's beginning to its end, this spelled controversy.

The work of DG-45 was on the arid Arizona Strip, where a stable water supply for a CCC camp was a rarity. Initially, the camp location was to be Black Rock Springs some thirty miles south of St. George, Utah.[1] However, that plan came flat up against the most dominant cattleman in the Arizona Strip, Preston Nutter.[2] By 1901, he reportedly owned twenty-five thousand cattle and controlled nearly all of the Arizona Strip. Besides being a shrewd businessman, Nutter acquired nearly every Arizona Strip water source by questionable but legal means, including Black Rock Springs.[3] Upon his death, the *Salt Lake Telegram* called him "Utah's last great cattle king."[4]

In May 1935, Milton E. Moody, secretary of the St. George Chamber of Commerce, wrote to Nutter inquiring of him if "we can depend on your cooperation" in running an Army-required telephone line to the potential Black Rock CCC location.[5] Apparently, Nutter protested to one Harry Ott, presumably a government official, and was told the camp would not be at Black Rock. Later, Nutter said he learned that the camp was still on track. Nutter wrote Secretary of the Interior Harold I. Ickes in protest. He complained to Ickes that he had been crowded out by sheep men overgrazing the land and that a camp at Black Rock would jeopardize his business even more. Nutter strongly opposed any need for CCC work on the Arizona Strip and stated, "I am very much opposed to any camp being located at Black Rock."[6]

On August 30, E. K. Burlew, Department of the Interior administrative assistant, wrote to Nutter indicating he was requesting a report from a field representative. On September 5, Nutter wrote a letter to Burlew. Unlike his earlier strongly worded letter to Ickes, this letter was more explanatory in tone. Nutter wrote that he now owned about eight thousand acres and that Black Rock was important to his business. All of the activity of a camp would scare the cattle from the spring he owned. "The whole Strip has been so overgrazed by the sheep these later years and so completely denuded in large sections that we are in a sad and precarious plight right now in spite of all that the Taylor Bill gave promise of."[7]

In early October, Depue Falck, acting director of the Division of Grazing, wrote Nutter that the Black Rock location had been abandoned and the camp would be at St. George. His letter was somewhat conciliatory in tone, stating that the Division of Grazing was to do projects on the Strip to benefit all. "It is not the intention of the Division of Grazing to make any unnecessary developments or to make any improvements which may upset the orderly use of the range or the rights of the stockmen using these lands," he wrote. He said that work projects were still in a formative stage under the direction of Donald D. McKay, regional CCC supervisor, and that McKay would consult with Nutter.[8]

Three days later, CCC Regional Inspector W. A. Rupea met for two hours with Nutter and his wife. Rupea wrote to McKay that he found Nutter "to be well informed, high-class gentleman and stockmen of the old school, perfectly in accord with the Taylor Grazing Act, and most anxious to place at our disposal his vast knowledge gained through actual experience and a lifelong study of the range." Whereas earlier Nutter was uncooperative, he now suggested CCC projects, including the Wolf Hole Road and Pierce Wash Bridge. Mrs. Nutter was to have said the "CCC camps were doing more for young manhood than any other one thing which had ever been attempted."[9] The next day, McKay wrote to Falck that Nutter would consider a spike camp at Black Rock. He summarized by saying the "incident [is] closed, and that work in this district will be harmonious with all parties concerned."[10] In November, Nutter wrote to Falck, stating that Rupea kindly consulted with him, he was glad his position was understood, and that he was in sympathy with the work of the Corps.[11] Nutter passed away the following year.

Two years after DG-45 was located at St. George, a controversy arose over the issue of the Utah work. J. E. Gavin, secretary to Senator Carl Hayden of Arizona, telegrammed Division of Grazing's Falck to say that Hayden understood that only a small number of the St. George enrollees were working in Arizona and he wanted the company to work completely in Arizona. The telegram also was intended to notify Secretary of Interior Ickes that Hayden wanted to be notified in advance of openings at Arizona DG camps so Hayden "can recommend to him competent supervisory personnel."[12] In a series of three telegrams from C. K. Caron to Falck, he indicated that the Ninth Enrollment Period (April 1, 1937, to September 30, 1937) work of the St. George camp was about 90% in Arizona, but that in the Tenth Enrollment Period (October 1, 1937, to March 31, 1938) it was possible to do only half of the work in Arizona because of weather and the distance from the camp to the Arizona work sites. Caron suggests the camp be moved to Black Rock in April, as the Wolf Hole to Black Rock Road would be done then.[13] The following day, Division of Grazing Acting

Director Julian Terrett wrote Gavin to say that it was only possible for DG-45 to do half of their work in Arizona, but the camp would be moved in April.[14]

April passed without a move, and in August, District Grazier Huling E. Ussery wrote the Division of Grazing director that Company 2558 would move to Black Rock by October. He indicated the new camp location would be called DG-129 and advised that the new buildings had not yet been arranged.[15] Two weeks later, Ussery was advised that the recommended move went all the way to CCC Director Robert Fechner and was marked disapproved. (No reasons for disapproval were given in the correspondence.) Ussery was told to keep the camp in its present location through March 31, 1939.[16]

On November 18, 1938, the Kingman newspaper reported that the Mohave County Board of Supervisors was seeking to have the St. George CCC camp moved to Black Rock Springs.[17] In mid-March 1939, confusion seemed to be the order of the day. Acting Regional Grazier John Ray Painter wrote the Division of Grazing director to say that the Black Rock site had not been inspected yet by the Army. The same day, Caron wrote the director to say that a move of DG-45 to Black Rock was not possible and made reference to a phone call from the War Department on March 13 saying the move from St. George would not happen. The letter concluded somewhat cryptically that "this change was instigated in Washington … not Ninth Corps."[18] However, the same day, the *Washington Country News* had a front page story titled "St. George CCC Camp to Be Transferred to Arizona," indicating the move was to Black Rock Springs.

On March 14, Terrett wrote H. E. Weatherwax, CCC Department of the Interior Advisory Council member, saying, "It is particularly desirable from the work standpoint that DG-132, Black Rock, be occupied on or about July 1, 1939."[19] A few days later, A. B. Molohon, chief of range improvements, wrote to Painter: "The situation pertaining to … DG-45 … is extremely involved. DG-45 is continuing and DG-132 is delayed to 13th period. Occupation of DG-132 should be no later than 7-1-39. Army should be inspecting site soon."[20]

In April, Terrett wrote to Senator Hayden that CCC Director Fechner had approved Black Rock for the period beginning April 1, 1939.[21] On April 5, K. Wolfe, liaison officer to the CCC, wrote to Ussery indicating the building materials for DG-132 were under contract. He suggested immediate action to locate and survey the camp's site.[22] Things seemed to be moving. But on May 1, in a radiogram from Caron to Wolfe, the Black Rock site was rejected by the Fort Douglas military. The message said the denial was "for numerous reasons, but primarily because of unsatisfactory roads which they feel will require several months work to bring to passable standard."[23]

So, now the barracks were apparently being assembled and a site had to be found. On May 3, Caron sent a radiogram to Wolfe asking that Fechner approve the Black Rock barracks for Short Creek, Arizona.[24] The following day, Molohon telegrammed Caron the following: "Fechner approved construction permanent type camp and barracks at Short Creek, Arizona, in lieu Black Rock with notation on request that this cancels construction DG-132. New camp numbered DG-135."[25]

Why was Black Rock never a full CCC camp location? In 1935 or 1936, and even in 1937, Black Rock would have been a somewhat reasonable location. Assuming that the road to the camp was up to military standards, Black Rock would have been convenient to the needed work, such as the Wolf Hole Road. However, once the projects nearby were close to completion, Black Rock became a less than desirable site, perhaps even a liability.[26] Was Senator Hayden's less than subtle pressing for Black Rock a factor? There is no evidence that Hayden's actions produced outright opposition. Surely, he did not endear himself to DG and CCC officials. Of course, the Short Creek site appeared to be satisfactory to Hayden.

It is this writer's opinion that a significant amount of delay took place regarding the administrative decisions to occupy Black Rock. The reasons may be numerous. St. George merchants would not have relished the camp moving out of town and their losing at least some of the income they were used to. From an Army perspective, even given that the Black Rock Road was acceptable, medical care would have been significantly inferior to St. George. Also, enrollee morale at such an isolated location would have always been a serious concern to the military. A telephone line to Black Rock, apparently an initial consideration in 1935, was still lacking. Perhaps Utah politicians attempted to influence the location of CCC camps, as Senator Hayden had.

1. U.S. BLM (Grazing Service), CCC, "Report of the 8th Period, DG-45, March 31, 1938," Narrative Reports of Individual Camps, 1936–1938, NARACO RG 49/15/C/6/1 Box 62.
2. Altschul and Fairley, *Man, Models and Management*, 195.
3. Ibid.

4. Evans, Max. "Preston Nutter Made Utah the Home of His Cattle Kingdom," http://historytogo.utah.gov/utah_chapters/pioneers_and_cowboys/presonnuttermadeutahhomeofhiscattlekingdom.html.
5. Moody to Nutter, 29 May 1935, Records of the BLM (Grazing Service), CCC Correspondence … 1935–1939, NARACO RG 49/15/6/2/1 Entry 2 Box 2.
6. Nutter to Ickes, 17 August 1935, ibid., Box 2.
7. Nutter to Burlew, 5 September 1935, ibid., Box 2.
8. Falck to Nutter, 3 October 1935, ibid., Box 2.
9. Rupea to Donald D. McKay, 9 October 1935, ibid., Box 2.
10. McKay to Falck, 10 October 1935, ibid., Box 2.
11. Nutter to Falck, 11 November 1935, ibid., Box 2.
12. Gavin to Falck, 13 October 1937, ibid., Box 4.
13. Caron to Falck, telegrams, 13 and 15 October 1937, ibid., Box 4.
14. Terrett to Gavin, 16 October 1937, ibid., Box 4.
15. Ussery to the Director, 4 August 1938, ibid., Box 5.
16. Chief, Range Improvements to Ussery, 18 August 1938, ibid., Box 5.
17. "Seek to Have CCC Camp at St. George Moved to the Strip," *Mohave County Miner,* October 28, 1938, 3.
18. Painter to the Director and Caron to the Director, 16 March 1939, Records of the BLM (Grazing Service), CCC Correspondence … 1935–1939, NARACO RG 49/15/6/2/1 Entry 2 Box 6.
19. Terrett to Weatherwax, 17 March 1939, ibid., Box 5.
20. Molohon to Painter, 21 March 1939, ibid., Box 6.
21. Terrett to Hayden, 11 April 1939, ibid., Box 6.
22. Wolfe to Ussery, 15 April 1939, ibid., Box 6.
23. Caron to Wolfe, radiogram, 1 May 1939, ibid., Box 6. The change appears to be the result of a military inspection of the Black Rock site the week of April 20 by Major Kent, district quartermaster, noted in the April 20, 1939, *Washington County News,* 7.
24. Caron to Wolfe, radiogram, 3 May 1939, Records of the BLM (Grazing Service), CCC Correspondence … 1935–1939, NARACO RG 49/15/6/2/1 Entry 2 Box 6.
25. Molohon to Caron, telegram, 4 May 1939, ibid.
26. The author acknowledges John M. Herron, St. George BLM archaeologist, for this cogent observation.

CHAPTER 16

Short Creek (G-135)

THE ABANDONMENT OF DG-45 at St. George, Utah, was announced formally in August (see chapter 15, *St. George, Utah [DG-45]*). However, the assembly of the new Short Creek buildings appears to have started as early as June 1939. In a "Short Creek" column in the June 1 issue of the St. George newspaper, Mrs. I.W. Carling, the Short Creek reporter, announced, "A CCC camp is being established here and some of our men are being employed to help build it." On June 2, the *Kane County Standard* (page 5) reported that Short Creek construction had begun on May 24 under Lieutenant Dildine of the St. George camp. Two Company 2557 crews from Pipe Spring were said to be digging a well and constructing the road into the camp. Two weeks later, Carling stated that construction was moving fast and expected to be completed by July 1.

While the Company 2558 men continued to salvage the St. George CCC buildings and haul them away through October, it appears the new buildings, intended for the Black Rock camp, were the nucleus of the Short Creek camp. Company 1820 was organized out of Fort Logan, Colorado, and officially occupied the camp on April 16, 1940. In the April 25 *Washington County News*, Carling reported that the CCC was to "stay indefinitely."

Unfortunately, unlike the detailed coverage of the St. George camp, the Short Creek camp was mentioned infrequently. The only other nearby newspaper, the Kanab-based *Kane County Standard*, made no mention of the Short Creek camp throughout its occupancy. No camp newspapers or narrative work reports have survived, and only one camp inspection report survives, so this discussion is based almost totally on BLM records from the St. George Field Office. This account is surely incomplete. Much of the camp's work consisted of fence construction. Although this camp was occupied for slightly more than a year, they completed numerous projects under Project Superintendent Paul H. Higdon.

1940

Company 1820 had previously worked at G-138, Ajo, Arizona. On April 30, they had 189 enrollees (all but 2 from Texas). On June 30, 1940, they had 146 enrollees. It appears their first work was completing the construction of camp buildings (Project #135-08), which continued until September 30.[1]

Early in June, the camp was inspected by CCC Special Investigator M. J. Bowen, and he noted the "Camp [is] in excellent condition." The "work projects [are] getting along very satisfactory" and making "good progress." He noted about half the enrollees were Spanish American and called them all "very satisfactory." He called the camp administration "very capable," mentioning that the camp commander, Capt. Edward B. Watson, had six years of CCC service, and the executive officer, 1st Lt. Standlee D. Roberts, had four and a half years of CCC service. He reported that there was no truck taking boys to town on Sundays for religious services due to the distance, but that soon there would be two monthly visits by chaplains. Bowen noted that there were three literacy classes meeting four hours per week, with total attendance of fifty-seven enrollees. Camp electricity was coming from three 5kw units. The report included comments from District Grazier Samuell regarding the camp's educational program. According to him, many of the camp's occupational needs were filled by the camp educational classes, such as truck drivers who had taken the auto mechanics classes. He said that all the camp cooks and clerks were coming from the camp classes. Samuell noted the job training classes had resulted in a 50% gain in the amount and quality of work.[2]

Early work projects for the camp included the 9.5-mile-long Brinkerhoff-Esplin Segregation[3] Fence (Project #135-15), which appears to have been started in 1939 but not finished until August 7, 1940. It required 2,802 man days and over 2,000 posts and 6,000 stays (BLMSTG JDR 010061). The 8.75-mile-long Esplin-Heaton-Prince Segregation Fence (Project #135-16) was estimated at 2,250 man days (BLMSTG JDR 010065). Records indicate it was begun on February 2, 1940, and finished on June 14, 1941, with a small part left unfinished. On May 1, work began on the 2-mile-long Atkin-Esplin Segregation Fence (or Short Gap Division Fence) (Project #135-09, BLMSTG JDR 010036), which was completed on May 20 in 424 man days. The 5.1-mile-long Heaton-Brinkerhoff Segregation Fence (Project #135-17) was estimated at 1,281 man days, but actually took 2,758 man days; it was started on May 6, 1940, and finished on September 30, 1940 (BLMSTG JDR 010071). This project was reported as having labor from the "Antelope Side Camp." It is unclear if this was a G-135 spike camp.

Other early camp work appears to have included improving the Wolf Hole spike camp (Project #135-10), the Quail Canyon Truck Trail (Project #135-11), and Short Creek Cattle Guards (Project #135-12).[4] Work began on the Heaton Troughs #1, 2, and 3 (Projects #135-19, -20 and -21) in July and was completed in October. No other details are known of these projects.[5]

The 1.26-mile-long Antelope–State Line Fence (Project #135-24) was started on August 7 and completed on September 30, requiring 935 man days (BLMSTG JDR 010097). Like with most of the G-135 fences, the local ranchers contributed the materials, such as barbed wire and staples, and the CCC contributed the labor. The 5.9-mile-long Brinkerhoff Class 2 Cattle Segregation Fence (Project #135-22) was begun on August 8, 1940, and completed October 31, 1940, taking 1,616 man days (BLMSTG JDR 010090). The Antelope–State Line Cattle Guard (Project #135-25) was begun September 1, 1940, and completed January 29, 1941. It was estimated at 160 man days, but took 183 man days (BLMSTG JDR 010104). The 5.3-mile-long Esplin-Brinkerhoff Segregation Fence No. 2 (Project #135-29) was begun on October 28 and completed on November 26, requiring 828 man days (BLMSTG JDR 010115).

During the period of July and August, camp strength stayed high at 190 enrollees (nearly all from Texas). During September and October, strength dropped to 114, with the ending of the enrollment period at the end of September, and ramped up to 207 with the beginning of the new enrollment period at the beginning of October.

The Hurricane Class 2 Cattle Allotment Fence (Project #135-31) was begun on November 28, 1940, and completed March 31, 1941. This 5.5-mile-long fence required 1,661 man days and 1,200 posts. The records indicate it was "abandoned in part," so it is unclear if it was completed to the original specifications (BLMSTG JDR 010121). The 1.2-mile-long Cane Beds State Line Fence (Project #135-32) was begun on December 11, 1940, and completed on January 31, 1941. It took 952 man days, and like many of this company's fence projects, had four barb wire strands with posts 25' apart (BLMSTG JDR 010127).

The Sullivan Corral (Project #135-39) was started some time in 1940, and records noted it was completed February 13, 1941 (BLMSTG JDR 010153). This project was estimated at 500 man days and has an element of mystery about it. Records note it was to be done from the "New Spring Side Camp" of the Short Creek Camp. Nothing more is known of this possible spike camp.

Camp strength was recorded at 165 on December 31, 1940 (all from Texas), with the typical two Army officers and an educational advisor. The camp physician was on contract.

1941

On January 11, the Short Creek–Tuweep Cattle Guard (Project #135-26) was begun and completed less than a month later. It was estimated at 160 man days, but only required 73 (BLMSTG JDR 010108). On January 31, 1941, Company 1820 had 197 enrollees (all from Texas). On February 2, the substantial 7.5-mile-long Lyle-Reeve Division Fence (Project #135-23) was begun. It was estimated at 2,100 man days. Almost 1,600 posts and 4,600 stays were also estimated (BLMSTG JDR 010098). It appears that all of this project, except for 1 mile, was done by Company 1820, but the abrupt closing of the camp in July meant it had to be completed by DG-173.

On February 6, the St. George newspaper (page 3) noted that camp educational advisor Eugene Briscoe was not only teaching classes at the camp but also teaching a first aid class to school children aged twelve and over every Friday. Between February and July, camp strength went from 190 to 111.

During February, the camp cut posts at Cane Beds (Project #135-34), started the Short Creek–Hurricane Cattle Guard (Project #135-27), maintained truck trails (Project #135-38), and began work on the Short Creek Shipping Corrals (Project #135-35).[6] The camp may have worked on the Esplin-Holgate Division Fence (Project #135-41).[7] On May 12, 1941, work began on the 4.75-mile-long Brinkerhoff-Yellowstone Segregation Fence (Project #135-43); it was completed on June 18, 1941 and took 718 man days (BLMSTG JDR 010167).

Company 1820's last known projects were the Point of Rocks Reservoir (Project #135-46, started on May 2, 1941, and finished on June 12, 1941), and building a map cabinet (Project #135-45).[8] The reservoir was about 125' across and 7' deep. It required 68 man days (BLMSTG JDR 010179). Enrollees were planning on doing seed collecting in the Short Creek area, but the project (#135-44) was not started.[9]

On July 1, 1941, the Short Creek camp was closed down. The abandonment of G-135 was the result of an economy move dictated by Washington. Nationwide, 264 camps were closed, with Arizona losing 4 camps.[10]

Unless noted otherwise, any reference to the number of enrollees in a company, the location of the company, or company supervisors are from U.S. War Department, Location and Strength of CCC Companies, 1933–1942, NARAMD RG 35 530/65/22/04/05.

1. BLMSTG-*RIRB*.
2. U.S. CCC, Camp Inspection Reports, NARAMD RG 35/530/65/23/04 Entry 115 PI #11 Box 10.

3. Segregation, in this context, generally means to keep sheep separate from cattle.
4. BLMSTG-*RIRB*.
5. Ibid.
6. Ibid.
7. Ibid.
8. Ibid.
9. Ibid.
10. "CCC Camps Will Be Closed in Arizona," *Prescott Evening Courier,* June 30, 1941, 1. The *Kane County Standard* also wrote of the camp closing due to lack of federal funds, July 3, 1941, 8.

CHAPTER 17

Pipe Spring (DG-44)

THE CCC CAMP AT PIPE Spring National Monument was an oddity in that most of the work load was oriented to grazing projects outside the national monument.[1] This would be a source of strain throughout the existence of DG-44.

1935–1936

The only reliable water supply in this area was Pipe Spring. On June 11, 1935, the CCC asked permission from the National Park Service to locate the camp at Pipe Spring National Monument, as the Army recommended it as the only "possible site."[2] The camp was constructed in July and August 1935[3]; however, enrollees did not arrive until the end of October. The first enrollees, members of Company 2557, were largely from Ohio and all were white. It appears that the full company arrived on November 1 and totaled 190 enrollees.[4] The first officers, including the medical officer, were all Army men. Aland Forgeon was the educational advisor, Capt. Earl S. Jackson was the first commanding officer, and Hamilton A. Draper was the project superintendent.[5] At year's end, the Army location and strength report indicated Company 2557 had a total of 169 enrollees (151 from Ohio).

Although Company 2557 accomplished a great deal of grazing work, Leonard Heaton, the Pipe Spring National Monument custodian, expressed frequent dissatisfaction with the CCC.[6] A reading of Heaton's monthly reports published in *Southwestern Monuments Monthly Reports* reveals common themes of dissatisfaction with the lack of CCC labor in the monument, enrollee misbehavior, and disagreements with camp Army officers. Heaton expected the enrollees to obey National Park Service rules, such as not abusing wildlife. But at times, enrollees ignored the rules and trapped birds and reptiles; one even attempted to send reptiles home in the mail. Did Heaton look upon the CCC personnel as an outside force foisted upon him? Suddenly, over 200 outside people were living close at hand on the monument's ten acres. As there were no nearby diversions, such as a town, enrollees were surely on the monument grounds much of their non-work time. Heaton, up to then, had been in charge of the monument, living and working under a specific set of rules. This new group had its own rules, history, and priorities. And, at times, they surely were not going to be told what to do. The Army and the National Park Service were both organizations with top-down management and a primacy of rules. So, it appears their likenesses would have resulted in some strain no matter who the monument custodian or Army officers had been. However, it is this author's observation that more diplomacy and communication on the part of Heaton would have lessened some of the strain.

Heaton was not the only dissatisfied person. On December 29, CCC Special Investigator James C. Reddoch noted that twenty-seven enrollees were administratively discharged for refusing to work. Reddoch noted that the commanding officer said they were "Communistically inclined," but Reddoch "found no Communistic propaganda in their possession.... I believe these men were simply dissatisfied and wanted an opportunity to go home."[7]

According to Katherine McKoy, the company's grazing work was not immediately authorized, so the company's first projects were often inside the monument.[8] The company's first narrative report, dated April 1, 1936, summarizes the previous monument work, totaling 884 man days, including diversion ditch work, transplantation of 150 trees, campground and road construction, flagstone walkway construction, and fence and parking lot construction.[9] During this early period, the enrollees constructed a tennis court, a baseball diamond, a basketball court, a volleyball court, and a boxing ring.[10]

A close look at this first narrative report reveals that substantial labor and resources went into road building and maintenance (BLMSTG-*RIRB* Projects #44-01, #44-03, and #44-28).[11] The widening and surfacing of the 12-mile-long Fredonia to Pipe Springs Road totaled 6,038 man days. Ten thousand cubic yards of gravel were hauled, nine culverts were constructed, and 3,500' of drainage ditches "were built entirely with hand labor." The road was widened "from a single track trail" to one with "ample room for the passing of two cars."[12] Custodian Heaton made no comment in his reports about this road work, which appeared to benefit the monument.

Other early work for DG-44 was a 1.5-mile-long drift fence from the southeast corner of the Kaibab Indian Reservation to Kanab Gulch (less than 300 man days) and the cutting and hauling of eight hundred cedar posts (106 man days).[13] The Cedar Knoll Dam (Project #44-02) and Truck Trail work (Project #44-04) began March 1, 1936, and was completed October 3. The latter project required 2,776 man days and was said to benefit 5,500 cattle and sheep (BLMSTG JDR 010009).[14] According to the *Kane County Standard* (February 14, 1936, page 4), the 3.7-mile-long Bull Rush Truck Trail was begun on January 27. Ultimately that project would take 1,691 man days to complete on April 11, 1936 (Project #44-20, BLMSTG JDR 014190). The same newspaper article noted the Heaton-Findlay Dam replacement (Project #44-30) was to start shortly. By March 8, the camp newspaper said the latter project was "progressing nicely."[15] It would replace washed-out sections, raise the dam, and add a spillway. In a front page story, the March 6 newspaper noted the reconditioning of the Heaton-Findlay Dam project was nearly done.

During April, the 7.5-mile-long Jensen-Heaton Fence was completed, as well as the 4-mile-long Foremaster Homestead Fence and the 1-mile-long Foremaster Segregation Fence. The House Rock spike camp as well as the 3-mile road leading into it was completed. The E. A. Curtis allotment and 1.25-mile-long Sand Hill Unit Fence were said to be completed.[16]

During May, the camp swimming pool was completed, a successful dance was held, and the camp fielded a baseball team playing community and other CCC teams.[17] "This camp boasts one of the best baseball teams in the State … and the whole camp is very enthusiastic," wrote E. W. Samuell, CCC special investigator, in his July 15 report. He noted the Bull Rush Truck Trail had ten miles completed, with numerous stone culverts and a 30′ bridge with stone abutments. He reported that this truck trail would open up an area for new projects.[18]

In June, monument work included parking lot and road work, flagstone walkways, and curbing work.[19] On June 30, 1936, there were 125 enrollees (all from Ohio, Kentucky, or Indiana, except 8 from Arizona). During the remainder of the summer and early fall, work inside the monument included campground irrigation ditches, a campground parking lot, and curbing and landscaping.[20] Tragedy struck on July 25 when a CCC truck with twenty-one enrollees returning from a Saturday night dance in Kanab hit another vehicle head-on. Enrollee Robert Haverkamp, 17, of Cincinnati, Ohio, died in the Kanab hospital two days later of a ruptured spleen.[21]

Grazing work in the late summer included the beginning of the Antelope Valley Erosion (Control) Project (Project #44-32). By March 31, 1937, nearly 3,200 man days were logged on 1,200 acres. However, the entire project was estimated at 30,000 acres and 20,000 man days. This work consisted of building rock gully plugs, earth dikes, wire and rock spreaders, and wire and rock sausage.[22] On September 4, 1936, the 23-mile-long White Pockets Stock Driveway was completed (Project #44-07).[23]

Special Investigator Samuell inspected the camp November 13–14 and noted the Mt. Trumbull stockmen were saying the Bull Rush Truck Trail improvements had cut their travel time to Fredonia by two hours.[24] Preliminary work on the Bull Rush Bridge had begun with the milling of lumber at mills in the Buckskin Mountains. He pointed out that not having an educational advisor at such an isolated camp during the winter months was a real hardship and that a new advisor was needed soon. He reported that "the meals are much below par. This should be corrected because the boys have become dissatisfied and the morale is very low for this reason." He spoke at the dedication of the Cedar Knoll Stock Tank and reported three hundred in attendance.[25] The dedication was featured on the front page of the November 20 *Kane County Standard*. This was said to be the camp's first completed water project. Numerous speeches were made, and a barbecue followed at Pipe Spring, with a dance that went to midnight.

In the fall, relations between the monument and the CCC seemed to have reached a new low. In November, NPS Landscape Architect Alfred H. Kuehl reported that the CCC camp was more a detriment than a help. On December 3, the NPS director was advised that the CCC camp should be withdrawn.[26]

Figure 45. DG-44, Clay Hole, Partially Completed Corral Project, 1937. Courtesy NARA-CO, RG 49/15/C/6/1 Box 62.

Monument work included substantial landscaping in December.[27] Land surveys were being made at year's end for future projects. Plans were completed for the construction of the 75′ steel span bridge across Cottonwood Wash (Project #44-26), with the Indian Service furnishing all materials. "This project is of great importance to all stockmen of the district and preference has been requested."[28] On December 31, 1936, DG-44 had 157 enrollees (most from Kentucky and Ohio).

1937

The winter of 1936–1937 was the worst in memory for residents of southern Utah and northern Arizona. Snows started in mid-December and continued into January. Many

Figure 46. Pipe Spring Camp, Company 2557, 1936. Courtesy NARACO, RG 49/15/C/6/1 Box 62.

communities were cut off from the outside for weeks. Kanab's *Kane County Standard* opined: "Worst Storm in Dixie's History." It noted that temperatures of 30° and 40° below had been recorded and snow drifts between St. George Utah and the Nevada state line were 15′ high. The Short Creek correspondent for the St. George newspaper reported that Short Creek had not had a mail delivery in twenty days, men had been working two to three weeks to clear the roads, and because of lack of feed, cattle were dying.[29] The Kanab newspaper noted that a CCC truck had required two days to travel eight miles to reach a ranch near Cane Beds.[30] Pipe Spring was also cut off from the outside world from December 18 until late January, when the CCC obtained snow-clearing equipment from Utah.[31] As it turns out, food for the camp was delivered by truck convoy from Fort Douglas, Utah, to Fredonia, where the camp had to retrieve it.[32]

Although little regular project work was done during this period, the CCC accomplished significant rescue work totaling 748 man days. "During the months of January and February it was necessary for members of this camp to do practically all the work in assisting the stockmen of this district. The tractor and truck crews were kept busy all hours of the day and night in attempting to keep the roads clear of snow and haul feed and supplies for stranded stock and stockmen. Forty tons of feed were hauled to livestock and several loads of livestock were moved to places of shelter."[33] Significantly, Pipe Spring

Monument Custodian Heaton, in his February 1937 report in the *Southwestern Monuments Monthly Reports*, reported that "the CCC started work after eight weeks of rest."

In mid-February, DG-44 Range Examiner Floyd Allen and his crew of enrollees were temporarily stationed at the Round Valley CCC camp near Kingman to do range survey work.[34] In February through May, Custodian Heaton frequently had seven or eight enrollees working for him. (He wrote that he had been promised ten.) They worked on landscaping, cleanup, and building a watering trough and picnic tables.[35]

On April 27, Special Investigator Samuell spent one day at the camp and reported the Bull Rush Bridge work was "shaping up." The Cottonwood Wash Bridge project had begun, and a number of Company 2557 enrollees were staying at the St. George camp while they disassembled the bridge to be moved to Cottonwood Wash. The Bull Rush Truck Trail work was continuing. A range survey was going on at House Rock Valley. The Hack Canyon spike

Figure 47. Bull Rush Bridge Work, Hoist Is Equipped with Geared Drum and Hand Brake, 1937. Courtesy NARACO, RG 49/15/C/6/1 Box 62.

camp consisted of twenty-five men, and they had completed 15,000 acres of the Antelope Valley Erosion Project. The foreman at Hack Canyon was F. E. Maitland, and he had spent his money for baseball, volleyball, and other sporting goods for the enrollees. Samuell said the boys much preferred the spike camp to the main camp. Charles Black was the new educational advisor. Camp strength was down to 137, with 11 LEMs.[36]

Figure 48. Bull Rush Bridge on Completion, 1938. Courtesy NARACO, RG 49/15/C/6/1 Box 62.

Samuell re-visited the camp on June 3 and noted a "great improvement" in the mess. He observed the Army and Educational Advisor Black "were working toward success." Work projects included the Bull Rush Bridge and Truck Trail and construction of a corral for the upcoming wild horse roundup. He noted that the steel sections of the future Cottonwood Wash Bridge had been hauled from the Santa Clara River west though the Zion National Park tunnel using a large four-wheel drive truck borrowed from Albuquerque. The range survey continued at House Rock Valley, and erosion control work continued out of Hack Canyon. Samuell noted the latter had a five-hundred-gallon concrete water tank, the camp was exceptionally clean, and morale there was high.[37] On June 30, 1937, the camp had a total of 131 enrollees (100 from Ohio).

On July 2, Samuell again visited the camp and noted: "The enrollees are above average in work and seem more satisfied. The morale is high." He singled out the Hack Canyon spike camp men as so satisfied they did not want to come into the main camp even for Fourth of July events. The spike camp was constructing the Heaton Finley Corral (Project #44-10, BLM-STG JDR 010040). It required 531 man days and was completed July 6. Samuell noted that 90% of the national monument CCC projects were complete, with seven enrollees. Work continued on the Bull Rush Bridge, Cottonwood Wash Bridge, Ryan Ranger Station Range Survey, and Antelope Valley Erosion Control (35% complete.) The wild horse corral was completed.[38]

Figure 49. Hack Canyon Spike Camp, Twenty-five Miles Southwest of Main Camp, 1937. Courtesy NARACO, RG 49/15/C/6/1 Box 62.

Figure 50. Small Band of Wild Ones, Exhausted after a Forty-Mile Trip ... Just before They Were Rushed into the Canyon Leading to the Trap, 1937. Courtesy NARA-CO, RG 49/15/C/6/1 Box 62.

The camp's ninth period narrative report supplied the following roundup details. DG-44 constructed a very sturdy trap, along with 2.25 miles of drift fence leading into the trap. (The

Figure 51. Band of Eleven Wild Horses Already in the Trap, Three Hundred Eliminated during the Drive, 1937. Courtesy NARA-CO, RG 49/15/C/6/1 Box 62.

latter was removed at the end of the project.) The day of the drive, seventy-five horsemen were placed at advantageous points, and then two airplanes began, as much as forty miles away, to drive the horses toward the trap. Four hundred horses were said to have been eliminated during the drive. "When it is considered that a wild horse will use as much range as two head of cattle, this work was of a very beneficial value."[39]

On July 27, Samuell inspected again and noted continued bridge, truck trail, range survey, and national monument work. He reported the .4-mile-long Cedar Knoll Fence (Project #44-13, BLMSTG JDR 010052) was completed August 6, 1937, and took 314 man days. He reported the Hack Canyon spike camp was working on the June Heaton Corral (Project #44-12, BLMSTG JDR 010049), which was finished on July 30 and required 435 man days.[40]

Samuell returned on September 30 and reported the total number of enrollees at only 73. (This was common for the end of an enrollment period when new members were expected soon.) The Bull Rush Bridge was about 60% complete. It was described as a two-span timber truss bridge, with each span measuring 38′ with rubble masonry abutments. A rock quarry was opened nearby, and more than 400 slabs measuring 18″ thick, 2′ wide and 4–6′ long had been hauled to the bridge site.[41] The Cottonwood Bridge and Bull Rush Truck Trail work were both about 33% complete. He reported the House Rock Valley Sand Hill Division Fence (Project #44-16) as 90% complete.[42]

Other projects completed later in the year were the White Pockets Corral (Project #44-17, BLMSTG JDR 010074), completed October 30 and taking 208 man days; the Soap Creek Corral (Project #44-09, BLMSTG JDR 010035), completed November 3 and taking 420 man days; and the Clayhole Corral (Project #44-11, BLMSTG JDR 010045), completed October 29 and taking 506 man days. (The ninth period narrative report indicated that five corrals had been completed by September 30, 1937, and four more remained. The Two Mile Corral was started some time in 1937 [the date is uncertain] and completed in June 1938 [Project #44-08, BLMSTG JDR 010031]).

In the latter part of the year, the National Park Service became more resolute in demanding more benefits from the grazing camp for the national monument. On November 10, the Division of Grazing agreed to contribute $50 per month for the purchase of materials for CCC monument jobs. As Heaton had been complaining a great deal that CCC labor was often

Figure 52. House Rock Spike Camp, Sixty-five Miles from Camp, 1937. Courtesy NARACO, RG 49/15/C/6/1 Box 62.

useless without a truck, the agreement stated the monument would supply a truck to be shared equally with the Division of Grazing. Grazing agreed to supply ten enrollees daily.[43]

December CCC work at the monument included road maintenance, landscaping, irrigation ditch work, a drinking fountain, picnic tables, and a water trough.[44] In December, work was begun on the 7.3-mile-long Sand Hill–Kanab Fence (Project #44-33, BLMSTG JDR 010129). Originally estimated at 1,600 man days, it was not completed until December 22, 1938, and required 5,426 man days.[45] It was said to affect 10,000 head of livestock. On December 31, 1937, Company 2557 had 158 enrollees.

1938

On January 7, Company 2557 completed the Bull Rush Bridge, one of their more complex and lengthy projects. It took 6,980 man days and had no lost time accidents.[46] On January 24, Special Investigator Reddoch inspected the camp and called the camp well managed. He said the enrollees seemed to be contented and the relations between the Army and the technical services were harmonious. The day he was there, all 153 men available for work were held in camp due to poor road conditions. He noted that eleven of their trucks were in poor condition and in need of complete overhauls. The camp goal was to cut 8,000 posts, and so far 2,400 had been cut. The current Bull Rush Truck Trail[47] project of eleven miles had 7 miles completed, and 1.2 miles of the Sand Hill Fence was done. Work had started on the Chatterly Corral (Project #44-15, BLMSTG JDR 010059), originally estimated to take 400 man days and eventually completed on May 18, 1938. He noted four projects not yet started totaling 15,800 man days.[48] In January, a CCC crew assisted Custodian Heaton in planting cottonwood trees.[49]

In February, roads were frequently impassable, so fifty enrollees and five trucks assisted Heaton in hauling dirt to fill a drainage ditch.[50] On February 25, enrollees finished the Bull Rush Stock Driveway (Project #44-19, BLMSTG JDR 014190), which was 23 miles long and 1 mile wide and followed the Bull Rush Truck Trail. This "consisted of driving steel posts and then placing metal signs on the posts." It involved much walking over a two-week period and took 230 man days.[51]

Apparently the roads cleared by March, for the camp started two large jobs. Sunset Tank (Project #44-34, BLMSTG JDR 010135) was begun on March 14, estimated at 3,200 man days,

and ultimately completed October 1, 1938.

Figure 53. Typical CCC Fence Construction, Grand Canyon National Park, 1934. Courtesy Grand Canyon National Park Museum Collection, #29842.

The 5-mile-long State Line Fence No. 2 (Project #44-36, BLMSTG JDR 010142), affecting 5,000 cattle and 25,000 sheep, was begun on March 21 and completed August 12, requiring 1,153 man days.

On April 4, work started on the Two Mile Fence (BLM-STG-*RIBR* Project #44-31), and this 1-mile-long job was finished June 27, 1938. The March 31 narrative report reported that the House Rock Valley Sand Hill Division Fence was completed in 270 man days. The Cottonwood Wash Bridge work "has progressed very satisfactorily." Both abutments were completed, requiring about three hundred large stones, each weighing 1,000 to 1,200 pounds. "A high degree of perfection has been attained in the art of rock masonry."[52]

On June 1, the camp began work on the Seven Knolls Corral (Project #44-14, BLMSTG JDR 010057), estimated at 400 man days and completed on August 19. The Eight Mile Bridge project (#44-38) was completed on June 7.[53] On June 30, company strength was 117 (all but 1 from Ohio, Indiana, or Kentucky).

On July 1, work was begun on the 4.5-mile-long State Line Fence No. 1 (Project #44-35, BLMSTG JDR 010237). It took 957 man days to complete on September 8. Special Investigator Samuell visited camp on July 22 and reported that six enrollees were working at the monument hauling dirt and installing toilets. Twenty-six men were in the Buckskin Mountains cutting fence posts.[54] Three enrollees were surveying the Hack Canyon–Tuweep Truck Trail. The Kanab Stock Driveway Reservoir was ready to start. He also reported on the various fence projects. Samuell inspected Sunset Tank and found Foreman Lauritzen's work "un-satisfactory." At the House Rock spike camp, he "kept a dirty camp, the Army complained." His fence line work was unsatisfactory, as "line was poor and the holes were not deep enough. Work had to be done over, his corrals were very un-satisfactory."[55]

On August 8, E. A. Bickley inspected the camp and noted that Lauritzen was supervising twenty-six enrollees doing wheelbarrow work at Sunset Tank. Main camp work included fence and corral work. A twenty-man crew was cutting posts in the Kaibab Forest, and a twenty-eight-man crew was in the Buckskin Mountains cutting 1,100 posts per week. A twenty-five-man crew at the House Rock spike camp had completed 70% of the Sand Hill–Kanab Fence. He noted that the camp trucks were all in bad shape because of rough roads and extreme distances. He was preparing to have four stake trucks disposed of.[56] On August 22, enrollees began work on the Bull Rush Corral (Project #44-43, BLMSTG JDR 011767), completing this job on September 7 for a total of 216 man days. From September 9 to 27, enrollees worked the Kanab Unit Driveway (Project #44-40).[57]

Beginning October 17, Special Inspector Samuell spent four days inspecting the camp and its projects. He noted the Sunset Tank was good looking and complete. He reported an impressive summary of the company's post cutting: forty-two men were in the field, while thirty-three men in camp were peeling 6,000 posts there, another 3,500 posts were at the foot of the mountain, and 2,500 posts were cut down in the woods.[58] He noted the Two Mile and Chatterly Corrals were being reconstructed. (Were these Lauritzen-supervised corrals that he rated earlier as unsatisfactory?) Samuell was not happy with the mess, however. He said the enrollees away from base camp were "not properly fed" and the "breakfasts generally entirely too light."[59]

On October 17, the camp began work on Johnson Run Reservoir (Project #44-53, BLMSTG JDR 010199), and they completed work on December 23, using 1,340 man days. Improvement Supervisor Samuell, during his inspection, noted that thirty men had started work at the Johnson Run project, but he recommended a higher dam and clearing the brush from the spillway. Samuell returned on November 5 for three days of inspection and noted Johnson Run had thirty men with wheelbarrows and a "Cat" working there. He noted twenty-six men were working the Central Sheep and Cattle Fence No. 1 (Project #44-47, BLMSTG JDR 010182). (This fence extended 11.5 miles and was begun November 7, completed April 7, 1939, and required 2,565 man days.) The Fredonia Free Use Allotment Fence (Project #44-48, BLMSTG JDR 010185) was using part of a forty-three-man crew. (This fence extended 6.6 miles and was begun November 7, completed January 30, 1939, and required 1,170 man days.) The remainder of that forty-three-man crew was working the E. B. Pratt Fence (Project #44-486, BLMSTG JDR 010177). (This 3-mile-long fence was started November 7, completed December 27, and required 482 man days.) Samuell noted the Sand Hill–Kanab Fence was nearly done and the House Rock spike camp would then close. He reported the theft of tools from the House Rock and the Hack Canyon spike camps.[60]

Samuell returned for another three-day inspection on December 12. He reported in detail on the various fence projects, saying the Fredonia Free Use Allotment Fence was "a good job." The Central Sheep and Cattle Fence No. 1 needed some corrections. The Sand Hill–Kanab Unit Fence (Project #44-33) was just finished, and most of the holes for fence posts had to be dynamited. This fence, he said, is "the best in the country." He reported the camp had 16,000 to 18,000 posts on hand, so there would be plenty of posts for winter and spring work.[61] On December 19, the camp began work on the Short Creek Cattle Guard and finished this job on December 27, using 28 man days (Project #44-47, BLMSTG JDR 010188). At year's end, the camp had 140 enrollees (all but five from Ohio, Indiana, or Kentucky).

Figure 54. DG-44 Soap Creek ... Partially Completed Corral, 1938. Courtesy NARACO, RG 49/15/C/6/1 Box 62.

1939

The new year did not start off well for Pipe Springs enrollee Homer Hacker. Hacker was stabbed New Year's Eve in Kanab by a Seeps Springs spike camp enrollee for "saluting" the attacker's girl. The alleged assailant was Stephen (Babe) Davitto. Hacker recovered and returned to camp.[62] Davitto's fate is unknown.

On January 5, CCC Special Investigator M. J. Bowen visited camp and reported the camp had one spike camp sixty-five miles away and was responsible for an area of 1,200 square miles. He noted a number of older trucks out in the weather that were out of service. The camp latrine was rated as unsatisfactory because of numerous problems.[63]

With all the fence posts on hand, Company 2557 started the first new fence project of the year on January 16 with the 8.5-mile-long Thomas Jensen–June Heaton Fence (Upper Blue Cow Fence, Project #44-52, BLMSTG JDR 010196). This project was initially estimated at 2,000 man days, but ultimately took 3,028 man days when finished on June 29. The original budget for this project called for 180 rolls of barbed wire (contributed by the stockmen), 400 pounds of powder, and 1,900 posts.

On February 3, work was started on the 1-mile-long P. E. Church Fence (Project #44-51, BLMSTG JDR 010192). Finished on March 21, this project took 221 man days. Improvement Supervisor Samuell visited the camp on February 8 and noted that all work projects were snowed in. Consequently, the camp worked from February 6 to 28 doing emergency clearing of snow and ice (BLMSTG-*RIRB* Project #44-60). The House Rock spike camp was getting their supplies by horseback. He rated the camp educational program as "very satisfactory," with 90–95% of the enrollees participating.[64] On February 27, work started on the .5-mile-long House Rock–Ferry Swale Fence (Project #44-59, BLMSTG JDR 010219). It was completed on March 13 and required 169 man days.

In early March, enrollees completed the Sand Hill Kanab Cattle Guard (Project #44-58) and the Curtis South Cattle Guard (Project #44-56).[65] On March 6, enrollees began work on a rock culvert for the monument and continued that work until finished on May 17. During the same period, the monument used the $50 monthly grazing fee to purchase sewer system materials.[66] On March 13, Samuell inspected for three days and noted four ongoing fence projects. Although he found the garage dirty, he reported that enrollees and foremen had improved.[67] On March 22, work began on the Church-Rider Fence (Project #44-50, BLMSTG JDR 010190). Completed on March 31, it required 198 man days, less than the estimate of 360.

April work included repair to the Kanab Creek–Reservation Fence (Project #44-61, BLMSTG JDR 010017, begun April 10, completed April 18, and requiring 184 man days) and the 2-mile-long Button-Chatterly Fence (Project #44-65, BLMSTG JDR 010233, begun April 19, completed May 1, and requiring 184 man days).

Samuell returned April 16 for a three-day inspection and noted that the Mt. Trumbull spike camp was being erected by a foreman and four enrollees. According to former Company 2557 enrollee Millard Quesinberry, the spike camp consisted of three buildings: a mess hall and kitchen building, barrack, and officers' quarters.[68] Twenty-five men with the "Cat" were working the House Rock Truck Trail into the spike camp.[69] Four enrollees were doing culvert work at the monument. He declared that there were not enough vehicles available to get all the men to their work. He said that for three years complaints had been lodged about the mechanic, and his work was not satisfactory. He declared the mechanic must work nights to keep all the trucks available. The House Rock spike camp was criticized for a number of things, including a dirty camp.[70]

From May 2 through May 8, enrollees worked on the 1-mile-long Pratt-Findley Segregation Fence (BLMSTG-*RIRB* Project #44-67). On May 9, work was started on the Foremaster-Homestead Allotment Fence (Project #44-63, BLMSTG JDR 010231). Stretching 5.5 miles, it was completed on June 9 in 639 man days.

Samuell returned May 21–23 and again noted the House Rock spike camp was dirty, and the main camp's mechanic's shop was dirty and the tools needed maintenance. The House Rock spike camp was working the Two Mile Truck Trail and the Curtis–Sand Hill Division Fence.[71] Thirty-four men were surfacing the camp road into the Short Creek camp.[72]

May 22 marked the beginning of work on the 5.25-mile-long Foremaster Segregation Fence (Project #44-62, BLMSTG JDR 010227). It was finished on June 29 in 499 man days, well under the initial estimate of 1,150. On June 2, the Kanab newspaper reported two Company 2557 crews were working at Short Creek digging a well and building the camp road.[73] On June 9, work began on the 7.7-mile-long Central Cattle and Sheep Fence No. 2 (Project #44-69, BLMSTG JDR 010244, completed September 22, and requiring 1,748 man days.) The 2.5-mile-long Judd Division Fence was started on June 19 (Project #44-68, BLMSTG JDR 010240, completed October 4, and requiring 529 man days.)

According to the Kanab newspaper, the Mt. Trumbull camp goal was to cut four thousand posts.[74] On June 22, the St. George newspaper reported that the Mt. Trumbull spike camp "which is at White Springs, on the north side of Mt. Trumbull, gave a dance in honor of the completion of their mess hall. Everyone reported a nice time."[75]

On June 26, Samuell inspected for three days and noted that the Mt. Trumbull spike camp had sixteen men working on the water line. The House Rock spike camp had twenty-three men and had been cleaned up since the last visit. They were working on the Two Mile Truck Trail and had finished three cattle guards at the Ferry-Swale Fence, Buckskin Mountains, and House Rock–Sandhill Division Fence.[76] The mechanic's work was still not satisfactory, but the educational program was "well carried out."[77] On June 30, Company 2557 had 124 enrollees (from five different states). Also on June 30, the camp softball team was reported to have won two games in Kanab.[78]

On July 5, work started on the Central Unit Segregation Fence (Project #44-76, BLMSTG JDR 010260). This 3.25-mile-long job was completed on July 24 in 342 man days. The following day, the St. George newspaper reported Mr. Maitland, the Mt. Trumbull spike camp foreman, had brought a truckload of boys to the community dance on June 23.[79] In July, the CCC began monument work on the sewer system, including a concrete septic tank. This project required 79 man days, but was stopped on September 9.[80] Other CCC work in the monument in July included making signs from logs.[81]

On July 23, Samuell again visited for a three-day inspection. The Mt. Trumbull spike camp was closed for lack of water. The House Rock spike camp had twenty-three men, who were cutting posts[82] and working on the Two Mile Truck Trail. He reported that trucks and mechanic work seemed to have improved. A Milkweed Eradication project had begun.[83] Thirty-six enrollees were cutting posts southwest of the Junius Heaton Reservoir. He noted a new commanding officer had taken over three months ago, and it is "by far best mess this camp has ever had" and this "increases morale and the work output." The educational program had nearly 100% participation.[84]

On August 1, work was begun on the Kanab Unit Sheep and Cattle Fence, a 10.3-mile-long fence (Project #44-77, BLMSTG JDR 010262). It was finished on October 4 and required 1,835 man days. Two days later, enrollees started work on the Mt. Trumbull Segregation Fence (Project #44-75, BLMSTG JDR 010258). This 4-mile-long fence was completed on September 30, using 1,292 man days. On August 8, the Grand Canyon North Rim CCC Company 3318 invited Company 2557 to a day of games and barbecue, and forty Pipe Spring boys attended.[85] On August 15, work was started on the Bull Rush Cattle Guard No. 1 (Project #44-79, BLMSTG JDR 010267). It was completed August 28, using 123 man days.

On August 23, Samuell returned and spent seven days inspecting. He reported that thirty-six men were cutting posts in the Buckskin Mountains. The Mt. Trumbull spike camp was re-opened, with thirty-five men cutting posts[86] and building fences. He explained that rains had re-charged the Mt. Trumbull spring, and there was now a five-hundred-gallon tank with a ten-thousand-gallon overflow tank. The educational program reported 100% participation.

On August 29, work started on the Bull Rush Cattle Guard No. 2 (Project #44-78, BLMSTG JDR 010266). It was completed on September 30, using 124 man days. On August 31, work began on the Curtis-Hamblin Division Fence (Project #44-81, BLMSTG JDR 010270). Nearly 2 miles long, this job was finished September 28, using 185 man days. Between all the work projects, the enrollees still had time for fun, as some won a jitterbug contest in Kanab.[87] On September 8, the Kanab newspaper reported fence work and indicated that Curtis-Hamblin fence work was being carried out by men of the "Two Mile Side Camp."[88] It is unclear if this is a reference to the House Rock spike camp or to another spike camp of DG-44.

On September 29, the Kanab newspaper reported that enrollees were departing on October 1 for DG-122, Las Vegas.[89] Samuell made his last inspection of the camp on September 30 for three days. He reported on the fence and truck trail work. He reported the company was to move to Ajo.[90] Before moving, they finished the June Heaton Cattle Guard (Project #44-84) and the House Rock Corrals and Loading Chutes (Project #44-86).[91] The camp was officially abandoned on October 5, 1939.[92] Most of the buildings were dismantled and moved to NP-12, Walnut Canyon National Monument, with Pipe Spring National Monument retaining several that were adapted to monument use.[93] Apparently, a good deal of lumber from the buildings was given to the local Paiutes.[94]

Unless noted otherwise, any reference to the number of enrollees in a company, the location of the company, or company supervisors are from U.S. War Department, Location and Strength of CCC Companies, 1933–1942, NARAMD RG 35 530/65/22/04/05.

1. McKoy, *Culture at a Crossroads*, 569. "Pipe Spring would experience all the pitfalls of being occupied by an army of adolescent boys and very few of the benefits." Note: McKoy page numbers documented here are from the digital version.

2. Ibid., 701.

3. Ibid., 569.

4. "Pipe Springs Camp Now Occupied by Camp DG-44," *Washington County News*, November 7, 1935, 8.

5. McKoy, *Culture at a Crossroads*, 704, 705.

6. Ibid., 774–776.

7. U.S. CCC, Camp Inspection Reports, NARAMD RG 35/530/65/23/04 Entry 115 (PI #11) Box 10. "Communistic Activities," a category to be checked yes or no, was

8. McKoy, *Culture at a Crossroads*, 705.
9. U.S. BLM (Grazing Service), CCC, "Division of Grazing, Camp DG 44 … April 1, 1936," Records of the BLM (Grazing Service), CCC, Narrative Reports of Individual CCC Camps, 1936–38, NARACO RG 49/15/6/7.5/1 Entry 19 Box 74.
10. McKoy, *Culture at a Crossroads*, 706.
11. BLMSTG-*RIRB*.
12. U.S. BLM (Grazing Service), CCC, "Division of Grazing, Camp DG 44 … April 1, 1936," Records of the BLM (Grazing Service), CCC, Narrative Reports of Individual CCC Camps, 1936–38, NARACO RG 49/15/6/7.5/1 Entry 19 Box 74.
13. Ibid. This may be Project #44-05, the Loco Point–Kanab Gulch Fence in BLMSTG-*RIRB*.
14. This author visited the Cedar Knoll Dam on May 9, 2012, and it appeared to be functioning as intended. It was reported to be 400′ long and 15′ high and still looks impressive today. See "Pipe Springs CCC News," *Kane County Standard*, February 14, 1936, 6.
15. "Work Projects," *Pipe Post*, vol. 1, no. 4.
16. "Pipe Springs CCC News," *Kane County Standard*, April 10, 1936, 6.
17. "Pipe Springs CCC News," *Kane County Standard*, May 29, 1936, suppl.
18. U.S. BLM, Camp Inspection Reports, 1938–1942, NARACO RG 49 Entry 20 Box 84. It appears he is referencing two of the ultimate four projects on the Bull Rush Road, namely Project #44-23 (3.3 miles completed November 30, 1935) and #44-20 (3.7 miles completed April 11, 1936) in BLMSTG-*RIRB*.
19. McKoy, *Culture at a Crossroads*, 778.
20. Ibid., 779.
21. "Lights Blamed," *Ogden Standard*, July 28, 1936.
22. U.S. BLM (Grazing Service), CCC, "Division of Grazing, Camp DG 44 … Eighth Period," Records of the BLM (Grazing Service), CCC, Narrative Reports of Individual CCC Camps, 1936–38, NARACO RG 49/15/6/7.5/1 Entry 19 Box 74.
23. BLMSTG-*RIRB*.
24. Apparently referring to the addition of the third Bull Rush Road, Project #44-22, 6.7 miles long. BLMSTG-*RIRB*.
25. U.S. BLM, Camp Inspection Reports, 1938–1942, NARACO RG 49 Entry 20 Box 84.
26. McKoy, *Culture at a Crossroads*, 780.
27. Ibid., 781.
28. U.S. BLM (Grazing Service), CCC, "Division of Grazing, Camp DG 44…Eighth Period," Records of the BLM (Grazing Service), CCC, Narrative Reports of Individual CCC Camps, 1936–38, NARACO RG 49/15/6/7.5/1 Entry 19 Box 74.
29. "Short Creek, Ariz. Mrs. I. W. Carling Reporter," *Washington County News*, February 11, 1937, 5.
30. "CCC Opens Up Road to 25,000 Head of Livestock," *Kane County Standard*, February 19, 1937, 1. The headline was referring to CCC rescue work in the Escalante, Utah, area.
31. "January, 1937 Pipe Spring Narrative Report," *Southwest Monuments Monthly Reports*.
32. U.S. CCC, Camp Inspection Reports, NARAMD RG 35/530/65/23/04 Entry 115 (PI #11) Box 10.
33. U.S. BLM (Grazing Service), CCC, "Division of Grazing, Camp DG 44…Eighth Period," Records of the BLM (Grazing Service), CCC, Narrative Reports of Individual CCC Camps, 1936–38, NARACO RG 49/15/6/7.5/1 Entry 19 Box 74.
34. "Round Valley CCC Camp," *Mohave County Miner*, February 19, 1937, 11.
35. McKoy, *Culture at a Crossroads*, 896.
36. U.S. BLM, Camp Inspection Reports, 1938–1942, NARACO RG 49 Entry 20 Box 84.
37. Ibid.
38. Ibid.
39. U.S. BLM (Grazing Service), CCC, "Ninth Period Illustrated Narrative Report, September 30, 1937, Camp DG 44…," Records of the BLM (Grazing Service), CCC, Narrative Reports of Individual CCC Camps, 1936–38, NARACO RG 49/15/6/7.5/1 Entry 19 Box 74.
40. U.S. BLM, Camp Inspection Reports, 1938–1942, NARACO RG 49 Entry 20 Box 84.
41. U.S. BLM (Grazing Service), CCC, "Ninth Period Illustrated Narrative Report, September 30, 1937, Camp DG 44…," Records of the BLM (Grazing Service), CCC, Narrative Reports of Individual CCC Camps, 1936–38, NARACO RG 49/15/6/7.5/1 Entry 19 Box 74.
42. U.S. BLM, Camp Inspection Reports, 1938–1942, NARACO RG 49 Entry 20 Box 84.
43. McKoy, *Culture at a Crossroads*, 900.
44. Ibid., 902.
45. According to the BLMSTG-*RIRB*, this was Project #44-33 and ultimately cost $4,845.04.
46. U.S. BLM (Grazing Service), CCC, "Tenth Period Illustrated Narrative Report, March 31, 1938, Camp DG 44…," Records of the BLM (Grazing Service), CCC, Narrative Reports of Individual CCC Camps, 1936–38, NARACO RG 49/15/6/7.5/1 Entry 19 Box 74. This project, #44-22, ultimately cost $10,249.13 and, except for the total spent on the Bull Rush Truck Trail, was the most

expensive of the company's projects, per the BLMSTG-*RIRB*. This author visited the Bull Rush Bridge on May 9, 2012. One of the two spans remains, but it is closed to all traffic. The remaining span's support consists of nine wood beams 6.1 x 14.1″ and two beams 10 x 12.6″, with two cross beams 9.6 x 11.4″. All appear to be Ponderosa pine.

47. This appears to reference the fourth Bull Rush Truck Trail, Project #44-24, in the BLMSTG-*RIRB*. The four projects totaled $15,620.94, an extraordinary sum for the CCC.
48. U.S. CCC, Camp Inspection Reports, NARAMD RG 35/530/65/23/04 Entry 115 (PI #11) Box 10.
49. McKoy, *Culture at a Crossroads*, 945.
50. Ibid., 945.
51. U.S. BLM (Grazing Service), CCC, "Tenth Period Illustrated Narrative Report, March 31, 1938, Camp DG 44…," Records of the BLM (Grazing Service), CCC, Narrative Reports of Individual CCC Camps 1936–38, NARACO RG 49/15/6/7.5/1 Entry 19 Box 74.
52. Ibid.
53. BLMSTG-*RIRB*.
54. This appears to be Project #44-18, BLMSTG-*RIRB*.
55. U.S. BLM, Camp Inspection Reports, 1938–1942, NARACO RG 49 Entry 20 Box 84.
56. Ibid. Eleven days later, Samuell wrote to District Grazier Huling E. Ussery that he had personally inspected all the company trucks and that three of ten were unsafe.
57. BLMSTG-*RIRB*.
58. Apparently Project #44-42, BLMSTG-*RIRB*.
59. U.S. BLM, Camp Inspection Reports, 1938–1942, NARACO RG 49 Entry 20 Box 84.
60. Ibid.
61. Ibid. Project #44-37, BLMSTG-*RIRB*.
62. "CCC Boy Injured in Stabbing Fray," *Kane County Standard*, January 6, 1939, 1; "Hospital News," *Kane County Standard*, January 20, 1939, 6.
63. U.S. CCC, Camp Inspection Reports, NARAMD RG 35/530/65/23/04 Entry 115 (PI #11) Box 10.
64. U.S. BLM, Camp Inspection Reports, 1938–1942, NARACO RG 49 Entry 20 Box 84.
65. BLMSTG-*RIRB*.
66. McKoy, *Culture at a Crossroads*, 988.
67. U.S. BLM, Camp Inspection Reports, 1938–1942, NARACO RG 49 Entry 20 Box 84.
68. Letter of Millard, undated, Collection No. 930, SNMAHA.
69. Apparently Project #44-54, BLMSTG-*RIRB*.
70. U.S. BLM, Camp Inspection Reports, 1938–1942, NARACO RG 49 Entry 20 Box 84.
71. Curtis–Sand Hill Division Fence, Project #44-70, 1.5 miles long, begun May 22, completed June 2, 1939, BLMSTG-*RIRB*.
72. U.S. BLM, Camp Inspection Reports, 1938–1942, NARACO RG 49 Entry 20 Box 84.
73. "Pipe Springs CCC Camp News," *Kane County Standard*, June 2, 1939, 2. Short Creek Truck Trail is Project #44-74. Enrollees worked on the Short Creek Well, Project #44-66, from May 15 to June 12, 1939, per BLMSTG-*RIRB*.
74. "Pipe Springs CCC Camp News," *Kane County Standard*, June 30, 1939, 8. The July 14 (page 8) issue of the newspaper said their goal was 15,000 posts! Apparently, BLMSTG-*RIRB* Project #44-72, Mount Trumbull Post Cutting, was completed in August.
75. "Mt. Trumbull, Ariz., Roy Bundy Reporter," *Washington County News*, June 22, 1939, 3.
76. BLM records show the Ferry Swale Cattle Guard, completed June 22, Project #44-71 and the Buckskin Cattle Guard, completed June 20, Project #44-57, BLMSTG-*RIRB*.
77. U.S. BLM, Camp Inspection Reports, 1938–1942, NARACO RG 49 Entry 20 Box 84.
78. "Pipe Springs CCC Camp News," *Kane County Standard*, June 30, 1939, 8.
79. "Mt. Trumbull, Ariz., Roy Bundy Reporter," *Washington County News*, July 6, 1939, 3.
80. McKoy, *Culture at a Crossroads*, 989.
81. "July 1939 Pipe Spring Narrative Report," *Southwestern Monuments Monthly Reports*.
82. Apparently Project #44-39, started July 17 and finished September 30, 1939, BLMSTG-*RIRB*.
83. Project #44-80, BLMSTG-*RIRB*, July 25–27, covering twenty-three acres.
84. U.S. BLM, Camp Inspection Reports, 1938–1942, NARACO RG 49 Entry 20 Box 84. The *Kane County Standard* reported on May 19 (page 8) that Lt. Paul R. Hunt was appointed commanding officer on April 22.
85. Audretsch, *Shaping the Park and Saving the Boys*, 57.
86. Project #44-72, BLMSTG-*RIRB* indicates 759 posts cut by August.
87. *Happy Days*, September 9, 1939, 6.
88. "Pipe Springs CCC Camp News," *Kane County Standard*, September 8, 1939, 8.
89. "Pipe Springs CCC Camp News," *Kane County Standard*, September 29, 1939, 8. The camp newspaper *The Rattler* also reported Company 2557 was moving to Las Vegas in their September 19, 1939, issue.
90. U.S. BLM, Camp Inspection Reports, 1938–1942, NARACO RG 49 Entry 20 Box 84. McKoy, *Culture at a Crossroad*, 990, says Company 2557 was to go to Ajo, but lists no source. The Army *Location and Strength of CCC Companies* for Arizona does not list Company 2557 and lists Company 1820 at Ajo.

91. BLMSTG-*RIRB*.
92. "Civilian Conservation Corps Eighth Corps Area, Status Record of CCC Camps Authorized Since Inception of the Program up to … December 31, 1941 … Compiled by Office of Liaison Officer, CCC Fort Sam Houston…," NARACO BLM CCC Directories RG 49 Entry 33, 34 Box 132.
93. McKoy, *Culture at a Crossroads,* 1030.
94. Everett L. Minteer, interview in Stein, *New Deal at Walnut Canyon,* 11–12.

CHAPTER 18

Antelope Valley (G-173)

THIS CAMP, OCCUPIED BY COMPANY 1814, is not unlike its neighbor at Short Creek in that information about it is incomplete. No newspaper accounts, narrative work reports, or camp newspapers were found for this camp. Army reports indicate its buildings, like those at Short Creek, were "rigid," indicating the enrollees were not eating or sleeping in tents. And like the Short Creek camp, they did considerable fence work. However, Antelope Valley was more isolated, located out on the open range. (G-173 is sometimes called Bull Rush and located, incorrectly, at Pipe Spring or Fredonia.) It was about four miles south of Pipe Spring National Monument at the terminus of a cattleman's water pipeline. The Army leased one-third of the water in the pipeline, but that was insufficient at times. In those cases, water was hauled by truck from Pipe Spring.[1] A 1941 camp inspection report indicated it was twenty-two miles from the nearest town. However, travel over dirt roads would have been nearly impossible after significant rain or snow. (The Army initially wanted to locate this camp at Pipe Spring National Monument, but strained relations between DG-44 and the monument in the past resulted in the monument declining another CCC camp.)[2]

The men of Company 1814, like the men of Company 1820 at Short Creek, were experienced in Division of Grazing work. Before arriving at Antelope Valley, they occupied Camp G-136 near Duncan, Arizona. Much of what is known about this camp's work is based upon BLM records from the St. George Field Office and camp inspection reports.

1940

Camp buildings were constructed beginning May 21, 1940, when a crew of sixty-five enrollees and an Army officer arrived at Pipe Spring and stayed in the vacant DG-44 buildings. (According to the BLMSTG-*RIRB*, this work [Project #173-02] was not completed until September 30.)[3] Apparently, they remained at the DG-44 buildings until August 8, when they moved to the new DG-173 quarters.[4] Military reports indicate the camp, located at Bull Rush, was officially occupied on August 10, 1940, by 197 enrollees (all but 2 from Texas). The first staff was two Army officers, an educational advisor, and a contract physician. It was organized originally from Fort Logan, Colorado. Roy D. Wright was the project superintendent. Not unlike the Short Creek camp, they were to remain at this location for slightly more than one year, and they completed considerable projects.

The first report of the camp's work is a camp inspection letter from CCC Special Investigator Hamilton A. Draper dated August 20–21, 1940. He indicated the enrollees were assisting in the dismantling of the DG-44 buildings, cutting posts,[5] constructing two fence lines, hauling gravel, and rehabilitating the Mount Trumbull spike camp (Project #173-06).[6] He noted the latter was limited to thirty men, as the camp water supply, White Springs, was supplying only six hundred gallons per day.[7] The first BLM JDR on record for this camp is 010026 for the Jackson-Heaton Segregation Fence (Project #173-07), with work starting September 4, 1940, and finishing April 18, 1941. This 7.35-mile-long fence line was estimated at 2,000 man days and 1,650 posts.

In mid-September, Draper spent three days inspecting the camp and noted the latter fence project had twenty-six men working on it. He noted the Brooksby–Hacks Canyon Fence (Project #173-03) had twenty-three men working it, with 2.75 miles of "very good quality" completed of its total of 3.8 miles. It was started on August 13 and finished on November 8 and took 1,388 man days (BLMSTG JDR 010011). Also in August, enrollees had begun the Antelope Camp Fence (Project #173-10).[8] Draper said the camp was doing road construction as well as road repair near Fredonia. He reported the camp had "faithfully carried out" its education and safety program. The Mount Trumbull spike camp had twenty-four men erecting a recreation hall and cutting posts.[9] On September 30, the camp had a total of only 120 enrollees.

The isolation of the camp was no doubt responsible for a very popular company canteen. During September, the canteen grossed the astounding sum of $1,166 and was featured in the CCC national newspaper *Happy Days*.[10]

In mid-October, CCC Special Inspector E. W. Samuell evaluated the camp for three days and reported the camp was waiting for a large number of new enrollees. The Mount Trumbull spike camp continued post cutting, while the main camp was said to have nearly completed the Pipe Spring–Bull Rush Truck Trail (Project #173-12), using double shifts.[11] Beginning October 18, and lasting nearly a year, the camp began work on the Fredonia Moccasin Road No. 1 (Project #173-13). This project appears to have been substantial.[12] On October 31, the Army reported the camp at 218 enrollees (all but 1 from Texas).

During November and December, a small side camp of Company 1814 was set up in Grand Canyon National Monument (the present-day Toroweap area of Grand Canyon National Park). Under a cooperative agreement with Grand Canyon, the small side camp was set up, supervised by a Grand Canyon ranger. The enrollees assisted in the opening of the new ranger station—painting, digging a root cellar, and doing road maintenance. They returned to Antelope Valley on December 18, with a comment from the Grand Canyon National Park superintendent about "six high caliber boys who did a lot of work and did it well."[13]   On November 12, the 1.5-mile-long Hack Canyon–Jensen Segregation Fence (Project #173-05) was begun and ultimately took 521 man days (BLMSTG JDR 010018).

Draper again inspected November 19–20 and reported the camp's educational program as very good and its safety record as one of the best. He noted that the Mount Trumbull spike camp had already cut one thousand posts and six thousand stays. The Jackson-Heaton Segregation Fence had 1.8 miles completed, and work continued on the Pipe Spring–Bull Rush Truck Trail. They were also working on the Pipe Spring–Short Creek Road, having completed 2 miles on the west end of the road, with nine culverts installed in the first mile. He discussed with the Indian Service the construction of two tile bridges.[14]

On November 22, the camp began the Antelope Valley Fence Maintenance Project (#173-21), which would continue until March 28.[15] Camp strength at the end of November was 213 men, but dropped to 147 at year's end. On December 9, work began on the 3/8-mile-long Jackson–Hacks Canyon Segregation Fence No. 2 (BLMSTG JDR 010043, Project #173-11), ultimately taking 119 man days when completed on January 14, 1941. On December 10, the camp was inspected for two days, and the inspection letter noted the Hack Canyon–Jensen Segregation Fence was completed and called it "a very nice project." Twenty men were working the cooperative bridge projects, driving piling at Two Mile (Project #173-25) and Sand Wash. Men were working the Fredonia–Pipe Valley Road, including the installation of one 12′ cedar bridge. The Jackson-Heaton Segregation Fence had 1.5 miles completed. The Mount Trumbull spike camp was cutting posts and had begun the Mount Trumbull Division Fence. However, work was halted there, as Foreman Kelly and eighteen enrollees were stricken with the flu.[16]

1941

On January 9, the camp started a large fence project, the 4-mile-long Elmer Jackson Division Fence (Project #173-26, BLMSTG JDR 010105), which ultimately took 1,674 man days when completed on May 9. On January 21, Special Inspector Samuell inspected the camp for two days and noted that many men were sick with the flu. He reported that the weather had curtailed some of the normal projects, so enrollees had done a great deal of vehicle work. He said the pipeline on the east side of the Buckskin Mountains was not running due to snow. Two crews under Engineer Pratt of the Indian Service were working west of Sand Wash doing road construction, including installing culverts (Project #173-24).[17]

During March, the camp began the Pipe Springs Cattle Guard (Project #173-19) and the Kaibab Cattle Guard (Project 173-20).[18] Also in March, the camp worked on the Monument Bridge (Project #173-28) and the Foot Hill Bridge (Project #173-29).[19] In April, the camp again aided Grand Canyon National Park in the Toroweap area by setting up a six-man side camp that was hauling supplies down to a team of geologists on the Colorado River. Few other details are known of this special work.[20] Camp strength stayed near 200 men early in the year, but then dropped to 156 at the end of May.

May was a very busy month. The 5.1-mile-long Esplin–Mount Trumbull Division Fence (Project #173-23, BLM-STG JDR 010094) was started officially on May 5 and ultimately required 1,659 man days when completed on August 8. It was originally estimated to require 1,210 posts, 100 pounds of powder, and 60 detonators.[21] On May 5, the 6.8-mile-long Findlay-Brooksby-Heaton Segregation Fence (also called the Head of Hack Boundary Fence) was estimated at 2,630 man days. It was estimated to require 1,900 cedar line posts, 5,700 cedar stays, and 200 pounds of powder in addition to wire and a large amount of gasoline (Project #173-30, BLMSTG JDR 010117). Its completion date was uncertain. Work on the Antelope Camp Cattle Guard (Project #173-09) was done May 7–16.[22] On May 19, the 4-mile-long Charles Heaton and Sons Fence was begun. It was completed on July 31, requiring 1,452 man days (Project #173-31, BLMSTG JDR 010122).

Special Investigator Bowen filed a detailed report on May 14 about the camp. He reported the work completed since the camp's beginning included one building, four bridges, 17.9 miles of fencing, 26 miles of fence maintenance, 8.5 miles of road construction, 227 miles of road maintenance, 14,000 cedar posts, and 23,000 cedar stays, as well as re-seeding, stock reservoirs, and cattle guards. "The enrollees are farm type boys; very satisfactory," he reported. He said morale was very good. He noted the camp commander, George L. Furedy, had substantial CCC experience. He reported that winter weather or the rainy season isolated the camp completely, resulting in meat not being delivered for meals and over 3,550 man days lost to work in just four months! He recommended that the camp only be occupied in the summer. However, Bowen was not at the camp for a regular inspection.

About 1:00 a.m. on the morning of May 10, an Army truck loaded with thirty or so enrollees returning from a dance in Kanab overturned, injuring as many as twenty-five.[23] Bowen, at Grand Canyon at the time, revised his schedule to investigate. Army Sub-district Commander Brown was also on scene. At first, Bowen said there was a concern there would be more than one fatality. A total of sixteen enrollees were hospitalized in Kanab. After talking with the doctors and men, he reported all were expected to survive. Upon investigating, he found that the regular truck driver was intoxicated when it was time to return to camp. An enrollee, who did not have a license, although he was eligible for one, and who admitted to having one drink of wine, was designated to drive. After talking with all the enrollees, the driver, the doctor, and the camp staff, Bowen reported that "the enrollees were pretty well liquored up." Apparently, they obtained liquor "through a Utah resident." Bowen visited the accident site about four miles from camp, where there was a very sharp curve with a 20 mph speed limit. "It is my opinion that excessive speed was the cause of the accident."[24] The regular driver who was too intoxicated to drive was discharged. All the enrollees recovered. In his report, Bowen also noted that Sub-district Commander Brown had noted deficiencies in mess and lunches. This subject would come up again in the near future.

It is not clear when all the changes in camp staff occurred, but by June 10, the commanding officer and subaltern were transferred out, and all of the mess staff, numbering four, was new. In late May, Jim Currie, the father of one of the G-173 enrollees, wrote his congressman, Gene Worley, that the camp was serving moldy bread and meat with worms. Worley wrote to CCC Director James McEntee on May 24, who in turn had Assistant to the CCC Director Charles H. Kenlan investigate. On May 31, Kenlan responded to Worley that the recent inspection by the Army had noted the deficiencies and that immediate corrections had been assured by the commander.

On June 10, Currie wrote Congressman Worley that his son had returned home from camp "because of changes in attitude toward him in camp." (The implication was that once it was learned who the enrollee was who complained about the food he was retaliated against.) Kenlan immediately sent a telegram to Bowen, who returned to G-173. Bowen talked with forty enrollees in groups and individually. He examined some half-dozen lunches and found them "very satisfactory." Bowen stated the camp was very clean, he did not get a single complaint, and morale was greatly improved. The new commander was "doing a splendid job." Now, Bowen tried to find out why enrollee Currie had left so abruptly. In talking with other enrollees who claimed to know Currie quite well, three said Currie confided he had gotten a girl back home in trouble and his father was trying to get him an honorable discharge.

However, as Currie had left without permission, he was given a dishonorable discharge. On June 24, Kenlan wrote Congressman Worley that the camp had a new commander, and it appeared that enrollee Currie's leaving camp suddenly was not related to retaliation, but to "clandestine girl relations."[25]

During June, the enrollees performed maintenance at the Sunset Reservoir (Project #173-22) and did maintenance on the Antelope Valley Truck Trail (Project #173-32).[26] By the end of June, camp strength had dropped to 88, then rose to 169 on July 31, and then dropped to 161 on August 30 (almost all from Texas). During July, work included the Mount Trumbull Post Cutting No. 2 (Project #173-36) and the Nixon Fire No. 2 (Project #173-42).[27]

On July 30, the camp underwent a two-day inspection, and the inspection letter stated there were a number of problems with the water supply, which was an Army responsibility. The camp was said to be clean and orderly. The Esplin–Mount Trumbull Division Fence had thirty men working, and even though the work was slower than expected, it was "a nice job." The Boundary Bridge (June 30 to July 25) on the west side of the Indian reservation was said to be nearly complete (Project #173-33).[28] The Charles Heaton and Sons Fence was to be completed in a few days. That crew was then to move to the 3.5-mile-long Brooksby–Elmer Jackson Division Fence (BLMSTG JDR 010159), which ultimately took 898 man days to complete on September 12. Men were working on the Jensen–Hack Canyon Cattle Guard (Project #173-37). The inspection letter noted the Brooksby-Findley-Heaton Fence was delayed due to the lack of enrollees. Sunset Tank maintenance had been stopped so the "Cat" could begin Navajo Trail construction. Also in September, enrollees hauled posts for the Mount Trumbull Post Cutting (Project #173-36).[29] On September 30, the enrollee count was 141, dropping to 92 on October 31.

In October, the local newspaper announced the camp was to be closed for the season and then re-occupied in May of the following year, with enrollees transferring to Arlington, Arizona.[30] Five projects that were logged in at St. George, including two cattle guards, one reseeding project, and three projects, were left unfinished.[31] The camp was officially abandoned on November 6, 1941.[32]

Unless noted otherwise, any reference to the number of enrollees in a company, the location of the company, or company supervisors are from U.S. War Department, Location and Strength of CCC Companies, 1933–1942, NARAMD RG 35 530/65/22/04/05.

1. McKoy, *Culture at a Crossroads*, 1034.
2. Ibid., 1029.
3. BLMSTG-*RIRB*.
4. McKoy, *Culture at a Crossroads*, 1032–1033.
5. Sunshine Post Cutting, Project #173-04, BLMSTG-*RIBR*.
6. BLMSTG-*RIBR*.
7. U.S. BLM, Camp Inspection Reports, 1938–1942, NARACO RG49 Entry 20 Box 84.
8. BLMSTG-*RIBR*.
9. U.S. BLM, Camp Inspection Reports, 1938–1942, NARACO RG49 Entry 20 Box 84.
10. October 26, 1940, page 8. With the junior enrollees receiving $5.00 per month spending money and the month ending with only 120 enrollees, one wonders who the other canteen customers were.
11. U.S. BLM, Camp Inspection Reports, 1938–1942, NARACO RG49 Entry 20 Box 84.
12. BLMSTG-*RIBR*. Project dollars totaled $5,077.79, the largest in this record book.
13. Audretsch, *Shaping the Park and Saving the Boys*, 58.
14. U.S. BLM, Camp Inspection Reports, 1938–1942, NARACO RG49 Entry 20 Box 84.
15. BLMSTG-*RIBR*.
16. U.S. BLM, Camp Inspection Reports, 1938–1942, NARACO RG49 Entry 20 Box 84.
17. Ibid.
18. BLMSTG-*RIBR*.
19. Ibid.
20. Audretsch, *Shaping the Park and Saving the Boys*, 58.
21. A letter in this project's JDR file indicates it was started on April 28. The reference to work beginning in the December 10 camp inspection report may indicate enrollees were hauling posts and stays to the fence location, with actual fence construction beginning later.
22. BLMSTG-*RIBR*.
23. "Twenty-five CCC Enrollees Injured in Accident near Pipe Springs Camp—Nine Youths Still in Kanab Hospital with Various Injuries," *Kane County Standard*, May 15, 1941, 1.
24. Bowen to Kenlan, 13 May 1941; camp inspection report dated May 13, 1941, U.S. CCC, Camp Inspection Reports, NARAMD RG 35/530/65/23/04 Entry 115 (PI #11) Box 10.
25. Worley to McEntee, 24 May 1941; Bowen to Kenlan, 20 June 1941; and Kenlan to Worley, 24 June 1941, U.S. CCC, Camp Inspection Reports, NARAMD RG 35/530/65/23/04 Entry 115 (PI #11) Box 10.
26. BLMSTG-*RIBR*.
27. Ibid.
28. Ibid.
29. Ibid.
30. "Fredonia and Pipe Springs Camps Scheduled for Closing on Nov. 1st," *Kane County Standard*, October 23, 1941, 1.
31. Jensen–Hack Canyon and Elmer Jackson Cattle Guards, Antelope Valley Reseeding Project, Elmer Jackson Driveway Fence, Carrol-Esplin Segregation Fence, and Yellowstone-Heaton Division Fence (BLMSTG-*RIBR*).
32. "Civilian Conservation Corps Eighth Corps Area, Status Record of CCC Camps Authorized Since Inception of the Program up to … December 31, 1941 … Compiled by Office of Liaison Officer, CCC Fort Sam Houston…," NARACO BLM CCC Directories RG 49 Entry 33, 34 Box 132. When a camp was abandoned and expected to be re-occupied, Army practice was to assign a caretaker to guard the property.

CHAPTER 19

Fredonia (G-170)

COMPANY 847 OFFICIALLY OCCUPIED THE Fredonia site on August 10, 1940, apparently coming directly from G-109 at Arlington, Arizona. Their staff consisted of two Army officers, an educational advisor, and a contract physician. Palmer Schiele was their first project superintendent. Company 847 had a varied career, having worked previously at Gillette, Wyoming; Alpine and Yuma, Arizona; and Grand Canyon's South Rim.[1] There appears to be no surviving runs of the Kanab, Utah, *Kane County Standard* for 1940, so details of their camp construction and arrival are unknown.

The first camp inspection was August 21–22 by CCC Inspector Hamilton Draper. He noted that there were two crews of fifteen enrollees graveling the camp area and finishing the buildings. Thirty enrollees were in the Buckskin Mountains cutting posts and stays (Project #170-03). "General conditions in this camp are very good."[2] Work had already started on the 5.2-mile-long Chatterly-Findlay-Brooksby Segregation Fence (Project #170-05, BLMSTG JDR 010016), where Draper noted satisfactory progress. It was begun on August 14 and completed on September 30 in 1,057 man days. The 7.1-mile-long Hatch-Jensen Segregation Fence (Project #170-06, BLMSTG JDR 010022) was started on August 27 and completed on November 12 in 1,362 man days. On August 31, camp strength stood at 180 enrollees (almost evenly divided between those from Arizona and Texas).

Draper returned to inspect the camp for three days on September 16 and wrote that the camp had not progressed as fast as it should have in the new location. He also found a number of safety violations. The Chatterly-Findlay-Brooksby Segregation Fence was noted as 90% complete and "very good." He suggested putting more men to work cutting fence posts in the Buckskin Mountains to ensure there would be enough posts for winter work. Preliminary work was noted at the gravel pit for the upcoming surfacing of the Fredonia-Moccasin Road.[3]

In September, three new fence projects were started. The 2.4-mile-long Judd-Farnsworth-Brown Division Fence (Project #170-08, BLMSTG JDR 010030) was begun September 23 and finished November 29. This four-wire fence was completed in 361 man days. The same day, work began on the Farnsworth-Brown-Bunting Division Fence (Project #170-09, BLMSTG JDR 010034). The 1.5-mile-long fence was finished on December 10 in 279 man days. On September 24, work started on the 1.25-mile-long Rider Driveway Fence (Project #170-11, BLMSTG JDR 010041). It was completed on November 11 in 298 man days. Other projects begun in September included work on the Fredonia–Kaibab Indian Reservation Road (Project #170-07.)[4] Camp strength in September was only 82 enrollees, but increased to 200 on October 31 (nearly three-quarters of the enrollees were from Texas and the rest were from Arizona).

Inspector E. W. Samuell visited the camp twice in October and noted the water system was washed out and the camp was now hauling water. He noted engineer Earl Patterson's field and safety work were not satisfactory. Work projects included the Fredonia–Pipe Springs Road, including rock work and culverts and stub cutting for a power line.[5] The Two Mile spike camp (Project #170-04) was nearly ready.[6] On October 7, enrollees began periodic Kaibab Unit Fence Maintenance (Project #170-12), which would continue until March 31, 1941.[7]

Draper inspected for two days beginning November 27. He noted the ongoing fence projects and said that two tractors and eight men were doing good work reconstructing the Fredonia–Pipe Springs Road. The Two Mile spike camp was said to be clean and in good condition.[8] Thirty enrollees were in the Buckskin Mountains cutting posts, and six men were in camp making camp improvements. Six other men were in camp building cattle guard frames. Engineer Patterson was leading a crew installing two cattle guards southeast of Fredonia. The safety and educational programs were improving. Draper did recommend to the camp superintendent to have more projects planned and ready for future work.[9]

The camp started two new projects in December: the 3.2-mile-long Curtis-Houserock Driveway Fence (Project #170-23, BLMSTG JDR 010092) and the 8.5-mile-long Pratt Sheep Segregation Fence (Project #170-18, BLMSTG JDR 010075). The former was begun on December 2 and completed on February 20, 1941, in 511 man days. The latter started on December 5 and finished on April 15, 1941, in 1,853 man days. Draper returned to inspect the camp for two days on December 12 and noted the 1.2-mile-long Fredonia Power Line had just been completed. Enrollees were working on the Fredonia–Pipe Springs Road, building fences and cutting posts. The Two Mile spike camp was building the Curtis-Houserock Driveway Fence.[10] At year's end, camp strength was 147 enrollees (with most calling Texas their home).

1941

We have only a partial picture of the camp work in 1941, as only one camp inspection report survives and the holdings for the Kanab newspaper are incomplete. Nevertheless, like the other Arizona Strip Division of Grazing camps, they completed a great deal of long-lasting, valuable work. Although the camp was to be short-lived, closing down in November, they completed at least thirteen new projects before they left.

On January 31, the camp had 196 enrollees (22 from Arizona and the rest from Texas). On February 11, two projects were started: the Fredonia-Buckskin Cattle Guard No. 1 (Project #170-17, BLMSTG JDR 010069) and the Pratt Class 2 Cattle Division Fence (Project #170-30, BLMSTG JDR 010116). The 15′-wide cattle guard was completed in 17 days and took 152 man days. The 6-mile-long fence was completed on May 8 and required 1,023 man days. Records of this project indicate that 75% of the post holes were drilled and blasted in solid rock and 300 pounds of dynamite were required.

In February, the Kanab newspaper reported on illiteracy in the CCC in what appears to be a national story. It stated that early in the CCC program 3% of the enrollees were illiterate and, over seven years, eighty thousand enrollees were taught basic reading and writing. The goal was to have the new readers "read a newspaper and write a letter in about three months."[11]

On February 15, work was started on the Brooksby Stock Driveway Fence (Project #170-27, BLMSTG JDR 010109). This .9-mile-long fence was completed on April 15 and required 100 man days. The Fredonia Shipping Corrals (Project #170-26) were begun February 15 and completed on November 1, 1941 and took 130 man days.[12] In mid-February, enrollees constructed a horse trailer (Project #170-25).[13] At the end of February, Company 847 had 192 enrollees (most from Texas). During March, the Fredonia-Buckskin Cattle Guard No. 2 (Project #170-22, BLMSTG JDR 010089) was completed.

Beginning April 1, and lasting through the end of September, enrollees did truck trail maintenance in both the Kanab and House Rock Units (Project #170-33).[14] On April 10, work started on the Two Mile Division Fence (Project #170-24, BLMSTG JDR 010096). This 8.8-mile long fence was finished on August 25, using 2,721 man days, and it appears the Two Mile spike camp did the work. From April until July, the camp was listed as doing "Well Drill Transportation" (Project #170-35). No other information was provided.[15] At the end of April, the camp had 151 enrollees (nearly all from Texas).

On May 6, the Hatch Free Use Fence (Project #170-37, BLMSTG JDR 010146) was started. Under 1 mile long, it required 345 man days to complete. Two days later, the Kanab newspaper announced that G-170 was holding an open house the following day with talks and dinner.[16] For four days beginning May 9, the camp worked on, and finished, the .55-mile-long Judd-Mace Division Fence No. 2.[17] On May 12, enrollees began work on the 3.75-mile-long Muggins Flat Division Fence (Project #170-39, BLMSTG JDR 010151). This job took 856 man days and was finished on June 11.

The same day the Muggins Fence was started, Inspector M. J. Bowen visited camp and filed an impressive report. Since the camp opened, he said the completed work included 35 miles of fence construction, 1.25 miles of fence maintenance, 1.25 miles of telephone line, 8 miles of truck trail construction, 132 miles of truck trail maintenance, and 20,000 cedar posts cut. In addition to the projects noted in this chapter, he reported the camp had constructed reservoirs and concrete watering troughs. (No records were found for these projects.) He said the water supply was not reliable, with water hauling taking place on seventeen days since the camp opened. He mentioned that the Catholic priest from Cedar City was visiting camp once a month. Bowen was quite positive in this report, saying morale was "very satisfactory." He singled out the commanding officer, 1st Lt. Eino M. Jacobson, and the subaltern, Roy J. Autry (a civilian coming up through the technical services), as "doing very good." He asserted the camp was enabling enrollees to gain useful employment after CCC life: "Many enrollees have secured jobs as mechanics, carpenters, truck drivers, and clerks from the [camp] education and experience."[18]

On May 20, the camp began assisting with the Spence Two Mile Fence (Project #170-49, BLMSTG JDR 010042). The actual fence work was done by a contractor, with the CCC hauling materials, for a total of 23 man days. On May 31, Company 847 had 157 enrollees (nearly all from Texas).

On June 12, work began on the Jensen Free Use Division Fence (Project #170-19, BLMSTG JDR 010079). This 2.75-mile-long fence was completed on June 23, using 356 man days. The .5-mile-long Bunting Division Fence (Project #170-44, BLMSTG JDR 010171) was started on June 25, took only one day, and used 92 man days. From July through October, fence post cutting continued (Project #170-42).[19] During June and July, company strength varied from 105 on June 30 to 156 on July 31. Work commenced on the Baker–Badger Creek Division Fence (Project #170-43, BLMSTG JDR 010166) on August 27 and ceased on September 21, taking 382 man days. On August 31, camp strength was 165 enrollees.

The Two Mile spike camp apparently did the work on the 6.1-mile-long Spence Division Fence (Project #170-51, BLMSTG JDR 010193), starting on September 19 and finishing on October 20 in 648 man days. Camp strength on September 30 was 153 enrollees. House Rock Reseeding began September 24 and was completed October 22 (Project #170-47).[20] DG-170 began the Pigeon Tank Corral (Project #170-53, BLMSTG JDR 010200), starting on October 3 and finishing on October 7 in 108 man days. This woven wire corral measured 300 x 248'. On October 10, work started on the 2,560-acre Jensen Allotment Reseeding, which was listed as completed November 5.[21]

On October 23, the local newspaper announced the closing of the Fredonia camp. It was to be effective November 1, with the remaining enrollees to go to Arlington, Arizona. The camp was said to re-open on May 1.[22] Camp G-170 was listed as officially abandoned on November 13, 1941.[23] Although it was anticipated the CCC would return, the outbreak of World War II would spell the end of the CCC.

Unless noted otherwise, any reference to the number of enrollees in a company, the location of the company, or company supervisors are from U.S. War Department, Location and Strength of CCC Companies, 1933–1942, NARAMD RG 35 530/65/22/04/05.

1. Their accomplishments at Grand Canyon were considerable. See Audretsch, *Shaping the Park and Saving the Boys*, 11–20.
2. U.S. BLM, Camp Inspection Reports, 1938–1942, NARACO RG49 Entry 20 Box 86.
3. Ibid. Project #170-10. According to BLMSTG-*RIRB*, this was begun on September 25, 1940, and completed on August 17, 1941.
4. BLMSTG-*RIRB*.
5. Fredonia Power & Telephone Line (Project #170-13), BLMSTG-*RIRB*.
6. U.S. BLM, Camp Inspection Reports, 1938–1942, NARACO RG49 Entry 20 Box 86.
7. BLMSTG-*RIRB*.
8. Work there included post cutting (Project #170-16) per BLMSTG-*RIRB*.
9. U.S. BLM, Camp Inspection Reports, 1938–1942, NARACO RG49 Entry 20 Box 86.
10. Ibid.
11. "CCC Establishes School for Uneducated Campers," *Kane County Standard*, February 27, 1940, 3.
12. BLMSTG-*RIRB*. Shipping corrals were also listed as a House Rock project (#170-20) in the *RIBR*, but with no starting and ending dates, so their existence is uncertain.
13. BLMSTG-*RIRB*.
14. Ibid.
15. Ibid.
16. "Fredonia CCC Camp Holds Open House Tomorrow Afternoon," *Kane County Standard*, May 8, 1941, 1.
17. BLMSTG-*RIRB*.
18. U.S. CCC, Camp Inspection Reports, NARAMD RG 35/530/65/23/04 Entry 115 PI #11 Box 10.
19. BLMSTG-*RIRB*.
20. Ibid.
21. Ibid.
22. "Fredonia and Pipe Springs Camps Scheduled for Closing on Nov. 1st," *Kane County Standard*, October 23, 1941, 1. The November 30 Army location and strength report shows Company 847 at G-109, Arlington, effective November 14.
23. U.S. BLM (Grazing Service), CCC, Camp Histories, 1933–45, NARACO RG 49 Entry 5 Box 22.

CHAPTER 20

The End of the CCC in Arizona

THE CCC WAS THE MOST popular New Deal program. However, when the United States entered World War II in 1941, any program not deemed essential to the war effort was evaluated. President Franklin D. Roosevelt wanted to preserve the CCC. Congress debated in April and May 1942, and a final vote occurred in June. The vote was close, but the CCC was ordered to disband on July 1, 1942.[1] Even before the congressional debates, the number of Arizona CCC camps was decreasing dramatically. Between May 31, 1941, and May 31, 1942, the number of Arizona camps dropped from twenty-seven to just five. Two of the final camps were in the area covered by this study: Company 822 (F-75, Coconino National Forest, Pivot Rock) and Company 1826V (F-19, Prescott National Forest, Fairgrounds).

During the life of the CCC, Arizona hosted ninety-eight individual companies. On December 31, 1935, Arizona reached its highest number of camps with fifty-five. The heyday time for Arizona was from January 31, 1935, to December 31, 1937, when the state averaged forty-two camps.[2] Nearly all of the companies were juniors, with the exception of three veterans' companies and one "colored" company. The latter, Company 1871C, located at Fort Huachuca, was made up of mostly Texas enrollees and was listed on only one report. Its existence in Arizona was short-lived due to economy moves. Almost all companies serving in Arizona were from the 8th Corps, with the exception of eight 5th Corps companies (Ohio, West Virginia, Indiana, and Kentucky), nine 3rd Corps companies (Pennsylvania, Maryland, Virginia, and the District of Columbia), and one 7th Corps company (Kansas, Arkansas, Iowa, Nebraska, North Dakota, South Dakota, Minnesota, and Missouri). Significant movement of enrollees from the eastern to western United States did not begin until late 1935.

Looking at the number of CCC camps by individual enrollment period reveals that about 42% of the Arizona camps were National Forest camps. National Park Service and state park camps were 25%, Division of Grazing camps were about 17%, Soil Conservation Service camps were 12%, and Bureau of Reclamation camps were 4%. There were three Fish and Wildlife Service camps and one military camp reporting.[3]

The total number of Arizona men serving in the CCC in Arizona from April 1933 to June 30, 1942, was 41,362. Of this total, 17,407 were juniors and veterans. Indians and Territorials in Arizona totaled 19,520, and the number of personnel in this category was exceeded only by Oklahoma.[4] When men who served from other states are added, a total of 52,905 men served in Arizona.

The work finished on a statewide level is staggering. For the fiscal year ending June 30, 1936, 1,512 miles of telephone line were strung; 3,658 miles of roads and trails were built; 1,125 miles of fence were constructed; 1,758,549 acres were controlled for rodents; 700 useless range stock were eliminated; 4 fire lookout towers were constructed; 237,907 acres were controlled for erosion; 270 buildings were constructed; 10,153 man days were spent fighting forest fires; 20,330 man days were spent in emergency work such as searching for missing persons; and 3,140 man days were spent in educational and contact station work in Arizona.[5] By the end of the CCC in 1942, total Arizona CCC work included 3,559 miles of telephone lines; 7,071 miles of roads and trails; 7,045 miles of fence; 45 lookout towers; 1,768 buildings; 51,249 man days spent fighting forest fires; 7,451,000 trees planted; 184,239 predatory animals eliminated; 48,186 man days spent in emergency work such as searching for missing persons; and 33,190 man days spent in educational and contact station work.[6]

This nine-year period of intense activities occurred throughout public lands across Arizona. These undertakings halted economic collapse. They saved many young men from lives as hobos and drifters; nay, some were saved from a life of crime. By sending home $25 of their pay each month, many of their families were saved from hunger and homelessness. The CCC, and the other New Deal programs, saved the state's farming, ranching, and timber industries, according to historian Peter MacMillan Booth. The CCC spurred the expansion of the state's service industries, such as tourism, he says. And finally, the state's aging bureaucracies were modernized to work with the expanding post–World War II federal bureaucracy.[7]

The boys built trails and bridges,

Telephone lines and fire breaks,

They fought forest fires on a thousand fronts,

They built cabins, fire towers,

Built up public campgrounds and parks,

Piped in pure water, built dams and dykes,

They terraced eroded farms and planted young trees in the gullies,

Honorable Discharge
from the
Civilian Conservation Corps

TO ALL WHOM IT MAY CONCERN:

This is to Certify That* CLIFTON V. BOWNDS   CC8-3838901

a member of the CIVILIAN CONSERVATION CORPS, who was enrolled

April 17, 1941 (Date) at San Antonio, Texas, is hereby

HONORABLY DISCHARGED therefrom, by reason of**

TO ACCEPT EMPLOYMENT THAT WILL BETTER HIS CONDITION...

Said Clifton V. Bownds was born in San Antonio in the State of Texas. When enrolled he was nineteen years of age and by occupation a Laborer. He had Brown eyes, Brown hair, Ruddy complexion, and was Five feet eight inches in height. His color was White.

Co. 3838 Camp NP-12-A
Given under my hand at Flagstaff, Arizona, this sixth day of September, one thousand nine hundred and forty-one.

Mr. Clifton Bownds
420 W. 8th St.
Liberal, KS 67901-2604

(Name) (Title)
WALLACE W. CAYWOOD, CCC Subaltern
Commanding Co. 3838, CCC

* Insert name, as "John J. Doe."
** Give reason for discharge.

C. C. C. Form No. 2
April 5, 1937

Figure 55. Honorable Discharge from Civilian Conservation Corps, Clifton V. Bownds, 1941. Courtesy Kaibab National Forest.

They built ponds and brought back water to waterfowl marshes,
    Counted the deer, and planted deer feed,
    Restored marshes for mallards and Canada honkers.
    They climbed trees for nuts and seed,
    They cleared land for forest nurseries,
    Planted the forest seed they collected,
    Watered and weeded the young seedlings,
    They set out young trees by hundreds of millions
    On bare lands that knew no shade.
    All working for America.
    —by John D. Guthrie, *What They Did* [8]

---

1. For a more detailed account of the debate, see Audretsch, *Shaping the Park and Saving the Boys,* 97–98.
2. U.S. War Department, Location and Strength of CCC Companies, 1933–1942, NARAMD RG 35 530/65/22/04/05.
3. U.S. War Department, Camp Directories, 1933–1942, Records of the CCC, NARAMD RG 35/530/65/11/1.
4. U.S. Federal Security Agency, *Final Report of the Director of the Civilian Conservation Corps,* 108.
5. U.S. CCC, *Annual Report of the Director of Emergency Conservation Work Fiscal Year Ending June 30, 1936.*
6. U.S. Federal Security Agency, CCC, "A Brief Summary of Certain Phases of the CCC Program Arizona April, 1933 to June 30, 1942," NARAMD RG 35 PI-11 Entry 67, Pictographs, 1933–1942, Box 1, Folder: Pictographs–United States to Wyoming.
7. Booth, *Civilian Conservation Corps in Arizona,* chapter 6, 29–35.
8. Excerpted from Guthrie, *Saga of the CCC,* 25.

APPENDIX 1

CCC Enrollment Periods

CCC Period	Dates
1	April 5, 1933 to Sept. 30, 1933
2	Oct. 1, 1933 to Mar. 31, 1934
3	Apr. 1, 1934 to Sept. 30, 1934
4	Oct. 1, 1934 to Mar. 31, 1935
5	Apr. 1, 1935 to Sept. 30, 1935
6	Oct. 1, 1935 to Mar. 31, 1936
7	Apr. 1, 1936 to Sept. 30, 1936
8	Oct. 1, 1936 to Mar. 31, 1937
9	Apr. 1, 1937 to Sept. 30, 1937
10	Oct. 1, 1937 to Mar. 31, 1938
11	Apr. 1, 1938 to Sept. 30, 1938
12	Oct. 1, 1938 to Mar. 31, 1939
13	Apr. 1, 1939 to Sept. 30, 1939
14	Oct. 1, 1939 to Mar. 31, 1940
15	Apr. 1, 1940 to Sept. 30, 1940
16	Oct. 1, 1940 to Mar. 31, 1941
17	Apr. 1, 1941 to Sept. 30, 1941
18	Oct. 1, 1941 to Mar. 31, 1942
19	Apr. 1, 1942 to June 30, 1942

APPENDIX 2

List of CCC Camps in Study Area

(Locations, when listed, from War Department *Location and Strength* reports)

BR-17 Parker Dam (5.4 miles north of Topock)
    11-6-35   1849   1-12-36

BR-18 Upper Parker Dam (5.4 miles north of Topock)
    11-6-35   2833   4-20-36

DG-8 Yava (7.3 miles northeast of Hillside)
    10-24-35   2541   1-5-36
    1-13-36   1849   5-2-37

DG-44 Pipe Spring
    10-30-35   2557   10-5-39

DG-45 St. George, UT
    10-27-35   2558   8-21-39

DG-46 Round Valley (26.8 miles southeast of Kingman)
    8-21-35   2865   6-30-38?
    7-12-38   340   6-5-39

DG-47 Congress Junction (Date Creek, 16 miles north of Congress Junction)
    8-17-35   2854   5-5-36
    10-16-36   852   5-2-37

DG-133, G-133 Kingman (4.3 miles southwest of Kingman)
    6-5-39   340   6-25-41?
    6-25-41   4812   5-13-42

F-5 Schultz Pass (5 miles north of Flagstaff)
    5-28-33   821   11-2-33
    5-1-34   821   10-29-34
    5-19-35   821   11-7-35
    5-1-36   821   10-19-36
    5-15-37   821   10-16-37
    5-22-38   821   6-29-38?
    7-12-38   311   10-22-38
    5-20-39   311   10-28-39

F-6 Double Springs (Mormon Lake, 30 miles south of Flagstaff)
    6-2-33   863   11-1-33
    5-1-34   863   10-29-34
    5-14-35   863   11-1-35
    6-1-36   863   10-16-36

F-9 Wood Springs
    6-3-33   860   11-1-33

F-18 Groom Creek (7 miles southeast of Prescott)
    5-28-33   820   12-1-33
    5-1-34   820   11-5-34
    5-15-35   820   10-22-35

5-16-36	2870	10-29-36
5-16-37	2847	9-30-37
5-22-38?	3320?	10-25-38?

F-19 Thumb Butte (4.5 miles west of Prescott)

7-12-33	1823V	12-1-33
5-1-34	822	10-29-34
5-19-35	822	11-3-35
5-22-37	822	10-31-37

F-19 Fairgrounds (1 mile northwest of Prescott)

5-5-36	835	11-2-36
10-31-37	822	6-24-41
6-28-41	1826V	7-24-42?

F-20 Walnut Creek

5-29-33	822	12-1-33

F-27 Bellemont

5-25-33	851	10-31-33

F-28 Williams (9 miles south of Williams)

5-26-33	848	10-31-33
4-30-34	1826V	10-27-34
5-16-35	1838	8-16-35?
4-30-36	2833	10-22-36
7-23-37	2848?	10-23-37
5-26-38	3346	10-22-38
5-14-39	3348	10-21-39
5-5-40	3348	10-12-40

F-32 Clear Creek, Sedona (27.7 miles northeast of Clarkdale)

11-1-33	860	5-1-34
11-5-34	860	5-15-35
11-7-35	821	5-1-36
10-19-36	821	5-15-37
10-16-37	821	5-22-38
10-22-38	311	5-20-39
10-28-39	311	6-30-40
11-30-40	311	4-16-41
1-4-42	822	5-21-42

F-33 Mayer (.5 miles south of Mayer)

12-1-33	822	5-1-34
10-29-34	822	5-19-35
11-3-35	822	5-22-37
10-25-38	3320	6-30-39
11-11-39	3320	6-29-40
11-15-40	3320	6-21-41

F-35 Clarkdale, Clear Creek (35 miles southeast of Clarkdale)

11-2-33	821	5-1-34
10-29-34	821	5-19-35
10-16-37	863	5-28-38
10-22-38	863	5-27-39
10-28-39	863	5-11-40
11-17-40	863	5-17-41

F-39 Verde No. 1 (14 miles southeast of Clarkdale)

12-1-33	820	5-1-34
11-5-34	820	5-15-35
7-24-37	1840	5-22-38

F-51 Beaver Creek (30 miles east of Clarkdale)

11-1-33	863	5-1-34
10-29-34	863	5-14-35
11-1-35	863	6-1-36
10-16-36	863	5-19-37

F-62 Lynx Creek (12.9 miles southeast of Prescott)

5-1-34	860	11-5-34
5-19-35	860	10-21-35
5-16-36	2855	10-29-36
5-16-37	2861	10-23-37

F-75   Pivot Rock (75 miles south of Flagstaff)

5-19-37	863	10-16-37
5-28-38	863	10-22-38
5-27-39	863	11-28-39
5-11-40	863	11-1-40
5-17-41	863	11-1-41
5-21-42	822	7-23-42?

F-79 Walnut Creek (43.6 miles northwest of Prescott)

6-30-39	3320	11-11-39
6-29-40	3320	11-15-40

F-80 Flagstaff (3.5 miles north of Flagstaff)

6-30-40	311	11-30-40
4-16-41	311	6-24-41?
6-24-41	822	1-4-42

FWS-1 Parker Dam

9-14-41	3840	7-42?

G-135 Short Creek

4-16-40	1820	7-1-41

G-170 Fredonia

8-10-40	847	11-13-41

G-173 Antelope Valley

8-10-40	1814	11-6-41

NM-1 Petrified Forest National Monument (19.6 miles southeast of Holbrook)

7-3-34	831	5-6-36?
10-11-36	805	7-30-38?

NM-2 & NP-8 Petrified Forest Monument/National Park (35 miles east of Holbrook)

8-2-38	3342	6-21-41?
6-22-41	1837	3-7-42

NM-5 & NP-12 Flagstaff Area National Monuments (4.5 miles east of Flagstaff)

8-2-38	3345	4-30-41?
5-10-41	3838	3-21-42

SCS-27 John A. Thompson Ranch (22 miles northwest of Prescott)

7-20-40	2863	1-31-41
5-17-41	2863	3-42?

SP-8 & CP-2 Hualapai Mountain Park (20 miles southeast of Kingman)

6-10-34	830	10-26-34
7-1-35	1837	10-20-39
5-19-40	1837	11-3-40

SP-9 Hualapai Mountain Park

7-3-34	874	10-25-34

APPENDIX 3

Camp Newspaper Poems and Song

My Hitch in Hell by B. J. Williams

I am sitting here thinking, of the things I've left behind,
And I would hate to put on paper what is running through my mind.
I've dug a million ditches, I've cleaned ten miles of ground,
A meaner place this side of hell, is waiting to be found.
I've cut a thousand twig blight, I've climbed a thousand trees,
I've done a little of everything, while in the CCC's.

The number of trees I've climbed is hard for me to tell,
But I won't climb trees in Heaven, for I've done my hitch in hell.
I've washed a thousand mess kits, I've peeled a thousand spuds,
I've rolled a hundred bedrolls, I've washed the Captain's duds.
I've been a rear rank soldier, striving to stand at ease,
But all I ever got, is Saturday and Sunday on KP's.

Some boys say, "it's a great life and can't be beaten,"
But they really mean, it's a great life if you don't weaken.
I've washed a million pots for our cooks to stew our beans,
I've done a million washings, I've cleaned the camp latrine.
The other day I went to see the Cap, and he says to me,
 "Well son, I guess I will be forced to give you a great big DD."***
But when the final taps are blown, and I lay aside life cares,
Saint Peter will welcome me, upon the golden stairs.
And when I reach the golden gates, the harps will start to play,
I'll draw a million furloughs, I'll spend them in a day.
And when I enter the golden gates, Saint Peter will loudly say,
"TAKE A FRONT SEAT ROOKIE, 'YOU HAVE DONE YOUR HITCH IN HELL.'" [1]

***Dishonorable Discharge

Camp F-18, Company 2847, *Pine Needle*, July 1937

****

A CCC Prayer

Now I lay me down to sleep
While the CCC's around me creep
May no other CCC take my shoes
Or socks before I wake.
Oh, Lord, protect me in my slumber
And keep my bunk upon it's [sic] number
And let me dream of places,
Pretty shapes and pretty faces.
And in the morning Lord, let us wake
To the joyful smell of a surlein [sic] steak
Cleo (Arkey) Fullen[2]

Camp F-33, Company 822, *Turkey Creek Gobbler*, November 1935

****

Antelope Springs Theme Song
(Dedicated to William Murphy, words by Mrajazynaki & Jordan)

Hey! Boy, clear that line……………
Top away, bring the bottom to ya'…….
Top away, bring the bottom to ya'…….
Hey! Boy, we're going to swing tonight.

Swing that bar, get the shovel moving,
Swing that bar, get the shovel moving,
Hey! Boy, we're going to swing tonight.[3]

Camp G-133, Company 340, *The Cattle Guard News*, April 15, 1940

****

The C.C.C. Prayer
Roosevelt is my shepherd I shall not want
He maketh me lie down on straw mattresses
He leadeth me inside a mess hall
He restoreth to me a job
He leadeth me on the path of Division of Grazing for his country's sake
Yea, though I walk through the prairie grass and cactus I will fear no evil for he asketh it of me
His blankets and O-D uniform they comfort me
He prepareth a shovel and pick before me
In the presence of my commanding officer he anointeth my mind with discipline
My shoes runneth over from marching
Surely bonus and employment shall follow me all the days of the Roosevelt Administration
And I shall dwell in a barrack forever.
Valton "Missouri" Fowler[4]

Camp DG-44, Company 2557, *Pipe Post*, vol. 1, no. 1, December 24, 1935

1. Fiche MN #1682, CRL Newspapers.
2. Fiche MN #0519, CRL Newspapers.
3. Fiche MN #0181, CRL Newspapers.
4. Fiche MN #1423, CRL Newspapers.

Sources

Researching the CCC for Arizona has been a bit like a treasure hunt. There were frequent dead ends, even a few false leads. As the main objects of this monograph were to establish the most basic data—what CCC company was located where and when and what work they did—the most likely places for a bonanza were federal and state records depositories. I quickly learned that the National Parks were the best keepers of records. Close behind were the National Monuments. Division of Grazing (now Bureau of Land Management) was a mixed bag, depending on what appeared to have been saved by the particular regional offices. Forest Service records appear to have been almost totally neglected, both at the local and national levels. At the National Archives at College Park, College Park, Maryland, records for only one national forest in Arizona, one in Colorado, etc., have been retained. In the case of Arizona, about forty boxes of Coconino National Forest records are on file. Records for the other seven national forests appear to have been destroyed.

All was not lost, however, as I realized from my earlier monograph on Grand Canyon National Park that newspapers offered an alternative research source that varied from town to town. As I had already scanned and indexed the Williams and Flagstaff newspapers for 1933 to 1942, I spent nearly a year scanning and indexing the newspapers in Holbrook, Snowflake, Prescott, Ash Fork, and Kingman, Arizona, as well as St. George and Kanab, Utah. The two Phoenix newspapers were dailies at that time and that proved a bit more daunting. The *Arizona Republic* was scanned and indexed for the period March 1933 to May 1937, and the *Phoenix Gazette* was scanned and indexed for March 1933 to January 1934. I had earlier scanned and indexed *Happy Days*, the national CCC daily, for Arizona stories. The newspapers, although never totally thorough, are critical in telling the CCC story in Arizona. If one imagines the CCC story as a jigsaw puzzle, we have been able to find nearly all the edge pieces, and we have many sections of the puzzle nearly complete. However, there are a few significant places where we have no pieces to the puzzle. And we may never have. However, I view my work as a signpost, not a road map. I hope it points the way for others, whether they be high school students or PhD candidates, to those CCC goldfields.

Selected Bibliography

The numerous government reports researched for this book, such as those from the CCC and the National Archives, are generally not included in this bibliography. Full information for the reports can be found in the endnotes throughout the book.

Alter, Jonathan. *The Defining Moment: FDR's Hundred Days and the Triumph of Hope.* New York: Simon & Schuster, 2006.

Altschul, Jeffrey H., and Helen C. Fairley. *Man, Models and Management: An Overview of Archeology of the Arizona Strip and the Management of Its Cultural Resources.* Washington, D.C.: USDA FS & DOI BLM, 1989.

Audretsch, Robert W. "Literacy in the CCC." *CCC Legacy Journal* (September–October 2010): 7.

———. *Shaping the Park and Saving the Boys: The Civilian Conservation at Grand Canyon, 1933–1942.* Indianapolis, IN: Dog Ear Publishing, 2011.

Baker, Robert D., et al. *Timeless Heritage: A History of the Forest Service in the Southwest.* College Station, TX: USDA, 1988.

Baldridge, Kenneth W. *Nine Years of Achievement: The Civilian Conservation Corps in Utah.* Doctoral dissertation, Brigham Young University, Provo, 1971.

Bermingham, Peter. *The New Deal in the Southwest, Arizona and New Mexico.* Tucson: University of Arizona Museum of Art, [1980?].

Booth, Peter MacMillan. *The Civilian Conservation Corps in Arizona, 1933–1942.* Master's thesis, University of Arizona, Tucson, 1991.

Butler, Ovid, ed. *Youth Rebuilds: Stories from the C.C.C.* Washington, D.C.: American Forestry Association, 1934.

Civilian Conservation Corps Legacy. "CCC Camp Lists." http://www.ccclegacy.org/camp_lists.htm.

Cohen, Adam. *Nothing to Fear: FDR's Inner Circle and the Hundred Days That Created Modern America.* New York: Penguin Press, 2009.

Collins, William S. *The New Deal in Arizona.* Phoenix: Arizona State Parks Board, 1999.

Cornebise, Alfred Emile. *The CCC Chronicles: Camp Newspapers of the Civilian Conservation Corps. 1933–1942.* Jefferson, NC: McFarland & Co., 2004.

Danner, James W. "C.C.C. Slang." *American Speech* 15 (1940): 212–213.

Davidson, Levette J. "C.C.C. Chatter." *American Speech* 15 (1940): 210–211.

Delahoyde, Barbara Jane. *The Best Thing That Ever Happened to Me: Memories of the Civilian Conservation Corps.* Honors thesis, Arizona State University, Tempe, 1998.

Egan, Timothy. *The Worst Hard Time: The Untold Story of Those Who Survived the Great American Dust Bowl.* Boston: Mariner Books, 2006.

Engbeck, Joseph H., Jr. *By the People, for the People: The Work of the Civilian Conservation Corps in California State Parks, 1933–1941.* Sacramento: State of CA, CA State Parks, 2002.

Ermentrout, Robert Allen. *Forgotten Men: The Civilian Conservation Corps.* Smithtown, NY: Exposition Press, 1982.

Fahlman, Betsy. *New Deal Art in Arizona.* Tucson: University of Arizona Press, 2009.

Guthrie, John D. *Saga of the CCC.* Washington, D.C.: American Forestry Association, 1942.

Hinton, Wayne K., with Elizabeth A. Green. *With Picks, Shovels & Hope: The CCC and Its Legacy on the Colorado Plateau.* Missoula, MT: Mountain Press Publishing Company, 2008.

Hivert-Carthew, Annick. *Proud to Work: A Pictorial History of Michigan's Civilian Conservation Corps.* Manchester, MI: Wilderness Adventure Books, 2006.

Jackson, Jane E. "Monumental Tasks: Flagstaff's Mt. Elden Civilian Conservation Camp." *Journal of Arizona History* 48 (Autumn 2007): 289–304.

Johnson, Charles W. *The Civilian Conservation Corps: The Role of the Army.* Doctoral dissertation, University of Michigan, Ann Arbor, 1968.

———. "The Army and the Civilian Conservation Corps, 1933–42." *Prologue: The Journal of the National Archives* 4 (1972): 139–156.

Jolley, Harley E. *"That Magnificent Army of Youth and Peace": The Civilian Conservation Corps in North Carolina, 1933–1942.* Raleigh: NC Department of Cultural Resources, 2007.

Kennedy, David M. *Freedom from Fear: The American People in Depression and War, 1929–1945.* New York: Oxford University Press, 2005.

Kolvet, Renee Corona, and Victoria Ford. *The Civilian Conservation Corps in Nevada: From Boys to Men.* Reno: University of Nevada Press, 2006.

Kylie, H. R. *CCC Forestry.* Washington, D.C.: GPO, 1937.

Kyvig, David E. *Daily Life in the United States, 1920–1940: How Americans Lived through the Roaring Twenties and the Great Depression.* Chicago: Ivan R. Lee, 2002.

Leuchtenburg, William E. *Franklin D. Roosevelt and the New Deal, 1932–1940.* New York: Harper & Row, 1963.

Lowitt, Richard. *The New Deal and the West.* Norman: University of Oklahoma Press, 1993.

Lubick, George M. *Petrified Forest National Park: A Wilderness in Time.* Tucson: University of Arizona Press, 1996.

Maher, Neil M. *Nature's New Deal: The Civilian Conservation Corps and the Roots of the American Environmental Movement.* New York: Oxford University Press, 2008.

Major, Duncan K., Jr. "Mobilizing the Conservation Corps: The Army Does a Gigantic Job in Record Time." *Army Ordnance* 14 (1933): 33–38.

Malach, Roman. *Home on the Range: Civilian Conservation Corps in Kingman Area.* Kingman, AZ: Roman Malach, 1984.

McBride, Dennis. *Hard Work and Far from Home: The Civilian Conservation Corps at Lake Mead.* Boulder City, NV: Boulder Images, 1995.

McDonald, William F. *Federal Relief Administration and the Arts: The Origins and Administrative History of the Arts Projects of the Works Progress Administration.* Columbus: Ohio State University Press, 1969.

McFadden, Jackie, and Jean Wells. *The Civilian Conservation Corps: A Bibliography.* Lewiston, NY: Edwin Mellon Press, 2005.

McKoy, Kathleen. *Culture at a Crossroads: An Administrative History of Pipe Spring National Monument.* Denver, CO: US DOI, 2000. http://www.nps.gov/pisp/historyculture/upload/PISP_adhi.pdf.

Melzer, Charles. *Coming of Age in the Great Depression: The Civilian Conservation Corps Experience in New Mexico, 1933–1942.* Las Cruces, NM: Yucca Tree Press, 2000.

Merrill, Perry H. *Roosevelt's Forest Army: A History of the Civilian Conservation Corps.* Montpelier, VT: P. H. Merrill, 1981.

Moore, Robert J. *The Civilian Conservation Corps in Arizona's Rim Country: Working in the Woods.* Reno: University of Nevada Press, 2006.

Moose, Clyde P. "Memoirs of Clyde P. Moose." Unpublished typed manuscript, USDA Forest Service, Southwestern Region.

Moose, Clyde P., et al. *People and Places of the Old Kaibab.* [Albuquerque, NM]: USDA Forest Service, Southwestern Region, 1990.

New Deal Network. "African Americans in the Civilian Conservation Corps, Documents." http:// newdeal.feri.org/aaccc/index.htm.

Nolte, M. Chester, ed. *Civilian Conservation Corps: The Way We Remember It, 1933–1942: Personal Stories of Life in the CCC.* Paducah, KY: Turner, 1990.

Olson, James S., ed. *Historical Dictionary of the New Deal.* Westport, CN: Greenwood Press, 1985.

Otis, Alison T. et. al. *The Forest Service and the Civilian Conservation Corps: 1933–42.* Washington, D.C.: U.S. Department of Agriculture, Forest Service, 1986

Paige, John C. *The Civilian Conservation Corps and the National Park Service, 1933–1942: An Administrative History.* Denver, CO: National Park Service, 1985.

———. "The CCC: It Gave a New Face to the NPS." http://crm.cr.nps.gov/archive/06-3/6-3-all.pdf.

Pfaff, Christine. *The Bureau of Reclamation's Civilian Conservation Corps Legacy: 1933–1942.* Denver, CO: BR, 2010.

Protas, Josh. *A Past Preserved in Stone: A History of Montezuma Castle National Monument.* Tucson, AZ: Western National Parks Association, 2002.

Purvis, Louis Lester. *The Ace in the Hole: A Brief History of Company 818 of the Civilian Conservation Corps.* Columbus, GA: Brentwood Christian Press, 1989.

Putt, Patrick John. *South Kaibab National Forest: A Historical Overview.* [Williams, AZ?]: Kaibab National Forest & Colorado Plateau Studies at Northern Arizona University, 1991.

Reid, Connie. *The History of the North Canyon Creek Fish Dams.* Fredonia, AZ: USFS, 2009.

Rodriguez, Alexander F. *Civilian Conservation Corps: Concept to Mobilization.* San Jose, CA: Raider Press, 1992.

Rudeen, Marlys, comp. *The Civilian Conservation Corps Newspapers: A Guide.* Chicago, IL: Center for Research Libraries, 1991.

Salmond, John A. *The Civilian Conservation Corps, 1933–1942: A New Deal Case Study.* Durham, NC: Duke University Press, 1967.

Schlesinger, Arthur M. *The Age of Roosevelt: The Coming of the New Deal, 1933–1935.* Boston: Houghton Mifflin, 1958.

Scott, Winfield. "California's Unemployment Forest Camps Where 7,000 Jobless Men This Winter Are Earning Food, Shelter, and Clothes by Forest Protection and Improvement Work." *American Forests* 39 (1933): 51–54.

Sherraden, Michael W. "Military Participation in a Youth Employment Program: The Civilian Conservation Corps." *Armed Forces and Society* 7 (1981): 227–245.

Smith, Jean Edward. *FDR.* New York: Random House, 2007.

Smith, Terrance J. "The Army's Role in the Success of the CCC." *The Retired Officer* (1983): 30–34.

Sommer, Barbara W. *Hard Work and a Good Deal: The Civilian Conservation Corps in Minnesota.* St. Paul: Minnesota Historical Society Press, 2008.

Stein, Pat. *The New Deal at Walnut Canyon: An Oral History of the Civilian Conservation Corps.* Flagstaff, AZ: Flagstaff Area National Monuments, 1988.

Swain, Donald C. *Federal Conservation Policy, 1921–1933.* Berkeley: University of California Press, 1963.

Sypolt, Larry N. *Civilian Conservation Corps: A Selectively Annotated Bibliography.* Westport, CN: Praeger, 2005.

Trails, Rails and Tales: Kingman's People Tell Their Story, 1882–1982. Kingman, AZ: Mohave Graphics, 1981.

U.S. Civilian Conservation Corps. *Second Report of the Director of Emergency Conservation Work for the Periods April 5, 1933 to September 30, 1933 and October 1, 1933 to March 31, 1934.* Washington, D.C.: USGPO, 1934.

U.S. Civilian Conservation Corps. *Annual Report of the Director of Emergency Conservation Work, Fiscal Year Ending June 30, 1936.* Washington, D.C.: USGPO, 1936.

U.S. Federal Security Agency. *Final Report of the Director of the Civilian Conservation Corps April, 1933 through June 30, 1942.* Washington, D.C.: USGPO?, 1942.

U.S. War Department. *Civilian Conservation Corps Regulations.* Washington, D.C.: USGPO, 1937.

———. Location and Strength of CCC Camps and Companies, 1933–1942. NARAMD RG35/530/65/22/04/05.

———. Records of CCC Camp Directories, 1933–1942, NARAMD RG 35 530/65/11/1.

Unrau, Harlan D., and G. Frank Williss. *Administrative History: Expansion of the National Park Service in the 1930s.* Denver, CO: NPS, 1983.

Westerlund, John S. *Arizona's War Town; Flagstaff, Navajo Ordnance Depot, and World War II.* Tucson: University of Arizona Press, 2003.

Wirth, Conrad L. *Civilian Conservation Corps of the United States Department of the Interior, March 1933 to June 30, 1943.* Chicago, IL: NPS, 1944.

INDEX

Numbers in *italics* refer to illustrations.

8th Corps 19, 177
A Kimble Ranch 107
Abineau Spring 20, 37, 38, 42
Adams, Capt,. 77
Adams, Wiley 76
Addams, C.E. 6 (n. 38)
African Americans 19, 30, 31 (n. 1), 31 (n. 11), 84
alcohol 16 (n. 31), 76, 80
Alcott, Earl 95
Allison, R.B. 76
American Indians 3, 30, 31
Anderson, E. A. 141, 142
Antelope Reservoirs 8, 9
Apache Indian Agency 11
Apache Maid Ranger Station 42, 51
Archer, L.F. 64
Arizona Strip xi, 1-2, 146-147, 151
Army 5, 6 (n. 35), 19 (n. 2), 65, 71, 88, 93 (n. 193) (n. 194), 110, 112, 151-152, 157, 170, 172, 173 (n. 32)
Ashurst, Henry F. 4, 6 (n.33) (n. 34)
Ashurst Lake 39
Aspen Spring 114, 115, 117
Bailey, Stuart 4, 33
Baird, D.S. 108
Baker Butte Lookout 51
Baldwin, Harvey C. 82
Baldwin's Ranch 47
Banjo Bill Campground 44, 45
Barber, S.E. 98
Barney Flat 64
Barrel Springs Spike Camp 85, 87
Baumgartner, Creston F. 16 (n. 10), 41, 60-62
Bear Spring 65
Beaubien, Paul 22, 24, 25
Beaver Creek Ranger Station 37, 39, 40, 41, 42, 45, 47, *50*
Bellemont, Arizona 5, 6 (n. 35), 20, 43, 55, 63-64, 69
Bergfield, George 78

Best, Dan C. 65, 66, 67, 82
Big Dry Wash 43, 46, 47, *51*
Bill Williams Lookout 68, 73 (n. 64)
Bill Williams Mountain 67, 68, 69, 73 (n. 98)
Bill, H. L. 11, 17 (n. 55)
Billingsley Ranch 95
Black Rock Springs 151-152
Black Spring 38, 42
Blair, Eldridge "Cowboy" 141
Blair, J.D. 128
Blankenagel, Emil 144
blizzard of 1936-1937 1-3, 83, 96, 97, 98, 116, 117, 127, 142-143, 158-159
Bobby, Andrew 69, 73 (n. 107), 74 (n. 122)
Bolo Cattle Company 126
Bowen, M.J. 52, 53, 54, 70, 87, 88, 107, 110, 119, 122, 137, 154, 165, 171, 172, 173 (n. 24) (n. 25), 175
Boynton Canyon 49
Bradshaw Mountains 78
Brian, William T. 82
Britt, John C. 82
Bruni, Albert V. 87
Bryant, B.H. 140
Buck and Doe Side Camp 28, *128,* 129, 130, 131, 134, 135, 136, 137
Buck Spring 68, 69
Buck Springs Spike Camp 52, 53
Buckskin Mountains 158, 163, 166, 171, 174
Bull Basin 73 (n. 98)
Bundy, James 140, 141, 142, 143, 145, 146
Bundy, Roy 168 (n. 75) (n. 79)
Burlew, E.K. 151, 153 (n. 7)
Burnett, B.H. 116
Burnett, Jack W. 80
Burris Ranch 46
Byers, Roland 103
CWA. *See* Civil Works Administration
Cady, Gilbert L. 40, 43
Calkins, Fred 78

Camp Spark 78
Campbell, E.A. 8, 9, 115, 116, 122
Campbell Ranch 40
Cane Springs Ranch 125
camp canteens/exchanges 49, 116, 170, 173 (n. 10)
Camp Clover 66, 67, 72 (n. 48)
Carlson, Edward 94
Caron, C.K. 151, 152, 153 (n. 13) (n. 18) (n. 23 through 25)
Carter, C.D. 20
Caulkins, Ford 103
Cecil White Ranch 107
Central Drug 70, 71
Chatwin, K.C. 10
Cheatham, William E. 67, 109, 110
Cheek, James 82
Cherry Creek Recreation Area 82
Chilson 96
Chloride 117, 127, 128
Civil Works Administration xi, 8, 15, 20, 34, 60, 62 (n. 9), 77
Clear Creek Ranger Station 39, 42, 47
Clover Springs 34
Cocke, Troy W. 97
Coconino Caverns 26 (n. 6) (n. 7)
Cofer Ranch 125
Coffee Creek 37, 41
Coffee Creek Ranger Station 46
Coleman, William 23, 27 (n. 67)
Collie, W.H. 8, 11
Collins, James T. 44
Colter Ranch Experimental Station 39
Communistic activities & propaganda 78, 122, 157, 166 (n. 7)
Company 311 47-53, 101
Company 340 130, 134, 136, 137
Company 805 5, 10-12
Company 806 5
Company 807 5
Company 818 30, 31
Company 819 30, 31, 60, 101
Company 820 38, 75-80, 154-155, 168 (n. 90)
Company 821 34-47, 56 (n. 59), 60, 61
Company 822 30, 53-54, 75-88, 94, 177
Company 830 114-115
Company 831 8-10, 60
Company 835 81-83
Company 847 67, 105, 174-176

Company 848 19, 64-65
Company 851 5, 19, 63-64
Company 860 34, 36, 40, 78-80
Company 863 30, 34-48, 50-53
Company 874 114-115, *114*
Company 1814 170-171
Company 1820 154-155, 168 (n. 90)
Company 1823V 31, 76-77
Company 1826V 19, 30, 31, 65-66, 88, 119, 177
Company 1837 14-15, 115-119, 122, 126
Company 1838 66
Company 1840 84-85
Company 1849 96-98, 109
Company 2541 96
Company 2557 101, 154, 157-1159, 162, 165-166, 168 (n. 89) (n. 90)
Company 2558 140-147, 152, 154
Company 2833 66, 101, 109-110
Company 2847 83-84
Company 2848 68
Company 2854 94-95
Company 2855 81-83
Company 2861 83-84
Company 2863 107-108
Company 2865 125-128, 130-131
Company 2870 81-83
Company 3318 166
Company 3320 85-88, 101
Company 3342 12-14
Company 3345 21-22, 27 (n. 47)
Company 3346 68-69
Company 3348 69-70
Company 3838 22
Company 3840 110
Company 4812 137
conditioning 4, 21, 64, 76, 140
Conley, Leo 68, 73 (n. 93)
Corbyn, Richard C. 97
Cowden Springs 97, 98
Cox, Kenneth S. 86
Crazy Basin 79, 80
Crook National Forest 33
Crown King, Arizona 75, 77, 78, 79, 80, 81, 85, 86
Crown King Ranger Station 81, *81,* 82, 90 (n. 72)
Crozier, Bruce 13, 22
Dalton, H.E. 116
Daniels, L.C. 38, 56 (61)
Darry (or Darrey), Earl 8, 60, 61

Davis Ranch 113
Davitto, Stephen (Babe) 165
Deadman Lookout 43
Dean Mine 113, 114
Democrat Mine 1, 126, 127
Dildine, Lt. 154
discipline 3, 64, 84, 88, 122
Dorsey, James W. 108
Doson, L.W. 108
Double O Ranch 76
Draper, Hamilton 122, 134, 135, 136, 146, 157, 170, 171, 174
Dry Creek 11, 49
drunkenness 54, 75, 109, 122
Duncan, Scott 81, 83
dynamite 114, 163, 175
Eddy, M.R. 65
education 3
Elden Ranger Station 47
Elk Springs, Arizona 69, 95
Elmore, L.R. 35, 51
Engel, Edmund L. 126, 127
Engle, Archie 140
environmental issues 35
Epstein, David 82
Esplin, Charles 144
Ezel, Paul 25
Falck, Depue 151, 153 (n. 8) (n. 10) (n. 11) (n. 12) (n. 13)
Farley, James A. 65, 72, (n. 42) (n. 43)
Fechner, Robert 3, 4, 5 (n. 18), 8, 12, 22, 30, 38, 49, 52, 56 (n. 57), 59 (n. 156), 62 (n. 4), 94, 122, 152
Felder, Charles K.. 44
Fernow Ranger Station 47
fish seining 39, 41, 45, 46, 51
Flask, Frank 66
Fleming, George 34
fly camps. *See* spike camps
Ford, Gordon 80
Forgeon, Aland 157
Fort Douglas, Utah 140, 152, 159
Fort Huachuca, Arizona 16, 17, 6 (n. 35), 30, 34, 82, 99 (n. 24), 177
Fort Pierce Wash Bridge 141, *143*
Fort Tuthill 4, 6 (n. 35), 40, 52, 59 (n. 56)
Fort Valley Experimental Station 35, 38, 40, 42, 43, 45, 47, 48, *48,* 50, 57 (n. 87), 58 (n. 103)
Fort Whipple Veterans Hospital 36, 40, 41, 42, 57 (n. 73), 64, 75, 76, 77, 79, 80, 84

Foster Springs 40
Fosworth-Falbraith Lumber Co. 83
Francis Creek Spike Camp 1, 126, 127
Fruebel, G.H. 67
Fulton Spring 47
Furedy, George L. 171
Garland Prairie 64, 67, 69
Gavin, J.E. 151
Gay, J.L. 96
Gebby, Francis 117
Geisser, H.H. 8
General Spring 43, 47, 48, 51
Gibbs, John M. 110
Gilliam, Porter H. 84, 91 (n. 136)
Golden Eagle Mine 79
Good, Wealty W. 49
Gordon, Col. 53, 59 (n. 168)
Grand Canyon 6 (n.35), 15, 20, 21, 22, 23, 27 (n. 34), 30, 32, 60, 63, 66, 67, 68, 69, 70, 72 (n. 60), 74 (n. 122), 77, 79, 82, 89 (n. 36), 101, 103, 106 (n. 28), 171, 172, 174, 176 (n. 1)
Grand Canyon Caverns 20
Grandview Lookout 67, *67*
Granite Basin 82, 83, 85, 86, 87, 91 (n. 113), 92 (n. 62) (n. 181)
Greer, Jason 82
Greenlaw Mill 20, 40
Greenway, Isabella S. 66, 99 (n. 25), 109-110, 113, 125
Griffin Spring 47
Griffith Spring 38, 52
Groesbeck, Edward 48, 50
Grubb, Frank 68, 75, 76, 77, 78, 89 (n. 51)
Gulick, E. Leeds 127
Hack Canyon Spike Camp 144, 159, 160, *160,* 161, 163
Hacker, Homer 165
Haffa, Milton C. 82
Haile, John H., Jr. 12
Hall, Charles L. 64
Hall, Sharlot M. 95
Hallmark, Floyd 140, 142
Halsey, Frank W. 63
Hance Spring 37, 42, 45
Hanna, Frank 67, 68, 70
Hansson, Knute 94, 95
Hardin, Richard F. 82
Hart, Roy L. 40
Hart Prairie 50

Haverkamp, Robert 158
Hay Lake 34, 42
Hayden, Carl 59 (n. 168), 113, 119, 134, 151-152, 153 (n. 21)
health 111-112
Heaton, Leonard 157-158, 159, 162
Heiser Spring 20, 23
Henry Ritter Ranch 96
Higdon, Paul H. 154
Higehock, Floyd 103
Hilldring, Major 49
Hillside Cattle Company 98
Hinton, E.L. 115
Hispanics 31
Hitt Spring 65, 69
Hjalmarson, Dori 95
Hollinger, Charles 125
Holmes, Thomas P. 43
Hook, C.P. 107
Horse Thief Basin Recreation Area 81, 83, *83*
Horse Thief Basin Spike Camp 30, 81, 83, 87
Hotchkiss, H.H. 6
House Rock Spike Camp 158, *162,* 163, 165
Howe, C.R. 65
Hualapai Mountains 113
Hualapai Valley Spike Camp 126, 127, 128, 129
Hubbard, W.M. 84
Hull, Don R. 113
humor 101
Hussey, Ralph W. 33, 41, 49, 50, 53, 57 (n. 77)
Hutmaker, Mathew 49
Ickes, Harold I. 98 (n. 5), 151, 153 (n. 6)
Indian Creek Recreation Area 78, 81, 82, 85, 86
Indian Creek Ski Run 85, 86
Indian Creek Spike Camp 81
Inner Basin 20, 37, 38
inspections 112, 122
Iron Springs 83, 86, 87, 91 (n. 129)
JD Dam 64, 65, 66, 67, 68, 69, 70, 71
J.R. Williams Ranch 86
Jackson, Earl S. 157
Jahnke, William H. 80
James Reese Ranch 94
Jamieson, Ed 97
Janak, John 81
Japanese-American Relocation Camp 88, 93 (n. 194) (n. 195), 110
Johnson, John W. 95
John A. Thompson Ranch 107-108

John Lee Spring 36
Johnson Wash Ranger Station 78
Jolly, E.B. 76, 80, 81, 86, 96
Jones, Calvin 9
Joyce, Edward M. 97
Kaibab Indian Reservation 157
Kehl Spring 48, 51
Kelly Mine, Nevada 1
Kendrick Mountain 38, 65
Kenlan, C.H. 107, 172, 173 (n. 24) (n. 25)
Kennedy, James 64
Kennedy Dam 65, 66, 67, 72 (n. 31) (n. 44)
Kieling, Henry J. 22, 27 (n. 43)
Kimball, G.W. 64, 65, 68
Kinnerly, George B. 36
Kinnikinick Lake 35, 42
Kirby, Lee 4, 33
Kirkland, Ernest L. 127
Kit Carson Recreation Area 42, 45, 47, 48, 50
Klenk, Fred 141
Kneeland, William J. 78
Knob Hill Ranger Station 45, 47, 48, 51, 53
Koogler, W.G. 77
Kuehl, Alfred H. 11, 17 (n. 68), 158
LEMs 3, 19, 95, 98
Lake Mary 34, 38, 39, 40, 41, 45, 46, 50, 52, 66
Lakin, Lloyd C., farm 107
Lamb, Sherman 143, 145
Lane, W.W. 4, 6 (n. 26)
Lauritzen, Supervisor 163
Leach, Clifford 145
Lee, Oscar Terry 64
Lee Butte Lookout 36
Lee Johnson Spring 46, 48, 51
Leopold, Aldo 33, 55 (n. 8), 76
Leroux Spring 38, 57 (n. 81)
Leroux Spring Forest Nursery *48,* 53, 57 (n. 81)
Lewis, Ralph 141
Lewis Brothers 11
Lewis Dairy 131, 134
Link, R. C. 109
Linxwiler, Louis M. 9, 105
Lipan, Edward M. 82
literacy 175
Little Leroux Spring and Nursery 38, 43, *45,* 45, 46, 48, 50, 53, 54, 57 (n. 81)
Little Tank, Arizona 2
Littlefield, Arizona 143
Lloyd, J.V. 128

Lockett Spring 64, 67, 68
Lone Star Shop 70
Long, C. E. 85
Long Mountain 136
Long Valley Ranger Station 48, 51, 52
Lutz, Harry H. 70
Lynx Creek Spike Camp 78
Maddux, L.C. 40
Maggard, Schulyer 141
Maier, Herbert 27 (n. 34)
Major, Duncan 4
Malone, Elbert 79
Mann, Walter G. 66, 68, 69, 73 (n. 98)
Manusov, J. 71, 73 (n. 112) (n.113) (n. 115 through 120)
Manville Wells State Park 83, 115, 119
Marable, George 76
Marshall, Bob 46
Martinex, Gregorio P., Jr. 70
Massad, Ernest L 43
Mastalski, Chester S. 22, 27 (n. 42)
McBride, Howard L. 144
McConnico CCC Camp 138 (n. 34)
McDuff, C.E. 76, 77
McEntee, James 49, 109, 122, 172, 173 (n. 25)
McGavic, Louie 108
McKay, Donald D. 151, 153 (n. 9) (n. 10)
McMimimy, Earl 108
McNabb, Willis J. 82
McNamara, E.A. 34, 41, 55 (n. 29), 61
McNelty, John C. 80, 81
Meason, James 117
Mehle, Philip J. 82
Mehlhon, John A. 95
Mellor, James 87
Melton, Clarence 97
Mermel, Lester 24
Merriam, Dr. 63
Merrill, C.B. 82
Mileusnich, William 108
Miller, Andy 105
Miller, Charles E. 21, 49
Miller, E.G. 34
Miller, Hugh M. 20, 22, 27 (n. 46)
Mingus Mountain Lookout 78, 79, 80, 81
Mingus Mountain Recreation Area 82, 85
Mingus Mountain Spike Camp 81, 84, 85, 86, 87
Moeur, Benjamin B. 4, 5, 6 (n. 35), 63, 65

Mogollon Rim 37
Mohave County Livestock Association 97
Mohave County Miner 64, 105 (n. 7), 113, 114
Mokaac Spring 140, 141, 143, 144, 147 (n. 6)
Molohon, A.B. 152, 153 (n. 20) (n. 25)
Moody, Homer 71
Moody, Milton E. 151, 153 (n. 5)
Moore, Herbert W. 40
Moose, Clyde P. 63
Moqui Ranger Station 69, 70, *70,* 73 (n. 109)
Moretz Lake 45
Morrill, C.B. 82
Mostiero, Candido 36
Mt. Elden Water Users and Pipe Line Association 24
Mount Union Lookout 76, 81
Mt. Tipton 136
Mulligan, John S. 78
Murdock, John R. 108
Murray, Lt. 107
Mutz, George 85
National Audubon Society 35
National Defense Work 23, 88, 136
Nave, J.C. 33, 81, 83, 84, 85, 86, 87
Navajo Army Depot 55, 63
Neff, Bayard 82
Nelson, D.H. 113
Nelson, Greer B. 44, 51
Nelson, Lt. 77
Nemeck, Francis L. 82
Nemeck, X.C. 81
Nichols, Capt. 65
nicknames 103
Norman, Charles J. 21, 49
Nutter, Preston 151, 153 (n. 4 through 8), (n. 11)
O.K. Café 87
O'Connell, T.S. 4
Oatman, Arizona 122
Oldham, Ed 23, 34, 54
Olds Brothers of Winslow 11
Orr, Jack 85
Overstreet, Cecil 78
PWA. *See* Public Works Administration
PWAP. *See* Public Works of Art Program
Painted Desert Inn 11, 12, 13, 14
Painter, John Ray 135, 138 (n. 7) (n. 26), 146, 152, 153 (n. 18) (n. 20)
Papago Park 6 (n. 35), 66, 113, 114

Parker, Clay 23
Parker, Lester I. 140
pay 19, 177
Perkinsville Road 65, 66, 67, 68, 69
Peterson, Floyd 60, 61
Peterson, Vernon 142
Phelps Dodge Hospital 81, 96
pigeons, carrier 97
Pine Tree Flat Campground 36
Pirtle, Doler 41
Pivot Rock Spike Camp 42, 43, 45, 46, 47, 48, 50, 51, 52, 53, 54
Pooler, Frank C.W. 4, 33, 64, 87
porcupines 11, 35, 36, 38, 39, 56 (n. 36), 60, 64, 103
prairie dogs 35, 40, *44,* 64, 66, 76, 78, 80, 85, 89 (n. 25)
Prescott Evening Courier 3, 75
Pringle, Ray E. 94
Prisbrey, Marie 145
Public Works Administration 2, 8, 9, 11, 15, 20, 23, 24, 26 (n. 15), 34, 65, 66, 76
Public Works of Art Program 60
Puente, Louis, Jr. 67, 68, 109
Purvis, Louis 12, 30, 112
Putnam, Claude E. 127
Putsch, L.J. 75, 89 (n. 6)
Quesinberry, Millard 165
Quimby, M.B. 96, 134, 135, 138 (n. 7) (n. 26)
Raudebaugh, Ed 42, 67
radio 34, 55 (n. 30), 88, 97, 136
Randall, Frank J. 49
Ratliff, Donald 128
Ravello, Doinee 69, 84
Reddoch, James C. 8, 10, 38, 39, 40, 42, 65, 78, 79, 80, 95, 96, 109, 110, 116, 122, 125, 142, 143, 145, 157, 162
Reed, Stanley J. 82
Richie, Charles .A. 27 (n. 50)
Ringgold, William K. 116
Roberts, Edgar C. 116
Roberts, Standlee D. 154
rodent control 36
Rodriguez, Antonio P. 84
Roer, Supt. 10
Rogers, Isaac 22
Rogers Lake 35, 50, 63
Roosevelt, Elanor 60

Roosevelt, Franklin Delano 3, 17 (n. 41), 60, 105, 177
Rose, Benjamin F. 84
Rose, Clifton F. 121 (n. 56) (n. 58) (n. 60) (n. 64) (n. 66) (n. 67) (n. 68)
Rotty, Roland 50, 54, 59 (n. 155) (n. 175)
Rowan, Edward B. 60, 61, 61 (n. 4) (n. 13)
Rucker, Edward W. 79
Rucker Canyon 107, 115
Ruland, Walter 40
Runser, Albert 69
Rupea, W.A. 151, 153 (n. 9)
Rutherford, Ray C. 33
Sachen, Joe V. 21
safety 111-112
Sagaser, Lt. 21
Sainte Agathe Ski Course 85
Salazar, Casiano 9
Salazar, Ray 116, 120 (n. 45) (n. 46) (n. 53)
Sallenger, J.R. 125, 126, 127, 130
Samuell, E.W. 95, 96, 97, 98, 122, 126, 127, 128, 129, 130, 131, 134, 135, 136, 137, 141, 144, 145, 146, 147 (n. 22), 149 (n. 91), 154, 158, 159, 160, 161, 163, 165, 166, 168 (n. 56), 170, 171, 174
Sanchez, John F. 21
sanitation 3, 64, 111, 122
Schenebley, Ellsowrth 22
Scherer, Lt. 64
Schiele, P.J. 144
Schiele, Palmer 174
Schlotzhauer, W.S., Jr. 126
Sedona Ranger Station 36, 40, 41, 44
segregation 30
Seviers, E.R. 80
Self, Tommy 141
Shirley, G.O. 110
Shoemaker, D.A. 33
Sias, Harold E. 108
Sias, Richard 118
side camps. *See* spike camps
Sitgreaves National Forest 11, 12, 33, 81
Ski runs 50, 51, 54, 55, 85, 86, 87
slang 103
Smith, Charles J. 11, 105,
Smith, J.A. 35
Smith, John R. 44
Smith, Lt. 109
Smith, Ralph T. 97, 109

Snow Bowl Road & Ski Area 23, 50, 51, 52, 53, 54, *54*, 55
South Mountain Park 88, 115, 119
Sparkes, Grace M. 77, 89 (n. 50), 90 (n. 86), 99 (n. 25)
Spearman, F.S. 67
Spencer, Thomas A. 79, 80, 90 (n. 94)
Sperati, Paolo 8, 65, 113
spike camps 43
Spiney, George H. 65
Spring Valley Spike Camp 45, 54, 68, 69
Spring Valley Range Station 68, 69, 70
Spruce Mountain Lookout 76, 78, 80
Spudy, Albert 27 (n. 44) (n. 47), 29 (n. 118)
Spurlock 11
Squire, Guy O. 109
Stephens, Roscoe 109-110
Stevenson, M.B. 22, 23, 27 (n. 46) (n. 50)
Stevenson, William 24
Stevenson, R.G 49
Stewart, Stanley L. 82
Stockman, A.W. 11, 12, 21, 49, 50, 67, 81, 82, 84, 85, 96, 116, 117, 118, 122, 126, 130
Stonesplice, Capt. 64
Stuart, Robert Y. 33
Sultana Buffet 70
Sultana Theater 65
Summit Spring 64, 65, 67
Supai 1
Sweet, J.P. 82
Swift, T.T. 33
Sycamore Ranger Station 87
tamarisk 37
Taylor, Charles H. 110
Taylor Grazing Act xi, 94, 96, 125, 140, 151
Teague, Philip 102
Terrett, Julian 152, 153 (n. 14) (n. 19) (n. 21)
Thomas, Pearl L. 34, 75
Thomas, Rufus L. 78
Thomason, Jeff P. 115
Thompson 11
Thompson, D.M. 2, 5 (n. 10), 140, 141, 143, 147 (n. 18), 148 (n. 55)
Thompson, E.L.? 64
Thompson, Engineer 135
Tillotson, Miner 65, 68
Timblin, Merle 70, 73 (n. 114)
Tonto Ranger Station 85, 86

Toohey, Frank 115
Towers Mountain Lookout 81
Townsend Campground 42, 45, 47, 50
transient camps 34, 66, 79, 80, 81, 82
Turville, F.S. 97, 99 (n. 60)
Tway, Thomas 84, 122
twig blight 40, 41, 42, 43, 45, 48, 75, 76, 77, 78, 80, 81, 82, 83, 84, 85
Tyson, George W. 22, 82
U.S. War Relocation Authority 88
Ussery, Huling E. 144, 152, 153 (n. 15) (n. 16) (n. 22), 168 (n. 56)
V Bar B Ranch 47
veterans 3, 4, 19, 31, 177
Volunteer Mountain Lookout 67, 68, 69
WPA. *See* Works Progress Administration
Walker, S.M. 82
Walkup, J.D. 41
Wallace, Henry 4
Wallace, Robert M. 82
Walsh, James M. 43
Walthall, F.E. 125
Warner, Florence 4
Watson, Edward B. 154
Watson, Hugh 142
Wayne Ritter Ranch 96
Weatherwax, H.E. 152, 153 (n. 19)
Webb, Naomi 36
West Cataract Dam 66, 72 (n. 62)
Whalen, Walter F. 111, 112 (n. 2)
Whipple, Maurine 142
White Horse Lake 66, 67, 68, 69, 70, 72 (n. 67)
Whiting, John B. 67
Whitlock, Maj. 10
Whitlock, Wilburn T. 23
Whitlow, Doyle 84
Wild Horse Basin Spike Camp 98
Williams, R.P. 113
Willow Creek Ranger Station 81, 85, 87
Wingren, Oscar 22
Winn, Fred 33
Wirt, W.H. 9, 10, 15 (n. 6) (n. 16) (n. 25) (n. 30) (n. 34) (n. 38)
Wisniewski, Frank T. 25, 28 (n. 89)
Wolf, Edward T. 97
Wolf Creek Recreation Area 78, 81, 82, 85, 86
Wolf Hole Road 140, 141, 142, 143, 144, 147 (n. 6) (n. 9) (n. 19) (n. 22), 148 (n. 41) (n. 57), 151, 152

Wolf Hole Spike Camp 2, 141, 142, 143, 144, 145, 146
Wolfe, K. 152, 153 (n. 22) (n. 23) (n. 24)
Woolums, Q.B. 143
Worley, Andy 103
Worley, Gene 172, 173 (n. 25)
Works Progress Administration 20, 26 (n. 15), 34, 69, 70, 82, 86, 92 (n. 170), 107
Worthington, J.R. 8
Wright, J.B. 4, 20, 34, 65
Wright, Oscar B. 86, 92 (n. 164)
Wright, Roy 142, 145, 170
Yeager Canyon Ranger Station 85
Young, Kelsey 128
Yount, Robert 107

CPSIA information can be obtained at www.ICGtesting.com
Printed in the USA
LVOW090837260413

331057LV00005BA/28/P